A History of
Scientific Computing

A History of Scientific Computing

Edited by
Stephen G. Nash

with special acknowledgment to
Gene H. Golub

ACM PRESS
New York, New York

ADDISON-WESLEY PUBLISHING COMPANY

Reading, Massachusetts ∎ Menlo Park, California
New York ∎ Don Mills, Ontario ∎ Wokingham, England
Amsterdam ∎ Bonn ∎ Sydney ∎ Singapore
Tokyo ∎ Madrid ∎ San Juan

This book is in the **ACM Press History Series**

Many of the designations used by manufacturers and sellers to distinguish their products are claimed as trademarks. Where those designations appear in this book, and Addison-Wesley was aware of a trademark claim, the designations have been printed in initial caps or all caps.

Library of Congress Cataloging-in-Publication Data

A History of scientific computing / edited by Stephen G. Nash.
    p.   cm. — (ACM Press history series)
   Based on papers presented at the Conference on the History of Scientific and Numeric Computation, held in Princeton, N.J., 1987.
    ISBN 0-201-50814-1
    1. Electronic data processing—History. 2. Science—Data processing—History. I. Nash, Stephen. II. ACM Conference on the History of Scientific and Numeric Computation (1987 : Princeton, N.J.) III. Series.
    QA76.17.H59   1990
    004′.09—dc20   90-6
                                                                               CIP
#20934277

ABCDEFGHIJK–HA–943210

This book is dedicated
to the memory of
Peter Henrici
and
James Wilkinson

Series Foreword

As the computer approaches its first half-century and increasingly informs the structure and quality of modern life, its past becomes an ever more important part of our national and human heritage. ACM Press's History Series aims at the preservation, recovery, and interpretation of the historical record of computers and computing. In addition to proceedings of ACM Conferences on the History of Computing and of similar conferences sponsored by other organizations, the series encompasses autobiographies, memoirs, and biographies; general historical surveys and monographs on special topics; and bibliographies and guides to archives, collections, and other sources for historical research. In conjunction with the Anthology Series, it will also include annotated collections of classic papers documenting the development of various areas of computing. Through the History Series the ACM means not only to honor the pioneers whose achievements constitute the history of computing but also encourage collaboration between computer professionals and the growing number of professional historians who are seeking to discern the developmental patterns that link those achievements with one another and with wider technical and social contexts and thereby give them their historical meaning. As Editor of the Series, I invite proposals and inquiries from both communities.

Michael S. Mahoney
Series Editor

Book Foreword

This volume, *A History of Scientific Computing*, arises out of the Conference on the History of Scientific and Numeric Computation held at Princeton in 1987 and reflects the goal, expressed by Adele Goldberg in proposing the Conference series, of "promot[ing] a better understanding of the visions that led to some of the most compelling past research efforts, the impact of this work on the current state of the art, and the potential for impact on the future." Written by those who had the visions and carried out the research, these articles take stock of the subject itself, at the same time that they serve as a resource for historians interested in the people who, individually and collectively, created it. Offering valuable insight into the formation of new scientific disciplines, the volume includes accounts of European installations and thus brings a corrective balance to a subject overwhelmingly viewed through American lenses.

In moving from conference to book, Editor Stephen G. Nash has regrouped the papers according to People, Problems, Methods, Journals and Meetings, and Places, which should help readers with different backgrounds and concerns to focus their use of a volume that those who are not specialists in the field may find difficult to comprehend as a whole. Neither the book nor the conference was meant as an introduction to scientific computing. As specialists talking to specialists, the participants took much of the mathematics for granted. Indeed, part of the historical value of the papers lies in seeing what contributors to a forty-year retrospective felt needed no explanation, because it has become common knowledge.

Viewed in that light, it is striking how many of the papers take the computer itself as a given. The Editor's general introduction explicitly brings out what perhaps seemed to all participants to be too obvious to mention: the computer was central to the development of scientific computing. In a real sense, the computer defined the field of numerical analysis as the study of numerical algorithms designed to be run without intervention and hence to avoid or to contain accumulating errors that arise from the finite nature of digital computation. Some of the papers discuss directly (others raise implicitly) the question of how the pioneers recognized and formulated that central problem;

for example, what was the balance between empirical and theoretical investigation, and what role did the computer itself play?

It is an important question, if only because the computer originated as a tool for high-speed numerical computation but then gradually assumed its own identity. As James Wilkinson observed in his 1970 Turing Award Lecture,

> The use of electronic computers brought with it a new crop of problems all perhaps loosely associated with "programming" and quite soon a whole field of new endeavors grew up around the computer. . . . Many people who set out originally to solve some problems in mathematical physics found themselves temporarily deflected by the problems of computerology and we are still waiting with bated breath for the epoch-making contributions they surely will make when they return to the fold, clothed in their superior wisdom.

Some did not return, but instead laid the foundations of computer science as distinct from scientific computing. In the present volume we hear from those who continued to focus on the numbers. In future volumes we look forward to learning from those who were deflected by the machine.

Michael S. Mahoney

Introduction

In a sense, computing is as old as mathematics itself, and a history of scientific computing would diverge from a history of mathematics only in its later chapters. The Pythagorean theorem, the beginning of mathematics as an intellectual endeavor, is a computational formula.

Most of us would agree that scientific computing has emerged as a separate enterprise only in the last 40 years. Its reputation has so risen that numerical solutions are now often preferred to analytic solutions. Vast sums are spent on computer software and hardware for use in scientific calculations. Research journals are devoted to research on numerical methods. Many mathematicians and computer scientists devote their working lives to solving its problems. It is clear that scientific computing is highly valued. But is it of greater value than in Pythagoras' time? And what price has it exacted for the understanding that it provides?

Let us attempt an appraisal of the Pythagorean theorem. There is an apocryphal story that Pythagoras, when he discovered his theorem about right triangles, sacrificed 100 oxen to thank the gods. What a glorious celebration.

We no longer sacrifice oxen, but we value our algorithms nonetheless. New software for linear programming is being marketed, together with the computer that runs it, for more than $8 million. Is this more valuable than Pythagoras' sacrifice?

At today's prices, $8 million would buy about 16,000 oxen, far more than Pythagoras was willing to sacrifice on his island. But the value of an ox has decreased since Pythagoras' time. To get a better sense of relative values over these many centuries, consider that in Pythagoras' time 100 oxen would be worth 180,000 man-days. In Virginia, where this is being written, $8 million would translate into 100,000 man-days. So in this sense, scientific computing has declined in value.

The Pythagorean theorem imposed costs in addition to those 100 oxen. Pythagoras' joy was short-lived. The simple right triangle that inspired him to his discovery also revealed an unsettling mystery. Pythagoras and his followers studied not only geometrical shapes, but also music. From stringed instruments, they had learned the laws of harmonics—that if a string is divided into two equal parts, its pitch rises an octave, a harmonious interval. The same is true if the string is divided into three or four equal parts, an integral number of parts, suggesting a relationship between the integers and "natural" harmonies. The integers (and their inverses, corresponding to the division of the vibrating string) assumed a special significance for their cult.

Right triangles with *integral* sides were thus special, and motivated an investigation of their properties, hence the Pythagorean theorem. However, attention was also drawn to the simplest of right triangles, the one with both legs of length one. Its hypotenuse has length equal to the square root of two, and they immediately wondered about its representation as a fraction, its representation in terms of integers. They quickly discovered that it could not be represented as a fraction.

Thus their integers and their right triangles, which had offered them so much joy of discovery, also led them outside their concept and understanding of number. It precipitated an intellectual crisis more troubling than their earlier questions about triangles.

This volume is concerned with more recent events, primarily with events of the last few decades. The nature of computation changed in the 1940s with the invention of the computer. Before that, calculations were done by hand, possibly with the aid of a calculator, but certainly with human supervision. This had two consequences: First, calculations were usually short, limited in most cases to a few hundred steps; and second, any difficulties (such as cancellation) could be noticed as they happened, and the accuracy of particular steps adjusted as needed.

With the computer, lengthy calculations suddenly became possible, allowing thousands or millions of steps. Tiny errors, irrelevant in short calculations, could now accumulate and possibly overwhelm the desired answers to the problems. Also, algorithms suitable for small problems might no longer be workable as problem size increased. Nevertheless, the expectations of those posing the problems grew at least as quickly as the power of the computers they were using. In addition, the calculations went on without supervision, and computational crises would pass without notice.

These facts, which were observed immediately, created doubts about the safety of particular algorithms. In particular, the doubts led to the publications by von Neumann, Turing, and others on the solution of linear equations via Gaussian elimination. In the minds of many, these papers generated as many worries as they settled, suggesting that Gaussian elimination could produce large errors in the solutions of linear equations. This, combined with the physical limitations of the machines, led people to use other methods and led to skepticism about the utility of many methods. But the capabilities of the new machines were such that people were eager to use them and to find ways to use them effectively.

Today, there is little doubt about the value of scientific computing. Its use has spread throughout science and engineering and is the basis for medical imaging, automotive design, and other technologies that affect the public. It has offered many insights into the world around us, especially into phenomena not amenable to classical techniques of analysis.

Recently, simple numerical models have revealed remarkable complexity—fractal structure and chaotic behavior. Although originally regarded as anomalies of the calculations and models—points where the model broke down—they were eventually noticed to be different modes of behavior, consequences of the model. The calculations have also resulted in a search for such behavior in nature. This search has had its successes: the fractal nature of coastlines and snowflakes and the chaotic behavior of Pluto, for example. The models have also found practical application in computer graphical imaging.

They have also opened a chasm of doubt. Chaotic behavior has been found in the simplest of models, suggesting that it may be present in many other models, in particular models that approximate the behavior of the world around us, such as models of the weather. Since chaos, in both its popular and technical senses, is by nature unpredictable and unstable, it suggests that the world around us may also be unpredictable, frightening to a degree unimagined a generation ago.

The earlier crises have been resolved. In Pythagoras' case, the Greeks realized that a number could be represented by the length of a line segment, rather than by a fraction. Hence, the square root of two corresponds to the side of a square with area equal to two (hence the terms *squared* and *square* root, which are still in use). Geometry replaced numerical representation in Greek mathematics and may have led to the Greeks' excellence in geometrical reasoning, and hence to Euclid's *Elements*—the consolidation of their studies in geometry and the most used mathematical book in man's history.

In the case of computer arithmetic, the solution also came from taking a different point of view. Instead of asking about the accuracy of the solution, we now ask instead how much the algorithm alters our original problem, so-called *backward* error analysis. Thus, instead of asking how close the computed solution is to the true solution, we ask how well the computed solution solves the given problem. In addition, we have learned to use a few basic principles in designing algorithms, such as the use of orthogonal transformations in linear algebra, that tend to produce algorithms of good quality.

We have not yet come to terms with chaotic behavior. It does not seem amenable to standard forms of analysis, classical techniques based on simple local approximations. It suggests a mystery in our world for which we have no explanation. We can hope, however, that its resolution leads to a richness of development such as that inspired by these other two crises in computing.

Stephen G. Nash
Fairfax, Virginia
February, 1989

Preface

This volume grew out of the Conference on the History of Scientific and Numeric Computation held at Princeton University in 1987. Many leading participants in this field were attracted to the meeting and are represented here. Their essays chronicle the development of scientific computation *on the computer*, with all its possibilities and difficulties. We can read about John von Neumann's activities in promoting and explaining the new computer, James Wilkinson's investigations into the subtle properties of computational error, and the efforts of other influential individuals to clarify the nature of scientific computation. Sometimes a place rather than a person is the focus, such as the Los Alamos Laboratory in the period during and after World War II. In other cases, a particular problem or algorithm is described, such as the extraordinary impact of the simplex method on business and military planning, or the importance of solving differential equations in modeling physical phenomena. Finally, there is a discussion of the role of professional societies, journals, and meetings in promoting and publicizing work in scientific computing, such as *BIT* and the Society for Industrial and Applied Mathematics (SIAM) journals and the Gatlinburg meetings, which influenced the development of numerical linear algebra.

Neither the conference nor this book would have come about were it not for the work of the Conference Program Chairman, Gene H. Golub. From the first discussions with his Program Committee through the completion of the editing of this book, Gene consistently demonstrated a remarkable concern for detail and a product of the highest quality. For those of us who were privileged to have been a part of this effort, it was indeed a learning experience of the highest form. With the publication of this book, a part of this experience will live on—a written documentary of the history of the social, economic, political, and scientific forces that resulted in the blending of the genius of mathematicians and computer scientists from around the world into the formulation of new theories and practices in mathematics and computation.

It has been the goal of the ACM History of Computing Conference Series to bring together the pioneers and major contributors in each

Participants in the conference: [back row, left to right] John Herriot, Norman Schryer, Beresford Parlett, Bastiaan Braams, Tinsley Oden, Charles Gear, David Wheeler, Takashi Nodera, John Rice, Garrett Birkhoff, Carl-Erik Fröberg, Ivo Babuška; [middle row] Richard Varga, Martin Gutknecht, Robert Funderlic, Oscar Buneman, Tony Chan, Herman Goldstine, Magnus Hestenes, Donald Peaceman, Eugene Isaacson, Nicholas Metropolis, Frank Friedman, Gene Golub; [front row] David Young, James Cooley, Alston Householder, John Todd, Olga Taussky-Todd, Leslie Fox, Herbert Keller, M. L. Juncosa, Robert Skeel.

of a variety of fields to further explore and revisit the major events influencing the development of these fields. Thanks to Gene Golub, the Conference on the History of Scientific and Numeric Computation was tremendously successful in achieving this goal.

It is also appropriate to thank a number of other people who assisted in producing the conference and this book. George Crane was a great help in contacting authors and assembling the program during the preparations for the conference. Bonny Hilditch has provided endless resourcefulness in tracking down information from a great many reference sources. And, of course, Mike Mahoney and Frank Friedman have provided their support from the start.

Contents

xvii

Contents   xix

E.T. Whittaker (1873–1956).

PEOPLE

The inspiration of gifted individuals has always been an important factor in the development of scientific computing. Two such giants, Peter Henrici and James Wilkinson, would have been a part of this volume had their deaths not intervened. Instead, they were represented only by memories.

In this chapter, Herman Goldstine describes the activities of John von Neumann and his early understanding of the importance of computing in science. Von Neumann, in addition to his many other gifts, was a catalyst for developments in the United States, publicizing the new technology, encouraging the computer industry, and illuminating the new understanding that computing could provide. He was among the first to understand the differences between human and machine calculations, the nature of rounding errors, and also the new opportunities that calculation revealed through techniques such as the Monte Carlo method.

Beresford Parlett examines the work of James Wilkinson and assesses his contribution to numerical analysis. This work began in the period after World War II, in connection with the building of the first electronic computers in England, and developed into the many publications that established our current understanding of numerical linear algebra. He is especially remembered for his discussions of rounding errors and the insight he provided into the nature of machine calculations.

James Varah discusses the influence of George Forsythe, particularly via his position at Stanford University. At Stanford, Forsythe helped establish the Computer Science Department, which became a center for graduate training in numerical analysis. This tradition has been continued by the people that he hired, for example Gene Golub and Joseph Oliger, and has been widely disseminated through the work of the students who studied there.

Finally, Bernard Cohen tells us about Howard Aiken's electromechanical machines and their influence on the development of the computer. These machines are not, for technical reasons, always accepted as computers, but they were reliable and long-lived computing devices that illustrated the power of automatic computation.

Remembrance of Things Past

Herman H. Goldstine

In preparing a paper for this symposium on the topic of scientific and numeric computation, I have been forced once again to think over what these terms mean now and what they have meant throughout time. In my case this is a worthwhile task requiring me to reappraise the subject and ask myself if this is what was intended by the fathers of the field.

I think that with very many branches of mathematics we can well ask the perfectly proper questions: What is the purpose of this subject? Why did its creators choose to go in one direction rather than another? After all, even though mathematics is a magnificent creation of the human intellect, it is not merely a collection of complicated but arbitrary topics lumped together in an inchoate whole. We know that there are remarkable threads and themes that run through many of the topics and that many others are there to provide us with the tools needed to make yet other studies. The unities present are remarkably abundant, and the sense of arbitrariness that people sometimes mention seems to me often a reflection of their lack of understanding of the topics in question.

At this point it is perhaps relevant to quote some of von Neumann's views on mathematics and mathematicians. He said, "Most people, mathematicians and others, will agree that mathematics is not an empirical science, or at least that it is practiced in a manner which differs in several decisive respects from the techniques of the empirical sciences. And, yet, its development is very closely linked with the natural sciences. One of its main branches, geometry, actually started as a natural, empirical science. Some of the best inspirations of modern mathematics (I believe, the best ones) clearly originated in the natural sciences."

The subject of mathematics is very different, however, from, say, theoretical physics, and it is perhaps worth pausing for a bit to understand just how this is so. As we know, mathematics falls naturally into a large number of more or less distinct fields, and almost no one today has any reasonable grasp of the whole. On the contrary, physics seems to be a very different sort of topic. A crucial difficulty is met in the experimental area: Whatever anomaly this presents must be cleared up before the practitioners of the field can go forward. It is not possible for them to do what we very often do: drop the problem as being intractable and proceed to an entirely different challenge. As we can appreciate, certain critical experiments in the real world cannot be ignored if their results contradict existing theories. All the best scientists in the field are forced to face up to the challenge and to make whatever modifications are necessary to reestablish equilibrium in their science. Thus, experiments such as Michelson's led to the introduction of special relativity, and the conflict between that subject and classical celestial mechanics led to general relativity.

Let us look back at the beginnings of our subject, at the works of Hipparchus and Ptolemy, who worked in the period from about 150 B.C. to A.D. 150. Obviously they were not the first men to make significant use of mathematics. The great geometers—many of whose names have been lost to us because of Euclid's remarkable efforts to pull together all the empirical, semiempirical, and pure mathematical efforts in geometry—certainly developed one of the most noteworthy structures in the ancient world. We need not concern ourselves here with how much was empirical and how much purely mathematical. All that we need to know is that Hipparchus and later Ptolemy used the Euclidean apparatus to explain the motions of the heavenly bodies with excellent accuracy. I believe that it was they (and perhaps especially Ptolemy) who were mainly responsible for the initiation of our subject. Ptolemy was faced at the beginning with the problem of explaining the motions of the visible planets, the sun, and our moon with sufficient accuracy so that an observer armed with the astronomical instruments of that day could locate the body in question. The paper construct that Ptolemy created in his *Almagest* is in some ways like an elaborate mechanical device or rather a series of these devices, one for each of the visible planets, the sun, and the moon. These devices are made out of circles with smaller circles mounted on their perimeters. Each of these was, so to speak, handmade so that the particular body moved in accordance with observational data that in many cases went far back in time and enabled Ptolemy and his colleagues to determine many parameters with considerable exactitude.

Ptolemy did not, of course, develop the basic mathematics that he used to explain or rather to predict the locations and times of various celestial events. He obviously decided that he would accept the mathematics available at that time, Euclidean geometry, and went on to develop a means for using it in a practical way to give results in numerical form. The apparatus that he and Hipparchus put together is what we call trigonometry. Its utility has been so great that it has survived as a standard topic in school curricula for almost two millenia. Let me hasten to point out that very few things in our magnificent western culture have such survival times; therefore, let us not sneer at this subject. Ptolemy made two essential observations to establish his computational tool. He saw that a table of the sines—actually the subtended chords—of a series of equally spaced angles was just what was needed. This is quite clear, but what I think is remarkable is that he did not measure these chords or sines by physical means. Instead, he developed the lovely relations of trigonometry and coupled these with the knowledge of the number of degrees in the angles of certain regular polygons. By these means he was able to build up virtually all the needed entries in a table of sines with a half degree spacing. He needed, however, one more thing: the sine of $1/2°$. To obtain this he developed a neat scheme for interpolation based on an elegant inequality of Archimedes that says that if $A > B$ then $A/B > \sin A / \sin B$. He applied this to obtain the result

$$(2/3) \sin(3/4) < \sin(1/2) < (4/3) \sin(3/4)$$

This gave him $\sin(1/2)$ with a relative error of 2×10^{-6}.[1]

In addition to giving Ptolemy his table, this study gave us a whole way of viewing mathematics. It meant that the scientist who wants to explain the world need not go off into an experimental study, but can seek out a mathematical tool to use instead. This has reduced the need for experimentation to the determination of physical fundamentals such as physical constants whose values are very properly the subject for experimentation. If Ptolemy had not seen how to use mathematics to fill in his table but had constructed various-sized angles and actually measured chords, heaven knows what applied mathematics in general and computation in particular would have become.

In any case, so great was this success—through its remarkable predictive powers—that to try to emulate applied mathematics by becoming more mathematical in nature became and has continued to be a desideratum of virtually all sciences. So, for example, we see that some of the very great advances in theoretical physics have been made possible at least in part by the highly mathematical form that the subject has assumed. That the model stems from Ptolemy and his great predecessor Hipparchus also reminds us that our particular subject has been for a long time very much a handmaiden of mathematical astronomers.

It is perhaps not without some interest to note what the distinguished Arab astronomer al-Kashi, who lived during the time of Tamerlane in Samarkand (1400), did in his observatory. He was concerned with seeking a more elegant way to find the sine of $1/2°$ than Ptolemy had produced. To this end he noticed that there is a simple cubical relation between the sine of $3A$ and the sine of A:

$$\sin 3A = 3 \sin A - 4 \sin^3 A$$

so that if he had the sine of $3°$ he could then find the sine of $1°$. This led al-Kashi to develop an iterative scheme for solving the cubic equation and very likely led to the subject that was known as the Theory of

Equations. This was a field that was often taught at an elementary level in a number of universities. One of the most noteworthy topics in that field, at least for me when I was a student, was the so-called Newton-Raphson method for iteratively solving functional equations.

Let us now leave this ancient history and move forward into more modern times, and let us discuss my doings. Back in the days before World War II, Gilbert Bliss at the University of Chicago was interested in exterior ballistics and announced a course in the topic. He also was planning to write a book on the subject, which he in fact did. But the teaching of his graduate courses had fallen to me in those days because his health was uncertain. In this I was very fortunate. In the course of teaching the students at Chicago, I had to take them through a certain amount of numerical analysis so that they could learn how to solve the differential equations of motion for a projectile-fuse combination. This was a skill that I had acquired more or less painfully from an astronomer at Chicago named Walter Bartky. We had tables of logarithms and little else besides a method first named after Adams and Moulton.

This and similar methods played a major role at the Ballistic Research Laboratory at the Aberdeen Proving Ground in Maryland. They are characterized by the calculation and recording of many differences, since linear operations are cheap to perform by hand and paper for storage of partial results is inexpensive. These methods make use of as few nonlinear operations, such as multiplications and divisions, as possible, because these involve the use of log tables and entail many table look-ups and interpolations.

Therefore, when I arrived at Aberdeen and was assigned to the department that had to produce all the firing and bombing tables for the Army and the Air Force, I found myself back home again with the techniques that I had been teaching young people at Chicago. Fortunately from my point of view, I was put in charge of a substation of the laboratory at the University of Pennsylvania's Moore School of Electrical Engineering. I was in touch with several men who were keen on the problem of automating dull tasks that could be done better by machine than by human. In fact the staff included a number of faculty and at least one graduate student who had been involved in precisely this topic for some years in connection with a differential analyzer built at the school in the mid 1930s, with a copy made for Aberdeen. This was one of the reasons why Aberdeen and the Moore School were contractually related during the war.

The differential analyzer was an electromechanical device invented by Vannevar Bush in the early 1930s to integrate the differential equations arising in the field of electrical engineering. The equations for the motion of a projectile were readily adaptable to these machines, which afforded a fast way to solve them. The machines' accuracy was not high; about 5 parts in 10,000 was the best one could get. It took about 10 to 20 minutes to integrate the average trajectory. To illustrate, let me remark that such a trajectory involved about 750 multiplications and would take a human at least seven hours. Our main aim was to reduce this 10- to 20-minute time by an order of magnitude and to provide at the same time a nonhuman way to perform all the interpolations and other numerical steps that were needed to produce a firing table.

Fortunately for me, Grist Brainerd, then a young professor at the Moore School, proposed a solution to the problem first raised by a colleague of Brainerd named John Mauchly. His idea was to build an electronic digital computer to replace the differential analyzer and bring two enormous advantages to us: the speed of electronics and the accuracy of the digital principle. The Army accepted this proposal, and the Moore School actually built the device, the ENIAC, under Brainerd's aegis and with a superb young engineer named Presper Eckert. It is not my place here to spend more time on the details of this essential advance in our field. Suffice it to say that it immediately changed the face of the computational world.

Since the ENIAC and its successors had very small memories for intermediate results, the entire economy of computing changed overnight. Instead of being in a world of expensive multiplication and cheap storage, we were thrown into one in which the former was very cheap and the latter very expensive. (In fact we are only now getting into an economy in which storage is becoming exceedingly cheap.) This meant that virtually all the algorithms that humans had devised for carrying out calculations needed reexamination. In addition many areas of numerical analysis, such as the numerical solution of partial differential equations, were suddenly potentially open to us. This was the world in which we found ourselves at the end of World War II.

It was into this world that Johnny von Neumann projected himself with the gusto and élan that characterized all his activities. He went at something either with "full speed ahead and damn the torpedoes" or not at all. Nothing was ever so complete as the indifference with which Johnny could listen to a topic or paper that he did not want to hear.

At this time he was gung ho for the wonderful world that the electronic computer was opening up. We decided that we should set up at the Institute for Advanced Study a full scale effort to have a major hand in creating this brave new world. To do this we instituted what we called the electronic computer project and decided that our thrust needed to be multipronged.

We accordingly had a group devoting itself to a study that might now be called computer architecture and science. Here our main aim was to discover the right way to organize a computer so that it would be flexible and easily responsive to its users. This effort resulted in a series of papers on planning and coding of problems that had a fundamental role in shaping the architecture of the modern computer. We also pushed in a small way into topics such as merging and sorting of data and into the question of the least number of operations needed to perform a given function.

Another group was devoted to numerical methods (more on this later), and a third group was created to engineer and fabricate a computer embodying our architectural ideas. As one might suppose, the results of this third enterprise were transitory; the changes taking place in the engineering field were so great that the machine was perhaps obsolete within a year or so of its completion.

Finally we envisaged a group that would use the results of the others to solve some important problem that even the lay public could grasp to show the significance of the electronic computer to the world around us. Johnny chose the field of meteorology and set up a first-rate group of men around Jules Charney, who formulated the equations for the motion of climatic phenomena as partial differential equations. They of course had to make many simplifying assumptions, both to formulate the problem and to get it into such a size that our computer could calculate the motion of the weather at speeds in excess of the real speed so that forecasting into the future became possible.

It is not our business to discuss here the details of this project beyond remarking that the results of that effort were taken up by the weather bureaus of all the leading nations of the world. In fact, here in Princeton there is a laboratory established by our weather bureau that devotes its activities to the development of accurate long-range forecasting techniques.

Let us now take up some of the topics that engaged our attention during the period from 1946 to 1957 and that relate to our field. Obviously one of the first and most likely topics to be discussed was the solution of large systems of linear equations, since they arise almost everywhere in numerical work. V. Bargmann and D. Montgomery collaborated with von Neumann on a paper on this subject.[2] Then H. Hotelling, the well-known statistician, wrote an interesting paper in 1943 in which he studied a number of numerical procedures, including the Gaussian method for inverting matrices. He pointed out in a heuristic and as it turned out, inaccurate, way that the Gaussian method for inverting statistical correlation matrices would require about $k + 0.6n$ digits during the computation to obtain k-digit accuracy. Thus to invert a matrix of order 100 would in his terms require 70 digits be used if one wanted 10-digit accuracy.[3]

Johnny and I never quite believed that Gauss would have used a procedure so lacking in elegance, given his great love for computation. Indeed, his collected works contain a considerable amount of material on both astronomy and geodesy that shows his love for and great skill at calculation. As some partial evidence of this, we know he certainly used the so-called Cooley-Tukey method to handle Fourier transforms. Taking his skill as a given, we looked closely at the procedure and wrote a paper on the subject that we used as an elaborate introduction to errors in numerical calculation.[4] We tried in that paper to alert the practitioners in the field to a phenomenon that had not been particularly relevant in the past but was to be a constant source of anxiety in the future: numerical instability. In the course of the analysis we also brought to the fore the now obvious notion of well- and ill-conditioned matrices. Since then, of course, people such as Wilkinson have greatly simplified the very complicated analysis we went through to arrive at our final results.

In a second paper we raised a question that we thought might become more important than in fact it ever became.[5] We said, let us not worry so much about what might happen in a very small number of pathological cases; instead let us see what occurs on the average, what we can expect if we need to do this same task many times. To achieve this probabilistic result I had to develop proofs for several theorems in probability theory, which I did with considerable difficulty, only to receive a letter from a statistician named Mulholland after the paper appeared in which he showed me how to do one part with the slightest work: A mere flip of his wrist sufficed to demonstrate some obvious thing. My only consolation was that Johnny had not seen how to do it simply either. In the event, I suppose that our second paper scared practitioners of the subject away from the field of probabilistic estimates instead of bringing them in, or perhaps it simply was not a very important idea. Human egotism being what it is, I naturally hope it was the former, but honesty makes me think it was the latter.

Other things that one might reasonably want to know about a symmetric matrix are its eigenvalues or, as Veblen used teasingly to say, its proper-*Werte*. At that time Frank Murray, a mathematician from Columbia who had collaborated with von Neumann at one period on operator theory, was in Princeton for a term. The three of us set ourselves the goal of considering all reasonable ways that one might find the eigenvalues and discover which seemed the best in the sense of numerical stability. We made an extensive search and came up with one that pleased us very much. Since I seem to have had some priority on this scheme, it was agreed that I would present it at a 1951 meeting to be held at UCLA, where the National Bureau of Standards had a western numerical institute. There I presented the paper, which was very well received, and then Ostrowski got up and asked me if I knew that this method had first been worked out by Jacobi in 1846.[6] Of course the answer was no. Jacobi was interested in finding a better way to analyze some data of Leverrier in the *Connnaissance des temps* and did it by finding the eigenvalues of a symmetric matrix of order seven. His results significantly improved Leverrier's. I shall not discuss the improvements that Householder and then Givens made to our knowledge of how to find eigenvalues.

Instead I must turn now to the field of partial differential equations. There are several other papers in this volume on this topic, written by people who collaborated with Johnny during his lifetime and continued to make major thrusts after his death. One of Johnny's early interests was hydrodynamics, which he understood profoundly. I must tell you that some, indeed perhaps most, applied mathematicians know a great deal about the mathematical tools that they can use to solve problems but have little deep knowledge of the physics, chemistry, biology, or what have you that underlies their subjects. Not so Johnny. His grasp of the physics, the theory, the apparatus, and the experiments were all food for his interest. It is this that made his interest in the computer so profound. He was very concerned about the electrical characteristics of each type of vacuum tube, and about what resistors, capacitors, and inductances were made of and why. One had the impression that when he entered a field he had to encompass it all, however elaborate it might be.

In any case he was one of the very few people, outside of its three authors, who knew the 1928 paper on the solution of partial difference equations.[7] Here Courant, Friedrichs, and Lewy considered how to solve partial differential equations and in the course of their analysis based on the characteristic curves of hyperbolic difference systems, showed that certain inequalities had to be satisfied. These inequalities now go by the name of Courant conditions. In any case Johnny was a consultant to Los Alamos, where his expertise in hydrodynamics was of great value. He was a leader there for numerical calculation and gathered around himself a group of keen physicists, including Nicholas Metropolis, who became his apostles. His "object all sublime" was to replace experimentation by computation in so far as possible in fields where the equations for a problem could be unambiguously formulated. He even did this using Howard Aiken's electromechanical machine at Harvard to show the feasibility of such procedures.

His enthusiasm and vitality were so great in this connection that I agreed to let Los Alamos put what was then a huge problem on the ENIAC. The task was horrendous: People such as Metropolis and his then colleague Frankel worked like mad to get results. Whether this particular calculation was of any real use to Los Alamos I never asked, but it certainly caused that laboratory and all the other Atomic Energy Commission laboratories to take a vital interest in numerical work.

A look at von Neumann's collected works will show the most casual reader how much effort he and his collaborators (such as Goldstine, Metropolis, Richtmyer, Taub, and Ulam) put into hydrodynamic calculations. This meant, in effect, studies of hyperbolic and parabolic partial differential equations. One of the most interesting things for von Neumann in the study of hyperbolic equations was the truly anomalous and remarkable emergence of shocks—discontinuities—in otherwise thoroughly smooth situations, brought about by very slight and continuous motions. A number of his papers relate to precisely this point. One we wrote analyzed what happens if a very powerful explosion takes place at a point in a homogeneous medium.[8] The result is a spherical blast wave that emanates from the point. The shock was handled by making use of an iterative procedure originally used by Peierls for solving the Rankine-Hugoniot equations. Another intriguing method for coping with shocks was developed by Johnny and Robert Richtmyer, who conceived the idea of arbitrarily introducing some viscosity into an otherwise inviscid fluid.[9] This is the same thing as introducing artificial dissipative terms into the equations, giving the shocks a thickness roughly comparable to the mesh size of the numerical net. This changes the shocks into near discontinuities that propagate at essentially the right speeds and across which the temperatures and pressures change by nearly the right amounts. This meant that one could totally ignore the Rankine-Hugoniot equations and proceed in a simple numerical fashion.

Von Neumann's interest in hydrodynamic and related calculations arising at Los Alamos and other places where nuclear particles were under study also resulted in the development of a lovely and perhaps totally unexpected gem of a field: Monte Carlo.

This was a nice example of von Neumann's combining interests in a number of subjects. He saw here how Newton's brilliance had enabled people to express in continuous form equations relating discrete particles, so that instead of horrible systems of unmanageable equations one could write down a few elegant conservation relations and solve the equations that they embody. Now the numerical revolution caused the analyst to replace the continuous equations by systems of discrete ones. Johnny and Ulam got the idea of returning to finite systems and playing repeated games according to the rules of probability theory.

Instead of saying more on this, perhaps I can just mention some work that we did on a conjecture of Kummer.[10] This was part of an idea that we had of using the computer as a new and improved form of scratch pad to develop examples and counterexamples. Artin had mentioned to us this conjecture of Kummer which was based on a very few—in fact on 45—cases. Artin believed that it was too difficult to undertake a proof of the conjecture without more evidence of its truth. We accordingly ran a test for about 10,000 values and found that there was little evidence from our results to justify Artin or anyone else in undertaking a major effort to try to establish the result.

I often think that in addition to all the individually remarkable things that Johnny did in our field, he did something else that may almost be more important. This is a matter that I have skirted in what I have said to this point and which I find difficult to discuss without someone's thinking that I am making a pejorative remark. I believe that von Neumann's great status in the world of the physical and social sciences was sufficient so that when he told people to compute digitally and not to make analog computations by means of various sorts of physical experiments they believed him. I think that this in large measure accounted for the early acceptance of the digital computer. I do not imply by my remark that it was necessary for the ultimate use of the computer by the scientific world at large; I simply mean that he caused it all to happen at a rate that was much accelerated over what it would have been had he not influenced the field so decisively. I should like to give two examples of this. First, young Tom Watson, Jr., just back from being a pilot in the CBI (China, Burma, India) area and having heard of Johnny and his interest in electronic computing, came to the Institute for Advanced Study to see for himself what the new world was all about. I feel very certain that this had an extremely important impact on IBM and hence on the world at large. The other example arose from the fact that Johnny, after joining the Atomic Energy Commission, exerted great influence on the laboratories of the Commission to use computers and to authorize both IBM and Sperry-Rand to undertake a sort of competition that resulted in two monster machines for their era—the Stretch and the Larc computers. Out of these, many great advances in our modern world arose.

Instead of continuing I think that this is perhaps a good point to close by illustrating Johnny's expository style when applied to a technical subject that he wanted to make clear to a nontechnical audience. To do this I include some paragraphs from an address that he gave at the dedication of a large electronic computer built by IBM for the Naval Ordnance Research Laboratory.[11]

> The three main areas of geophysics are, of course, air, water, and earth. Let me begin with the air, i.e., with the phenomena in the atmosphere. I am referring to dynamical, or theoretical, meteorology. This subject has for a number of years been accessible to extensive calculations. It is therefore worthwhile to estimate what NORC could do in this area.
> We know today, mainly due to the work of J. Charney, that we can predict by calculation the weather over an area like that of the United

States for a duration like 24 hours in a manner, which, from the hydrodynamicist's point of view may be quite primitive because one need for this purpose only consider one level in the atmosphere, i.e., the mean position of the atmosphere.

We know that this gives results which are, by and large, as good as what an experienced "subjective" forecaster can achieve, and this is very respectable. This kind of calculation, from start to finish, would take about a half minute with NORC.

We know, furthermore, that this calculation can be refined a good deal. One cannot refine the mathematical treatment *ad infinitum* because once the mathematical precision has been reached at a certain level, further improvements lose their significance, since the physical assumptions which enter into it are no longer adequate.

In our present, simple descriptions of the atmosphere, this level, as we know, is reached when one deals with approximately three or four levels in the atmosphere. This is a calculation which NORC would probably do (for 24 hours ahead) in something of the order of 5 to 60 minutes.

We know that calculations of meteorological forecasts for longer periods, like 30 to 60 days, which one would particularly want to perform, are probably possible but that one will then have to consider areas that are much larger than the United States. In a duration like 30 days—in fact in much shorter durations, like 10–15 days—influences from remote parts of the globe interact. We also know that interaction between the Northern and Southern Hemispheres is not very strong. Therefore, one can probably limit the calculation in the main to one entire hemisphere, but not to a smaller area.

Such calculations have so far only been performed in tentative and simplified ways and all those who have worked on these problems have done so in the sense of a preliminary orientation only. . . .

A calculation of this order on NORC would, I think, require something of the order of 24 hours' computing time. This can be off by a factor of perhaps two, one way or other, but in any event this order of magnitude is acceptable for research purposes.

In this area, therefore, an instrument like NORC becomes essential at about this latter level. Indeed, whether one does a simple 24-hour forecast in half an hour or in two minutes is not decisive. But in a 30 day hemispheric calculation it is very important whether one needs 24 hours or a month. If it takes a month one will probably not do it. If it takes 24 hours, one may be willing to spend several months doing it 20 times, which is just what is needed.

Notes

1 Ptolemy worked with chords, not sines, with chord $2\alpha = 2\sin\alpha$, constructing a table of chords in increments of a degree rather than of sines in increments of half a degree. In addition, it may appear odd that $\sin(3/4)$ would be easier to compute than $\sin(1/2)$. Ptolemy knew the values for $72°$ and $60°$. Also, given the values for A and B, he could

calculate results for $A + B$, and hence for 12°. From a half-angle formula, he was able to obtain the values for 6°, 3°, $^3/_2$°, and finally $^3/_4$°. (ed.)

2 J. von Neumann, "Solution of Linear Systems of High Order," *Collected Works* V (1963): 421–77.

3 H. Hotelling, "Some New Methods in Matrix Calculation," *Ann. Math. Stat.* 14 (1943): 1–34.

4 J. von Neumann, "Numerical Inverting of Matrices of High Order I, II," *Collected Works* V (1963): 479–572.

5 J. von Neumann, "Numerical Inverting of Matrices of High Order II," *Collected Works* V (1963): 558–72.

6 C. G. J. Jacobi, "Über ein leichtes Verfahren die in der Theorie der Säcularstörungen vorkommenden Gleichungen numerisch aufzulösen," *J. Reine Angew. Math.* 30 (1846): 51–95.

7 R. Courant, K. O. Friedrichs, and H. Lewy, "Über die partiellen Differenzengleichungen der mathematischen Physik," *Math. Ann.* 100 (1927): 32–74.

8 J. von Neumann, "Blast Wave Calculation," *Collected Works* VI (1963): 386–412.

9 J. von Neumann, "A Method for the Numerical Calculation of Hydrodynamic Shocks," *Collected Works* VI (1963): 380–85.

10 J. von Neumann, "A Numerical Study of a Conjecture of Kummer," *Collected Works* V (1963): 771–72.

11 J. von Neumann, "The NORC and Problems in High Speed Computing," *Collected Works* V (1963): 241–44.

The Contribution of J. H. Wilkinson to Numerical Analysis

B. N. Parlett*

1. A Brief Outline of His Career

James Hardy Wilkinson died suddenly at his London home on 5 October 1986 at the age of 67. Here is a very brief account of his professional life.

When he was 16 years old, Wilkinson won an open competition scholarship in mathematics to Trinity College, Cambridge. He won two coveted prizes (the Pemberton and the Mathison) while he was an undergraduate there and graduated with first class honors before he was 20 years old.

Throughout World War II he worked as a mathematician for the Ministry of Supply, and it was there that he met and married his wife, Heather. In 1946 he joined the recently formed group of numerical analysts at the National Physical Laboratory in Bushy Park on the outskirts of London. He was to stay there until his retirement in 1980. Soon after his arrival he began to work with Alan Turing on the design of an electronic digital computer, in addition to his work with the numerical analysts using mechanical computing machines. That work led to the pilot (prototype) machine ACE which executed its first scientific calculations in 1953. Wilkinson designed the multiplication unit for ACE and its successor DEUCE.

One could say that the decade 1947–1957 was the exciting *learning* period in which Wilkinson and his colleagues at NPL discovered how automatic computation differed from human computation assisted by desk-top calculating machines. By dint of trying every method that they could think of and watching the progress of their computations on punched cards, paper tape, or even lights on the control console, these pioneers won an invaluable practical understanding of how algorithms behave when implemented on computers.

Some algorithms that are guaranteed to deliver the solution after a fixed number of primitive arithmetic operations *in exact arithmetic* can produce, on some problems, completely wrong yet plausible output on a digital computer. That is the fundamental challenge of the branch of numerical analysis of which Wilkinson became the leader: matrix

* The author gratefully acknowledges partial support from Office of Naval Research Contract ONR N00014–85–K–0180.

computations. He was the first to see the pattern in the bewildering mass of output.

The period 1958–1973 saw the development, articulation, and dissemination of this understanding of dense matrix computations. It was in 1958 that Wilkinson began giving short courses at the University of Michigan Summer College of Engineering. The notes served as the preliminary versions of his first two books. The lectures themselves introduced his work to an audience broader than the small group of specialists who had been brought together in 1957 by Wallace Givens at Wayne State University, Michigan, for the first of a sequence of workshops that came to be called the Gatlinburg meetings. These conferences are discussed in more detail in the paper by R. S. Varga in this volume. The year 1973 saw the beginning of the NATS project (at Argonne National Laboratory, USA), whose goal was to translate into FORTRAN and test in a most exigent manner the ALGOL algorithms collected in the celebrated *Handbook* of 1971. That book, written essentially by Wilkinson and Reinsch, embodied most of what had been learnt about matrix transformations. There is more on this topic in the following sections.

By 1973 Wilkinson had received the most illustrious awards of his career. He was awarded a Doctor of Science Degree at Cambridge in 1963. He was elected to the Royal Society of London in 1969. In 1970 he was awarded both the A. M. Turing award of the Association for Computing Machinery and the John von Neumann award of the Society for Industrial and Applied Mathematics. Both these professional groups are in the United States. It was not until 1977 that he was made an honorary fellow of the (British) Institute for Mathematics and its Applications.

The final period, 1974–1986, may be marked by Wilkinson's promotion to the Council of the Royal Society. Indeed he served as secretary for the physical sciences section for two or three years, and these duties absorbed much of his energy. When that obligation was discharged he accepted a professorship in the Computer Science department at Stanford University, California (1977–1984). He was only in residence for the Winter quarter, however, and was not able to take up his position every year. His research now focused on more advanced but less urgent numerical tasks, such as computing the Jordan form, Kronecker's form for matrix pencils, and various condition numbers. During the last four years of his life he was absorbed in the still-open problem of how to determine the closest defective matrix to any given square matrix. He also gave much attention to the task of explaining to the wider mathematical community the nature of the subject with which his name is indissolubly linked: roundoff error analysis. The following sections will say more on this expository problem.

2. Background

People are awed at the prodigious speed at which the digital computers of the 1980s can execute primitive arithmetic operations: sometimes millions of them per second. Yet this speed is achieved at a price; almost every answer is wrong. When two 14-decimal digit numbers are multiplied together, only the leading 14 digits are retained, and the remaining 13 or 14 digits are discarded forever. If such a cavalier attitude to accuracy were to make nonsense of all our calculations, then the prodigious speeds would be pointless. Moreover it requires little experience to discover how easily a digital computer can produce meaningless numbers.

Fortunately there are procedures that can survive these arithmetic errors and produce output that has adequate accuracy. Consequently computers can be useful. The difficult task is to discern the robust algorithms. A poor implementation can undermine a sound mathematical procedure and this simple fact has extensive and unpleasant consequences. It suggests that clean, general statements about the properties of numerical methods may not always be possible. Here is an example: Will the process of iterative refinement improve the accuracy of the output of a good implementation of Gauss elimination on an ill-conditioned system of linear equations? The answer turns out to depend on whether certain intermediate quantities are computed with extra care. Considerations of this sort make it difficult to present the results of an error analysis, and Wilkinson became more and more concerned with this problem.

Before embarking on a list of Wilkinson's contributions, five points must be emphasized.

1. Only a minority of numerical analysts pay attention to roundoff error. For example, in his influential book [16], R. S. Varga mentions in the introduction that he will not be considering the effects of roundoff error. Virtually every publication concerned with the approximate solution of differential equations invokes exact arithmetic. The tacit and warranted assumption is that the approximation errors are so much greater than the effect of roundoff that the latter may be ignored without risk.

Let us pause a moment. The foregoing remarks seem paradoxical at best. If most numerical analysts, including those who model fluid flows, can legitimately ignore roundoff error, then perhaps these little inaccuracies in the basic arithmetic operations are not of much consequence and Wilkinson's work, though clever, concerns only a limited part of the subject.

This anomaly warrants a full discussion, but that would distract us from Wilkinson. Suffice it to say that scientific computation can be divided into two parts according to the role of roundoff error. Yet it is odd how these tiny arithmetic inaccuracies leap sharply from being negligible in one domain to critical in the other. A dozen roundoff errors, even a single one in the wrong place, can cause totally misleading output. That is why statistical treatment of roundoff has not found favor in matrix calculations.

Wilkinson's brand of numerical analysis is perhaps best regarded as an extra layer in the analysis of approximate solutions. It slips in just above the arithmetic facilities themselves but below the discretization of partial differential equations.

2. The pages that follow give the erroneous impression that Wilkinson single-handedly showed the world how to analyze the effect of roundoff error on the procedures used to solve matrix problems. Yet this mode of expression is no worse than the familiar statement that William of Normandy won the battle of Hastings in 1066. Wilkinson did receive all the honors and most would agree that he became the leader of the group. Yet he was not working in isolation. Other people independently came to understand how roundoff errors can destroy a computation. I would like to insert my personal opinion that had Wilkinson returned to classical analysis at Cambridge in 1947, our present state of understanding of roundoff would not be significantly changed. F. L. Bauer of Munich could have become the dominant figure, or H. Rutishauser of Zurich.

3. The production of the *Handbook* was a remarkable achievement. It testifies to cordial and close cooperation between leading experts in several European countries, the United States, and Australia. In contrast, consider the application of the simplex algorithm to linear programs and the finite element method to analyze structures. There it was the habit for engineers with debugged programs to form companies around those programs. The quest for profit stifled cooperation for improvement. Wilkinson's friendly yet exacting personality played no small part in the success of the *Handbook* venture. I am aware of no disharmony among the leading researchers on matrix problems.

4. A digital computer works with a finite set of representable numbers, which may be combined using operations $\oplus$, $\ominus$, $\otimes$, $\oslash$ that mimic the familiar $+$, $-$, $\times$, $/$. Unfortunately, some basic properties of the rational number field fail to hold for the computer's system. For example, the associative law fails for both addition and multiplication: $a \oplus (b \oplus c)$ is not always the same as $(a \oplus b) \oplus c$. Nevertheless, there is some algebraic

structure left and it seemed quite likely during the 1950s that rigorous error analysis would have to be carried out in this unattractive setting. Indeed there have appeared a number of ponderous tomes that do manage to abstract the computer's numbers into a formal structure and burden us with more jargon.

To those who work in the field of matrix computations, Wilkinson's least appreciated achievement, perhaps, was to deflect analysis of algorithms from jargon-laden formality into a mode in which insight and simplicity can survive. He made no use of the pseudo-operators, preferring to work with the exact relations satisfied by the computed quantities.

5. In contrast to many mathematicians (and despite his more than 100 published papers), Wilkinson's fundamental contribution to numerical analysis is contained in the three books of which he is an author. In the remainder of this essay we shall attempt to give the flavor of his work.

3. Roundoff Error Analysis

Wilkinson is honored for achieving a very satisfactory understanding of the effect of rounding errors during the execution of procedures that are used for solving matrix problems and finding zeros of polynomials. He managed to share his grasp of the subject with others by making error analysis intelligible, in particular by his systematic use of the "backward," or inverse, point of view. This approach asks whether there is a tiny perturbation of the data such that execution of the algorithm in exact arithmetic using the perturbed data would terminate with the actual computed output derived from the original data. This approach is mentioned in an article by Turing [15], but not developed.

Wilkinson did not invent backward error analysis, nor did he refrain from using the natural (or forward) error analysis when appropriate. Although his name is not associated with any particular method, he performed rigorous analyses of almost every method that was under discussion and trial. This work led him to become one of the leaders of an activity known as mathematical software production. The collection of Algol procedures contained in the *Handbook* (see the reference list) is a seminal contribution to this branch of computer science.

Most of what follows is amplification of the preceding paragraphs. If the reader is impatient for a theorem or delicate inequality, the following quotation from *Modern Error Analysis* (1971) may engender a little forbearance. This is from the published version of Wilkinson's von Neumann lecture.

There is still a tendency to attach too much importance to the precise error bounds obtained by an a priori error analysis. In my opinion, the bound itself is usually the least important part of it. The main object of such an analysis is to expose the potential instabilities, if any, of an algorithm so that, hopefully, from the insight thus obtained one might be led to improved algorithms. Usually the bound itself is weaker than it might have been because of the necessity of restricting the mass of detail to a reasonable level and because of the limitations imposed by expressing the errors in terms of matrix norms. A priori bounds are not, in general, quantities that should be used in practice. Practical error bounds should usually be determined by some form of a posteriori error analysis, since this takes full advantage of the statistical distribution of rounding errors and of any special features, such as sparseness, of the matrix.[9]

We would add that there is as yet no satisfactory format for presenting an error analysis so that its message can be summarized succinctly. Could we say that the analysis is the message?

To the mathematical reader of the following sections both the idea and application of backward error analysis may seem rather straight-forward. Readers may ask themselves whether the honors given to Wilkinson are warranted. In response we would say that despite its apparent simplicity, the *significance* of backward error analysis did not occur to either Alan Turing or John von Neumann despite the fact that both of them were thinking about related matters. To my mind an even better illustration of the elusive nature of this idea is Wilkinson's own observation that he explicitly made a backward analysis of Horner's method for evaluating a polynomial *three years* before he thought of applying the technique to Gaussian elimination.

One surprising implication of Wilkinson's researches is that the number of significant digits in the intermediate numbers generated in a computation may be quite irrelevant to the accuracy of the output.

To be specific, suppose that an eigenvalue algorithm generates from a square matrix A_0 a sequence of matrices $\{A_1, A_2, \ldots, A_n\}$ each of which is similar to A_0. If the effect of roundoff error is to produce a sequence $\{B_1, B_2, \ldots, B_n\}$ such that B_n bears little or no resemblance to A_n, then there is no cause for alarm *provided that B_n is very nearly similar to A_0*. The number of correct digits in each element of B_n is irrelevant to the accuracy of the eigenvalues.

4. The Linear Equations Problem

Given an $n \times n$ real invertible matrix A and $b \in R^n$, the task is to compute $x = A^{-1}b$. The familiar process known as Gaussian elimination lends itself to implementation on automatic digital computers. It is also well known that Gaussian elimination is one way to factor A into the product LU where L is lower triangular and U is upper triangular. Once L and U are known, the solution x is obtained by solving two triangular systems: $Lc = b$, $Ux = c$. Roundoff is the only source of error.

In 1943, Hotelling published an analysis showing that the error in a computed inverse X might well grow like 4^{n-1} where n is the order of A. Alan Turing was making similar analyses informally in England. The fear spread that Gaussian elimination was probably unstable in the face of roundoff error. The search was on for alternative algorithms.

In 1947 Goldstine and von Neumann, in a formidable 80-page paper [12], corrected this false impression to some extent. Some scholars have chosen the appearance of this paper as the birthday of modern numerical analysis. Among other things, this paper showed how the systematic use of vector and matrix norms could enhance error analysis. However, it had the unfortunate side effect of suggesting that only people of the calibre of von Neumann and Goldstine were capable of completing error analyses and, even worse, that the production of such work was very boring. Their principal result was that if A is symmetric and positive definite, then the computed inverse X satisfies

$$\| AX - I \| \le (14.2)n^2\epsilon \operatorname{cond}(A)$$

where $\operatorname{cond}(A) = \| A \| \cdot \| A^{-1} \|$; $\| \cdot \|$ is the spectral norm; and ϵ denotes the roundoff unit of the computer. Only if A is too close to singular will the algorithm fail and yield no X at all, but that is as it should be. The joy of this result was getting a polynomial in n, and the pain was obtaining 14.2, a number that reflects little more than the exigencies of the analysis. Some nice use of "backward" error analysis occurs in the paper, but it is incidental. There was good reason for this attitude.

A backward error analysis is not guaranteed to succeed. Indeed, no one to this day has shown that a properly computed inverse X is guaranteed to be the inverse of some matrix close to A, that is,

$$X = (A + E)^{-1} \text{ and } \| E \| / \| A \| \text{ is small}$$

Indeed, it is likely that no such result holds in full generality. What is true is that each column of X is the corresponding column of the inverse of a matrix very close to A. Unfortunately, it is a different matrix for each column.

The success of their analysis of the positive definite case prompted von Neumann and Goldstine to recommend the use of the normal equations for solving $Ax = b$ for general A; that is, $x = (A^TA)^{-1}A^Tb$. However, that was bad advice for several reasons.

The fact is that careful Gaussian elimination, if it does not break down, produces computed solutions z with tiny residuals. It was practical experience in solving systems of equations using desk-top calculators (with n as large as 18!) that persuaded Wilkinson and his colleagues (L. Fox and E. T. Goodwin) that Gaussian elimination does give excellent results even when A is far from being symmetric, let alone positive definite. In his 1959 IFIP talk, we find for the first time a clear statement of the situation. The result is also presented on page 108 in his first book [1]. The computed solution z satisfies

$$(A + K)z = b$$

If inner products are accumulated in double precision before the final rounding, then

$$\| K \|_\infty \le g\epsilon(2.005n^2 + n^3 + \tfrac{1}{4}\epsilon n^4)\| A \|_\infty$$

where g is the element growth factor, namely the ratio of the largest intermediate value generated in the process to a maximal element of A. The corresponding bound on the residual is

$$\| b - Az \|_\infty \le g\epsilon(2.005n^2 + n^3)\| z \|_\infty$$

provided that $\epsilon n \ll 1$. The important quantity g is easily monitored during execution of the algorithm. In his celebrated 1961 paper on matrix inversion [4], Wilkinson obtained an a priori bound on g when A is equilibrated and the "complete" pivoting strategy is employed. This is a clever piece of analysis and yields

$$g^2 = g(n)^2 < n(2^1 3^{1/2} \cdots n^{\frac{1}{n-1}})$$

which is a slowly growing function of n. Being a man of intellectual integrity, Wilkinson hastens to show that the bound cannot be sharp and indeed is not realistic at all. For certain Hadamard matrices, $g(n) = n$, but apart from these cases Wilkinson reports that he has *never* encountered a value of g exceeding 8 despite intensive monitoring of the programs in use at NPL.

At this point we wish to emphasize that all the results quoted so far do a disservice both to Wilkinson and to the topic of error analysis. Neither the powers of n that appear in the inequalities quoted above nor the coefficients in front of those powers convey genuine information about the process under analysis! It could be argued that the residual bound $\|b - Az\| < g\epsilon n^3\|z\|$ is very weak indeed. *Wilkinson's contribution cannot be conveyed by quoting such theorems.* His achievements in regard to Gaussian elimination were to show the following:

- ☐ The effect of roundoff errors is not difficult to analyze. Indeed, the analysis is now presented in undergraduate courses.
- ☐ If the element growth factor g is small (say, $g < 100$) then the computed solution will have a residual norm scarcely larger than that belonging to the representable vector closest to $A^{-1}b$.

- When A is ill-conditioned, that is, when $\| A \| \cdot \| A^{-1} \| \sqrt{\epsilon} > 1$, then g is very likely to be 1 if a reasonable pivoting strategy is used. In fact, for many ill-conditioned matrices the complete pivoting strategy produces factors L and U with elements that diminish rapidly as the algorithm proceeds.

- The technique known as iterative refinement may be employed to obtain an accurate solution provided that the system is not too ill-conditioned for the precision of the arithmetic operations. Moreover, if the iteration converges slowly, then the coefficient matrix A must be ill-conditioned.

- The partial pivoting strategy cannot guarantee that g will be small. There exist matrices for which $g = 2^{n-2}$.

The following very specific result of the 1961 paper is, to me, more interesting and more informative than all its theorems. The following Hilbert matrix was a favorite test example in the 1940s and 1950s.

$$H = (h_{ij}), h_{ij} = (i + j - 1)^{-1}$$

H_n denotes the leading principal $n \times n$ submatrix of H. Formulas are known for H^{-1}. Wilkinson showed that when Gaussian elimination was used to invert H on a binary machine, then the act of rounding the fractions $1/3, 1/5, 1/6, 1/7, 1/9$ to the closest representable numbers caused more deviation in the computed inverse than all the rounding errors that occur in the rest of the computation. That computation involves more than 100 multiplications and 100 additions.

Despite several significant insights, the celebrated 1961 paper still does not make clear just how stable Gaussian elimination is for solving $Ax = b$. The contrast between this paper and the 1963 book is instructive. The paper follows the lead of von Neumann and Goldstine and concentrates exclusively on the problem of matrix inversion. Not only are the error bounds rather large, but backward error analysis fails. However, the problem of matrix inversion is not very important. The overwhelming demand is for solving systems of equations, and here the backward analysis is simple and very satisfactory. The computed solution z satisfies some equation $(A + K)z = b$, and the insight comes in seeing how K depends on L, U and other quantities. The insight vanishes when norms are taken. Too much information is discarded.

5. The Eigenvalue Problem

Nearly three quarters of Wilkinson's publication list is devoted to this subject. No specific method bears his name, yet every available method was analyzed by him and most of the published implementations of the better techniques owe something to his careful scrutiny.

The eigenvalue problem comprises many subproblems. The primary distinction is between symmetric matrices and the rest. For both classes the eigenvectors may or may not be needed. It is easy to describe Wilkinson's contribution to this topic: It is his magnum opus, *The Algebraic Eigenvalue Problem* [2]. However, that gives only half the picture. That book gave the understanding needed to produce the eigenvalue programs that appeared in the *Handbook* [3]. The latter was edited jointly with the gifted but self-effacing Dr. Christian Reinsch. The *Handbook* gave rise to the collection of Fortran programs called EISPACK that first appeared in 1974. The later version of these routines (1977) is available in virtually every scientific computer center in the world. It is pleasant to report that this useful product was achieved by the willing cooperation of many experts. To some extent this happy outcome is due to Wilkinson's generous and agreeable personality, for he was certainly the leader of the group.

At a more technical level we now discuss some of his "results." Journal articles are given in the brief reference list at the end of this essay.

□ His study of polynomials, and the sensitivity of their zeros to changes in their coefficients, helped to stop the quest for the characteristic polynomial as a means of computing eigenvalues. See [1].

□ In 1954, W. Givens explicitly used backward error analysis to demonstrate the extreme accuracy of the Sturm sequence technique for locating specified eigenvalues of symmetric tridiagonal matrices. His analysis was for fixed-point arithmetic and was never published. Wilkinson showed that the result also holds for standard floating-point arithmetic and that contrary to popular wisdom, backward error analysis of most algorithms is easier to perform for floating-point arithmetic. Even more interesting was his demonstration that Givens' Sturm sequence algorithm could be disastrous for computing eigenvectors though simultaneously superb for locating eigenvalues. The point is worth emphasizing. Given an appropriate eigenvalue that is correct to working precision, the eigenvector recurrence can sometimes produce an approximate eigenvector that is orthogonal to the true direction to working accuracy though the signs of the computed components are correct. The contribution here was a well-chosen class of examples.

□ Wilkinson showed that the backward error analysis of any method employing a sequence of orthogonal similarity transformations can be made clear and simple. In particular, the final matrix is similar to a small perturbation of the original matrix. This perturbation is essentially the sum of the local errors at each step: There is no propagated error.

An important consequence of this analysis is the following. Let C denote the equivalence class of matrices orthogonally similar to the original matrix. For the computation of eigenvalues, it does not matter if roundoff errors cause the computed sequence to depart violently from the exactly computed sequence *provided that* the computed sequence lies close to C. A naive forward analysis can miss vital correlations between computed quantities.

Indeed a number of efficient, stable algorithms do regularly produce intermediate quantities that differ significantly from their exact counterparts. Nevertheless, eigenvalues are preserved to within working accuracy. The QR algorithm is an example of this phenomenon.

☐ Although it was invented in 1959 and 1960, the QR algorithm of J. G. F. Francis did not achieve universal acceptance until about 1965. It provides an ideal way to diagonalize a symmetric tridiagonal matrix because it produces a sequence of symmetric tridiagonal matrices that converge to diagonal form. However the QR algorithm requires a strategy for choosing shifts. Let

$$
T = \begin{bmatrix}
\alpha_1 & \beta_1 & & & \\
\beta_1 & \alpha_2 & \beta_2 & & \\
& \beta_2 & \cdot & & \cdot \\
& & \cdot & & \cdot & \beta_{n-1} \\
& & & \beta_{n-1} & \alpha_n
\end{bmatrix}
$$

be a typical matrix in the QR sequence. Wilkinson's shift w is defined to be the eigenvalue of

$$
\begin{bmatrix}
\alpha_{n-1} & \beta_{n-1} \\
\beta_{n-1} & \alpha_n
\end{bmatrix}
$$

that is closer to α_n. It is the favorite strategy (rather than choosing α_n), but when it was first introduced there was no proof that it would always lead to convergence. Convergence here means that $\beta_{n-1} \to 0$ as the algorithm is continued without limit. The Rayleigh quotient shift α_n causes the β_{n-1} to be monotone decreasing, but the limit need not vanish. Wilkinson's shift sacrifices the monotonicity and gains convergence.

In a tour-de-force in 1971, Wilkinson proved that with his strategy, convergence is assured (in exact arithmetic) and is usually cubic. A tricky argument showed that the product $\beta_{n-2}\beta_{n-1}$ is monotone decreasing to zero though initially the rate could be very slow.

This was not the last word, however. In 1979 Parlett and Hoffman discovered an elementary proof that $\beta_{n-1}^2 \beta_{n-2}$ decreases geometrically at each step by a factor that is at most $1/\sqrt{2}$. Convergence of β_{n-1} to 0 follows readily.

□ In 1976, Wilkinson and Golub published a definitive article on the Jordan canonical form. They discussed its discontinuous dependence on the matrix elements in the defective case and showed how to go about computing robust bases for the associated cyclic subspaces (the numerical analyst's Jordan chains of principal vectors). They also explained the limitations of this form in practical calculations.

A natural extension of this research was to the computation of the Kronecker form of a pair of matrices (A, B). This form arises in the study of systems of differential equations with constant coefficients:

$$B\dot{u} = Au \qquad u(0) \in R^n \text{ is given}$$

□ In the last decade of his life, Wilkinson's attention was more and more attracted to the difficult and still-open problem of determining, for any given A, the closest defective matrix B. The article [10] gives some penetrating insights into the subtleties of this task.

6. The Zeros of Polynomials

Until near the end of the 1950s, the computation of the zeros of polynomials was regarded as a vital ingredient in scientific computation. It is not surprising, then, that a significant part of Wilkinson's work of this period was devoted to this task. His contribution is consolidated in Chapter 2 of *Rounding Errors* [1]. Thanks in part to his discoveries, polynomials no longer attract much attention. It was the advent of digital computers that drove people to think in detail about general polynomials of large degree: say 20 or 100 or even 1000.

Since isolated zeros are analytic functions of the coefficients, one may consider the derivative of any isolated zero with respect to each coefficient. As the degree rises, these derivatives can hardly avoid becoming huge. The presence of such an ill-conditioned zero can make it difficult to compute comparatively well-conditioned zeros.

By use of well chosen examples, Wilkinson brought these facts home to numerical analysts. Of considerable personal interest is the fact that Wilkinson was led to an explicit appreciation of the importance of backward error analysis when he investigated the reliability of Horner's method (also known as nested multiplication) for *evaluating* a polynomial. He realized that with floating-point arithmetic, the output of Horner's recurrence is, in all cases, the exact value of a polynomial whose coefficients are each tiny relative perturbations of the original ones. The relative change in the coefficient of x^r is less than

$$(1.01)(r + 1)2\epsilon$$

where ϵ is the roundoff unit. In the majority of cases the inherent uncertainty in each coefficient will exceed this given worst case error. In this way a fearsome error analysis melts away into classical perturbation theory.

One of Wilkinson's final works, "The Perfidious Polynomial," [11], sums up his experience with polynomials in a way that is designed for readers outside numerical analysis. This pellucid essay was awarded the Chauvenet prize for mathematical exposition. Unfortunately, Wilkinson died before he could receive it.

Selected References

Books by J. H. Wilkinson

[1] *Rounding Errors in Algebraic Processes*, Notes on Applied Science, No. 32 (National Physical Laboratory, England: HMSO, 1963). Also published in 1964 by Prentice Hall.

[2] *The Algebraic Eigenvalue Problem* (Oxford University Press, 1965).

[3] Edited with C. Reinsch, *Handbook for Automatic Computation, Volume II: Linear Algebra* (New York: Springer-Verlag, 1971).

Selected Articles by J. H. Wilkinson

[4] "Error Analysis of Direct Methods of Matrix Inversion," *J. Assoc. Comput. Mach.* 8 (1961): 281–329.

[5] "Error Analysis of Eigenvalue Techniques Based on Orthogonal Transformations," *SIAM J.* 10 (1962): 162–95.

[6] "Global Convergence of Tridiagonal QR Algorithm with Origin Shifts," *Linear Algebra Appl.* 1 (1968): 409–20.

[7] With G. H. Golub, "Ill-conditioned Eigensystems and the Computation of the Jordan Canonical Form," *SIAM Rev.* 18 (1976): 578–619.

[8] "Kronecker's Canonical Form and the QZ Algorithm," *Linear Algebra Appl.* 28 (1979): 295–305.

[9] "Modern Error Analysis," *SIAM Rev.* 14 (1971): 548–68.

[10] "On Neighbouring Matrices with Quadratic Elementary Divisors," *Numer. Math.* 44 (1984): 1–21.

[11] "The Perfidious Polynomial," in *Studies in Numerical Analysis*, Gene Golub (ed.) (Washington, DC: Mathematics Association of America, 1984): 1–28.

Works Not by J. H. Wilkinson

[12] H. H. Goldstine and J. von Neumann, "Numerical Inventing of Matrices of High Order," *Bull. Amer. Math. Soc.* 53 (1947): 1021–1099.

[13] W. Hoffman and B. N. Parlett, "A New Proof of Global Convergence for the Tridiagonal QL Algorithm," *SIAM J. Numer. Anal.* 15 (1978): 929–37.

[14] H. Hotelling, "Some New Methods in Matrix Calculations," *Ann. Math. Stat.* 14 (1943): 1–34.

[15] A. M. Turing, "Rounding-off Errors in Matrix Processes," *Q. J. Mech. & Appl. Math.* 1 (1948): 287–308.

[16] R. S. Varga, *Matrix Iterative Analysis* (Englewood Cliffs, NJ: Prentice Hall, 1962).

The Influence of George Forsythe and His Students

James Varah

1. Introduction

It is a pleasure to have the opportunity to comment on the influence of George Forsythe from my point of view as one of his students and from a perspective 15 years after his death. This article owes much to earlier commentaries on George, published immediately following his death, and also to material made available to me by George's daughter, Diana Forsythe, and by the Stanford Archives.

2. His Life

The facts concerning George's life are easy enough to list: He was born in 1917 in State College, Pennsylvania, and spent most of his formative years in Ann Arbor, Michigan. He attended Swarthmore College, graduating with a major in Mathematics in 1937. He attended graduate school at Brown University and received his Ph.D. in 1941. During World War II he worked for the Air Force as a meteorologist; following the war he worked principally for UCLA and the National Bureau of Standards before going to Stanford University as a professor of Mathematics in 1957.

It was for the period at Stanford, from 1957 to his untimely death in 1972, that George is probably best remembered. His interest in computing (scientific and otherwise), which had begun at NBS, developed and flourished at Stanford—he was instrumental in forming a computer science division within the Mathematics Department in 1961 and was Director of the Stanford Computation Center from 1961 to 1965. Then, in 1965, he became the first head of the newly formed Department of Computer Science. During his headship, the department developed into one of the truly outstanding departments of computer science anywhere, a position it has continued to hold.

George died suddenly of cancer in the spring of 1972. His untimely death was a shock to all his many colleagues and friends and resulted in numerous memorials and dedications: an article in the SIGNUM Newsletter [3]; two articles in the CACM [1,2]; a special Stanford memorial resolution by Herriot and colleagues, available from the Stanford archives; and a special issue of the SIAM Journal on Numerical Analysis (April 1973) with a dedication by Alston House-

FIGURE 1.
George Forsythe.

holder. Moreover, when a new building to house the Computation Center was built in 1980, it was named after him. Two national awards bear his name: the ACM undergraduate paper competition and the SIGNUM memorial lecturer award for leadership in numerical mathematics.

3. His Research

George's early interest in scientific computation was fostered by the meteorological problems he was involved with during the war. Then, while at NBS, he interacted with many of the early pioneers in scientific computation when this group was coming to grips with the intricacies of basic floating-point computation. His early work on the numerical solution of partial differential equations culminated in his 1960 book with Wasow, *Finite Difference Methods for Partial Differential Equations*. This book remained a standard in the field for many years.

He also made contributions to the use of orthogonal polynomials in scientific computation and to our understanding of various aspects of the solution of linear systems. Two other textbooks remain in use today: *Computer Solution of Linear Algebraic Systems*, with Cleve Moler (1967), and *Computer Methods for Mathematical Computations*, with Moler and Michael Malcolm (1973).

He was instrumental in pointing out the significance of finite precision arithmetic in the computational solution of fundamental mathematical problems—his article "Pitfalls in Computation," published in the *American Mathematical Monthly* in 1970, for example, is still an excellent source of instructional material on the subject. A full list of publications (4 books, 83 articles) is given in [2].

Besides his own research in numerical computation, George was one of the early pioneers in computer science education. He advocated the introduction of computing into mathematics education at an early stage; moreover he was one of the first proponents of Computer Science as a separate discipline. The concept of algorithms as central to Computer Science was clear in his mind: he was Algorithms Editor for the *Communications of the ACM* from 1964 to 1966 and was president of the ACM for the same period. I can recall as a graduate student helping him with the editing of the algorithms section, jogging referees and examining new algorithm proposals. He was remarkably diligent and enthusiastic about this work, believing the algorithms to be an essential part of the CACM.

4. His Students

Besides the Stanford Computer Science Department, George's most enduring legacy is his Ph.D. students. In his 15 years at Stanford, George had 17 students receive their Ph.D. in Mathematics or Computer Science. A complete list is given in Appendix I. Some of these people have pursued careers in industry or government; others have stayed in an academic environment and produced Ph.D. students of their own. A (incomplete) "tree" of these students is reproduced as Appendix II and includes 71 names.

One of the striking aspects of George's interactions with his students is the lack of joint authorship. Apart from the two books with Moler, he did not produce joint research papers with his students. This was a conscious decision on his part: He believed that the student's research belonged to the student, who should get full credit for it.

Yet this is not to say that George didn't play a large role in the development of the thesis research. Far from it: George's approach was to be so interested in the problem at hand that the student would naturally be inspired to pursue the topic thoroughly. He had a very good sense of when to go into detail and when to leave the work for the student, so that in the end the student felt it was his or her own work though in fact George had played a large part in the development.

Here is a direct statement I received recently from one of his students. I'm sure the rest of his students would agree with the sentiments expressed.

Forsythe opened my eyes to the compelling excitement of research and scholarship. Above all, he gave so very generously of his time and talent. Every week I would send him a written summary of my research ideas, then we would meet for an hour to discuss them. He even had the patience to correct every single spelling and grammatical mistake. He helped steer me clear of my bad ideas, and his numerical instincts were uncanny. I have tried to use him as a role model for my relations to students, but I do not expect to attain his degree of patience and generosity.

The Ph.D. research topics covered by George's students ranged all over the map of scientific computation—from basic numerical linear algebra to optimization and zero-finding to numerical techniques for partial differential equations. One general theme that he liked to pursue was the development of precise, sharp, computable error bounds for various algorithms and problems. In his graduate course in numerical computation, he focused this theme on a particular problem involving zeros of the first Bessel function, using a Taylor series expansion. He would insist that the students produce both an algorithm to find the zeros and error bounds for them using roundoff error bounds for each step of the computation. If we were careful about the work, we could obtain rather sharp bounds, and we all found the exercise very illuminating. I still use this example when I teach roundoff analysis.

Another theme that emerges from reviewing the thesis work (and subsequent research) of George's students is the use of the computer as an essential tool in the understanding of mathematical phenomena. George emphasized the development of algorithms more than theorems—and thus made us (his students) feel at home in the Computer Science Department. His famous statement given during his IFIP address in 1971, "Numerical analysts have gone over the last 15 years from being queer people in mathematics departments to being queer people in computer science departments," remains true today. But I believe that he would still think that there is a place for numerical analysis, or as we prefer to call it today, scientific computation, in computer science departments.

5. The Work of His Students

As mentioned earlier, George passed on to all his students a belief in the importance of actual, hands-on computation. Mathematics and mathematical theorems were not neglected, but they were not the central issue. That was computation, or algorithms for computation—and a deep understanding of the algorithms was at the heart of his brand of numerical analysis.

His students' work certainly has continued this theme—for example, Ortega's work on understanding algorithms for nonlinear systems of equations; Parlett's work on understanding algorithms for matrix eigenvalue problems; Moore's work on algorithms for interval arithmetic; Moler's work on the algorithms of LINPACK, EISPACK, and MATLAB; Alan George's work on algorithms for sparse linear equations; and Brent's work on algorithms for zero-finding. All of this work is highly regarded by the scientific computation community.

Besides the hundreds of scientific papers contributed by George's students, there have also been highly regarded textbooks. For example:

- □ *The Numerical Solution of Nonlinear Systems of Equations*, by Ortega and Rheinboldt (San Diego: Academic Press, 1970).

- □ *The Symmetric Eigenvalue Problem*, by Parlett (Englewood Cliffs, NJ: Prentice Hall, 1980).

- □ *Interval Analysis*, by Moore (Englewood Cliffs, NJ: Prentice Hall, 1966).

- □ *Computer Solution of Linear Algebraic Systems*, by Forsythe and Moler (Englewood Cliffs, NJ: Prentice Hall, 1967).

- □ *Computer Methods for Mathematical Computations*, by Forsythe, Malcolm, and Moler (Englewood Cliffs, NJ: Prentice Hall, 1977).

- □ *Computer Solution of Large Sparse Positive Definite Systems*, by George and Liu (Englewood Cliffs, NJ: Prentice Hall, 1981).

Moreover, many of his students have held administrative positions with universities and national organizations. Several have been members of the SIAM Council and Board, for example. Jim Ortega is currently Chairman of Applied Mathematics at the University of Virginia; Beresford Parlett served a term as Chairman of Computer Science at Berkeley; Cleve Moler was Chairman of Computer Science at New Mexico; Jim Daniel was Chairman of Mathematics at Texas; Jim Varah was Head of Computer Science at British Columbia; Alan George was Dean of Mathematics at Waterloo and is currently Provost; and Richard Brent is Head of Computer Science at Canberra.

6. His Legacy

It is now 15 years since George died; scientific computation has grown enormously in this period, and its applications are felt over a wide range of disciplines. Yet his approach to the subject and his attitude toward research remain as relevant as ever. His insistence on a fundamental understanding of the basic mechanics of floating-point arithmetic, his emphasis on algorithm development, his keen interest in any new unsolved problem, and his generous, open manner regarding research problems are just a few examples. Those of us who were fortunate enough to work with him are charged with the responsibility of carrying on his spirit of inquiry and his essential humanity and conveying them to future generations of scientists.

References

[1] J. Herriot, "In Memory of George E. Forsythe," *Comm. ACM* 15 (1972): 719–20.

[2] D. E. Knuth, "George Forsythe and the Development of Computer Science," *Comm. ACM* 15 (1972): 721–26.

[3] C. Moler, "A Memory of George Forsythe," *SIGNUM Newsletter* 7 (1972): 8–9.

APPENDIX I
Ph.D. Students

Here is a complete list of the Ph.D. students of George Forsythe, together with their thesis topics.

1. Eldon Hanson (1960): presently with Lockheed Aerospace Corporation, Sunnyvale, California
   Thesis: Jacobi methods and block-Jacobi methods for computing matrix eigenvalues

2. James Ortega (1962): presently Chairman, Department of Applied Mathematics, University of Virginia
   Thesis: an error analysis of Householder's method for the symmetrical eigenvalue problem

3. Betty Jane Stone (1962): presently living in Washington, DC
   Thesis: (a) best possible ratios of certain matrix norms
   (b) lower bounds for the eigenvalues of a fixed membrane

4. Beresford Parlett (1962): presently Professor of Math and Computer Science, University of California at Berkeley
   Thesis: application of Laguerre's method to the matrix eigenvalue problem

5. Donald Fisher (1962): presently at Oklahoma State University, Norman, OK
   Thesis: calculation of subsonic cavities with sonic free streamlines

6. Ramon Moore (1963): presently Professor of Computer Science, Ohio State University
   Thesis: interval arithmetic and automatic error analysis in digital computing (joint supervision with McGregor)

7. Robert Causey (1964): presently Professor and Chairman, Department of Computer Science, Chris Newport College, Newport News, VA
   Thesis: on closest normal matrices

8. Cleve Moler (1965): presently with Intel Corp., Beaverton, OR
   Thesis: finite difference methods for the eigenvalues of Laplace's operator

9. James Daniel (1965): presently Professor of Math, University of Texas
   Thesis: the conjugate gradient method for linear and nonlinear operator equations (joint supervision with Schiffer)

10. Donald Grace (1965): presently at Oklahoma State University, Stillwater, OK
    Thesis: computer search for nonisomorphic convex polyhedra (joint supervision with Polya)

11. Roger Hockney (1966): recently retired from University of Reading, England
    Thesis: the computer simulation of anomalous plasma diffusion and the numerical solution of Poisson's equation (joint supervision with Golub and Buneman)

12. James Varah (1967): presently Head, Computer Science Department, University of British Columbia
    Thesis: the computation of bounds for the invariant subspaces of a general matrix operator

13. Paul Richman (1968): presently with Bell Laboratories, Chicago, IL
    Thesis: (a) e-calculus (b) transonic fluid flow and approximation of the iterated integrals of a singular function (joint supervision with Herriot)

14. Alan George (1971): presently Distinguished Professor, University of Tennessee and ORNL
    Thesis: computer implementation of the finite element method (joint supervision with Dorr)

15. Richard Brent (1971): presently Head, Department of Computer Science, Australian National University
    Thesis: algorithms for finding zeros and extrema of functions without calculating derivatives (joint supervision with Dorr and Moler)

16. David Stoutemyer (1972): presently Professor of Computer Science, University of Hawaii
    Thesis: numerical implementation of the Schwartz alternating procedure for elliptic partial differential equations

17. Michael Malcolm (1973): presently President, WMI, Waterloo, Ontario and Adjunct Professor, University of Waterloo
    Thesis: nonlinear splines

APPENDIX II
Student Tree

Given here is an incomplete "tree" of students "descended" from George Forsythe, either through supervision or hiring.

Forsythe

1. Hansen, Eldon, 1960
2. Ortega, James, 1962
    2.1 Elkin, Richard, 1968
    2.2 Caspar, Joseph, 1969
    2.3 Stepleman, Robert, 1969
        2.3.1 Shoosmith, J., 1973
    2.4 Voigt, Robert, 1969
    2.5 Moré, Jorge, 1970
        2.5.1 Thomas, Steve, 1974
    2.6 Lambiotte, Jules, 1975
    2.7 Adams, Loyce, 1982
    2.8 Romine, Charles, 1986
    2.9 Poole, Eugene, 1986
3. Stone, Betty, 1962
4. Parlett, Beresford, 1962
    4.1 Johnson, Olin, 1968
    4.2 Bunch, James, 1969
    4.3 Poole, William, 1970
    4.4 Nazareth, Larry, 1973
    4.5 Chen, N. F., 1975
    4.6 Wang, Ying, 1975
    4.7 Scott, David, 1978
    4.8 White, T., 1980
    4.9 McCurdy, A., 1981
    4.10 Greenbaum, A., 1981
    4.11 Nour-Omid, B., 1982
    4.12 Simon, H., 1982
    4.13 Taylor, D. L., 1983
    4.14 Ng, K. C., 1983

5. Fisher, Donald, 1962
6. Moore, Ramon, 1963
    6.1 Talbot, Thomas, 1968
    6.2 Wittie, Larry, 1974
    6.3 Athavale, M. L., 1974
    6.4 Lee, Y. D., 1980
    6.5 Jones, Sandie, 1978
7. Causey, Robert, 1964
8. Moler, Cleve, 1965
    8.1 Schryer, Norman, 1969
    8.2 Cline, Alan K., 1970
    8.3 Crawford, Charles, 1970
    8.4 Kammler, David, 1971
    8.5 Eisenstat, Stanley, 1972
    8.6 Kaufman, Linda, 1973
    8.7 VanLoan, Charles, 1973
    8.8 Burris, Charles, 1974
    8.9 Sanderson, James, 1976
    8.10 Starner, John, 1976
    8.11 Davis, George, 1979
    8.12 Dongarra, Jack, 1980
    8.13 Jones, Ronal, 1985
    8.14 Dubrulle, Augustin, 1986
    8.15 Madrid, Humberto, 1986
9. Daniel, James, 1965
10. Grace, Donald, 1965
11. Hockney, Roger, 1966
    11.1 Brownigg, David, 1975
12. Varah, James, 1967

12.1 Doedel, E. J., 1976
12.2 Benson, Maurice, 1978
12.3 Foreman, Michael, 1984
13. Richman, Paul, 1968
14. George, Alan, 1971
    14.1 Liu, Joseph, 1976
    14.2 Gonnet, Gaston, 1977
    14.3 McIntyre, David, 1981
    14.4 Ng, Esmond, 1983
    14.5 Rashwan, Hamza, 1985
15. Brent, Richard, 1971
16. Stoutemyer, David, 1972
17. Malcolm, Michael, 1973
    17.1 Cheriton, David, 1978
        17.1.1 Zwaenepoel, W.
    17.2 Piquer, Alfredo, 1982

Golub

1. Bartels, Richard, 1968
2. Jenkins, Michael, 1969
3. Smith, Lyle, 1969
4. Ramos, George, 1970
5. Saunders, Michael, 1972
6. Palmer, John, 1974
7. Underwood, Richard, 1975

8. O'Leary, Dianne, 1976
   8.1 Fisher, David, 1985
   8.2 Conroy, John, 1986
9. Lewis, John, 1976
10. Wright, Margaret, 1976
11. Heath, Michael, 1978
12. Luk, Franklin, 1978
13. Overton, Michael, 1979
14. Bjorstad, Petter, 1981
15. Boley, Daniel, 1981
16. Grosse, Eric, 1981
17. Nash, Stephen, 1982

Oliger

1. Strikwerda, John, 1976
2. Chan, Tony, 1978
3. Bube, Ken, 1978
4. Coughran, Bill, 1980
5. Higdon, Robert, 1981
6. Gropp, Bill, 1981
7. LeVeque, Randy, 1982
8. Trefethen, Lloyd, 1982
9. Bolstad, John, 1982
10. Berger, Marsha, 1982
11. Caruso, Steven, 1985

Howard H. Aiken and the Computer

I. Bernard Cohen

Howard Aiken's contributions to the development of the computer[1]—notably the Harvard Mark I (IBM ASSC) machine[2] and its successor the Mark II—are often excluded from the mainstream history of computers on two technicalities. The first is that Mark I and Mark II were electromechanical rather than electronic; the second, that Aiken was never fully convinced that computer programs should be treated as data in what has come to be known as the von Neumann concept, or the stored program.

I don't propose to discuss here the origins and significance of the stored program.[3] Nor do I wish to deal with the related problem of whether the machines before the stored program were or were not "computers." This subject is complicated by the confusion in actual names given to machines. For example, the ENIAC, which did not incorporate a stored program, was officially named a computer: Electronic Numerical Integrator and Computer.[4] But the first stored-program machine to be put into regular operation[5] was Maurice Wilkes's EDSAC: Electronic Delay Storage Automatic Calculator. It seems to me to be rather senseless to deny many truly significant innovations the important place in the history of computers (such as the innovations by Atanasoff and Berry and by Stibitz in this country, by Zuse in Germany, by the designers of "Colossus" in Britain, and by Aiken and by Eckert and Mauchly) on the arbitrary ground that they did not incorporate the stored-program concept. Additionally, in the case of Aiken, it is significant that there is a current computer technology that does not incorporate the stored programs and that is designated (at least by Texas Instruments) as "Harvard architecture," through it should more properly be called "Aiken architecture." In this technology the program is fixed and not subject to any alteration save by intent—as in some computers used for telephone switching and in ROM.

Aiken is often presented in the historical literature on computers as a man who was not abreast of the times. He not only turned his back on the stored program, but he allegedly distrusted electronics, preferring slow-working electromechanical relays because of their supposed great reliability. I confess that I myself was long puzzled by Aiken's apparent preference for relays over vacuum tubes. Accordingly, when Henry Tropp and I conducted an oral history interview with Aiken on 24 February 1973, a few weeks before he died,[6] I was poised to discuss with him his reasons for choosing to build his computing machine with relays rather than vacuum tubes. Early in the interview Aiken told us that the subject of his doctoral research was an aspect of "space charge" in relation to the physics of vacuum tubes; he observed that "this is a field where one runs into cylindrical coordinates, or in a parallel case, into ordinary differential equations — in nonlinear terms, of course." Actually, he continued, "the object of the thesis almost became solving nonlinear [differential] equations: not completely, but there was some of that in it." The only methods then available for dealing with such systems of differential equations required very laborious sequences of hand calculations or calculations with a desk calculator, which "were extremely time consuming." It became apparent "at once that this [process] could be mechanized and programmed and that an individual didn't have to do this."[7] Before long Aiken had gone well beyond the immediate needs of his thesis problem and had begun to think about large-scale calculation by machine.

By at least April 1937 Aiken had progressed sufficiently far in his general thinking and design to be ready to seek support from industry. Knowing Aiken's work habits, it is not difficult to imagine that he would have drawn up a careful memorandum stating the features of a proposed machine, its mode of operation, and its general method of solving problems. His philosophy was later expressed in a student's assignment that was drawn up for one of Aiken's classes — the design of an inexpensive laboratory computer (or calculator): "The 'design' of a . . . computing machine is understood to consist in the outlining of its general specifications and the carrying through of a rational determination of its functions, but does not include the actual engineering design of component units."[8]

Aiken thus assumed that the design of a computing machine included the specification of the logic or the sequence of controlled operations that the machine would be programmed to perform. Unlike the present concept of computer architecture, such a design was not concerned with the "physical or hardware structure of computer systems and the attributes of the various parts thereof," nor with the consequent physical or hardware problem of "how these parts are connected."[9] To judge from all the information available, Aiken's design would not have necessarily specified which particular components (nor even what sorts of components) would be used. The design could apply equally to a machine that would be constructed of mechanical, electromagnetic, or electronic components.

Once Aiken had his plans worked up, he proceeded to seek industrial support for the construction of his machine. The first company he approached was the Monroe Calculating Machine Company, one of America's foremost manufacturers of desk calculators. On 22 April 1937 Aiken had an interview with George C. Chase, a distinguished inventor in the calculator field, who was then Monroe's director of research. Chase has recorded how Aiken outlined his conception and "explained what it could accomplish in the fields of mathematics, science, and sociology."[10] The plan he outlined, according to Chase, "was not restricted to any specific type of mechanism; it embraced a broad coordination of components that could be resolved by various constructive mediums."[11] This accords well with Aiken's philosophy embodied in the earlier quotation from a student's assignment.

As part of my preparation for the interview with Aiken, I reread Chase's discussion of his encounter with Aiken. There was no hint in Chase's recollections that Aiken had in mind anything other than "the construction of an electromechanical machine." I had a copy of Chase's article in my pocket as reinforcement for my pressing Aiken on the choice of electromechanical parts for his machine. Early in the interview I raised the question I had prepared. Since Aiken's thesis was on the physics of vacuum tubes, specifically on space charge in the field of electronics, had he even considered using electronic systems rather than electromechanical systems? Why had he not contemplated using vacuum tubes? I confess that I had expected Aiken to frame his replay in terms of his great often-expressed ideal: reliability.[12] I will even confess that I had, in part, prepared the question less as a means of obtaining information than as an opportunity to record on tape—directly from Aiken's mouth—his thundering condemnation of supposedly unreliable vacuum tubes and his preference for slower and more reliable relays. So you may imagine my astonishment when he replied that he had not been wedded to any particular technology. He had been aware that to make his computer a reality would require "money and a lot of it." Since he was not then—nor was he ever—primarily interested in technological innovation, it had seemed to him that the most sensible course was to "build the first machine out of somebody's existing parts," rather than to have to invent or construct parts on his own. Electromechanical relays and step switches were already in wide use, teletype had been developed, and punched tape or punched cards could be used for input. "The tape," he said, "was harder to edit and you couldn't sort with it, but nevertheless it would work and it had advantages." These "different techniques—printing telegraph techniques, telephone switching techniques, communications industry techniques—were," he added, "all grist for my mill." At that time, Aiken said, he was "largely a promoter, trying to find out where to get these pieces so that the machine could be put together."[13]

Aiken described his "first step": his visit to the Monroe Calculating Machine Company.[14] "Chase was Chief Engineer at Monroe, and a very, very scholarly gentleman. He took an almost immediate interest and we kept up an association for quite a few years thereafter. He wanted, in the worst way, to build Mark I. He would supply me with the parts and we would collaborate and do it together; that's what he wanted to do." Chase's management, however, "after some months and months of discussion turned him down completely."[15]

I was not completely satisfied by Aiken's presentation. Accordingly, a little later in the interview, I returned to the subject of why Aiken had chosen to have Mark I built of electromechanical components—why he had not made use of vacuum tubes.[16] This time I stressed the fact that this had always seemed astonishing to me in view of the fact that Aiken had been a student at Harvard of E. L. Chaffee, under whom he had written his doctoral dissertation; Chaffee's specialty was vacuum tubes and vacuum tube circuits. To be specific, I asked whether at one time there hadn't been some thought given to having quenching circuits in Mark I, using vacuum tubes. Aiken replied, "Yes. But your question really is: Since I had grown up in 'space charge' in a laboratory like Cruft [at Harvard], why wasn't Mark I an electronic device? Again the answer is money. It was going to take a lot of money. Thousands and thousands of parts! It was clear that this thing could be done with electronic parts, too, using the techniques of the digital counters that had been made with vacuum tubes, just a few years before I started, for counting cosmic rays." And then he concluded with the following dramatic assertion: "But what it comes down to is this: If Monroe had decided to pay the bill, this thing would have been made out of mechanical parts. If RCA had been interested, it might have been electronic. And it was made out of tabulating machine parts because IBM was willing to pay the bill."[17]

Before leaving the subject of relays, another myth about Aiken ought to be expunged from the record. This involves the topic of relays and reliability. Aiken's fierce insistence on the highest standards of reliability is well-known.[18] What is not so well-known is that the original Mark I/ASCC, as it came to Harvard from IBM's assembly system at Endicott, was very unreliable. The worst feature of this unreliability was that it seemed to occur in a random or sporadic way. Eventually Bob Campbell[19] and the operating staff traced the source of the unreliability to the relays supplied to the Mark I from IBM's off-the-shelf inventory.

Designed for the relatively light load of IBM tabulators and cumulators, these relays simply could not stand up under the 24-hours-a-day, 7-days-a-week assignment of the Mark I and had to be replaced by heavy-duty components.[20] When Aiken planned the successor Mark II, he asked the Autocall Company to design and manufacture wholly new types of relays to take the place of those that had not lived up to his standards for the Mark I.[21]

Mark I was constructed and assembled by IBM and then disassembled and shipped to Harvard, where it was put into operation in August 1944. It was installed in the old "battery room" in the basement of Harvard's Physics Research Laboratory, now known as the Lyman Laboratory—not in the basement of the Cruft Laboratory, as is usually stated.[22] The main feature of the machine was that its operations were controlled by a paper tape that contained the program. Its full name was the IBM "Automatic Sequenced Control Calculator." It was automatic to the degree that it could perform thousands of calculating operations one after another, according to the sequence punched into the program, without human intervention.

Mark I had devices for numerical input and output and for storing and operating the numbers that were either fed in during a calculation or that were the result of previous (or intermediate) operations. There were 60 constant registers, each consisting of 24 ten-pole switches that could be individually set by hand to one of 10 marked positions from 0 to 9. There were 23 significant digits;[23] the 24th position was set at 0 or 9 to indicate a positive or negative number. There were, furthermore, 72 adding or storage registers, where the arithmetic operations were performed.[24]

The output consisted of either a sequence of punched cards or typed results. The output for tables consisted of typewritten columns of numerical results that could then be placed in a transparent form, so as to make a page to be photographed and then printed directly by photolithography. This series of steps eliminated any source of error in copying out numerical results by hand, having numbers typed by a human operator, typesetting, and proofreading. This was a practical realization of Charles Babbage's ideal for his proposed Difference Engine and Analytical Engine.[25] It may be noted that Aiken always complained that the electric typewriter was the slowest part of the system.

In order to solve a problem on Mark I, the problem had to be reduced to a form in which a mathematically literate programmer could render it as a sequence of numerical codes that could then be punched into the control tapes, with provision for entering numerical information (e.g., values of constants). This programming operation was described precisely and tersely in the Manual of Operations:

> When a problem is referred to the Computation Laboratory, the first step in its solution is taken by the mathematician who chooses the numerical method best adapted to computation by the calculator. This choice is made on the basis of the accuracy desired, the possible checking operations and the speed of computation. Such functional, value, and control tapes as are required are then computed, coded, and punched. Since the mathematician cannot always be present while the calculator is running, instructions must be prepared to guide the

operating staff. These must include switch settings, the list of tapes to be used, plugging instructions, manual resets, information concerning checks, starting, stopping and rerun instructions.[26]

The mathematician or programmer worked with the code book at his or her side.[27] Before long, it was seen that certain parts of the instructions occurred again and again. So the practice began of writing such partial programs into a notebook. The most extensive such collection was assembled by Dick Bloch, who was the primary programmer. Aiken told us that Bloch was so fabulously skilled a programmer that he would (and was perhaps the only person ever to do so) write out his programs in ink! Grace Hopper informs me that she and others also kept private libraries of partial programs. Years later, such collections of partial programs became known as libraries of subroutines, but their origin goes back to the actual programming practices of those who were working on Mark I. These coded subroutines, or "canned" elements of programs, are to be distinguished from the subroutines built into the machine, such as those for logarithms, exponentials, and trigonometric functions.

As originally conceived, Mark I had no conditional or branching circuits.[28] These were added later.[29] Other later enhancements included an electronic multiply/divide unit, additional storage registers, and an improved interpolator tape unit. Throughout its whole life, Mark I operated with a fixed decimal point. Needless to say, Mark I was a strictly decimal machine.

One of Aiken's students (in 1949/50), Jack Palmer, remembers his experience in programming (coding) Mark I, which he found to have been very "similar to coding modern stored-program computers."[30] The programmer would write down sequences of codes for addresses and operations in the appropriate columns of a coding form, following which these codes or their equivalents would be punched in a program tape—"a strikingly similar procedure to that which programmers who programmed the early stored-program computers did when they were programming in machine language." They too "needed to know the codes for the addresses of the words in storage and the codes for the operations to be performed," Palmer said, which they would write down "in a strict instruction format on a coding form" and which would later be punched on cards.[31] In both, Mark I and the later stored-program computers, the numerical codes were obtained from a coding book.

There is no doubt in the minds of anyone who programmed Mark I that in many ways it was more like a modern computer than other early machines. Mark I differed in a fundamental way from later computers, therefore, not so much in its slower speed (as compared with electronic machines), as in its initial lack of conditional branching and complete separation of data and instructions. This latter feature, more than the choice of electronics over electromagnetic relay systems, was and remained central to Aiken's thinking about computers.

Mark I was an extraordinary machine in many ways. It had a long, active life from 1944 until it was dismantled 15 years later. No other of the early giants operated continuously, as Mark I did, for so long a time. Mark I ran 24 hours a day for 7 days of the week. What is even more significant is the fact that Mark I could run so constantly and so long and be relatively free from the kinds of errors that plagued such machines. I have mentioned that Aiken's key word in all his career was reliability. He would gladly sacrifice speed for reliability, if he had been forced to make a choice between them.

In our interview, Aiken recalled that he always tried to find "an identity or some kind of algorithm in the mathematics so that when you compute the number x, you can subject the number x to mathematical scrutiny to show that it's right." As a simple example, he recalled the computation of trigonometric tables "for our own use." "We wanted $\sin x$," but "we computed $\cos x$ too, and we squared and added them to make sure they were equal to one." Even when Mark I was tabulating results for internal use, that is, for direct storage on tape or cards, the same results were also typed out so that the operators could watch the results being typed and make a check. Aiken also noted, "We had a check counter, and if you subtracted two numbers in that check counter, and the absolute value of the difference was greater than the preassigned counters, the machined stopped."

Mark I was a landmark machine in many ways, and many authors have testified to its significance. An encyclopedia article on "Digital Computers: History, Early" by Maurice V. Wilkes begins: "The digital computer age began when the Automatic Sequence Controlled Calculator (Harvard Mark I) started working in 1944."[32] Another statement on the history of computers begins: "The Harvard Mark I, also called the IBM Automatic Sequence Controlled Calculator . . . marked the beginning of the era of the modern computer."[33] When in 1964 the American Federation of Information Processing Societies (AFIPS) decided to honor its second president, Harry H. Goode (who died in 1963), by establishing the Harry Goode Memorial Award for "outstanding achievement in the field of information processing,"[34] the first pioneer to be so recognized was Howard H. Aiken.

Significant as the Harvard architecture has been and is, Aiken's ideas about machines never became influential (to use the words of Fred Brooks) "in the same sense as those of Eckert and Mauchly and the UNIVAC family and way of thinking," nor as "those of the parallel binary machine group, the so-called von Neumann machines." Brooks finds that in machines and machine architecture, Aiken's "greatest legacy" was "an emphasis on machines as things which one uses," which naturally led to "a conservative approach to their design."[35]

In assessing Aiken's fundamental contributions to the computer, therefore, primacy of place must go to Mark I, the IBM Automatic Sequence Controlled Calculator, not as a machine that set design standards for an industry, but rather as a first real public demonstration[36] that such machines were practicable. Mark I may not have been an absolute "first" in every department, but it was the machine that did the job of first proving to the world at large that a complex calculating engine could function automatically, performing operations in sequence and following a predetermined program from the entry of the data to the production of the final results. The world-wide publicity attendant on these achievements, aggrandized by the stark fact of its regular and continuous operation to produce reliable and accurate results, convinced any last doubters that large-scale automatically sequenced calculators were here to stay and could perform a major, needed role in our technical world. In this sense, it is certainly correct to say that when the switch on Mark I was thrown, the Computer Age began.

A second major pioneering activity of Aiken's was his establishment at Harvard of the first academic program in what we would today call "computer science."[37] Fred Brooks, Ken Iverson, and others agree that perhaps Aiken's most important influence was therefore not on machine design but rather on the curriculum. Brooks finds "amazing" the "degree to which today's computer science programs mirror the program" that Aiken had in place in the early 1950s.[38] This program had three parts: instruction (courses) for undergraduate and graduate students, a master's degree program in applied mathematics centering on computer theory and applications, and the Ph.D. program.

Brooks also reminds us that another fundamental contribution was Aiken's "attention to applications":

> He was one of the very first to realize the important potential of computers for business, and that business applications would completely dominate scientific applications. He insisted that the business applications would require usability of decimal among other things, and he turned his attention to forging the ties with the utilities, the business organizations, that would first have the need—insurance companies, and that kind . . . in order to make sure that the mathematical approach was carried over into the business problem.[39]

Aiken's research under contracts with the American Gas Institute and the Bell Telephone Laboratories inaugurated the present system of computer billing.

In a summation of the lasting contributions of Aiken, an important place must be given to his service in publicizing the new instrument and making men and women in all walks of life aware that a revolution was in the making. The celebrated Harvard symposiums[40] that he organized were part of his general campaign to advance the new computer art and science, to bring pioneers together from all over the world so they could share their skills and knowledge and stimulate one another. His driving impact on the first stages of the modern computer was indeed so great that we can agree with the Harvard Faculty Memorial Minute on "The Life and Services of Howard H. Aiken": "He was a giant among us, figuratively and literally."

Aiken was a visionary, a man ahead of his times. Grace Hopper and others remember his prediction in the late 1940s, even before the vacuum tube had been wholly replaced by the transistor, that the time would come when a machine even more powerful than the giant machines of those days could be fitted into a space as small as a shoe box. His students and associates did not know whether to take him seriously. Toward the end of our interview, just weeks before his death in 1973, Aiken made another prediction. We were talking about how the cost of computing power had been constantly and rapidly decreasing. He pointed out that hardware considerations alone did not give a true picture of computer costs. As hardware has become cheaper, software has been apt to get more expensive. And then he gave us his final prediction: "The time will come," he said, "when manufacturers will give away hardware in order to sell software." Time alone will tell whether or not this was his final look ahead into the future.

Notes

1 This article is based on two larger works in progress, to be published by MIT Press. One is my book about Aiken, to be titled *Howard H. Aiken, Computer Pioneer*. The other is a collection of essays about Aiken: *Makin' Numbers: Howard H. Aiken and the Computer*, primarily to be on his career and his influence by those who knew or worked with him.

2 IBMers still prefer to call Mark I the IBM ASCC. See, for example, Charles J. Bashe, Lyle R. Johnson, John R. Palmer, Emerson Pugh, *IBM's Early Computers* (Cambridge: The MIT Press, 1986), Ch. 1.

3 On von Neumann and the stored program see Herman Goldstine, *The Computer from Pascal to von Neumann* (Princeton University Press, 1972); Nancy Stern, *From ENIAC to UNIVAC* (Bedford, MA: Digital Press, 1981).

4 Stern, *From ENIAC to UNIVAC*, 15.

5 The first operational machine to use the stored program principle was built to the design of F. C. Williams and Tom Kilburn at Manchester University; this was an experimental model intended to test the Williams tube memory and the ability to operate according to instructions. EDSAC, however, was built at Cambridge, England, specifically for the purpose of "solving realistic problems" and successfully performed a great variety of practical calculations. It "first ran a program on 6 May 1949" and continued in full operation until 1958. On the Manchester machine see Simon Lavington, *Early British Computers* (Manchester University Press; Bedford, MA: Digital Press, 1980), 37; on the EDSAC see Lavington, *Early British Computers*, Ch. 6. See

also M. V. Wilkes, "EDSAC," *Encyclopedia of Computer Science and Engineering*, 2d ed., Anthony Ralston (ed.) (New York: Van Nostrand Reinhold Company, 1983), 584a–585a.

6 This 24 February 1973 interview was conducted as part of the AFIPS-Smithsonian project of taped interviews with selected computer pioneers. Excerpts from this interview will be published in *Makin' Numbers*.

7 Transcript of oral history interview.

8 This assignment dates from the academic year 1949/50; the text was made available to me by John Palmer of the IBM history project.

9 See D. J. Frailey, "Computer Architecture," in *Encyclopedia of Computer Science*, 275–88.

10 George C. Chase, "History of Computing Machinery," *Ann. Hist. Comput.* 2 (1960): 198–227.

11 Ibid.

12 Anyone who was acquainted with Aiken quickly learned that he placed great store on reliability. This aspect of his point of view cannot be overstated.

13 Oral history interview.

14 Aiken could not at first remember the name of the chief engineer at Monroe, whom he had gone to see almost forty years earlier. "Chase," I told him, "George Chase." Aiken was curious about my knowing Chase's name. I told him that the only reason I knew about Chase was that I had discovered and had read his account of Aiken's visit to him. I showed Aiken the photocopy I had with me of Chase's article and read aloud the sentences I have just quoted about Aiken's plans. Aiken commented, "He's just saying what I said a moment ago, only much better." Then, he added, "I went to Chase, and I did just what he said."

15 Oral history interview.

16 This was part of the Aiken "folklore" at Harvard.

17 Oral history interview.

18 See note 12.

19 Robert Campbell has contributed a chapter on the design, construction, and operation of Mark I for *Makin' Numbers*, in which this aspect of Mark I is documented.

20 To be published in Campbell's chapter of *Makin' Numbers*.

21 On Mark II, see the Staff of the Computation Laboratory, *Description of a Relay Calculator*, in *The Annals of the Computation Laboratory of Harvard University* 24 (Cambridge: Harvard University Press, 1949).

22 This error probably arose because Aiken had been associated with E.L. Chaffee's "Cruft group" in the adjacent Cruft Laboratory; there was no obvious internal or physical barrier, staircase, causeway, or wall that isolated (or marked off) the Research Laboratory from Cruft.

23 The choice of 23 significant figures was originally dictated by a plan to perform extensive calculation of planetary orbits and other problems in celestial mechanics.

24 See the Staff of the Computation Laboratory, *A Manual of Operation for the Automatic Sequence Controlled Calculator*, with forward by James Bryant Conant, in *The Annals of the Computation Laboratory of Harvard University*,

(Cambridge: Harvard University Press, 1946). Reprint with a new foreword by I.B. Cohen and an introduction by Paul Ceruzzi in the Charles Babbage Institute Reprint series for the History of Computing 8 (Cambridge, London: The MIT Press; Los Angeles, San Francisco: Tomash Publishers, 1985).

25 Babbage proposed that the output be imprinted on papier-maché moulages, from which stereotype plates could be directly cast. On Aiken and Babbage, see I.B. Cohen, "Babbage and Aiken," *Ann. Hist. Comput.* 10 (1989): 171–93. On the first printing calculator, see Uta Merzbach, *Georg Scheutz and the First Printing Calculator* in Smithsonian Studies in History and Technology 36 (Washington, DC: Smithsonian Institution Press, 1977).

26 The Staff of the Computation Laboratory, *Manual of Operation*, 50.

27 Ibid., 405ff.

28 On the lack of branching circuits in Mark I, see I.B. Cohen, "Babbage and Aiken," 197b.

29 *Proceedings of a Symposium on Large-Scale Digital Calculating Machinery,* jointly sponsored by the Navy Department Bureau of Ordnance and Harvard University, at the Computation Laboratory, 7–10 January 1947 in *The Annals of the Computation Laboratory of Harvard University* 16 (Cambridge: Harvard University Press, 1948). Reprint with a new introduction by William Aspray, in the Charles Babbage Institute Reprint Series in the History of Computing 7 (Cambridge: The MIT Press; Los Angeles: Tomash Publishers, 1985) 29, para. 2.

30 Taped interview at the Thomas J. Watson Research Center, Yorktown Heights, NY, 1987.

31 Taped interview, 1987.

32 See Frailey, "Computer Architecture," 535b.

33 See ibid., 916b, in which Mark I is designated "the first completed, operational, automatic, general-purpose, digital calculator." To be absolutely precise, the machines designed and constructed in Nazi Germany by Konrad Zuse antedate Aiken's Mark I, especially Zuse's Z–3. But no one knew of these machines until well after World War II, at which time their priority became a historical curiosity—too late to influence the immediate next stages of computer development. By contrast, news of the Mark I was spread worldwide and brought the world's attention to the power of the new invention. Zuse informed me that he learned of the Mark I during wartime when his daughter, who worked in the Nazi Army's military intelligence, came upon a newspaper picture of Mark I with an accompanying article, apparently a cutting from a Swiss newspaper. She (illegally) informed her father of the American invention of a machine very much like his. On Zuse's work, see Stan Augarten, *Bit by Bit: An Illustrated History of Computers* (New York: Ticknor & Fields, 1984), 88–97; Michael R. Williams, *A History of Computing Technology* (Englewood Cliffs, NJ: Prentice Hall, 1985).

34 See Frailey, "Computer Architecture," 61a.

35 From a talk by Frederick P. Brooke, Jr., at the Pioneer Day celebration in honor of Aiken at the National Computer Conference in Anaheim, California, 1983. The text will be published in *Makin' Numbers*.

36 Augarten, *Bit by Bit*.

37 The roster of his students reads like an early "Who's Who" of computing. Details will be available in Cohen, *Howard H. Aiken*, and *Makin' Numbers*.

38 To be published in Brooke's chapter of *Makin' Numbers*.

39 Ibid.

40 *Proceedings of a Second Symposium on Large-Scale Digital Calculating Machinery*, jointly sponsored by the Navy Department Bureau of Ordnance and Harvard University at the Computation Laboratory, 13–16 September 1949, in *The Annals of the Computation Laboratory of Harvard University* 26 (Cambridge: Harvard University Press, 1951).

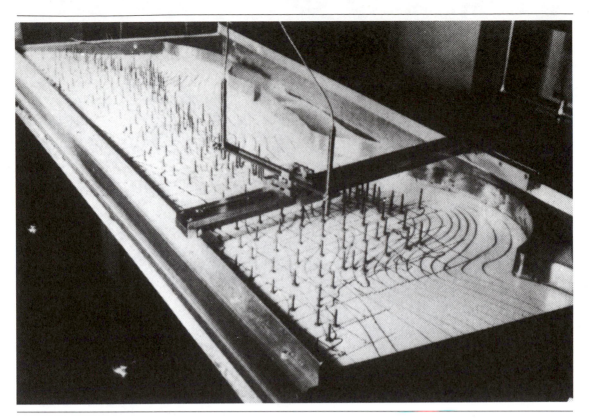

Electrolytic model of East Texas oil field.

PROBLEMS

Scientific computing has always been at the service of other disciplines and has always been driven by the need to solve problems. The idiosyncracies of these problems drive research and influence the development of algorithms, software, and at times even the computers themselves.

Oscar Buneman describes the computational analysis of particles in self-consistent fields, with such applications as the study of microwave generators and plasmas. This work began almost as soon as the mathematical models had been developed, starting with Hartree's "differential analyzer" built out of toy Meccano parts. Although initially performed primarily on a small scale with human calculators, it continues to be a challenging problem, as evidenced by Buneman's recent research using modern supercomputers.

Garrett Birkhoff discusses the work of himself and many others on fluid dynamics and related problems. This includes the work of von Neumann in transforming this into a computational problem, the applications to weather prediction and ship design, and the development of effective algorithms for multidimensional data fitting, particularly as applied to the automotive industry. This essay illustrates several of the topics that are central to the history of scientific computing: the accumulation of rounding errors, the influence of von Neumann, methods for solving linear equations (taken up later in the essays by Fox and Young), and the importance of faster and more powerful computers in the development of scientific computing.

C. W. Gear and Robert Skeel give a history of methods for solving ordinary differential equations. They begin in the precomputer era with hand calculation, move on to analog machines such as the differential analyzer, describe the first digital-computer methods, and finish with a treatment of stiff equations.

The chapter concludes with Donald Peaceman's view of reservoir simulation techniques. He describes the development of the alternating-direction method and its implementation on primitive punch-card calculators. This work has had important application to the oil industry and has led to numerical methods of more general usefulness.

Particles in Their Self-Consistent Fields: From Hartree's Differential Analyzer to Cray Machines

Oscar Buneman

After the early success of astronomers in rigorously solving the problem of two gravitationally interacting bodies, it became quite a disappointment that the notorious "problème de trois corps" could never be solved by elegant nineteenth century mathematics. Computations were practical (and respectable) only for the evaluation of series. Finite difference calculus made its way very slowly during the first few decades of this century. Størmer struggled hard calculating orbits of charged particles in the earth's magnetic field (not even a self-consistent field!)—for which he earned pity, if not ridicule.

Strangely, it was a change in physics that brought the next advance: Quantum theory changed particle dynamics from ordinary differential equations to partial differential equations, thus putting field and particle dynamics on the same footing. The combination of Schroedinger's equation for electron density with Poisson's equation for the electric potential results in coupled nonlinear PDEs. As a first step taken in the 1920s, one eliminated the angle variables and reduced the problem to two nonlinearly coupled ODEs in the radial variable.

This meant that an efficient integrating machine or procedure was called for, and Hartree built his "differential analyzer"—making the first model with a Meccano set (American: "erector set"). It uses the principle of a continuously variable gear, and its prinicipal element is shown in Figure 1. One rotating disc rolls in contact with another. We note that at constant engine speed, one's distance travelled would be the time-integral of the continuously varying gear ratio. The power for this delicate transmission device was provided by a "torque amplifyer" that slipped whenever the drive became slower than the load and tightened otherwise.

With initially only four such integrators, Hartree solved the problem of self-consistent electronic wave functions and atomic energy levels. Later, Metropolitan Vickers built him a well-engineered model with eight integrating tables. Figure 2 shows Hartree bending over that machine in the basement of the Physics building at Manchester University. With him is an assistant whose various roles I shall have

FIGURE 1.
Integrating table in
differential analyzer.

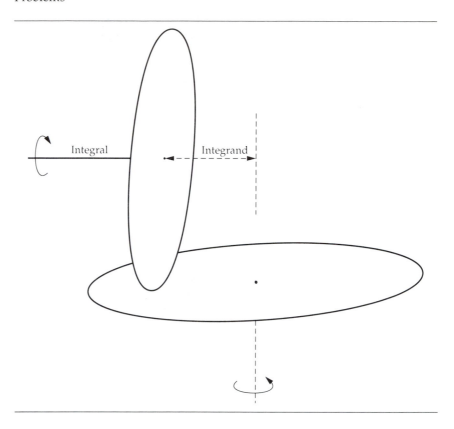

occasion to describe later. The little Meccano model was sitting by the
side of the M-V machine.

Solving quantum mechanical problems as an exercise in coupled
PDEs has since become a subject of chemistry with, of course, great
strides being made through the availability of more powerful digital
computers. However, Hartree's own next important contribution to
self-consistent field computation came during World War II and was
in classical (meaning nonquantum) dynamics.

The "magnetron," a now very familiar microwave generator, had
been invented by Boot, Randall, and Sayers in Birmingham. It was of
paramount importance to Britain's defense: The Germans could not
jam the magnetron frequencies used for early detection of Luftwaffe
take-offs. The magnetron is a fine example of "swords into plough-
shares." It is replacing the human tradition of many millennia to cook
food with incandescent heat.

Initially it was something of a mystery exactly how and why the
magnetron worked. The scientific staff at the British Admiralty realized
that in order to unravel the workings of the magnetron, they would
have to solve a self-consistent field problem (namely that of motion of

electrons in the electric field that the electrons themselves produce) in addition to the externally applied electric and magnetic fields.

The Admiralty therefore approached Hartree, who promptly initiated classical particle simulation. He integrated, numerically, the orbits of large numbers of particles in a field that was revised in accordance with the instantaneous charge density either at each step, or only occasionally, in the hope of reaching a steady field by iteration.

Both one- and two-dimensional simulations were performed by Hartree and the team that he collected for the purpose. The hardware consisted of three Marchant mechanical add-and-shift machines, rather like the mechanical cash registers that have just disappeared from popular use. There were three "CPUs": Phyllis Lockett, who is shown in the picture with Hartree; David Copley, a schoolmaster from Sheffield; and myself. We were about a billion times slower than modern CPUs, but Phyllis was the fastest. Hartree addressed the multitasking, or parallel, CPU problem by sharing out the several hundred orbits among the three of us, at least for the case in which the field was revised only occasionally.

He also provided an elegant solution to the difficulty that becomes implicit with time-centered differencing the Lorentz equation of motion in a magnetic field: His algorithm is used to this day in particle simulations. The instructions for the three CPUs had been set out by Hartree in the form of a program, with go-tos and loops. We did not call it looping, though: Phyllis named it "knitting."

The idea of space-time centering in finite difference work was very important to Hartree. When, at another stage in World War II, the

FIGURE 2.
Douglas Hartree with Phyllis Lockett leaning over the output plotting table of the differential analyzer at Manchester University. From M. Wilkes, *Memoirs of a Computer Pioneer* (MIT Press, 1985).

Sheffield steel firms wanted to know how long they should cook their ingots, he got Phyllis and another assistant to undertake the numerical integration of the heat equation, which also becomes implicit under time-centering. Phyllis had by this time become Mrs. Nicolson, and the other assistant's name was Crank: That was the origin of another famous algorithm!

In the two-dimensional simulations it turned out very beneficial for me to be a human CPU. Unlike electronic CPUs, which will grind out billions of trivial zeros without objecting or giving us a warning, I observed that my particles shunned certain regions in the field. This made me discover that there exists a new kind of potential, in a rotating frame of reference. It led to the "threshold" criterion for magnetron operation—now an important design tool.

The one-dimensional simulations had yielded a steady state that was approached in transience, but this could not account for magnetron operation or for the observed currents that flow across the magnetic barrier. I found that this state was two-dimensionally unstable, in a mode similar to the Kelvin-Helmholtz instability. A (linear) differential equation had to be solved to get the growth rates: We programmed that into the differential analyzer. The importance of going into at least two dimensions when there are magnetic fields has dominated charged particle simulation ever since.

We had a major problem with solving Poisson's equation in two dimensions. Hartree introduced us to Southwell's relaxation technique and provided us with hardware in the form of large plastic sheets on which we could record the two-dimensional potential array and on which we could easily rub out our work to improve our guesses.

We found this far from relaxing and in fact very frustating to try to chase residuals away to the boundaries. Iterative methods were abandoned at that point (this was in 1944!), and Hartree changed to the direct Fourier method. It turned out that a very modest number of harmonics was adequate: The FFT was not yet known.

Eventually, plausible particle-field configurations emerged, showing the four- or six-spoke wheel that rotates in the magnetron and excites the high frequencies in the resonators.

During the late forties and early fifties a small community of electron device engineers maintained self-consistent charged particle simulations while many of us drifted into other areas such as nuclear and fundamental particle physics. However, the quest for fusion brought new impetus to the subject: simulation of plasma electrons and ions in their self-consistent field and the physics of magnetic barriers.

In the late fifties Dawson at Princeton and I at Stanford began numerical plasma particle simulations. I drew attention to another instability, namely the electron-ion interstreaming instability in high-current plasmas. The nonlinear evolution of this had to be calculated by a one-dimensional simulation, and the publication of two pages of graphic computer output in *Physical Review,* showing electron and ion space-time orbits, made quite a stir. It showed how the plasma randomizes directed energy (in the absence of close collisions) and how "anomalous resistivity" comes about. That simulation had been done at Lockheed on an early electronic digital computer, an 1103 AF. There were 256 electrons and 256 ions.

These early simulations were one-dimensional with no transverse magnetic field, and in view of the importance of magnetic barriers in fusion plus what one sees in magnetrons, two-dimensional simulations were needed urgently. Fortunately, at that point a research student appeared at Stanford who wanted to do plasma physics as well as numerical analysis. He was Roger Hockney, and he fit neatly between his supervisors, Gene Golub and myself.

Hockney embarked on the first serious two-dimensional particle simulation of magnetized plasma. He wrote the program (in Fortran) to advance several thousand particles in the magnetic field by the Hartree algorithm. (Coincidentally, Hockney had grown up in a house opposite the Hartree's in Manchester, but by this time Hartree was no longer with us.)

When it came to field solving, I drew Hockney's attention to a centerfold in an old text, *Calculus of Observations*, by Whittaker and Robinson [1]. It gives a program for the efficient execution of a 24-point discrete Fourier transform. (Twenty-four signifies the hours in the day and results in the numerically convenient angles of 30 or 60 degrees.) The FFT was still unknown to us—or rather, no one had unearthed Gauss' original FFT program, written in Latin.

The 24-point transforming seemed a bit skimpy for our simulation. The several thousand particles deserved somewhat finer field resolution (particle and field data should balance). This is where Gene Golub stepped in and inspired Hockney with recursive doubling: The first simulation was done on a 48-point grid in the angle direction. The fast direct field solver allowed Hockney to update the field after every particle step. The results, displayed by a movie, showed how just like the electron cloud in the magnetron, the plasma develops spokes that allow it to penetrate and conduct across the magnetic field in what is known as "anomalous diffusion."

Hockney left Stanford for IBM, where he started galactic simulations. Many of his ideas and computer practices are documented in his text *Computer Simulation Using Particles* (written jointly with J. Eastwood). Having to pick up the threads of his work made me learn Fortran and go more deeply into recursive doubling in application to Poisson solving. I found that Gene's principle of recursive doubling could be extended and used for both rows and columns and that one could arrange things so that errors would not build up. I left a few copies of my program (plus sketchy report) at a conference at Los Alamos. They were picked up, and later R. Morse told me gleefully: "We've cracked your code." C. Nielssen and B. Buzbee had studied the algorithm, and things got back to Gene Golub. The three wrote a profound paper about it.

Particle simulation has since taken a step forward with every advance in computer technology. "Bigger" machines have allowed more particles and better resolution. The Illiac, for instance, became popular as a tool for galactic simulations (R. Miller): A large number of stars could be time-stepped in parallel. On the other hand, a code like the Hockney code can now be run on a PC.

Having experienced very early how the inclusion of another dimension can reveal important new physics, researchers had strong motivation to go from two to three dimensions. This became possible with the advent of the CRAY, which combines speed with the benefits of parallelism and pipelining. We have now a TRI-dimensional STANford code, TRISTAN, which traces some five million particles through a field recorded over $160 \times 160 \times 160$ data points. It is fully electromagnetic and relativistic. A time step takes about two minutes. When writing this code, the deep problems did not arise from the physics or numerical analysis, but from the data management. The architecture of the machine heavily affected the choice of simulation methods.

In the code the fields are advanced by Fourier transforming in all three dimensions. At one point there is a distinct bottleneck, owing to the fact that Fourier methods are global, not local. We have encountered that bottleneck also in simulations on other highly parallel machines of recent design. Looking into the future, we can see an increasing demand for local algorithms, because data path lengths must be minimized. We may want to return to the old "local" method of solving for the field, which we discarded in 1944 when we got tired of rubbing out calculations on the plastic sheets. Luckily, it turns out that we can discard the eraser as well, and that in a fully electromagnetic simulation, each of the local updates is physically significant!

Reference

[1] E. Whittaker and G. Robinson, *The Calculus of Observations* (London: Blackie and Son, 1924).

Fluid Dynamics, Reactor Computations, and Surface Representation

Garrett Birkhoff

1. Background

Having been fascinated by the challenges of scientific computing for over 40 years, I take pleasure in sharing with you some impressions of developments that took place between 1945 and 1970 in three areas of this very broad field: numerical fluid dynamics, nuclear power reactor modeling, and computerized surface representation. All of these developments expanded the usefulness of mathematics by *numerical* methods designed to exploit large-scale, increasingly high-speed computers. As is the case for most important developments in applied mathematics, my own efforts were highly collaborative. Moreover, their value was due largely to my previous experience in applying mathematics and in watching it be applied by others to related questions. Therefore, I shall sometimes digress to describe this previous experience.

To provide continuity, I shall follow a roughly chronological order. I shall begin by reminding you how much smaller and less specialized the scientific community was in 1945 than it is today! This smallness is reflected in the "chatty, anecdotal account"[1] of "Computer Developments 1935–55, as Seen from Cambridge, U.S.A." which I gave eleven years ago in a taped talk [20, pp. 21–30]. Here, I shall concentrate in Sections 1–5 on some developments in scientific computing during the second of these decades, with special reference to von Neumann's influence.

1.1. FLUID DYNAMICS IN 1940

Although papers on *analytical* fluid dynamics (hydrodynamics, aerodynamics, acoustics) were systematically reviewed in *Mathematical Reviews* in 1940, as were papers on "numerical and graphical methods," I think they excited very few readers. Like Lamb's classic treatise [18], they dealt with mathematical solutions of the partial differential equations of Euler-Lagrange and Navier-Stokes, with little reference to physical reality or problems of practical interest.

For various reasons, mathematicians had achieved very limited success in deducing from these equations the observed behavior of real fluids, such as the observed resistance to flow through pipes or, most important, the observed forces on airplane wings. As a result, in 1940 most experts regarded fluid mechanics "as a complex mixture of theory and experiment, in which mathematics by itself should not be taken too seriously."[2] Aeronautical engineers and naval architects relied primarily on wind tunnel and towing tank experiments in their design work, judging mathematical models by their success in simulating observed flows.

Prominent among such models were the "jets" and "wakes" ably reviewed by von Kármán in his Gibbs lecture of 1940 [17]. These divide flows into regions of *potential flow* (having a harmonic velocity potential) and regions of *stagnant fluid*, separated by *free streamlines* at constant pressure, along which the flow speed is therefore constant (by Bernoulli's law). Unfortunately, as Helmholtz showed, such free streamlines are highly unstable in single phase flow. As a result, the theoretical "wakes" calculated by Kirchhoff and others are rarely realized in nature.

1.2 WORLD WAR II

However, *two-phase* potential flows with "free" boundaries had two important new practical applications in World War II. First, the cavities formed behind torpedoes entering water looked quite like Kirchhoff-type "wakes." And second, the jets from bazookas and other antitank weapons utilizing hollow explosive charges with conical metal liners could be explained as reversed impinging coaxial jets.[3] By coincidence, it was with these two-phase flows that my most sustained wartime research was concerned.

Von Neumann had made the more glamorous subject of shock waves his primary wartime interest. As late as 1950, he chose "Shock Interaction and its Mathematical Aspects" as the title of his address at the International Mathematical Congress in Cambridge, but supplied no manuscript. Among the papers listed in his bibliography, papers 81, 88, and all but one of 92 to 100 were devoted to their properties. Of these, his joint paper 97 for Los Alamos especially foreshadowed later developments.

Late in the war, von Neumann also became fascinated by the ENIAC, as Herman Goldstine has already mentioned.[4] His combined interest in shock waves and in computation led him in 1944 to attempt a numerical simulation of "simple" shocks by a Lagrangian particle model,[5] and by March of 1945 he had already made a major contribution (his joint paper 102) to the design of the EDVAC [20, p. 339]. Three months later, before the war was completely over, he gave an audacious and unforgettable sales pitch for the future importance of numerical fluid dynamics. He based this on the inadequacy of analytical fluid dynamics, and claimed that wind tunnels, on which hundreds of millions of dollars were currently being expended, were in principle just analog computers!

1.3 VON NEUMANN'S VISION

Specifically, von Neumann gave a memorable speech called "High-speed Computing Devices and Mathematical Analysis" at the First Canadian Mathematical Congress in June of 1945. There he claimed, as he would write a year later [21, v, p. 4], "Indeed, to a great extent, experiments in fluid mechanics are carried out under conditions where the underlying physical principles are not in doubt, where the quantities to be observed are completely determined by known equations. The purpose of the experiment is not to verify a proposed theory but to replace a computation from an unquestioned theory by direct measurements. Thus wind tunnels are . . . used at present, at least in large part, as computing devices of the so-called analogy type."

This prophetic 1945 talk first identified *numerical* fluid dynamics, to be carried out on electronic digital computers, as a major area of future research. It suggested that with the help of ingeniously designed (and programmed) electronic computers, fluid mechanics might even become the mathematical science that Euler had envisioned two centuries earlier. More generally, it characterized the whole field of scientific computing, to whose development von Neumann himself later contributed so much. In the following Sections 1–6 and 12, I shall try to indicate by example the extent to which computing has increasingly replaced classical analysis as a research tool in fluid dynamics, as well as mentioning some of its limitations.

2. Dawn of a New Era

After the war ended in 1945, a new era began to dawn for scientific computing. Resources previously devoted to urgent wartime needs were now liberated and devoted to basic science. In particular, the U.S. Navy Department and the Atomic Energy Commission decided to continue to support the development of computers and scientific computation on a longer-range basis.

Aware of this potential support, von Neumann decided to have a major hand in creating the wonderful world of scientific computing that it encouraged. Instead of publishing his ideas in the *Proceedings* of the First Canadian Mathematical Congress, he developed them in collaboration with Herman Goldstine into a much more ambitious manuscript entitled "On the Principles of Large Scale Computing Machines" [21, v, pp. 1–33]. There, in Section 2, it was emphasized that "successful work in both pure and applied mathematics . . . deals in the main with linear problems. . . . The advance of analysis is, at the moment, stagnant along the entire front of nonlinear problems." Many examples of this stagnation were given, especially from analytical fluid dynamics. The best hope for a breakthrough, it was suggested, would be provided by digital electronic computers.

As is stated in *Collected Works* [21, v, p. 1], the content of this paper was presented orally to the Office of Research and Inventions of the Navy Department in May of 1916 and to other similar audiences, and it helped to secure support for the machine built under von Neumann's direction at the Institute for Advanced Study.

A month later, Burks, Goldstine, and von Neumann also submitted to the U.S. Army Ordnance Department a "preliminary discussion" of the "logical design of an electronic computing instrument" [21, v, p. 34]. Goldstine and von Neumann followed this up with three long reports on "the planning and coding of problems" for it [21, v, pp. 35–235]. None of the preceding reports were published until after von Neumann's death in 1957; they led to the "Computer Developments at the Institute for Advanced Study" described by Herman Goldstine [15, Part III] and by Julian Bigelow [20, pp. 291–310].[6]

Likewise, after developing his electromechanical Mark I computer in collaboration with IBM during the years 1939 to 1945, Howard Aiken had by 1946 completed for the Naval Proving Ground at Dahlgren a faster Mark II based on similar principles. He also obtained funds from the Navy to construct the Harvard Computation Laboratory. Moreover, IBM had produced similar machines by 1946 for the Ballistic Research Laboratory in Aberdeen [21, v, p. 7]. Finally, under the creative leadership of Mina Rees, our Office of Naval Research was sponsoring from 1947 on much of the early academic research on scientific computing.[7] Thus our Defense Department and Atomic Energy Commission funded a large fraction of the development of electronic computing in the postwar years 1945 to 1950.

Today, scientific computing is sometimes condescendingly referred to as "number crunching," because the applications of computers to business data processing and word processing are so much more lucrative. However, one should remember that the primary motivation for all this government support was provided by a desire to explore the possibilities of scientific computing. This was also von Neumann's main motivation, and he had published several papers on the subject by 1950.

Indeed, scientific computing as envisioned by von Neumann had begun to take on substance by then. As A. G. Oettinger would write in 1962 in the preface to the "Proceedings of a Symposium" dedicated to computer-aided academic research:

> Fifteen years have passed since Professor Howard Aiken organized the first Symposium on large-scale Digital Calculating machinery at Harvard University in response to a "need of better channels of communication

among those mathematicians, physicists, and engineers interested
in the design, construction, operation, and application of large-scale
digital calculating machinery." Sixty persons were expected to attend,
over 300 came.[8] A second Symposium, held in 1949 to summarize
then recent and current developments, was attended by over 700
participants. . . .

All but one session of the first Symposium was concerned with the
new tool itself, since only a very few had had experience with its
applications. Although the balance went the other way in the second
Symposium, the applications were restricted to the realm of the natural
sciences and to certain aspects of the economic and social sciences
which readily lent themselves to quantification. [2]

The table of contents of the "Proceedings" of the 1949 Symposium gives some idea of the state of scientific computing at the time.
Business data processing received little attention there. Indeed, published material on the mathematics of computation was still largely
concerned with classical numerical analysis, partly because so much
scientific computing was related to classified projects supported in
connection with the Cold War then taking shape and was not published for that reason.

2.1 NUMERICAL WEATHER PREDICTION.

By 1950, von Neumann had published a now famous paper with
Jules Charney and R. Fjörtoft entitled "Numerical Integration of the
Barotropic Vorticity Equation" [21, vi, number 30]. Using the ENIAC at
the Ballistics Research Laboratory in Aberdeen, they had made a first
substantial attack on "the problem of numerical weather prediction."
In summarizing what this attack had achieved, von Neumann would
state at the first public showing of the IBM Naval Ordnance Research
Calculator (the NORC) in December, 1954:

We know today, mainly due to the work of J. Charney, that we can
predict by calculation the weather over an area like that of the United
States for a duration like 24 hours in a manner which, from the
hydrodynamicist's point of view, may be quite primitive because one
needs for this purpose only consider one level of the atmosphere. . . .

We know that this gives results which are, by and large, as good as
what an experienced "subjective" forecaster can achieve, and this is
very respectable. This kind of calculation, from start to finish, would
take about a half minute with NORC. [21, v, p. 24]

Although this assessment may have been somewhat optimistic,
and although in 1968 Arakawa would refer more modestly to "numerical simulation of large-scale atmospheric motions" in reviewing much
more elaborate computations [7, pp. 24–40], von Neumann's vision of
1945 has led to major progress in applied meteorology.

Von Neumann did not attend Aiken's 1949 Symposium. Indeed, after the outbreak of World War II in 1939, he had less and less time for attending meetings. And after the war, his many-sided lecturing, consulting, and advisory activities forced him to rely increasingly on collaborators for developing his ideas. For example, his ideas about the stability of difference approximations to initial value problems for partial differential equations were written up by G. G. O'Brien, M. A. Hyman, and S. Kaplan [22].

Lax and Richtmyer [23, Part 1] gave five years later a now classic derivation of "von Neumann's stability criterion" in terms of Banach space concepts. They related it to the "Lax equivalence theorem," that stability is a necessary and sufficient condition for the convergence of difference approximations to the solution of a well-posed, linear, time-independent initial value problem. In 1965, Varga and I showed how to construct difference approximations having an arbitrarily high order of accuracy.[9]

2.2 INVERTING MATRICES

As his papers show, von Neumann realized how much had to be done to computerize effectively the solution of even *linear* partial differential equations. Especially for elliptic DE's, standard elimination methods seemed questionable for solving the large systems of simultaneous linear difference equations to which the usual approximations lead. In addition, in their Navy report of 1946, von Neumann and Goldstine had already emphasized that "no machine . . . is really carrying out the operations of real arithmetic in the rigorous mathematics sense" [21, v, p. 16]. Actually, von Neumann had coauthored during the war a 55-page report to the Navy on the accumulation and amplification of roundoff errors incurred in solving large systems of linear equations by "direct" elimination methods [21, v, pp. 421–78]. Von Neumann and Goldstine followed up on these reports in two long joint papers published by the American Mathematical Society in 1947 and 1951 [21, v. pp. 479–572]. These papers gave "the first detailed analysis of the rounding errors made in . . . fixed point arithmetic."[10]

A decade later, Wilkinson published his now classic reinterpretation of the "matrix inversion" problem, based on his formula $LU = A + E$ where E is a small "error matrix," and on a clearly formulated "condition number" concept.[11] However, it took much longer for the conceptual basis of the preceding papers to be reexamined carefully.

2.3 RANDOM MATRICES

Throughout, von Neumann's papers had assumed a model population of $n \times n$ "random matrices" A, whose entries a_{ij} were independently normally distributed with mean $\overline{a_{ij}} = 0$ and variance $\overline{a_{ij}^2} = \alpha^2$. For such a population of matrices, with $n = 400$, von Neumann and Goldstine concluded that A^{-1} could be computed with satisfactory accuracy with 99.9 percent probability by using fixed-point arithmetic having 12 decimal digits of precision. They showed that by using two more decimal digits of arithmetic precision, n could be increased by a factor of at least 4.5 to about 1800.

By 1976, it was possible (using a good random number generator) to test experimentally in floating point arithmetic the bounds derived theoretically 25 years earlier by Goldstine and von Neumann. I organized a series of such experiments,[12] and found out that as expected, these bounds were very conservative. In attempting to rationalize our experimental results, I assumed that $A = A(\omega)$ was a random matrix having the specified distribution, with column vectors $a_1, \ldots, a_n$. One can triangularize A by the (Gram-Schmidt) orthogonal transformation whose jth unit (column) vector is in the direction of the component of a_j perpendicular to the subspace spanned by $a_1, \ldots, a_{j-1}$. This transforms A into a random upper triangular matrix $B = B(\omega)$ whose jth diagonal entry $b_{jj}(\omega)$ is the square root of a χ^2_{n+1-j}-distribution, with $b_{ij}(\omega) = 0$ if $i > j$, and $b_{ij}(\omega)$ for $i < j$ normally distributed with mean 0 and $b_{ij}{}^2 = 1$. Moreover, $B(\omega) = Q^T A(\omega) Q$ (Q orthogonal) has the same eigenvalues and singular values as $A(\omega)$.

The largest of these singular values is obviously at least b_{11}, which is $\sim \alpha \sqrt{n}$ asymptotically, and the smallest is at most b_{nn}, whose normal distribution is independent of n. This led me to believe that $\kappa(A) \sim \sqrt{n}$. Since then, Smale, Edelman, and others have made a much more precise asymptotic analysis of the distribution of the Euclidean condition numbers $\kappa(A) = \sigma_n / \sigma_1$ of $n \times n$ random matrices having the specified normal distribution. They concluded that the largest singular value, σ_n, is asymptotically $\sim 2\alpha \sqrt{n}$, while the smallest has a density near 0 proportional to $1/\sqrt{n}$. Hence, to keep $\kappa(A)\epsilon < 0.1$ with 99.9 percent probability (for example), one should make the arithmetic precision ϵ asymptotically proportional to $1/n$,[13] and two extra digits of precision should allow one to increase n by a factor of nearly 100.

3. Automating Relaxation

As Professor Fox has explained,* Southwell and his group had shown by 1946 that one could solve by hand, using "relaxation methods," a large variety of elliptic boundary value problems. Many such solutions are carefully reviewed in *Relaxation Methods in Theoretical Physics* [26], the power of such methods is acknowledged in von Neumann's *Collected Works* [21, v, p. 12], where it is estimated that "about 20 relaxation steps [are] required" to solve a problem involving 400

---

* See the essay by Fox in this volume.

unknowns. (The basis for this estimate is not clear, because 20 iterations using the Gauss-Seidel method would only reduce the error by a factor e.)

It has recently been discovered by Pesi Masani [19] that Norbert Wiener had proposed solving such problems on a "rapid electrical adding machine" of unspecified design, essentially by the point-Jacobi method, in an imaginative 1940 memorandum to Vannevar Bush. In 1947, however, when David Young asked me to suggest a Ph.D. problem to him, the only competitor to Southwell's highly intuitive relaxation methods of which I was aware was Stefan Bergman's "kernel method," which Bergman had publicized in two papers [6, Chapter 8, Section 3]. Southwell's approach, based on physical intuition, seemed much more promising to me.

Having vaguely in mind the possibility of implementing relaxation on Aiken's Mark I computer, I therefore proposed that Young try to *automate* relaxation methods, beginning with the Laplace equation with given boundary values (the Dirichlet problem), because of its simplicity and importance for classical mathematical physics. Since he has described his now classic solution of this problem himself,* I will here only recall a few relevant circumstances (but see Section 8).

When I called on him at Imperial College in 1948, I found out that Southwell himself did not believe that computers could compete with human intuition and ingenuity in applying relaxation methods. He emphasized "the freedom . . . left to the [human] computer, to decide the nature of his next step" by relaxation methods.[14] And indeed, it is only in the past 15 years that Babuška and Rheinboldt have made substantial progress in automating the construction of good local mesh refinements, such as were used routinely by Southwell's coworkers [26, Figs. 113, 114, 116]. However, as they themselves kindly informed me, these same coworkers had also discovered through practical experience the advantages of overrelaxation and block relaxation [25, Section 54], and I communicated this information to David Young when I returned to Cambridge that September.

Soon after, Young and Stanley Frankel independently discovered how to automate the SOR ("successive overrelaxation") method, in the special context of the "model problem" (the Poisson equation in the unit square). By 1950, Frankel had published his discovery, and Young had developed a rigorous *general* theory of SOR in his thesis.

During those years, the robustness of large electronic digital computers had not yet been conclusively established, and my own main concern was with the extent to which the Young-Frankel SOR method

---

* See the essay by Young in this volume.

would prove to be more practical than other methods. These included not only hand relaxation à la Southwell, but also the electrolytic tank.

Especially for solving potential flow problems, electrolytic tanks had been used as analog computers since at least 1927,[15] and were being successfully applied to many engineering problems in a large Paris laboratory directed by Joseph Péres. When visiting this laboratory in 1948, I was able to persuade Lucien Malavard to spend three months in setting up and operating an electrolytic tank at Harvard, using funding supplied by the Office of Naval Research. Discussions with Malavard in Cambridge about the practical difficulties involved convinced me of the correctness of von Neumann's conclusion (cf. [21, pp. 489–90]) that digital computers had a more promising future than analog computers.

4. Jets, Wakes, and Cavities

During the years of postwar recovery, 1945 to 1950, although I was intrigued by the problem of automating relaxation methods, I devoted at least 10 times as much time and effort to fluid mechanics. The first edition of my book [4], which presents the main fruits of this effort, did not even mention computing! Its second chapter, entitled "Recent Progress in Free Boundary Theory," deals with applications of the Helmholtz-Kirchhoff model of potential flow with "free streamlines" to *real* jets, wakes, and cavities; I had presented most of these applications in 1947 at the first Symposium on Applied Mathematics sponsored by the American Mathematical Society (cf. [3, v. I]).

Encouraged by Young's success, however, I decided in 1950 to investigate the computability of potential flows with free boundaries as part of a major study. This study, funded by the Office of Naval Research, eventuated in a 1957 book called *Jets, Wakes, and Cavities*,[9], coauthored by E. H. Zarantonello; I shall next summarize our computational experience.

Because preliminary studies by Southwell's collaborator Miss Vaisey and by Malavard's collaborators in Paris had indicated that neither relaxation calculations nor an electrolytic tank could treat the axially symmetrical cavity flow past a disk with satisfactory accuracy,[16] we concentrated on *plane* flows with free streamlines. Specifically, we used Aiken's Mark I Calculator in 1949, IBM machines at the Naval Ordnance Laboratory in 1950, and the Mark II Computer at Dahlgren around 1952 to compute streamlines and equipotentials for jet and cavity flows past *polygonal* obstacles.

We then extended and applied conformal mapping formulas due to Levi-Civita (1907) and a related integral equation formulation due to Villat (1911) to compute the stream functions and velocity potentials of plane cavity flows past curved obstacles. These more sophisticated computations were performed in 1953 on the von Neumann machine at the Institute for Advanced Study in Princeton.[17]

All the programming was done in machine language by Princeton experts, and the computing was largely organized by Douglas Hartree, Herman Goldstine, and David Young among others. See *Jets, Wakes and Cavities* [9, Chap. 9] for details. Concurrently, David Young acted as coauthor with me of three papers on numerical conformal mapping and complex numerical quadrature. Of these, the most substantial was G. Birkhoff, D. M. Young, and E. H. Zarantonello, "Numerical Methods in Conformal Mapping," [3, v. IV, pp. 117–40], coauthored also by Zarantonello. Presented at a 1951 Symposium on "Fluid Dynamics" cosponsored by the Naval Ordnance Laboratory, this was the only paper given there concerned with numerical methods. (The 1953 Symposium [3, v. VI], cosponsored by the Bureau of Standards, would have "Numerical Analysis" as its main theme and would contain a paper on numerical conformal mapping by S. Warschawski, for which the computing was organized by John Todd.)

4.1. SHIP WAVE RESISTANCE

During these years, I also collaborated with Jack Kotik (then an M.I.T. graduate student), in trying to develop improved methods for computing ship wave-making resistance. Assuming a potential flow model and an otherwise undisturbed ocean surface, Michell had shown in 1898 [18, Section 256a] that in the linearized "thin ship" approximation, this resistance is expressible analytically as a quintuple integral.

As our contribution, Kotik and I proposed two "improved methods for computing Michell's integral for a given hull shape." Although the Society of Naval Architects and Marine Engineers published our analysis,[18] I doubt if it has ever been used in practice! One reason may be that, quite apart from the linearization made in Michell's model and its neglect of storm waves, propeller-hull interaction, and sinkage and trim variations, it is not clear "how to resolve the total resistance into the parts resulting from waves, skin friction, and eddies, respectively, even in towing tank tests." Curious readers interested in 1954 views about wave resistance can consult our paper and the discussion following it. Progress since then has been enormous.

Besides supporting the research on *numerical* fluid dynamics reported above, which utilized considerable graduate student assistance, the U.S. Office of Naval Research made possible repeated visits to Harvard by Douglas Hartree, J. Kampé de Fériet, and Eduard Stiefel, as well as single visits by Sir Harold Jeffreys, Louis Rosenhead, and Fritz Ursell. These visits had a great educational value for me and a number of graduate students (including Jack Kotik and Richard Kronauer, who later became my colleagues).

5. Numerical Fluid Dynamics[19]

Because they involved so much classical analysis, the computations of potential flows with free boundaries described in Section 1 are more typical of what Henrici has called "constructive analysis" than of modern numerical fluid dynamics. Far more typical of recent work, and closer in spirit to von Neumann's original ideas, were computations performed at Los Alamos in the 1950s based directly on difference *approximations* to partial differential equations.

Similar highly classified computations, essential for the design of atomic bombs, had been made already during World War II. However, until the late 1960s, published work was restricted to fluid dynamics in one space variable.[20] Thus it constituted only the "tip of an iceberg," stimulated by relevance to weapons calculations.

A 1950 paper by von Neumann and Richtmyer [21, vi, number 28] suggested an important new idea: the use of *artificial viscosity* to damp out the oscillations that had been produced behind shocks in previous molecular models and difference approximations. This paper stimulated later improvements by Peter Lax (1954), Godunov (1959), Lax-Wendroff (1960), and many others.[21]

I first visited Los Alamos in 1951, during the Korean War, and was invited to be a consultant because of my expertise on shaped charges. Although I never became involved in bomb calculations, I did try to keep track of the exciting new ideas about computational physics that were evolving during the 1950s in the extremely stimulating Los Alamos atmosphere and will recall a few of them.

A whole series of such ideas emerged from a now famous 1954 study by Fermi, Pasta, and Ulam[22] of the evolution in time of a circular "dynamical system" of 64 identical particles. By letting each particle repel the two adjacent particles by the same *nonlinear* force law, such a system can be interpreted as semidiscretizing a circular ring of fluid. Everyone expected, from the principle of equipartition of energy, that the oscillations initiated by a sinusoidal perturbation would soon evolve into a random motion in which all wave lengths $2\pi/n$ had about the same energy. Instead, a nearly recurrent oscillation having quasiperiods of quite moderate lengths was observed!

This seminal paper stimulated many other numerical experiments, including one by Charney[3] on point-vortex semidiscretizations of the "potential vorticity" model of his 1950 paper with von Neumann on numerical weather forecasting. Of all these experiments, the most fascinating concerned the *soliton* concept associated with the Kortweg-de Vries equation.[22]

5.1. Particle-in-cell Method

Other 1953/54 Los Alamos reports (LA–1557 and LA–1867), by Pasta and Ulam and by Harwood Kolsky, dealt with semidiscretizations of two-dimensional compressible flow problems. From these evolved notable "particle-in-cell," or PIC methods, developed by Francis Harlow and collaborators. Harlow has described the underlying idea in these words:[23]

> The general features of the PIC method can be described as follows. There are two computing meshes; one is Eulerian, the other Lagrangian. The domain through which the fluid is to move is divided into a finite number of computational cells which are fixed relative to the observer. This is the Eulerian mesh. In addition the fluid itself is represented by particles or mass points which move through the Eulerian mesh, representing the motion of fluid. This is the Lagrangian mesh. Associated with the mesh points of each system are certain variables whose history the calculation develops. Thus for each Eulerian cell there is kept the velocity, the internal energy, and the total mass of each kind of material. For the Lagrangian mesh of particles, individual masses and positions are kept.[24]

My own study of historical examples of such semidiscretizations by Cauchy, Kelvin, Born, Brillouin, and others led me to the conclusion that they should be regarded as defining "molecular models of synthetic materials," having a great variety of possible physical properties.[25]

6. Taylor Instability

"Taylor instability" refers to the instability of the interface between the two adjacent fluids of different densities, when the light fluid is accelerated toward the heavier fluid. This instability was recognized by G. I. Taylor and R. M. Davies during World War II as damping out the radial oscillations of the gas sphere formed by an underwater explosion; for a summary of their results, see *Underwater Explosions* [11, pp. 302–4].[26] In 1950, combined theoretical and experimental studies by Taylor and D. J. Lewis called attention to the general scientific interest of this phenomenon.

The same Taylor instability arises during the (spherical) *implosion* phase of an atomic bomb, initiated by explosives surrounding heavier fissile materials.[27] In this situation, as with shaped charges, models from fluid mechanics are applicable because explosive pressures so greatly exceed shear strength.

This application evoked considerable interest at Los Alamos in computer simulations of Taylor instability. Thus, in 1953, Fermi and von Neumann analyzed a very simple model of Taylor instability having two degrees of freedom [21, vi, pp. 431–6]. Later, von Neumann suggested computing the evolution of the interface of a much more elaborate model of doubly periodic Taylor instability, using vorticity-stream function difference equations in a rectangular domain with rigid walls. Suitably modified by Metropolis and others, this model (with 518 interior mesh points) was successfully handled by the Maniac, and the results were published in 1959 (see [21, v, pp. 611–50], which summarizes Los Alamos Report LA–2165).

In earlier Los Alamos reports (LA–1862 and LA–1927), I had proposed a system of integroDEs for computing the evolution in time of a spatially periodic interface separating two incompressible fluids under Helmholtz and Taylor instability. In a 1960 expository article on the subject, I noted that the numerical solution of these integroDEs "represents a formidable problem, even with high-speed computing machines." This article also reviewed contemporary applications of vortex methods.[28]

My writings on Taylor instability in the years 1953 to 1960, like most of my work on fluid dynamics, attempted to treat the subject as an exact mathematical science. As a result, their spirit differed essentially from that of the more heuristic calculations recalled in Section 5, which were more typical of numerical fluid dynamics as practiced in Los Alamos. Among these, especially remarkable was the simulation of periodic "vortex streets" that form behind cylinders at intermediate Reynolds numbers. This was achieved by Fromm and Harlow in 1963.[29] I shall discuss the different roles played by these two types of calculations at the end of my talk.

7. Nuclear Power

I now come to my second main theme: the reactor computations that have played such an essential role in the design of nuclear power reactors. Before 1951, the design of these was based on sophisticated analytical models of the neutron chain reactions that govern their power level. As in the case of fluid dynamics, these models were fitted to experimental observations, but with the major difference that whereas the study of analytical fluid dynamics was 200 years old, analytical models of nuclear reactors were brand new.[30] Moreover, to build experimental reactors (which had to be full-scale) was extremely expensive: There are no nuclear analogs of wind tunnels!

My acquaintance with reactor computations began late in 1954. Five years earlier, H. L. Garabedian and Sidney Krasik had joined the staff of the Westinghouse Atomic Power Division (WAPD), which had been assigned—together with the Argonne National Laboratory (ANL)—the task of designing a nuclear power reactor for submarine propulsion. These two men were joined in 1950 by "two able young theoretical physicists from Yale":[31] Allan Henry (later Chairman of the Nuclear Engineering Department at MIT) and Robert Hellens (who moved to an important position at Combustion Engineering).

Within a few years, the group headed by Garabedian and Krasik succeeded in designing (in cooperation with the ANL) the power plant for the submarine *Nautilus*. The relevant "two-group" computations were initially performed by a select group of desk machine operators, aided by a cumbersome analog computer consisting of "two huge coupled wall-like configurations of soldered resistors, each representing one group-diffusion equation."[32] However, by 1954 Garabedian and Krasik had decided that the new high-speed electronic digital computers that had just become available, such as the IBM 704 and the NORC at the Taylor Model Basin, were what they needed.

To write the necessary codes in machine language, many desk computer operators were retrained. Five fresh Ph.D.'s were recruited to design the codes, most notably Richard Varga, who had participated in the ONR-sponsored scientific computing at Harvard as a graduate student, Eli Gelbard, and Jerome Spanier. I served as a part-time consultant to advise these last. We all had to accept on faith the physical validity of the analytical models assumed; the problem was to solve *numerically*, with acceptable accuracy, the systems of elliptic partial differential equations constructed by physicists and claimed by them to provide realistic models.

Varga was put in charge of numerical solution of the multi-group diffusion equations used to simulate neutron chain reactions. Mathematically, these determine the neutron flux up to a scalar factor (the power level) as the positive eigenvector of a system of linear elliptic difference equations of the general form

$$L_k[\phi_k] = \sum S_l[\phi_l], \qquad l \bmod n \tag{1}$$

Here n is the number of energy groups, the L_k are self-adjoint operators, and the S_l are matrix multiplicands.

Within three years, Varga succeeded in designing a robust, widely used code PDQ-4 for designing nuclear reactors. Because he has published a description of its main features himself,[33] and my space is limited, I shall refer you to his paper for them.

8. Reactor Computations

In the system shown in equation (1), each individual equation is of the form

$$L_k[\phi_k] = -\nabla \cdot [D_k(\mathbf{x}) \nabla \phi_k] + \sigma_k(\mathbf{x}) \phi_k = f_i(\mathbf{x}) \tag{2}$$

where the D_k, σ_k, and f_k are known or previously computed positive functions. The standard five-point difference approximation to such elliptic equations satisfies the hypotheses of SOR theory. Young's 1950 thesis was finally published in 1954 [32], and Varga made it his "immediate goal to master Young's paper and all related papers in this area."[34]

By 1954, several competitors to SOR had been proposed for solving elliptic difference equations, in addition to Frankel's "second-order Richardson" method. Indeed, in his invited address at the 1954 International Mathematical Congress in Amsterdam, Eduard Stiefel had concluded that: "Among all scalar iteration algorithms, the method of conjugate gradients . . . is the best strategy," and in a 1956 paper [27], he had proposed a more specific Chebyshev method with similar virtues of "optimality." In a sharp 1957 sequel [30], Varga defended the virtues of SOR as used in PDQ-4, but I should add that Stiefel had written his paper during a visit to Harvard sponsored by the Office of Naval Research, and everything was done in a most friendly spirit.

Another competitor was the elliptic ADI method developed by Peaceman, Rachford and Douglas in 1955/56 for petroleum reservoir calculations, in which DEs of the form shown in equation (2) also arise. Indeed, for the "model problem" (the Poisson equation in a square or rectangle), elliptic ADI converges faster by an order of magnitude than SOR, a fact that at first suggested that it would soon make SOR obsolete! However, as Varga and I showed, this advantage is lost unless $HV = VH$, an equation that does not hold in general.[35]

Actually, for reactor applications, most successful for many years was the CCSI method of Golub and Varga (1961), which was a synthesis of the SOR and Chebyshev methods. I have mentioned other methods primarily to illustrate the great activity in related aspects of scientific computing that was going on in the mid-1950s, and to stress the high quality of some of it.[36]

A final, and most important feature of the system in equation (1) of multigroup diffusion equations, and indeed of the more basic transport integroDEs which these are intended to approximate, is that they are associated with positive linear operators. This fact has valuable computational consequences, for which I refer you to Varga's landmark book of 1962. These extend the Perron-Frobenius theory of nonnegative matrices. It also has interesting more general implications, for which I refer you to my own papers.[37]

By 1959, I felt knowledgeable enough about nuclear reactor theory to ask Eugene Wigner to join me in organizing a conference on mathematical problems in this field. The *Proceedings* of our conference were published [8], and a fair impression of the great advances in reactor computation that had occurred since 1955 may be had by comparing this volume with volumes three and five of the *Proceedings of the First International Conference on Peaceful Uses of Atomic Energy*. These volumes include discussions of many analytical models of neutron chain reactions, but do not even mention computers or numerical mathematics. This omission seems ironic since von Neumann, as an AEC Commissioner at the time, must have joined in sponsoring the conference.

In *Nuclear Reactor Theory* [8], in contrast, one may find three outstanding surveys of applications of numerical methods to reactor problems, written by leading experts. Varga reviewed numerical methods for solving multigroup diffusion equations. Richtmyer reviewed applications of Monte Carlo methods, with special reference to their use for deducing absorption coefficients for neutrons being slowed down in a medium that has known absorption coefficients. Bengt Carlson (from Los Alamos) spoke on the numerical solution of transport problems. These papers, taken together, give an excellent picture of the "state-of-the-art" as regards reactor computations at that time.

Within the next few years, moreover, reactor computations would become merged with numerical fluid dynamics in "plant codes" containing "thermohydraulic" subprograms designed to model variations in the rate of coolant flow and temperature distribution. By coupling these variations with control rod positions, operators could control the power level of a reactor. Thus, by 1963 or so, the numerical simulation of nuclear power reactors under normal operating conditions, however imperfect, was an accomplished fact.

9. Automobile Modeling

At the time, the 1950s were widely regarded as ushering in an "atomic age" in which nuclear energy would become the dominant source not only of electricity, but also of power in general. Thus, a major study was made by General Electric of the potentialities of nuclear aircraft propulsion. In the same optimistic spirit, a Nuclear Engineering Department was set up in 1956 at the General Motors Research Laboratory (GMR) by its new director, Lawrence Hafstad, previously head of the Reactor Development Division at the AEC. H. L. Garabedian served as a full-time physics consultant.

Not long after, Westinghouse set up an Astronuclear Division to exploit nuclear propulsion for space exploration, with "Sid" Krasik as a key scientific administrator. Unfortunately, these moves left the WAPD scientific computing activity without leadership. To compound the problem, Varga left WAPD for the Case Institute of Technology (as full professor) in 1960. Although Eli Gelbard and Jerome Spanier continued to provide Bettis with high quality expertise in the computer modeling of submarine reactors, no new mathematician of Varga's stature was added to its staff. Instead, Louis Hageman (who had written a Ph.D. thesis supervised by Varga) continued to develop Young's and Varga's ideas, coauthoring 20 years later with David Young the monograph *Applied Iterative Analysis* (Academic Press, 1981).

By 1959, General Motors had decided that it would be unduly expensive to maintain a Nuclear Engineering Department with an experimental reactor and replaced it with a small Physics Department and a minute Mathematics Department. The latter was headed by Garabedian, who promptly invited me to act as consultant, even before his department had well-defined missions. Carl de Boor, who had computed for me at Harvard (with ONR support) the steady flow with free surface *and* gravity under a sluice gate, soon joined the staff.

The first substantial mission of the fledgling GMR Mathematics Department was suggested by John Campbell, a GM chemist who had played an important role in developing "no-knock" leaded gasoline and was Associate Director of GMR. In a carefully planned briefing session, he described to Garabedian and me the slow and costly process required to put glamorous new car designs into mass production. He suggested that the process might be sped up by computerizing the definition of car body surfaces, especially since computer-controlled milling machines had become available. Might not a suitably programmed large computer replace the "acres of drafting boards" that were currently required to produce mechanical drawings? He arranged for us a conducted tour of the Styling Division, "a division cloaked with secrecy," headed by Peter Kyropoulos. It was fascinating "to observe the steps involved in creating . . . a new model automobile, from the artist's drawing, the clay model, a wooden model of the new design, the creation of dies for stamping out the pieces of sheet metal forming the exterior of the new model, and finally the . . . actual car, three years later."[38]

We were shown there the "Harley curves," traditionally used by draftsmen to produce attractive lines, and even visited a stamping plant. We were also given some reports from Boeing, where M. Donald MacLaren (a recent Harvard Ph.D.) was already using cubic spline curves for aircraft design. Armed with all this information, we started thinking about the problem of computerizing the representation of smooth (sheet metal) surfaces.

Being already aware of the use of splines by naval architects for designing horizontal sections of ship hulls, and having long admired a 1946 paper by I. Schoenberg on splines,[39] after learning of Boeing's work I immediately envisaged fitting a rectangular network of intersecting cubic spline curves to sections $z = f(x, y_j)$ and $z = f(x_i, y)$ of pieces of car body surfaces $z = f(x, y)$ that had rectangular plane projections. It was easy to computerize the interpolation of a cubic spline $z = g_j(x)$ through given offsets $z_{i,j} = g_j(x_i)$.

Concurrently, Garabedian looked into the possibility of applying the ideas of my father's book *Aesthetic Measure* to automobile styling, as did Russell Donnelly, an experimental physicist from the University of Chicago. Knowing how long it had taken my father to apply his ideas to single polygonal tiles and the fact stressed in the preface to his book that no one aesthetic formula can successfully predict transient tastes, I was not surprised when this project was soon abandoned.

10. Bicubic Splines

The idea of interpolating a smooth surface through a rectangular network of cubic spline curves seemed much more promising, and we decided to pursue it. We soon learned about so-called "Coons patches," which interpolate smoothly in any one mesh rectangle to smoothly varying boundary values on its edges by suitably superposing linear interpolants to pairs of corresponding points on opposite edges. They were taught as a "trade secret" in drafting schools for many years previously and are solutions of the boundary problem defined by the hyperbolic differential equation $\partial^4 u / \partial x^2 \partial y^2 = 0$ of Mangeron. Unfortunately, when applied to a rectangular network of spline curves, this scheme produces angular ridges along the curves separating adjacent mesh rectangles.

The GMR Computing Department, which had been given a five-year $10 million grant and several IBM graphics terminals to solve the problem of computerizing surface representation, was also aware of these "Coons patches." Ed Jacks, who headed this parallel effort, brushed aside our proposal to cooperate with him and told us he would "add three or four mathematics Ph.D.'s to his staff" when he felt he was "ready for mathematical assistance."

Undaunted, Garabedian and I developed a reasonably practical piecewise polynomial interpolation scheme which did interpolate a "smooth" (i.e., continuously differentiable) surface through a rectangular network of cubic spline curves, and we published it.[40] Knowing from mechanics[41] that cubic splines come from the linearized Euler-Bernoulli (one-dimensional) theory of point-loaded thin beams, I was also hoping for inspiration from the two-dimensional theory of thin planes and shells. However, an informative letter kindly sent me by Eli Sternberg convinced me that such a scheme would be too complicated to be practical.

The elegant technique of bicubic spline interpolation was discovered a year later by Carl de Boor. This interpolates a piecewise polynomial surface having continuous second derivatives through $z_{ij} = f(x_i, y_j)$ for given edge slopes and corner cross-derivatives. Previously a student of Collatz, de Boor had just spent a year at Harvard as a graduate student before joining the GMR staff, computing potential flows with free boundaries under gravity as a part-time research assistant to me under an ONR contract. For a mathematical description of his "tensor product" scheme in context, I refer you to de Boor's and my paper in *Modern Developments in Fluid Dynamics* [14, pp. 164–190].

Besides discovering bicubic spline interpolation, de Boor developed it into a working algorithm. To do this, he had to construct a reasonably well-conditioned basis of bicubic spline functions and solve the resulting linear system for the coefficients of these basis functions. Because bicubic splines are tensor products of cubic splines, this can be done by a very efficient direct method [6, Chapter 1, Section 6]. In his first month at GM, de Boor "did write a program for this . . . producing a bicubic spline interpolant to data taken from a model of a rear quarter panel [of a Cadillac], and even got a display of the resulting mesh lines." To do this with the computing and graphics equipment then available was very arduous, and only possible because "FORTRAN programming, as it had then just become available, was a great improvement over the machine language programming I had made use of at Harvard and earlier."[42]

De Boor's program so impressed Kenneth Ruff and other able members of the GM Manufacturing and Development staff that they made it and later de Boor programs the core of their successful INCA system for using computer-controlled machine tools to produce dies from clay models. This system, already operational around 1962, was used for many years and may even still be used in modified form.

11. Concluding Remarks

I have so far been reviewing key developments in scientific computing prior to 1962 with which I was acquainted at first-hand, in three different areas: over a 15-year period in fluid dynamics, whose analytical study had begun two centuries earlier; over an eight-year period during which nuclear power reactor behavior was successfully computerized only two decades after neutron chain reactions had been discovered; and over a three-year period during which smooth curves and surfaces were treated by computerizing ideas of Euler, Gauss, and Hermite.

I have ignored parallel and overlapping contemporary work at other centers. For example, bicubic splines were discovered independently by Dr. Theilheimer at the Taylor Model Basin and James Ferguson at Boeing. Moreover, far more general techniques of piecewise polynomial interpolation and approximation were being developed in many centers from the late 1950s on, under the name of the finite element method.[43]

Instead of discussing such related developments, I wish to conclude with a few remarks relating the "Stone Age" developments that I have described to more recent progress. I shall begin with some further developments at General Motors in which I participated prior to 1970. Of greatest general interest is probably progress in the aesthetic problem of "sweetening" curves, a class of mathematical entities whose "aesthetic measure" was not discussed in my father's book. In the early 1960s, nobody in the GM Styling Division had enough mathematical background to work effectively with mathematically defined spline curves. But five years later, after de Boor had left GM and his place had been taken by his brother-in-law Hermann Burchard (also a Collatz student), this deficiency was corrected.

In cooperation with two members of the Styling Division and James Ayers, Burchard developed "a working program CSLP, based on the idea of a discrete curve (list of points) to be smoothed by linear programming, with the constraints representing linearized curvature conditions. The objective function to be minimized was the distance, in the l^1 norm, of the discrete curve from the data points. . . . Our constraints were meant to model . . . logarithmic convexity of curvature."[44]

As originally written at GM, the running time of this program was two minutes—too long for practical use. By following advice given by Ellis Johnson, an expert on linear programming, this was reduced to 20 seconds, after which CSLP became a very convenient tool of computer-aided design.

Another valuable discovery at GMR (by William Gordon) was the concept of *spline blending*, interpolating smooth surfaces through rectangular networks of intersecting curves. This can be used to replace "Coons patches" connected along angular ridges with "Gordon patches," which blend smoothly. In particular, it produces bicubic spline *surfaces* from rectangular networks of intersecting cubic spline *curves*.

For developing this idea, penetrating and highly original earlier papers by D. Mangeron and D. D. Stancu were very suggestive. The volume *Approximations with Special Emphasis on Spline Functions* [24] contains a paper by Gordon which gives references to these papers and explains some of their theoretical implications. The paper by Martin Schultz there shows that splines provide effective finite element methods. For many later developments, I refer you to Carl de Boor's book [10] and the *Journal of Approximation Theory*.

However, as is often the case in applied mathematics, there are also some simple questions to which no simple answer has yet been found.[45] Already in *Approximation of Functions* [13, pp. 185–7], de Boor and I called attention to "the problem of devising a 'well-set' piecewise bicubic interpolation scheme of class C^2 in a general (connected) regular polygon." This essentially algebraic problem has many intriguing generalizations. I discussed some of them in my article in the Schoenberg volume [see also 6, Chapter 7, Section 8]. Although no theoretically attractive interpolation scheme solving this problem has yet been found, so-called "spline *quasi*-interpolants" often provide satisfactory practical solutions to the corresponding approximation problem. Currently, the design goals which led de Boor and me to formulate this *interpolation* problem are approached in other ways— for example by fitting best *approximations* to boundary conditions in subspaces of linear combinations of B-splines.[46]

The problems of numerical fluid dynamics are more complicated than those of computerizing surface representation in a very essential respect. Whereas all nonrelativistic models of three-dimensional geometry are mathematically equivalent, many inequivalent systems of differential equations and boundary conditions have been proposed as models for the motions of fluids [5, pp. 12–13]. For this reason, I think that "numerical fluid mechanics has not and will not replace either analytical or experimental fluid mechanics as a research tool, but . . . it complements and supplements them invaluably" [5, p. 15].[47] I believe that this statement also expresses von Neumann's opinion when, for example, he designed his pioneer computations with Charney and Fjörtoft on numerical weather prediction.

In my opinion, the vast literature on numerical fluid dynamics, much of it contained in the first 77 volumes of the *Journal of Computational Physics*, contains too few critical comparisons of numerical experiments with physical reality and mathematical theorems. Heuristic simulations of vortex streets[48] represented a major breakthrough in 1963, but users of today's supercomputers should be trying to predict "the variation with Re in the point of flow separation and the $C_D = C_D(Re)$" [5, p. 28] for flows past cylinders. Many other heuristic simulations should also be subjected to the acid test of precise quantitative comparisons aimed at locating discrepancies rather than at extolling the merits of some new "method." The true scientific challenge is to convert as much of fluid dynamics as possible into a mathematical science [5, p. 1], like geometry and celestial mechanics. Too many authors seem to be simulating that prosperous pseudoscientist, Mr. Grant Swinger!

A similar criticism of reactor computations has been made by Weinberg and Wigner: "We believe strongly that only when there is a true understanding of the *physical* and *analytical* basis of a reactor calculation can the machine be used to full effect."[49] Here the physics involved, which includes fluid flow in coolant channels, becomes an order of magnitude more complicated than that involved in numerical fluid dynamics when real reactor dynamics is under consideration. Even the *linear* equations governing *static* critical neutron distributions, which involve neutron energies varying by a factor of 10^8, must be treated by very ingenious empirical approximations invented by physicists, often decades ago.

Journals like *Nuclear Science and Engineering* should, in my opinion, devote more space to articles that successfully rationalize such approximations. This might help to dissipate the distrust of nuclear energy which currently threatens the efficient use of the world's limited mineral resources, especially in our country.

Notes

1 Quoted from the Preface of [20], a book that makes an excellent companion piece to the present volume.

2 Quoted from my paper "Numerical Hydrodynamics as a Mathematical Science," from the Proceedings of a Workshop on Numerical Hydrodynamics, (National Academy of Sciences, 1975): 117–57.

3 See G. Birkhoff, D. P. MacDougall, E. M. Pugh, and G. I. Taylor, "Explosives with Lined Cavities," *J. Appl. Phys.* 19 (1948): 563–82.

4 For an authoritative history of the ENIAC and its influence on later computer designs, see the article by Arthur Burks in [20, pp. 311–44]. Fascinating reminiscences by Eckert and Mauchly fill pp. 525–61 of the same volume.

5 See [20, pp. 23–5], where I mistakenly said that the computations were done on the ENIAC. Incidentally, Cunningham was the discoverer of Cunningham's comet.

6 See also the article by W. Aspray in Esther R. Phillips (ed.), *Studies in the History of Mathematics* (Washington DC: Mathematical Association of America, 1987).

7 See the articles by Mina Rees in Dalton Tarwater (ed.), *The Bicentennial Tribute to American Mathematics* (Buffalo, NY: Mathematical Association of America, 1977): 101–16; and in *Comm. ACM* 30 (1987): 832–48.

8 See [1]. Numerical solutions of problems in fluid dynamics were discussed there by Howard Emmons (turbulence) and Raymond Seeger (explosions).

9 *J. Math. and Phys.* 44 (1965): 1–23.

10 See J. H. Wilkinson, *The Algebraic Eigenvalue Problem* (Oxford University Press, 1965), 187.

11 *J. Assoc. Comput. Mach.* 8 (1961): 281–330. For a very readable brief summary, see J. H. Wilkinson, *Rounding Errors in Algebraic Processes* (Englewood Cliffs, NJ: Prentice Hall, 1963), 102–10.

12 For the distribution of the condition numbers of "random matrices," see my paper with S. Gulati in *Z. Angew Math. Phys.* 30 (1979): 148–56.

13 See S. Smale, *Bull. Amer. Math. Soc.* 13 (1985): 87–121; and Alan Edelman, *SIAM J. Matrix Anal. Appl.* 9 (1988): 543–60.

14 See J.T. Oden (ed.), *Computational Methods in Nonlinear Mechanics* (New York: North Holland, 1980), Ch. 3.

15 See [29, vol. iii, pp. 107–27].

16 See [9, pp. 220, 229]. Cavity flows past a disk were computed successfully around 1970 by E. Bloch and A. D. Snider. See P. R. Garabedian, *Pure Appl. Math* 23 (1970): 313–27; and L. I. Sedov and G. Yu. Stepanov (eds.), *Non-Steady Flow of Water at High Speeds* (Moscow: Nauka, 1973): 197–9.

17 See G. Birkhoff, H. H. Goldstine, and E. H. Zarantonello, *Rend. Sem. Mat. Univ. Politec. Torino* 13 (1954): 205–23; [5, Section 9], and G. Birkhoff, in *Non-Steady Flow*, 19–38, Sections 7–8.

18 G. Birkhoff, B. V. Korvin-Kroukovsky, and J. Kotik, *Trans. Soc. Nav. Arch. Mar. Eng.* 62 (1954): 359–96. For a scholarly review of the whole subject, see J. V. Wehausen, *Adv. in Appl. Mech.* 13 (1973): 93–245.

19 See also [5, Section 12] for previous comments on the topics discussed in this section.

20 See [23, second ed., Ch. 12], which is entitled "Fluid Dynamics in One Space Variable."

21 Los Alamos Report LA–1940, republished in Alan C. Newell (ed.), *Nonlinear Wave Motion* (Providence, RI: American Mathematical Society, 1974), 143–56. For comments on related topics, see Ulam's 1962 article in [3, v. XIII, pp. 247–58].

22 See Martin Kruskal in [16, pp. 43–62], and N. Zabusky, *J. Comput. Phys.* 47 (1981): 195–249.

23 See [3 v. XV, pp. 289–309].

24 See [3, v. XV, pp. 269–88].

25 See [2, pp. 23–31] and Report LA–2618, both coauthored by Robert E. Lynch.

26 For the wartime reports by Taylor and Davies, see [29, iii, pp. 337–57].

27 *J. Appl. Phys.* 19 (1948).

28 See also my papers with David Carter in *J. Math. Mech.* 6 (1957): 769–80; and with Joseph Fisher in *Rend. Circ. Mat. Palermo* 8 (1959): 77–90.

29 See *Phys. Fluids* 6 (1963): 975–82; *Methods in Comp. Phys.* 3 (1964): 345–82; [16, pp. 195–216].

30 See the fascinating article by L. Badash et al. in the *Proc. Am. Phil. Soc.* 130 (1986), 196–231, which brings out how unlikely it seemed to many physicists that nuclear energy could be harnessed, before the discovery of neutron chain reactions around 1939.

31 In Sections 7–10, I have drawn freely on a handwritten memorandum kindly sent me by H. L. Garabedian, entitled "A Brief Account of my Experiences at WAPD, 1949–56, and at GMR, 1956–66, with Emphasis on Computational Aids and their Operators" (24 pp.).

32 For the preceding graphic description, and many other comments that follow, I have drawn on a memorandum kindly sent me by Richard Varga.

33 *IRE Trans. of the Professional Group on Nuclear Science, NS–4* (1957): 52–62.

34 Memo from Richard Varga.

35 G. Birkhoff and R. S. Varga, *Trans. Amer. Math. Soc.* 92 (1959): 13–24; and our article with D. Young in *Adv. Comput.* 3, 190–273; [31]; and [33].

36 See also [6] and my article in [25, pp. 17–38], which attempts to review the history of methods for solving elliptic equations numerically.

37 See my *Selected Papers on Algebra and Topology*, (Cambridge: Birkhäuser Boston, 1987): 401–3. In the bibliography on pp. ix–xv of that volume, numbers 99, 100, 101, 103, 104, 106, 116, 117, 119, 127, 136, 139, 149, 150, and 158 reflect my interest in nuclear reactor theory.

38 The preceding quotations are from the letter by H. L. Garabedian cited in note 31.

39 *Quart. Appl. Math.* 4 (1946): 45–99, 121–41. Schoenberg's landmark paper concentrated on *uniform* meshes. See also I. Schoenberg, *Selected Papers* two volumes ed. by Carl de Boor (Cambridge: Birkhäuser Boston, 1988).

40 *J. Math. and Phys.* 39 (1960): 258–68.

41 See J. L. Synge and B. A. Griffith, *Principles of Mechanics*, second ed. (New York: McGraw-Hill, 1949), Section 3.3.

42 These quotations are taken from a letter kindly sent me by Carl de Boor.

43 An outstanding survey of the finite element method as of 1968 is given in [7, pp. 210–52] by Carlos Felippa (then at Boeing) and his thesis supervisor, Raymond W. Clough.

44 Quoted from a very helpful letter sent me by Hermann Burchard.

45 See C. de Boor and G. J. Fix, *J. Approx. Theory* 8 (1973): 19–45.

46 For de Boor's latest thinking on the subject, see his paper, "What Is a Multivariate Spline?" in *ICIAM '87* (Philadelphia: SIAM Publications, 1988).

47 Similarly, I wrote that "von Neumann was mindful of there being three different tools of scientific investigation: physical experiment, mathematical analysis, and numerical computation" in the Proceedings of a 1974 Workshop on Numerical Hydrodynamics (National Academy of Sciences, 1975): 127.

48 *Phys. Fluids* 6 (1963): 975–82; *Methods in Comp. Phys.* 3 (1964): 345–82; [16, pp. 195–216].

49 *The Physical Theory of Neutron Chain Reactions* (University of Chicago Press, 1958): vi. See also my paper cited in note 2.

References

[1] "Proceedings of a Second Symposium on Large-Scale Digital Computing Machinery," *Annals of the Harvard Computation Laboratory* 26 (Harvard University Press, 1951).

[2] "Proceedings of a Symposium on Digital Computers and their Applications," *Annals of the Harvard Computation Laboratory* 31 (Harvard University Press, 1962).

[3] G. Birkhoff, D. M. Young, and E. H. Zarantonello, "Numerical Methods in Conformal Mapping," *Proceedings of Symposia in Applied Mathematics*, published by the American Mathematical Society from 1948 on.

[4] G. Birkhoff, *Hydrodynamics: A Study in Logic, Fact, and Similitude* (Princeton University Press, 1950).

[5] G. Birkhoff, "Numerical Fluid Dynamics," *SIAM Review* 65 (1983): 1–34.

[6] G. Birkhoff and R. E. Lynch, *Numerical Solution of Elliptic Problems* (Philadelphia: SIAM Publications, 1985).

[7] G. Birkhoff and R. S. Varga (eds.), "Numerical Solution of Field Problems in Continuum Physics," *SIAM–AMS Proc.* II (1970).

[8] G. Birkhoff and E. Wigner (eds.), "Nuclear Reactor Theory," *Proc. Sympos. Appl. Math.* XI (1961).

[9] G. Birkhoff and E.H. Zarantonello, *Jets, Wakes, and Cavities* (San Diego: Academic Press, 1957).

[10] Carl de Boor, *A Practical Guide to Splines* (Berlin: Springer Publishing, 1978).

[11] R. M. Cole, *Underwater Explosions* (Princeton University Press, 1948).

[12] G. E. Forsythe and Wolfgang Wasow, *Finite Difference Methods for Partial Differential Equations* (New York: John Wiley, 1960).

[13] H. L. Garabedian (ed.), *Approximation of Functions* (New York: Elsevier Science Publishing, 1965).

[14] Sydney Goldstein (ed.), *Modern Developments in Fluid Dynamics*, two volumes (Oxford University Press, 1938).

[15] Herman H. Goldstine, *The Computer from Pascal to von Neumann* (Princeton University Press, 1972).

[16] "Proceedings of IBM Scientific Computing Symposium on Large Scale Problems in Physics," *IBM Research Symposia Series* (1963).

[17] Th. von Kármán, "The Engineer Grapples with Nonlinear Problems," *Bull. Amer. Math. Soc.* 46 (1940): 613–83.

[18] Horace Lamb, *Hydrodynamics*, sixth ed. (Cambridge: The University Press, 1932). German translations of the third and fifth editions, 1907, 1931.

[19] Pesi Masani, B. Randell, D. K. Ferry, and R. Saeks, "The Wiener Memorandum on the Mechanical Solution of Partial Differential Equations," *Ann. Hist. Comput.* 9 (1987): 183–97.

[20] N. Metropolis, J. Howlett, and G. C. Rota (eds.), *A History of Computing in the Twentieth Century* (San Diego: Academic Press, 1968).

[21] John von Neumann, *Collected Works*, six volumes (Elmsford, NY: Pergamon Press, 1961–63).

[22] G. G. O'Brien, M. A. Hyman, and S. Kaplan, "Numerical Solution of Partial Differential Equations," *J. Math. Phys.* 29 (1951): 223–51.

[23] R. H. Richtmyer, *Difference Methods for Initial-Value Problems*, first ed. (New York: Wiley Interscience, 1957); second ed. coauthored by K. W. Morton (1967).

[24] I. J. Schoenberg (ed.), *Approximations with Special Emphasis on Spline Functions* (San Diego: Academic Press, 1969).

[25] Martin H. Schultz (ed.), *Elliptic Problem Solvers* (San Diego: Academic Press, 1981).

[26] R. V. Southwell, *Relaxation Methods in Theoretical Physics* (Oxford: Clarendon Press, 1946).

[27] Edward Stiefel, "On Solving Fredholm Integral Equations," *SIAM J.* 4 (1956): 63–85.

[28] Edward Stiefel, "Recent Developments in Relaxation Techniques," *Proc. Internat. Math. Congress* 1 Amsterdam (1954); Noordhoff (1957).

[29] G. I. Taylor, *Scientific Papers*, four volumes (Cambridge University Press, 1958–1971).

[30] Richard S. Varga, "A Comparison of the SOR Method and Semi-iterative Methods using Chebyshev Polynomials," *SIAM J.* 5 (1957): 39–46.

[31] Richard S. Varga, *Matrix Iterative Analysis* (Englewood Cliffs, NJ: Prentice Hall, 1962).

[32] David M. Young, "Iterative Methods for Solving Partial Difference Equations of Elliptic Type," *Trans. Amer. Math. Soc.* 76 (1954): 92–111.

[33] David M. Young, *Iterative Solution of Large Linear Systems* (San Diego: Academic Press, 1971).

The Development of ODE Methods: A Symbiosis between Hardware and Numerical Analysis*

C. W. Gear
R. D. Skeel

1. Hand Calculation

We begin with hand calculation because it is interesting in its own right and because it is important to appreciate what was known about numerical methods before the use of computers.

Analog devices for general calculations date from 1620 when Gunter invented a forerunner of the slide rule [1]. However, any engineer trained before the introduction of the inexpensive four-function calculator knows that a slide rule is not a particularly useful device for numerical integration. The first digital arithmetic tool was built at about the same time by Schickard [1] and reinvented in 1642 by Pascal (1623–1662), who built a digital adder/subtracter. Thirty years later, Leibniz (1646–1716) built a digital machine that surpassed Pascal's by also being able to perform multiplication and division. However, it seems that practical calculating machines were not available until the mid-19th century [2].

Moulton [3] states that "Newton in his *Principia* was the first to find approximate solutions of differential equations by numerical processes" and goes on to say, "The successors of Newton . . . applied the method to problems in celestial mechanics to which more general methods are not adapted. For example, if a comet passes near Jupiter . . . its motion can be most conveniently followed during the interval by numerical processes." This must be a reference to one of the very important calculations in the history of science, namely the prediction made by Clairaut, Lalande, and Lepaute in 1748 that the return of Halley's comet of 1682 would be delayed. Lalande wrote, "During six months we calculated from morning to night, sometimes even at meals; the consequence of which was, that I contracted an illness which changed my constitution for the rest of my life. The assistance rendered by Madame Lepaute was such that without her we should never have dared to undertake this enormous labour; in which it was necessary to calculate the distance of each of the two planets, Jupiter and Saturn, from the comet, separately for every successive degree, for 150 years" [4]. The differential equations they solved [5] were not for the orbit itself but rather for the perturbations due to the

* This work was supported by the Department of Energy under contract DOE DEFG02–87ER25026.

two large planets. However, logarithms were probably the only calculating aids they had. The result was a prediction that the comet would reach perihelion 13 April 1749, which was in error by only 31 days. Sagan and Druyan [6] state that this "powerfully supported . . . the Newtonian view that we live in a clockwork universe" and quote Laplace as saying that "the regularity which astronomy shows us in the movements of the comets doubtless exists also in all phenomena." The next return of Halley's, in 1835, was predicted with an error of only five days, and the prediction for 1910 was off by only 2.7 days [7]. This won a 1000-mark prize for P. H. Cowell and A. C. D. Crommelin, who took into account the influence of the seven planets from Venus outward to Neptune. Cowell is known for the formula

$$y_{n+1} - 2y_n + y_{n-1} = \frac{h^2}{12}(f_{n-1} + 10f_n + f_{n+1})$$

for the special second-order ODE $y'' = f(y, t)$ [8].

It is Leonhard Euler [9] in 1768, according to Goldstine, who "is basically responsible for the present-day methods" [10]. Euler's chapter on *De Integratione Aequationum Differentialium per Approximationem* not only gives a description of the "Euler" or "polygon" method for the general problem

$$\frac{dy}{dx} = V(x, y)$$

but in paragraph 660 gives a general description of the step-by-step Taylor series method. Several examples are given for the Taylor method, the first being $V(x, y) = x^n + cy$, but no numerical results are given. The Euler method was the basis of the first existence proof for ODEs given by Cauchy a century later.

The higher derivatives needed for the Taylor series method can become very complicated. G. W. Hill in 1878 gives a recursion that simplifies these calculations for the gravitational force potential [11]. He was interested in calculating the position of the moon, important in navigation for the determination of longitude, using two second-order ODEs. A sixth-order Taylor method was used to generate numerical tables and graphs, and Jacobi's integral was used as a check.

The so-called Adams-Bashforth and Adams-Moulton formulas were both derived [12] by John Couch Adams (1819–1892) in 1883 to assist an investigation by Bashforth of capillary action [10]. Earlier, Adams had shared in the discovery of Neptune by calculating its position based on the motion of Uranus. In the work with Bashforth, a fixed stepsize was used with its value sufficiently small so that fifth-order differences were negligible. The process for a scalar equation was to predict y, evaluate the first derivative f, and then perform a single Newton-Raphson correction without reevaluating f.

The implicit Adams formula was employed in a fairly sophisticated way in 1897 by Sir George H. Darwin [13], also of Cambridge, in an effort to calculate periodic orbits for a restricted three body problem. Jacobi's integral was used to reduce the problem to three coupled first-order ODEs with arclength as the independent variable. Darwin made no reference to the work of Adams, but derived the implicit Adams formula as a straightforward application of the calculus of finite differences. Variable stepsize is used with doubling and halving of the step length, based on the size of second- and third-order differences of derivative values. Darwin remarked that the ratio of the largest increment to the smallest was 32 because of sharp bends in some orbits. The integration was started using low-order formulas with small stepsizes. For most of the calculation, the fourth-order formula was used, but the order was lowered from four to three just after going through a "quasi-cusp." Little is said about prediction, but the corrector iteration is said to be repeated until convergence, which is "usually rapid." Darwin gave a detailed description of the computational process, including a "schedule for computation" that depended heavily on the use of five-figure tables of logarithms with some use of four-figure tables, and he gave pages and pages of numerical results. He also mentioned "the prodigious amount of work involved" and the early death of his first computer, as well as acknowledging the Royal Society for providing two-thirds of the expenses of these computations.

Forest Ray Moulton (1872–1952), a professor of astronomy at the University of Chicago, spent April to June 1918 "computing the trajectories of projectiles as a basis for the construction of range tables" for the U. S. Army. This experience resulted in the publication of his book *New Methods in Exterior Ballistics* [14] in 1926, which describes in great detail methods for computing ballistics tables, including anti-aircraft tables. The process was to use five-place tables to solve a simple nonlinear system that accounts for gravity and air resistance, and then to use four-place tables and larger stepsizes to solve complicated linearized equations for corrections that account for minor factors such as the rotation of the earth. The simple nonlinear equations are given by

$$\frac{d^2x}{dt^2} = -F\frac{dx}{dt}$$

$$\frac{d^2y}{dt^2} = -F\frac{dy}{dt} - g$$

where

$$F = \frac{G(v)e^{-ay}}{C}$$

$$v^2 = \left(\frac{dx}{dt}\right)^2 + \left(\frac{dy}{dt}\right)^2$$

and G is given by tables of empirical data. The fourth-order implicit Adams formula was used with the fourth-order explicit Adams as predictor. The stepsize was chosen on the basis of the difference between the predicted value of f_{n+1} and its corrected value. With no reference to previous use of these formulas, Moulton does a derivation for uniform stepsize. Step doubling and halving is performed as by Darwin; however, for starting his fourth-order scheme he used a block implicit method, an idea that has reappeared many times since. One chapter of the book is devoted to convergence theory. In 1930 he wrote *Differential Equations* [3] with little of additional interest. This book contains the idea of Adams' method based on the replacement of $f(x(t), t)$ by an interpolating polynomial, a discussion of the choice of initial stepsize, and a reference to Darwin [13].

William E. Milne in a 1926 paper [15,16] discusses several methods based on numerical integration, including the well known fourth-order implicit Milne-Simpson formula. A fourth-order explicit formula is proposed as a predictor, and an appropriate multiple of the predictor-corrector difference is taken as an estimate of the (local truncation) error—the *Milne device*. This technique has seen wide use for the Adams method, for which it can be rigorously justified; however, it is not valid for the Milne-Simpson method because of weak instability. Apart from the problem of error estimation, the poor stability of these methods becomes a problem when computations are performed on a large scale. Thus, increases in computing speed have led to greater concern and study of numerical stability and to the abandonment of methods like those of Milne.

Carl Runge (1856–1927), an applied mathematician, seems to have been the first to derive the popular type of method based on resubstitution. His 1895 paper [10,17] derives two popular second-order two-stage methods, one based on the midpoint rule and the other on the trapezoid rule. He also derived a third-order four-stage method of short-lived interest. Collatz [18] gives interesting biographical information and a photograph.

In 1900 Karl Heun [19] introduced a restricted class of what we know as Runge-Kutta methods and determined the coefficients for about a dozen formulas. His list includes the three formulas of Runge that we have just mentioned. He also manages to construct a fourth-order eight-stage formula, but the most interesting is his third-order three-stage formula:

$$k_1 = hf(y_n)$$
$$k_2 = hf(y_n + \tfrac{1}{3}k_1)$$
$$k_3 = hf(y_n + \tfrac{2}{3}k_2)$$

and

$$y_{n+1} = y_n + \tfrac{1}{4}k_1 + \tfrac{3}{4}k_3$$

Heun then goes on to discuss systems of equations, error analysis, and graphical methods for solving ODEs.

It was Wilhelm Kutta (1867–1944) in his 1901 paper [20] who introduced the general class of explicit Runge-Kutta methods as we know it today and wrote down the nonlinear equations for the parameters that must be solved in order to attain a given order of accuracy. He solves these equations for the one-parameter family of second-order two-stage methods, the two-parameter family of third-order three-stage methods, and the two-parameter family of fourth-order four-stage methods. As a special case he obtains the very famous "classical" Runge-Kutta formula based on Simpson's rule as well as a fourth-order four-stage formula based on the 3/8 rule, which he calls Kutta's method. The formula given in the previous paragraph he calls Heun's method. Also, he obtains a fifth-order six-stage formula.

Runge-Kutta-type methods were devised for general and special second-order ODEs by Nyström [16,21] in 1925.

To give some idea of the scale of the computations performed, we quote page 125 of Collatz concerning the Norwegian mathematician Carl Størmer:

> In order to confirm his theory of the aurora borealis, Størmer and his colleagues spent several years calculating numerous orbits of electrons in the earth's magnetic field. . . . The computed orbits were reproduced very closely by . . . experimental work. . . . [which showed that] 4500 working hours were needed for 120 orbits [18].

Størmer [22] is known for a family of explicit formulas for special second-order ODEs, the simplest of which is

$$y_{n+1} - 2y_n + y_{n-1} = h^2 f_n$$

Another large-scale computation was that of L. J. Comrie in 1929 [2]. Comrie used a punched card system to calculate future positions of the moon and in the process punched half a million cards.

Hand calculation was very important until the 1960s (and reemerged in the 1970s with the invention of the handheld calculator). The practical details of hand calculation are found in many numerical analysis books, such as those by Collatz [18] and Hartree [23].

In conclusion, we see that the use of numerical methods was, out of necessity, quite sophisticated at the time of the introduction of computers. Thus, we have that in 1947 Sir Richard Southwell is reported [24] to have said that "human beings get a feeling for their problems as they work with them; they develop intuitions which cannot be automated or communicated to a cold, heartless computer." And he was right, for 20 years at least. The use of automated computing machinery led to the use of simplistic numerical methods that continue to this day among many who do simulations. As Hartree explains in the first numerical analysis book to consider seriously the use of computers, "With an automatic machine it may be best to obtain the same results by a simple process involving a large number of steps to save the time that would be taken in planning, programming, and coding a less simple method using fewer numerical steps" [23].

2. Analog Computation in ODEs

When in 1822 Babbage invented the difference engine, it would appear that digital technology was in a better position to cope with the numerical solution of ODEs than analog computers. Indeed, although Babbage failed to implement his ideas in the available technology, a machine based on his ideas was completed by a Swedish printer, Scheutz, in 1853 [1]. The difference engine was capable of calculating successive values of a polynomial by constructing a difference table. It is surprising that such machines were not adapted to the solution of ODEs, since it was a short step from them to the digital differential analyzer. However, the planimeter (a device for measuring the area bounded by a simple curve) was in existence at that time. It was improved by various people, including Maxwell and Thompson. According to Goldstine, Thompson did not present his idea to the Royal Society for almost a decade because no one saw any use for it until his brother Lord Kelvin discussed the problem of a tide-calculating machine. Kelvin used the invention to construct a machine to compute Fourier coefficients by quadrature. He then went on to plan its application to the solution of the linear second-order ODE:

$$\frac{d}{dx}\left[\frac{1}{F(x)}\frac{dy}{dx}\right] + y = 0 \tag{1}$$

He considered the use of two of Thompson's mechanical integrators to compute successive iterates of

$$\frac{d}{dx}\left[\frac{1}{F(x)}\frac{dy_{m+1}}{dx}\right] + y_m = 0 \tag{2}$$

from

$$y_{m+1} = \int F(x)\left[c - \int y_m dx\right]dx$$

This requires the coupling of the output of the inner integrator to the input of the outer integrator. Unfortunately, the mechanical integrator of the time had no power gain, so that technology was insufficient to support the idea until Vannevar Bush [25] and his colleagues at MIT independently developed the idea half a century later.

It is interesting to speculate what might have been the developments had Babbage's difference engine been slightly more successful and available to Kelvin. Instead, Goldstine says about Kelvin's harmonic analyzer: "Here we see for the first time an example of a device which can speed up a human process by a very large factor, as Kelvin asserts. That is why Kelvin's tidal harmonic analyzer was important and Babbage's difference engine was not." Certainly, an analog integrator was far better suited to the harmonic analysis problem—a quadrature of a product of two functions, one of which was sinusoidal—than any simple adaptation of Babbage's difference engine could have been. Among other problems, the construction of a sinusoidal function is mechanically nearly trivial but digitally computationally intensive. The planimeter seemed to be popular in the first part of this century (e.g., [26]) in graphical methods for integrating a Picard iteration.

In his discussion of the integration of equation (1) using the iteration in (2), Kelvin wrote, "After thus altering, as it were, y_1 into y_2 by passing it through the machine, the y_2 into y_3 by a second passage through the machine, and so on, the thing will, as it were, become refined into a solution which will be more and more nearly rigorously correct the oftener we pass it through the machine. If y_{i+1} does not sensibly differ from y_i, then each is sensibly a solution." (Quoted from [1].) Such a device would still involve considerable human intervention, although Kelvin was "feeling satisfied, feeling I had done what I wished to do for many years." But at this point, he saw that the iteration could be avoided. "Compel agreement between the function fed into the double machine and that given out by it." He then showed, according to Hartree [27], how, in principle, this can be done by making a second interconnection between the two integrators so that the output of the second is used continuously as the integrand of the first. He also showed that this interconnected system of integrators evaluates a solution of the equation directly, so that the general differential equations of the second-order with variable coefficients may be solved by a machine in a single process. Thus, the analog computer for the solution of ODEs was designed, and it would appear that the ideas in the design were to have an initial impact on the organization of the digital computer.

In 1930 Bush built the first working differential analyzer, and by 1940 there were over half a dozen full-size differential analyzers in use [1]. In addition, there was the intriguing "Hartree Differential Analyzer" [28] built of (toy) Meccano parts at the University of Manchester, which, according to Hartree [1], gave an accuracy of 2 percent and was used for serious computation.* However, limited precision was a problem even for the best differential analyzers in applications such

---

* See also the essay by Buneman in this volume.

as astronomy. Moreover, until 1942 the "differential analyzer was programmed manually, with a wrench in one hand and a gear in the other" [29], the process often taking a day or two [1].

3. The First Digital Differential Analyzers and Computers

It was the numerical solution of differential equations [2] in his thesis work that in 1937 led Howard Aiken, a physics instructor at Harvard, to plan an automatic computing machine. The largely mechanical 50-foot long Mark I was demonstrated in 1943 and served from May 1944 to 1959. The solution of ODEs (by the Runge-Kutta method) was one of five suggested scientific applications. In the same period, Bell Telephone Laboratories built a series of computers using electromagnetic relays. Model III (1944–1958) was called the "Ballistic Computer" because it solved fire control problems. A copy of the Model V built in 1947 went to the Ballistic Research Labs at the Aberdeen Proving Grounds. Alt states that systems of ODEs "have so far furnished the main portion of problems for the machine. Both Picard's method and step-by-step methods have been tried, and the latter have so far been found more efficient. As an example, in a system of order five each step required about three minutes. . . . The machine can be directed to change the length of step. . . . [and] can handle systems beyond the capacity of differential analyzers and the ENIAC" [30]. The stepsize was adjusted according to the number of corrector iterations needed for convergence.

One of the early digital computers, the ENIAC (Electronic Numerical Integrator And Computer) was initially programmed using a technique similar to the plug-board wiring of the early card-calculating machines. Any of its 20 registers (or memory cells) could be used as an accumulator, much as each integrator in a differential analyzer is used to "accumulate" an integral. Just as the integrators in an analog computer operate in parallel, so did the arithmetic on each of the accumulators. In fact, it appears that the ENIAC was designed with the intention of solving ordinary differential equations by imitating the techniques used on analog computers, because the construction of the ENIAC was preceded by a "Report on an Electronic Diff.* Analyzer (2 April 1943)" by Mauchly, Eckert, and Brainerd. The "*" means either "-erential" or "-erence." The historical importance [29] of the ENIAC was its electronic hardware, which made it 10 times faster than a differential analyzer and 100 times faster than a human computer. The very first digital electronic computer of Atanasoff for solving linear systems of equations was also modeled after the differential analyzer [29].

The ENIAC was funded for the purpose of preparing firing and bombing tables, in particular for the aiming of anti-aircraft guns [2,29].

According to Goldstine [10], the first method used to solve differential equations on the ENIAC was the Heun method. This was a second-order three-stage method, not the better-known method described in Section 1. The program was written by Burks [29] to integrate a trajectory.

After the ENIAC had been in operation and it had been observed that it took considerable time to prepare a "program" and incorporate it in wiring, the machine was modified so that a sequence of instructions could be read as sequence of two-digit numbers that are set up manually on a function table. In order to keep the logic simple, one register was dedicated for use as an accumulator and the rest were relegated for use as memory registers. Hartree commented that "it seems likely that it will increase the scope and value of the ENIAC as a general purpose machine, but that the older form of control may be better for extensive work on comparatively simple problems such as the step-by-step integration of ordinary differential equations for which the ENIAC was originally designed" [27]. Was the new approach considered easier due to the tedium of wiring the program, or was it due to the difficulty of programming for parallel operations? It may have been that the problems of parallelism in digital computation were first encountered nearly 40 years ago.

Special purpose digital machines (DDAs) for the integration of ODEs continued to be built. However, unlike ENIAC, these DDAs used short wordlength fixed-point binary arithmetic. The first of these, MADDIDA [31] was built in 1950. It used the Euler method with a stepsize so small that only the last bit or two changed with each step, and it employed a "residue register" to minimize the accumulation of rounding errors. More specifically, for each operation of an integration step, a running sum of the rounding errors was maintained and each time that operation was performed, the result was rounded in such a way that the running sum was minimized. (It should be appreciated that the effects of the rounding errors are not simply additive and so this technique does not completely eliminate the accumulation of rounding errors.) However, because of their slowness, DDAs never became as widely used as analog differential analyzers, let alone general purpose digital computers. Apparently [32], they have seen some use in special purpose applications such as real-time control systems (and graphics); Adams and Heun integration have both been used in some DDAs.

4. Early ODE Programs: The Effect of Small Memories

The early stored-program computers had extremely small memories. The EDSAC had 512 words of 17 bits, and the first ILLIAC had 1024 words of 40 bits. Because of this, space for both code and intermediate results was at a premium, so the codes had to be simple, and methods that required little temporary storage were utilized. The Runge-Kutta-Gill (RKG) method was in that class. It is a particular case of a fourth-order Runge-Kutta method in which Stanley Gill chose the coefficients so that it was not necessary to store all of the intermediate derivatives at each step. In a general explicit Runge-Kutta implementation, we require $(q + 1) \times s$ storage cells, where s is the number of components in the system, and q is the number of function evaluations. For the conventional fourth-order RK method, this would be $5s$. Gill [33] pointed out that the number is only $4s$ because of linear dependencies and that it can be reduced to $3s$ by enforcing a further dependency. The method required only minor additional arithmetic, and, as an added bonus, could be performed in partial double precision. The code was designed for fixed-point machines and carried scaled quantities to improve precision.

The RKG method was implemented on the EDSAC [34] and later implemented by Wheeler as code #27 for the ILLIAC I, and was apparently its first ODE solver. ILLIAC was first operational on Labor Day, 1952. The extant documentation indicates that this code was "machine tested," but is dated June 1952 so may have been tested on the ORD-VAC or on the ILLIAC prior to its full operation. It was revised for the ILLIAC in October 1953 as code #114, apparently because of a change in the operating system. Then, in January 1954, it was renumbered as code F1 in the "Reorganization of the ILLIAC Library," a library naming system [35] whose initial letter indicated the general class of code. At the time, there were 81 programs extant in the library, although the numbering had reached 128. Only 23 of these subroutines were concerned with the numerical solution of problems, and an additional 17 with the evaluation of elementary functions. At that time, the library contained three subroutines for numerical solution of ODEs. Program F2 was a Milne method for initial value problems written by Gene Golub and was placed in the library in October 1953. It used a feature of the operating system called an *interlude*. Because of the lack of memory, sections of code could be executed during load time (the "interlude") so they did not occupy memory space during run time. The Milne code computed the required starting values prior to t_0 from user-supplied values of the first and second derivatives at t_0. This was done in the interlude. Routine FA1 was a boundary value problem solver known as a "floating-point auxiliary." It was called that because floating point was itself handled by a subroutine that interpreted a pseudocode, so a "subroutine" written in the interpretive language was then called an auxiliary subroutine. Although the interpreter also provided indexing (which was not available in the 1950-designed ILLIAC), only eight of the 40 numerical programs were floating-point auxiliaries. The remainder used the 40-bit fixed-point arithmetic.

The number of instructions was kept to a minimum in the early programs. The independent variable, t, was treated as an additional dependent variable with the defining equation $dt/dt = 1$. This added one memory location for the derivative value, but no code to compute it since it could be specified as a constant at load time. It also added the space for the k_i values. Although the technique added several slow multiplications to each step, this was a saving over the space that would have been needed for the instructions to treat t separately, since four sets of LOAD, ADD, and STORE would have been needed for the general four-stage RK method. On machines of that time, multiplication was about a tenth as fast as addition (for the ILLIAC I, fixed-point addition was 72 microseconds and fixed-point multiplication averaged about 700 microseconds), so this represented a considerable space-time trade-off.

5. Adaptive Programs

The development of adaptive codes for ODEs had to await an increase in memory capacity, either primary or secondary. We have attempted to determine where the first adaptive codes were developed, but without success. Here we mention a few of the developments of which we are aware.

There were undoubtedly many variable-stepsize one-step methods written. A method was described by Merson in a 1957 report [36] and came to be known as the Runge-Kutta-Merson method. At the University of Illinois in 1958, Nordsieck wrote the variable-stepsize routine F6 that used the "classical" fourth-order formula Runge-Kutta method on the point set (0, 0.5, 0.5, 1.0) and the error estimator

$$E = y_{n+1} - y_n - hk_3$$

which was held to be no larger than $2^{-\lceil 3e/4 \rceil}$ where e was the "number of bits of accuracy" required. (This was a fixed-point code.) As in many codes of the time, the stepsize was restricted to powers of 2 "to reduce roundoff error." It also saved time in the multiplication by h in machines of the time, since multiplication by a multiplier with many zero bits was faster due to the reduced numbers of adds in the add-and-shift implementation.

Two years prior to that, D. E. Muller (of "Muller's method" for rootfinding) had coded routine F5, which used the RKG method to integrate until a condition was satisfied. The condition was a zero value of a specified dependent variable.

One of the early variable-stepsize multistep methods was the Nordsieck modification of the Adams method, in which Nordsieck stored scaled derivatives. Fred Krogh has pointed out to us that the idea was essentially developed much earlier in a paper by Thomas [37] presented at a September 1950 ACM meeting in which he discussed the implementation of variable-stepsize Adams methods using divided differences. He proposed a method for computing the derivatives of a function from the divided difference table. From these derivatives, Thomas suggested using Taylor's series to advance the solution over one time step, chosen so that the error estimate was constant. This was proposed in the context of an explicit method such as Adams-Bashforth, and the divided differences were to be calculated for the derivative, f. After y_{n+1} had been calculated by Taylor's series, a value of f_{n+1} could be evaluated and the divided difference table could be extended one more line. He then went on to point out that it was not necessary to store differences, because the "divided derivatives" could be computed directly. This is essentially the Nordsieck implementation of the Adams method, although it appeared that Nordsieck [38,39] was unaware of Thomas' work when he devised the method that appeared in Illinois code F7 in August 1961. One other interesting remark in Thomas's 1952 paper states that the method "is convenient for differential equations in which the derivative is given implicitly." However, although he was at the Watson Scientific Computing Lab, Columbia University, there is no indication that Thomas was thinking of a computer implementation of his method, and it seems that his method was never actually used.

Thomas proposed using a variable-stepsize but fixed-order method: Adams methods, implemented in hand calculations with a fixed stepsize and a difference table, naturally lent themselves to variable order because it was relatively simple to add or drop differences according to their size. This was the basis of what is probably the first variable-order code development for multistep methods by Krogh. It was written in late 1966 and 1967 and was presented at the 1968 IFIP meeting [40] in a session that may have been the first numerical analysis meeting on stiff equations. Krogh's code used modified divided differences, an implementation that is generally viewed as the best for a general multistep code today. It handled higher-order ODEs, provided output at arbitrary points, and used a corrector formula of one order higher than the predictor formula in order to obtain a longer interval of absolute stability.

6. Stiff ODEs

The earliest paper on stiff differential equations, by Curtis and Hirschfelder [41], described the use of the BDF (backward differentiation formula) methods. The authors were interested in finding smooth solutions to problems whose Jacobian had very large eigenvalues, which is not quite what we mean by a stiff problem today. Soon after, Mitchell and Craggs [42] found that these BDFs were not (zero-)stable for orders greater than six. The next significant development was the seminal paper of Dahlquist [43], which defined A-stability and showed that the order of an A-stable multistep method cannot exceed two. This result was later extended to a larger class of methods in the Daniel-Moore conjecture [44], which essentially says that the order of an A-stable method cannot exceed twice its "degree of implicitness" (that is, the number of derivatives involved implicitly in each step). The result was shown for implicit Runge-Kutta methods by Ehle [45]. Although it is outside of the time period we are discussing, mention should be made of the beautiful results of Hairer, Norsett, and Wanner [46] on order stars that proved this conjecture for all cases.

Because of the order limitation implied by A-stability, people looked for less restrictive stability requirements that would permit higher-order, useful methods. $A(\alpha)$ stability was defined by Widlund [47] to mean that the stability region included a wedge of half-angle α symmetric about the real axis in the left-half plane. A-stability corresponded to $\alpha = \pi/2$, but Widlund showed that for any smaller α it was possible to find methods of up to fourth-order. (This was later extended to arbitrary order [48,49].) As α approaches $\pi/2$, the coefficients of such methods become large, as the error coefficient must approach infinity if the order exceeds two. A different approach was taken by Gear [50,51], who defined "stiff stability" to mean that the method was stable in a half-plane to the left of a negative real value and in a finite region from there up to the origin. Most important about both approaches was the fact that non–A-stable methods were explored and were realized to be the most effective for general stiff problems.

Until the late 1960s, stiff equations were often being solved on analog computers. Electrical engineers had problems of sufficient size that they could only be handled on digital computers, so there were a number of papers on methods for stiff equations beginning to appear in the literature [52]. Many problems arising in chemistry, however, were still sufficiently small that analog computers were adequate. It was due to the use of analog computers in the then Applied Mathematics Division of Argonne National Laboratory that the first author became involved in stiff ODEs. Gear was a summer visitor in 1965 and 1966 (a program that encouraged a lot of interactions between numerical analysts and computer scientists) and in 1965 had extended the Nordsieck ideas to higher-order methods. In 1966, a person using the analog computer at Argonne to solve a set of seven equations describing a chemical kinetics problem made the statement, "You people will never be able to handle these type of problems with your digital computers." This was enough of a challenge to encourage Gear to search for methods. The concept of stiff stability was more of an afterthought: At the time it was realized that the problem required a method that was stable in most of the left half-plane and especially around the origin. Multistep methods were examined, and since the stability far from the origin was determined by the polynomial $\sigma(\xi) = \overset{-}{} \beta_i \xi^{k-i}$, the "most stable" such polynomial, ξ^k, was investigated. Only later was it realized that these were just the BDF methods used by Curtis and Hirschfelder (but dismissed by Henrici [53] for the very valid reason that they had large error coefficients and were not even zero-stable for orders exceeding six). At the same time, Krogh was studying the problem and also settled on the BDF methods independently in a report that was unfortunately never published because Krogh received a copy of Gear's report [50] before completing his. A version of his report with subsequent revisions was printed later as a TRW internal report [54], but never appeared in the open literature.

To return to Argonne in the summer of 1966: Gear wrote a preliminary version of a stiff integrator using fixed-order BDF methods, but with stepsize control, using a Nordsieck vector implementation. The chemistry problem was run successfully, although the proponent of the analog computer was not prepared to accept the answers from a digital calculation "until they match the results obtained from the analog computer." They did, when free of programming errors, and to the chemists' delight they produced extremely good "mass balance" results, the mass balance being a linear invariant of the system representing the number of each atom present in the reaction. It was realized that linear invariants were preserved within roundoff error by the class of methods being considered (see [55] for a discussion) so that preservation of mass balance was meaningless. Nonetheless, for a while there was considerable debate whether the mass balance equations should be used to eliminate variables or to check on the computation. At one point during the Argonne visit, a program error caused a change of several percent in the answers; the mass balance remained good to the ten digits printed, however, and it was somewhat difficult to convince the user that the answers were wrong.

After the Argonne visit, Gear embedded the method in a package, ODESSY: Ordinary Differential Equation Solver System, written with three graduate students but never published. It accepted a set of ODEs in symbolic form, translated them to a machine language subroutine, differentiated them to obtain a machine language subroutine for the Jacobian needed in a stiff integration method, and then proceeded to integrate them automatically. Stiff methods were used in all cases because no one had yet thought of changing methods in midstream, and stiff methods would work on nonstiff equations at a modest penalty. The order had to be varied because it did not seem reasonable to expect the user to choose the order. The package was of little value because it was too restrictive—it was impossible to append programs to compute the coefficients of the system or use tabular data, for example. For this reason, users at Kirtland AFB were unable to make effective use of the program, and Gear removed the integrator from the package and made it into a subroutine for their use. Work would have stopped there (and have been of relatively limited value) had it not been for the suggestion of George Forsythe in 1969 when Gear was on sabbatical leave at Stanford. Gear was preparing the draft manuscript for a book in a Prentice Hall series edited by Forsythe [56]. Forsythe suggested that the book would be much more valuable if it included working programs, so Gear spent part of that year rewriting the earlier code for publication in *Comm. ACM* [57] and in the book. By today's standards, DIFSUB was a poorly written code since it went to great lengths for speed. At the time, subroutine calls were expensive (particularly on the IBM 360 series on which it was first implemented), and so no internal subroutines were used: The equivalent was achieved with assigned GO TOs. Furthermore, many computer systems were still using early FORTRAN II compilers, so the code was written in a subset of Fortran. The impact of this on the internal allocation of working space led to convoluted code.

Analog computers remained an important tool for chemical kinetic problems for some time. Around 1970 there was a meeting in Boston between chemists and numerical analysts to discuss the use of digital methods in chemical kinetics. There was a proposal to build a large analog computer with a price tag of several million dollars to solve some high-altitude kinetic problems. However, digital methods were accepted in time to avoid this effort.

References

[1] H. H. Goldstine, *The Computer from Pascal to von Neumann* (Princeton University Press, 1972).

[2] B. Randell (ed.), *The Origins of Digital Computers*, third ed. (Berlin: Springer-Verlag, 1982).

[3] F. R. Moulton, *Differential Equations* (New York: Macmillan, 1930).

[4] P. Moore and J. Mason, *The Return of Halley's Comet* (New York: W. W. Norton, 1984).

[5] F. R. Moulton, *An Introduction to Celestial Mechanics*, second ed. (New York: Macmillan, 1914).

[6] C. Sagan and A. Druyan, *Comet* (New York: Random House, 1985).

[7] R. S. Richardson, *Getting Acquainted with Comets* (New York: McGraw-Hill, 1967).

[8] P. H. Cowell and A. C. D. Crommelin, "Investigation of the Motion of Halley's Comet from 1759–1910," *Greenwich Observations 1909* (Bellevue, England: Neill, 1910).

[9] F. Engel and L. Schlesinger, *Leonhardi Euleri Opera Omnia*, Ser. 1, Vol. XI (Leipzig: B. G. Teubner, 1913).

[10] H. H. Goldstine, *A History of Numerical Analysis from the 16th Through the 19th Century* (New York: Springer-Verlag, 1977).

[11] G. W. Hill, "Researches in the Lunar Theory, Chapter II," *Amer. J. of Mathematics* I (1878): 245–60.

[12] F. Bashforth and J. C. Adams, *An Attempt to Test the Theories of Capillary Action* (Cambridge University Press, 1883).

[13] G. H. Darwin, "Periodic Orbits," *Acta Math.* 21 (1897): 99–242.

[14] F. R. Moulton, *New Methods in Exterior Ballistics* (University of Chicago Press, 1926).

[15] W. E. Milne, "Numerical Integration of Ordinary Differential Equations," *Amer. Math. Monthly* 33 (1926): 455–60.

[16] W. E. Milne, "Step-by-Step Methods of Integration," in *Numerical Integration of Differential Equations*, W. E. Milne, A. A. Bennett, and H. Bateman (eds.) (New York: Dover, 1956), 71–87.

[17] C. D. T. Runge, "Über die numerische Auflösung von Differentialgleichungen," *Math. An.* 46 (1895): 167–78.

[18] L. Collatz, *The Numerical Treatment of Differential Equations*, third ed. (Berlin: Springer-Verlag, 1960).

[19] K. Heun, "Neue Methode zur approximativen Integration der Differentialgleichungen einer unabhängigen Veränderlichen," *Zeit. Math. Phys.* 45 (1900): 23–38.

[20] M. W. Kutta, "Beitrag zur näherungsweisen Integration oder Differentialgleichungen," *Z. Math. Phys.* 46 (1901): 435–53.

[21] E. J. Nyström, "Über die numerische Integration von Differentialgleichungen," *Acta Soc. Sci. Fen.* 50 (1925): 1–55.

[22] C. Størmer, "Sur les trajectoires des corpuscules électrisés," in *Arch. Sci.* 24 (1907): 5–18, 113–58, 221–47.

[23] D. R. Hartree, *Numerical Analysis* (Oxford University Press, 1952).

[24] G. Birkhoff, "Computing Developments 1935–1955, as Seen from Cambridge, U.S.A.," in *A History of Computing in the Twentieth Century*, J. Howlett, N. Metropolis, and Gian-Carlo Rota (eds.) (New York: Academic Press, 1980), 21–30.

[25] V. Bush, "The Differential Analyzer: A New Machine for Solving Equations," *J. Franklin Inst.* 212 (1931) 447–88.

[26] H. Levy and E. A. Baggott, *Numerical Solution of Differential Equations* (New York: Dover, 1950).

[27] D. R. Hartree, *Calculating Instruments and Machines* (University of Illinois Press, Urbana, 1949).

[28] G. R. Stibitz and D. R. Hartree, "Calculating Instruments and Machines," *MTAC* 4 (1950): 114.

[29] A. W. Burks, "From ENIAC to the Stored-Program Computer: Two Revolutions in Computers," in *A History of Computing in the Twentieth Century*, J. Howlett, N. Metropolis, and Gian-Carlo Rota (eds.) (New York: Academic Press, 1980), 311–44.

[30] F. L. Alt, "A Bell Telephone Laboratories' Computing Machine—II," *MTAC* 3 (1948): 69–84.

[31] T. C. Bartee, I. L. Lebow, and I. S. Reed, *Theory and Design of Digital Machines* (New York: McGraw-Hill, 1962).

[32] R. B. McGhee and R. N. Nilsen, "The Extended Resolution Digital Differential Analyzer: A New Computing Structure for Solving Differential Equations," *IEEE Trans.* C–19 (1970): 1–9.

[33] S. Gill, "A Process for the Step-by-Step Integration of Differential Equations in an Automatic Digital Computing Machine," Proc. *Camb. Philos. Soc.* 47 (1950): 96–108.

[34] M. V. Wilkes, D. J. Wheeler, and S. Gill, *The Preparation of Programs for an Electronic Digital Computer* (Cambridge, MA: Addison-Wesley, 1951).

[35] S. Gill, "Reorganization of the Illiac library," University of Illinois Digital Computer Laboratory Internal Report 55, Urbana, IL (1954).

[36] R. H. Merson, "An Operational Method for the Study of Integration Processes," in *Proceedings of a Symposium on Data Processing* (Salisbury, South Australia: Weapons Research Establishment, 1957).

[37] L. H. Thomas, "The Integration of Ordinary Differential Systems," Ohio State University Engineering Experiment Station News 24 (1952): 8–9, 31–32.

[38] A. Nordsieck, "On Numerical Integration of Ordinary Differential Equations," University of Illinois Coordinated Science Laboratory Rep ·t R–127, Urbana, IL (1961).

[39] A. Nordsieck, "On Numerical Integration of Ordinary Differential Equations," *Math. Comp.* 16 (1962): 22–49.

[40] F. T. Krogh, "A Variable Order Multistep Method for the Numerical Solution of Ordinary Differential Equations," in *Inform. Process. Lett.* 68, A. J. H. Morrell (ed.) (Amsterdam: North Holland, 1969): 194–99.

[41] C. F. Curtiss and J. O. Hirschfelder, "Integration of Stiff Equations," Proc. *U. S. Nat. Acad. Sci.* 38 (1952): 235–43.

[42] A. R. Mitchell and J. W. Craggs, "Stability of Difference Relations in the Solution of Ordinary Differential Equations," *Math. Comp.* 7 (1953): 127–29.

[43] G. Dahlquist, "A Special Stability Problem for Linear Multistep Methods," *BIT* 3 (1963): 27–43.

[44] J. W. Daniel and R. E. Moore, *Computation and Theory in Ordinary Differential Equations* (New York: WH Freeman and Co., 1970).

[45] B. L. Ehle, "High Order A-Stable Methods for the Numerical Solution of Systems of Differential Equations," *BIT* 8 (1968): 276–78.

[46] G. Wanner, E. Hairer, and T. P. Norsett, "Order Stars and Stability Theorems," *BIT* 18 (1978): 503–17.

[47] O. Widlund, "A Note on Unconditionally Stable Linear Multistep Methods," *BIT* 7 (1967): 65–70.

[48] R. D. Grigorieff and J. Schroll, "Über A(α)-stabile Verfahren hoher Konsistenz-ordnung," *Computing* 20 (1978): 343–50.

[49] A. K. Kong, "A Search for Better Linear Multistep Methods for Stiff Problems," Report R–77–899, Department of Computer Science, University of Illinois at Urbana-Champaign (1977).

[50] C. W. Gear, "The Numerical Integration of Stiff Differential Equations," University of Illinois Department of Computer Science Report 221, Urbana, IL (1967).

[51] C. W. Gear, "The Automatic Integration of Stiff Ordinary Differential Equations," in *Inform. Process. Lett.* 68, A. J. H. Morrell (ed.) (Amsterdam: North Holland, 1969), 187–93.

[52] W. Liniger, "Optimization of a Numerical Method for Stiff Systems of Ordinary Differential Equations," IBM Research Report #RC–2198, Yorktown, NY (1968).

[53] P. Henrici, *Discrete Variable Methods in Ordinary Differential Equations* (New York: Wiley, 1962).

[54] F. T. Krogh, "The Numerical Integration of Stiff Differential Equations," TRW Report 99900–6573–R000, Redondo Beach, CA (1968).

[55] C. W. Gear, "Maintaining Solution Invariants in the Numerical Solution of ODEs," *SIAM J. Sci. Statist Comput.* 7 (1986): 734–43.

[56] C. W. Gear, *Numerical Initial Value Problems in Ordinary Differential Equations* (Englewood Cliffs, NJ: Prentice-Hall, 1971).

[57] C. W. Gear, "Algorithm 407—DIFSUB for Solution of Ordinary Differential Equations," *Comm. ACM* 14 (1971): 185–90.

A Personal Retrospection of Reservoir Simulation

Donald W. Peaceman

I discuss here some early history of reservoir simulation, from a personal point of view. I will give some history, some philosophy, and some numerical analysis. I will try to stress the interrelationship of the type of computing equipment that we had available at any given time, the kinds of calculations we were able to make, and the kinds of problems we were able to solve. So, if you will indulge me, we will take a look at what computing and numerical analysis were like 20 to 35 years ago, in the not-so-good old days.

I started in 1951 with Humble Oil and Refining Company, which at that time was a subsidiary of Standard Oil of New Jersey. Standard Oil of New Jersey became Exxon, and the Research Division of Humble Oil evolved into the present day Exxon Production Research Company (EPR).

When I came to work in 1951, we did not have any real computers available to us. Yet there was some reservoir modeling going on. I found some old pictures that illustrate how physical models were used.

Figure 1 shows the earliest one that I found. It was made in 1933, and it shows a sand-packed model that was used to study water coning. On top is an oil layer, with a water layer underneath it. You can see that wells were drilled just into the upper oil layer. The production of oil causes the pressure around the well to decrease, and that causes the water to cone up and be produced with the oil. Though oil fields have been produced since 1860, it was not until the 1930s that people in the oil industry started looking at reservoir mechanics in any kind of a scientific way. This was therefore one of the first attempts to understand why water starts to be produced with oil and why the produced water-oil ratio increases with time.

Sand-packed models were still in use some 25 years later—before computers took over. They became more sophisticated; for example, wedge shapes were used to take into account the radial geometry around a well.

The analogy between electric current flow and Darcy flow through sand had been recognized for quite a while, and electrolytic models were used in the late thirties and the forties to solve Laplace's equation for various geometries. The photograph on page 54 shows an example of how elaborate an electrolytic model could get. This was a model

106

FIGURE 1.
Early study of water
coning (ca. 1933).

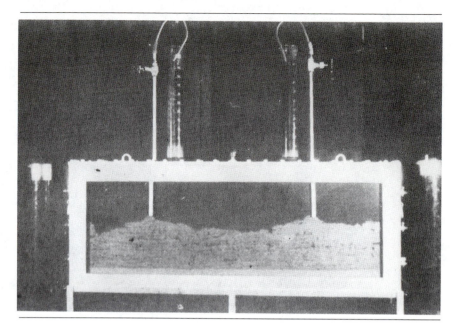

of the East Texas Field, which is still one of the largest fields in the United States. The model was made of plastic and covered with an electrolyte solution. The plastic was contoured to represent the shape and permeability distribution in the field, with the depth of the solution above the plastic being proportional to the thickness times permeability that was actually measured in the field. The object was to measure the potential distribution in the field in order to predict the water influx from the aquifer surrounding the field.

But electrolytic models were steady-state models. To get a better representation of unsteady-state flow, the reservoir analyzer shown in Figure 2 was devised, involving a scaled electrical network of resistors and capacitors. Voltages represented pressure, current flow represented fluid flow, resistors corresponded to permeability times thickness, and the capacitors corresponded to porosity times thickness times compressibility. With this representation, unsteady-state compressible flow could be taken into account. The electrical network corresponded, of course, to a finite-difference equation solved continuously in time.

In addition to these physical analog models, some mathematical methods were available in 1951. In the thirties and forties, three authors made the most significant contributions to applying the methods of mathematical physics to reservoir engineering. Muskat, of Gulf, wrote a book in 1937 that summarized his work, and that book is

FIGURE 2.
Electrical network
reservoir analyzer.

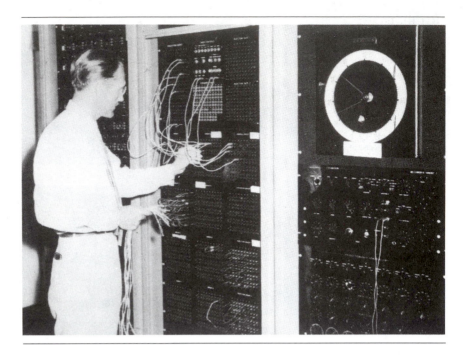

still very useful [1]. Hurst at Humble [2,3], and later Hurst and van Everdingen at Shell [4] also made significant contributions. Their methods were based primarily on infinite series solutions to Laplace's equation and the heat conduction equation. Although these methods were elegant, they suffered from serious limitations in their application to real reservoir problems—they assumed uniform properties and ideal geometries and could only be used on linear differential equations. Also, these methods required the tedious evaluation of infinite series, which had to be computed by hand.

So that was the state of reservoir modeling when I came to work at Humble in 1951. We had nothing that you could call a computer. We did have access to some accounting machines that the accounting department would let us use, but only at night. Henry Rachford had come to work a year before me and was already playing with an accounting machine called the IBM 604. He, along with the managers of the Production Research Division of Humble, had the vision to see that digital computation was going to be the way to do reservoir modeling and that by using finite-difference methods to solve partial differential equations, we could overcome the limitations of the analytical methods. We wanted to be able to include nonuniform properties, arbitrary geometry, and nonlinearities in the differential equations.

But that vision was still faint. The first partial differential equation that we tried to solve was one-dimensional gas flow, and the first limitation that we were trying to overcome was that of nonlinearity. If one assumes a perfect gas, then the equation for linear one-dimensional gas flow is

$$\frac{\partial^2 p^2}{\partial x^2} = \frac{2\phi\mu}{K}\frac{\partial p}{\partial t} \tag{1}$$

It looks a lot like the linear one-dimensional heat conduction equation, except that the second derivative term has p^2 in it instead of p, making that equation nonlinear. Because of that, there is no known analytical solution. The initial condition is uniform pressure; at one end is a fixed production rate q giving the nonlinear boundary condition

$$q = \frac{KA}{\mu RT}p\frac{\partial p}{\partial x} \qquad x = 0 \tag{2}$$

At the other end, the system is closed, so we have a no-flow boundary condition, with a zero derivative.

Of more practical interest was the radial problem, corresponding to the depletion of a circular gas reservoir with a well at the center:

$$\frac{1}{r}\frac{\partial}{\partial r}\left(r\frac{\partial p^2}{\partial r}\right) = \frac{2\phi\mu}{K}\frac{\partial p}{\partial t} \tag{3}$$

The initial and boundary conditions are similar.

When I came to work, Henry Rachford and John Rice were already at work on this problem, trying to use the accounting machine, the IBM 604. (See Figure 3.) Let me try to describe this gadget to you. It was called a multiplying punch—the only input/output that it had was a card reader and card punch. It could only handle fixed-point decimal numbers, with no alphabetic information. The way the accountants used it, say for a payroll application, would be to have some numeric data already punched on each card, such as an employee's identification number and salary. Each card would be read at the read station and would then travel to the punch station. On the way, the marvelous electronic multiply unit would calculate the withholding and social security taxes, subtract them, and then punch the taxes and take-home pay into the blank space on the card. After being punched, the card would then travel to the stacker. To see the results printed, an operator would have to carry the deck of cards to another machine to print the results.

The electronic multiply unit was really quite flexible, but programming it was done in a way that we would now consider quaint. There was a board with a lot of holes, and this board could be placed into a holder with terminals in the back. Programming was done by plug-

FIGURE 3.
IBM 604 multiplying
punch.

ging wires from one hole to another. Down one side of the board
was a series of holes called program steps. On the other side were
holes for various functions, such as reading from a card into electronic
registers, adding or multiplying the contents of two registers together,
and punching the contents of the registers onto the card. Remember
that in those days, all the electronics were done with vacuum tubes.

This device was certainly unsuitable for scientific computations,
yet it was all we had. John Rice and Henry Rachford programmed
it to solve the one-dimensional gas flow problem. They were already
familiar with the paper by O'Brien, Hyman, and Kaplan [5], published
in 1951, which discussed the finite-difference solution to the linear heat
conduction problem. That paper introduced us to the von Neumann
stability analysis as well as to the use of implicit equations. From the
stability analysis, they knew they could not use an explicit method
for the radial problem, so they attempted to solve it by this implicit
equation:

$$\frac{p_{i-1}^2 - 2p_i^2 + p_{i+1}^2}{\Delta x^2} = K\frac{p_i - p_i^{\text{old}}}{\Delta t} \tag{4}$$

We all were pretty naive in those days, so Rice and Rachford attempted to solve this equation sequentially from left to right using

$$p_{i+1}^2 = 2p_i^2 - p_{i-1}^2 + \frac{K\Delta x^2}{\Delta t}(p_i - p_i^{old}) \tag{5}$$

This required guessing the slope at the well and seeing if the slope came out to be zero at the closed end. If not, they would adjust the initial slope and try again (a shooting method). We found out the hard way that this sequence of calculations from one end to the other is unstable and must blow up. In retrospect, this is obvious from an error analysis. But as I said, we were pretty naive, so that was one of our first experiences with an unstable calculation.

The fix, of course, is to solve for all of the pressures at all of the nodes simultaneously. We saw how to do that when we came upon an unpublished note by L. H. Thomas of IBM. In that note, he outlined what we now know as the tridiagonal algorithm. I believe our paper on gas flow was one of the first to present this algorithm in the published literature.

In order to use this algorithm, the nonlinear difference equation (4) had to be linearized. We did that by factoring the second-difference term into the form

$$\frac{(p_{i-1}^k + p_i^k)(p_{i-1}^{k+1} - p_i^{k+1}) - (p_i^k + p_{i+1}^k)(p_i^{k+1} - p_{i+1}^{k+1})}{\Delta x^2} = K\frac{p_i^{k+1} - p_i^{old}}{\Delta t} \tag{6}$$

and iterating on each time step. Although the iteration converged only linearly, it did converge very rapidly—usually five iterations were sufficient. At that time, we were not aware of the Newton-Raphson method, which would have given quadratic convergence.

By the time we had this new approach worked out, we were onto our next machine. It was our own machine now, and not one that we had to borrow. This was the IBM CPC, or Card-Programmed Calculator, shown in Figures 4 and 5. That is Henry Rachford in Figure 4. IBM did not really develop the CPC. Several computing groups at various aircraft companies modified and hooked together some existing IBM accounting machines, which IBM adopted and marketed as the CPC. It was a real kludge. The 418 (in the foreground of Figure 4) was an electromechanical accounting machine that could read cards, perform simple additions and subtractions, and print results at 150 lines per minute. It had the capacity to store eight 10-digit numbers. The box at the rear was the card punch. The 605 (at the right rear) was an electronic calculator, an extension of the 604 that I discussed before. All of these required the wiring of large boards. In addition, there were three boxes (not shown in Figure 4) we called ice boxes, which could each hold 16 ten-digit numbers in electromechanical counter wheels, like the odometer on a car. We could open the top

FIGURE 4.
IBM card-
programmed
calculator (CPC).

FIGURE 5.
Components of
IBM CPC.

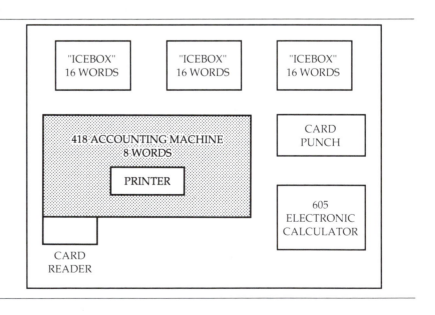

and actually read out the numbers while debugging. All of this was decimal. It was designed to be fixed-point, but Henry and I wired the machines to do floating-decimal arithmetic (two floating-point operations per card), so that we achieved the magnificent rate of five floating-point operations per second. We could store a total of 56 numbers. This was not a stored-program machine—instead the program had to be punched onto cards—so, in effect, we had an unlimited amount of storage available for programs, but only 56 words available for temporary data.

This, then, was the device on which we solved the gas flow problem for both the linear and radial cases [6]. Iteration was carried out by reading the same deck of program cards over and over, and the iteration was monitored by looking at the printed output. When the iteration converged, we switched to a new deck to start a new time step.

Although we were successful in solving the one-dimensional non-linear problem, we were aware that further progress toward solving realistic field problems would require going to higher dimensions—at least to two dimensions. At the very least, we knew that we needed to be able to solve the finite-difference analogs of Laplace's equation and the heat conduction equation (or better yet, the variable-coefficient versions of those equations) in an arbitrary geometry. To do this, we had to be able to solve a large system of simultaneous linear equations. Direct solution of these equations by Gaussian elimination was out of the question on the machines that were then available.

We had access in those days to several eminent consultants. One of them was John von Neumann, and he visited us a couple of times. He was very interested in the work we were doing, but when we asked him how to go about solving two-dimensional problems of this sort, he had no more to offer than the so-called extrapolated Liebman method, now known as successive overrelaxation, or SOR. We already knew about that method.

A breakthrough came, not while we were thinking about solving a problem in x-y coordinates, but while we were working on a flow problem in cylindrical coordinates:

$$\frac{1}{r}\frac{\partial}{\partial r}\left(r\frac{\partial p}{\partial r}\right) + \frac{\partial^2 p}{\partial y^2} = \frac{\partial p}{\partial t} \tag{7}$$

If we let $x = \ln r$, then the differential equation takes the somewhat simpler form

$$e^{-2x}\frac{\partial^2 p}{\partial x^2} + \frac{\partial^2 p}{\partial y^2} = \frac{\partial p}{\partial t} \tag{8}$$

Solving this equation implicitly would have had the same difficulty as solving the heat conduction equation implicitly. But the inherent dif-

Problems

ference between the radial and vertical directions suggested another approach. Suppose we make the difference equation implicit in just one direction, say the radial direction, and explicit in the other, vertical, direction. The half-implicit, half-explicit difference analog would then be

$$e^{-2x_i} \frac{p_{i-1,j}^{n+1} - 2p_{i,j}^{n+1} + p_{i+1,j}^{n+1}}{\Delta x^2} + \frac{p_{i,j-1}^{n} - 2p_{i,j}^{n} + p_{i,j+1}^{n}}{\Delta y^2} = \frac{p_{i,j}^{n+1} - p_{i,j}^{n}}{\Delta t} \qquad (9)$$

The advantage, of course, is that on each line we have just a tridiagonal system of equations, which is easy to solve. The von Neumann stability analysis is simple to do—we substitute this Fourier representation

$$p_{i,j}^n = \gamma_n e^{i\alpha x_i} e^{i\beta y_j} \qquad (10)$$

into the difference equation and examine the growth of γ. The amplification factor for γ is given by the ratio

$$\frac{\gamma^{n+1}}{\gamma^n} = \frac{1 - 4(\Delta t/\Delta y^2) \sin^2(\beta \Delta y/2)}{1 + e^{-2x_i}(\Delta t/\Delta x^2) \sin^2(\alpha \Delta x/2)} \qquad (11)$$

For the difference equation to be stable, the magnitude of this ratio has to be less than one for all α and β. Unless Δt is very small, that will not be true, so we have here a difference equation that is not much better than a fully explicit one.

Suppose we do the opposite by making the equation explicit in the radial direction and implicit in the vertical direction.

$$e^{-2x_i} \frac{p_{i-1,j}^{n} - 2p_{i,j}^{n} + p_{i+1,j}^{n}}{\Delta x^2} + \frac{p_{i,j-1}^{n+1} - 2p_{i,j}^{n} + p_{i,j+1}^{n+1}}{\Delta y^2} = \frac{p_{i,j}^{n+1} - p_{i,j}^{n}}{\Delta t} \qquad (12)$$

In that case, we would get the following ratio for the amplification factor

$$\frac{\gamma^{n+1}}{\gamma^n} = \frac{1 - e^{-2x_i}(\Delta t/\Delta x^2) \sin^2(\alpha \Delta x/2)}{1 + 4(\Delta t/\Delta y^2) \sin^2(\beta \Delta y/2)} \qquad (13)$$

and again, unless Δt is sufficiently small, this ratio will be bigger than one in magnitude for some α and β.

Somehow, and we do not remember exactly how, though it seemed natural enough, Henry Rachford and I came up with the idea of doing it one way for one time step, and then the other way for the next time step—a two-step procedure. We would then repeat the two-step procedure over and over.

It was not immediately obvious that this would be stable. We analyzed it independently overnight, however, and came to the same conclusion, that it is stable. It was necessary to recognize that we wanted to look at the amplification factor, not for either step alone, but for the entire process of going from step n to step $n + 2$. Now the second ratio (13) is really $\gamma^{n+2}/\gamma^{n+1}$, and we can multiply the two ratios (11) and (13) together and rearrange them to get

$$\frac{\gamma^{n+2}}{\gamma^n} = \frac{1 - e^{-2x_i}(\Delta t/\Delta x^2)\sin^2(\alpha\Delta x/2)}{1 + e^{-2x_i}(\Delta t/\Delta x^2)\sin^2(\alpha\Delta x/2)} \cdot \frac{1 - 4(\Delta t/\Delta y^2)\sin^2(\beta\Delta y/2)}{1 + 4(\Delta t/\Delta y^2)\sin^2(\beta\Delta y/2)} \quad (14)$$

Now a remarkable thing happens. The first ratio is always less than one in magnitude, no matter what the values of Δt, Δx, or α are. Similarly, the second ratio is always less than one in magnitude, no matter what the values of Δt, Δy, or β are. Hence, the product must be less than one in magnitude, and the two-step procedure must be stable. So that was how alternating direction was born.

Henry and I remember well the dates of this discovery, 30 and 31 December 1953. The reason we remember it so well is that we celebrated New Year's Eve at our house, along with Jim Douglas and his wife. Naturally we were very excited and could hardly talk about anything else. This shop talk was very distressing to the hostess, my wife. I think she finally forgave us a few years later.

There were several implications to the discovery that were immediately apparent. First, of course, was the fact that the asymmetry of the cylindrical problem had nothing to do with the success of the method, even though that was what triggered the idea. In particular, of course, it could be applied directly to the heat conduction problem in ordinary x-y coordinates.

The second implication, of even greater significance, was the fact that the alternating-direction method can also be used to solve a steady-state problem. The solution to Laplace's equation is, after all, the solution to the heat conduction equation at infinite time. We can imagine that if we take enough time steps, we will get the solution to Laplace's equation. We can think of accelerating the process by taking some short time steps and then some longer ones, and then if we are not close enough to the solution, repeating the sequence of short and long time steps. What that amounts to, of course, is nothing more than using alternating direction as an iterative method, with Δt serving as an iteration parameter. Well, Jim Douglas ran with that idea. He carried out an analysis that permits one to calculate an almost optimum sequence of iteration parameters. He also demonstrated convergence of the ADI method to the solution of the heat conduction problem. His results were published in a companion paper [7] to the paper that Rachford and I published in the SIAM Journal early in 1955 [8].

The first tests of ADI were on the Card-Programmed Calculator. For the SIAM paper [8], we solved both an unsteady-state and a steady-state problem on a 14 by 14 square grid. Why 14 by 14? Well, we had 56 words of data storage. As we calculated for each line, we needed to keep four numbers internally for each point. Thus, the longest line we could handle was 14. Most of the temporary data storage was punched out onto cards, and the direction was alternated using a card sorter. Because the data that were punched onto the cards had to be read back in reverse order, we punched the cards backwards and upside down, then turned them over, in order to facilitate the sorting process.

Jim Douglas and I wrote a second paper on ADI in which we solved some steady-state problems on geometries other than a square [9]. These were also done on the CPC. The first one, shown in Figure 6, was for heat flow around a corner, with the temperatures zero and one at two boundaries, and with no-flow boundaries elsewhere. Also shown is the grid numbering scheme that we used, in which the numbers correspond to the register numbers on the CPC.

Figure 7 shows a problem involving radiation from a square pipe. The inside of the pipe is at temperature T_1; the outside of the pipe has a nonlinear radiation boundary condition. We took advantage of the symmetry to solve the system in one-eighth of the cross-section. The computing grid is also shown.

The third problem, in Figure 8, was more related to reservoir engineering. We assumed an elliptical reservoir with no flow at the external boundary, with input wells at points A and B and output wells at points C and D. Again, we took advantage of symmetry and solved only one-quarter of the system. The computing grid for that problem is also shown. In all of these cases, the longest line was eight points long, which turned out to be very convenient on the CPC.

In 1955 we acquired a Bendix G-15, shown in Figure 9. This also had vacuum tube electronics, but its storage was almost completely on a magnetic drum. It came with fixed-point binary arithmetic, which was of limited scientific use, so I spent several months programming a floating-point interpreter for it. With that, we had the fantastic capability of doing 10 floating-point operations per second. It had 864 words

FIGURE 6.
Heat flow around corner.

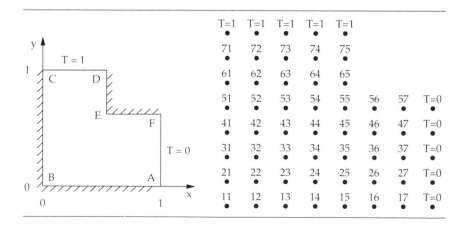

FIGURE 7.
Square pipe with radiation.

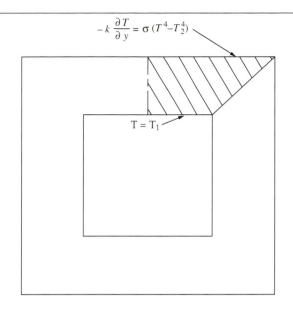

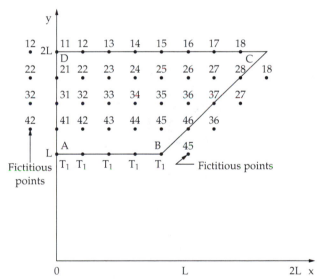

of memory available, for both data and program. Its input/output was paper tape, typewriter, and magnetic tape, none of which were particularly reliable by today's standards.

In addition, within the next few years we started using IBM's first widely used scientific computer, the 704, shown in Figure 10. It was a binary machine, with built-in floating-point hardware. Its electronics were based on thousands of vacuum tubes; its central memory was magnetic core; its secondary storage was magnetic tape. We never

FIGURE 8.
Flow in elliptical reservoir.

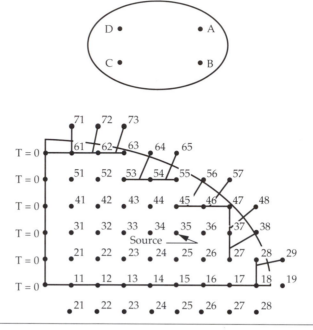

FIGURE 9.
Bendix G-15 drum computer.

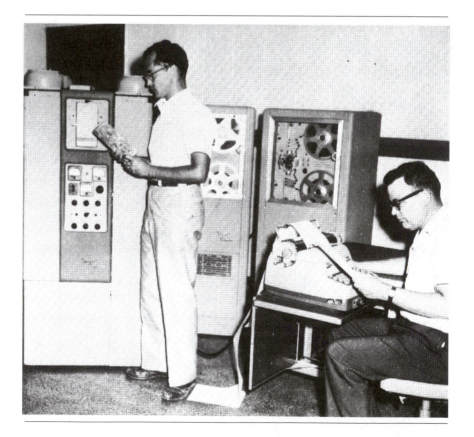

FIGURE 10.
IBM 704.

acquired a 704 of our own. The first one that we used was at the IBM Service Center in New York City, starting about 1956; after several years we started using 704s at various aircraft companies throughout the country that were selling excess time.

As you can see from Table 1, the 704 marked a major advance in our computing capability, and with it we were able to solve our first

TABLE 1
Humble/EPR Computing Equipment

Computer	Date Acquired	Storage (words)	Speed
IBM 604	Before 1950	8(?) + Cards	
IBM CPC	1952	56 + Cards	5 FLOPS
BENDIX G-15	1955	864	10 FLOPS
IBM 704	1956	8,192	10,000 FLOPS
	(away)		
BENDIX G-20	1961	8,192	20,000 FLOPS
IBM 7040/7044	1962	16,384	40,000 FLOPS
IBM 360/65	1967	256K	400,000 FLOPS
IBM 370/165	1971	1 M	1 MFLOPS
IBM 370/168	1975	2 M	1.2 MFLOPS
AMDAHL V8	1978	4 M	2 MFLOPS
IBM 3033	1979	4 M	2 MFLOPS
IBM 3081	1982	4 M	6 MFLOPS
CRAY 1S	1982	4 M	20–160 MFLOPS

real reservoir problem. That involved solving this variable coefficient version of the steady-state Laplace's equation:

$$\frac{\partial}{\partial x}\left[k(x,y)\frac{\partial p}{\partial x}\right] + \frac{\partial}{\partial y}\left[k(x,y)\frac{\partial p}{\partial y}\right] = q(x,y) \tag{15}$$

k was the value of permeability times thickness, which was known as a function of x and y. (See Figure 11.) As we still do today, we introduced the shape of the reservoir merely by setting k to zero for all grid points outside the reservoir. q is the input/output term. It was zero for most grid points and equal to the flow rate in or out wherever there was a well.

With internal storage of 8000 words, some of which was occupied by program, we could solve this problem core-contained on a 50 by 30 grid, or 1500 points. Alternating direction was used to iterate to the solution, and it took about five or ten minutes to converge. We could monitor the progress of the iteration on the slow on-line printer and modify the iteration parameter sequence by hand interactively, using switches on the control panel. Detailed output was taken on magnetic tape, which we took to an off-line printer for display of our results.

Fortran was not yet available. In fact, we saw the creators of Fortran using the same 704 in New York while we were there. Our program was written in assembly language, but that did not bother us because we were already used to dealing with machines that were much less user-friendly.

After the successful solution of this first field problem, the reservoir engineers wanted us to tackle a problem that required more defi-

FIGURE 11.
First field problem.

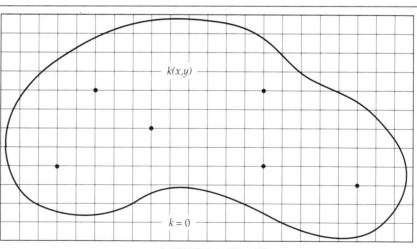

1. 1500 Points (50 × 30)
2. 6000 Points (100 × 60)

nition, one with 6000 grid points. We could not do this using only the 8000 words of central core memory, so we had to rewrite the program to use magnetic tape for secondary storage. Alternating direction using magnetic tape is very interesting to watch; you can actually visualize the calculations taking place. For each horizontal line, the tape moves forward slowly one block, as one line of the x-sweep and the beginning of the y-sweep takes place. This is repeated for each horizontal line. When all the lines are processed, the tape then quickly moves backward as the back solution of the y-sweep is carried out.

This illustrates one aspect of the computing environment that has changed considerably. In those days we loaded our own jobs and watched the calculations take place, with magnetic tapes and the on-line printer making the computations visible. Then, about 20 years ago, computing became much more invisible. Professional operators took over the actual operation of the machines. Secondary storage moved from tape to disk, which is not very visible. So, although we have gained in reliability, I think we have lost a feel for the computation process.

The next milestone of my career was the 1959 paper by Douglas, Rachford, and myself, on two-dimensional, two-phase immiscible displacement [10]. This involved the solution, in two dimensions, of these two simultaneous nonlinear differential equations:

$$\nabla \cdot \left[\frac{Kk_{ro}}{\mu_o} \nabla p_o \right] = \phi \frac{\partial S_o}{\partial t} \tag{16a}$$

$$\nabla \cdot \left[\frac{Kk_{rw}}{\mu_w} \nabla p_w \right] = \phi \frac{\partial S_w}{\partial t} \tag{16b}$$

Without going into too much detail, these equations model the displacement, in porous media, of oil by water. S is saturation, the fraction of the void space occupied by each fluid. S_o plus S_w add up to one. K is the rock permeability, a function of x and y. When oil and water flow together, they get in each other's way. To account for this, relative permeabilities, k_{ro} and k_{rw} are used. They are assumed to be known functions of saturation. In addition, the difference between the oil pressure and water pressure is the capillary pressure, also a function of saturation:

$$p_o - p_w = P_c(S)$$

These equations, (16a) and (16b), are coupled very nonlinearly. Again without going into detail, in that paper we presented two finite-difference methods for solving these equations that form the basis for reservoir simulation that is still in use today. These finite-difference methods have been extended to three dimensions and also to three phases: oil, gas, and water. Furthermore, the methods have been generalized to include fluid compressibility.

In looking back over this paper [10], however, I can see how naive we were. In particular, we did two things that we now recognize as unsatisfactory. First, we used midpoint weighting of relative permeability. In the difference equations, one needs values for relative permeability for each interval between grid points. It seemed reasonable to use an average value for this,

$$(k_r)_{i-1/2}^n = [(k_r)_{i-1}^n + (k_r)_i^n]/2 \tag{17}$$

and that is what we did. The other thing we did was to use old values for relative permeabilities.

We might ask two questions—what was naive about it, and why were we so naive? Let me answer the second question first. On the face of it, (16a) and (16b) look parabolic in nature—in other words, like extensions of the heat conduction equation. For the heat conduction equation, such a treatment of the nonlinear coefficients is usually satisfactory.

The fact is, for an incompressible system, these equations are not parabolic in nature; rather, they are elliptic and hyperbolic in nature. To see this, if we add (16a) and (16b), the time derivatives of saturation drop out, and we get this pressure equation:

$$\nabla \cdot [(Kk_{ro}/\mu_o) + (Kk_{rw}/\mu_w)]\nabla(p_o + p_w)$$

$$+ \nabla \cdot [(Kk_{ro}/\mu_o) - (Kk_{rw}/\mu_w)]\nabla(p_o - p_w) = 0 \tag{18}$$

The first term involves the sum of the two phase pressures, and the second involves their difference. But that difference is capillary pressure, which is usually very small. So the first term dominates, and (18) looks just like the variable coefficient Laplace equation, which is elliptic in nature. We get another equation by subtracting (16a) and (16b) and also by making these substitutions:

$$\vec{v}_t = -(Kk_{ro}/\mu_o)\nabla p_o - (Kk_{rw}/\mu_w)\nabla p_w \tag{19}$$

$$f(S) = (Kk_{rw}/\mu_w)/[(Kk_{ro}/\mu_o) + (Kk_{rw}/\mu_w)] \tag{20}$$

where $\vec{v}_t$ is a total velocity, and $f(S)$ is a fractional flow function. This gives us

$$-\nabla \cdot \left[\frac{Kk_{ro}}{\mu_o}f\frac{dP_c}{dS_w}\nabla S_w\right] - \vec{v}_t\frac{df}{dS_w} \cdot \nabla S_w = \phi\frac{\partial S_w}{\partial t} \tag{21}$$

On the face of it, (21) looks parabolic, but the first term involves P_c, the capillary pressure, and it usually is small. The second term is the convection term, with velocity times a first order derivative of saturation, and it dominates. So (21) is really almost first-order hyperbolic in nature.

It was not until much later that we realized that the appropriate differential equation to analyze for stability is

$$-v_t \frac{\partial f(S)}{\partial x} = \phi \frac{\partial S}{\partial t} \tag{22}$$

where we have assumed one dimension and zero capillary pressure. For midpoint weighting of relative permeability, the difference equation simplifies to

$$v_t \frac{f_{i-1}^n - f_{i+1}^n}{2\Delta x} = \phi \frac{S_i^{n+1} - S_i^n}{\Delta t} \tag{23}$$

A von Neumann stability analysis shows that (23) is unstable for any size time step. Indeed, people who started using our method discovered empirically that they were getting oscillatory solutions that could be avoided by using upstream weighting for relative permeability. In upstream weighting, the relative permeability at the upstream grid point is used for each interval between grid points. Within a few years, it became standard practice in the industry to use upstream weighting. In that case, the appropriate difference equation to look at is

$$v_t \frac{f_{i-1}^n - f_i^n}{\Delta x} = \phi \frac{S_i^{n+1} - S_i^n}{\Delta t} \tag{24}$$

A stability analysis shows that (24) is stable, provided the time step is small enough, according to the criterion

$$v_t \frac{\partial f}{\partial S} \frac{\Delta t}{\Delta x} \leq 1 \tag{25}$$

With the use of upstream weighting, the methods proposed in our paper and variations on them became quite popular for the solution of two- and three-dimensional problems. General-purpose reservoir simulators were developed by a number of companies over the next 10 years. But there was one class of problems that these simulators could not handle. These are coning problems, such as the one shown in Figure 12. Because of the radial geometry and the converging flow, the velocity is very high near the well. For any reasonable time step, inequality (25) is violated, and the calculated water-oil ratio produced into the well oscillates wildly.

About 1970, three papers were published almost simultaneously [11,12,13] that proposed essentially the same solution, which we call the semi-implicit approach. Instead of using the old value of relative permeability, an approximation for the new one is used:

$$k_r^{n+1} \approx k_r^n + \frac{dk_r}{dS}(S^{n+1} - S^n) \tag{26}$$

FIGURE 12.
Coning problem.

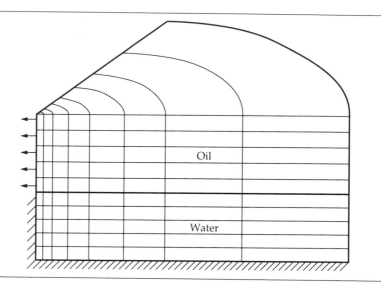

When this approximation is introduced into the saturation equation, in effect it makes the saturation equation implicit. The equation to analyze now looks like this:

$$v_t \frac{f_{i-1}^{n+1} - f_i^{n+1}}{\Delta x} = \phi \frac{S_i^{n+1} - S_i^n}{\Delta t} \tag{27}$$

It is stable for any size time step.

It might be useful to look now at how our computing equipment changed over the past 25 years. Refer again to Table 1. We finally got our own large-scale computer in 1961, a Bendix G-20 with 8192 words of core storage. It was twice the speed of the 704, with 20,000 floating-point operations per second. Bendix never came through with a Fortran compiler, so we continued to do all our programming in assembly language. We programmed a general-purpose, two-dimensional, two-phase reservoir simulator, with magnetic tape for secondary storage. Figure 13 shows Henry and me in front of the G-20 tape units, looking at some output. Bendix finally got out of the computer business, but before they did, we had sent back their G-20 and obtained an IBM 7040, a transistorized version of the 704, again with some increase in speed. Then, in the late sixties, we started with the new IBM 360/370 series, with disk storage and much faster arithmetic speeds. EPR now has several IBM machines, along with the IBM-compatible Amdahl, and the speed has been increasing significantly into the megaflops range, along with increases in the amount of central memory. EPR now also has a Cray 1-S, with four million words of storage. It is a vector computer with a theoretical maximum speed of 160 megaflops, although, like most users, we would get a sustained rate in the range of 20 to 40 megaflops. Later versions of the Cray have even higher speeds and larger memories. Now that I am retired from Exxon, however, I am reduced to having my own personal computer at home. It runs at about 30,000 floating-point operations per second, which puts it where the main-frame computers were 25 years ago. But, undoubtedly, we are seeing similar increases in speed and memory for personal computers.

One point I would like to make is that in designing a general purpose reservoir simulator, it was never safe to assume that the central random access memory would be big enough. Even though we have seen very large increases in memory size, the computation speed has also been going up drastically, and the unit cost of computation has been going down. As a result, the reservoir engineers who use our simulators keep wanting to make their models bigger and bigger, with more and more definition. Or, to put it another way, they tend

FIGURE 13.
Bendix G-20 tape units.

to run out of central memory before they run out of money. (At least, they did before the price of oil went down.) Consequently, we have found it necessary to program our simulators to use secondary storage to supplement the central memory. We used to use magnetic tape for that; now, of course, we use disk storage, which is faster and much more reliable.

But secondary memory is always much slower than central memory, so it has been necessary to learn how to use it in the most efficient way possible. This requires paying attention to the characteristics of the hardware. So you can see, we started out 30 years ago in a hardware-oriented way, and we have never gotten completely away from it. Even with the most modern machines, the effective use of the equipment still requires paying attention to the hardware. And with the advent of vector computers and other kinds of parallel computers, this has become even more true.

What has happened to the alternating-direction method? Our first paper on two-dimensional immiscible displacement [10] used alternating direction to solve for the two phase pressures on each time step. Although this worked fairly well, as we got into more difficult field problems with highly variable permeability distributions, it became more and more difficult to find a sequence of parameters that would make it converge quickly. And frequently it would diverge. In 1968, Herb Stone of Exxon published a new method [14] called SIP. This method also requires a sequence of parameters, but it is much more robust, and it is easier to make it work. So, at Exxon, SIP pretty much superceded ADI, while other companies tended to go more for successive line overrelaxation. At the present time, the trend is toward preconditioned conjugate gradient methods. However, the search for good iteration methods is far from over, and there is still a lot of research going on in the area of iterative solution of equations.

In earlier times, direct elimination methods were out of the question, but that is no longer true. For two-dimensional problems, they are now quite competitive with iterative methods. This also is an active area of research, with people looking particularly at sparse matrix methods as well as studying how best to make use of vector computers and other types of parallel machines.

I have just touched on the simplest of the reservoir flow equations that involve the flow of oil, gas, and water. These we now solve routinely, even in three dimensions, with thousands or sometimes tens of thousands of grid points. But now the industry is looking more and more at the simulation of enhanced recovery processes, which involve the injection of carbon dioxide, high-pressure nitrogen, steam, chemicals, or polymers. The calculations required to simulate these processes are much more demanding, so the needs and the opportunities for research in these areas are tremendous.

I will say a little bit about numerical methods in general, as applied to reservoir simulation. We started with finite-difference methods 25 years ago, and they still continue to be used throughout the industry today. There are a number of problems that arise from the use of finite-difference methods. The chief one is probably numerical dispersion, which smears the solution for saturation and concentration. Finite-element and other variational methods for solving reservoir problems are being studied by a lot of people, but the results they have obtained have not been impressive enough to cause the industry to stop using finite-difference methods. So the finite-element people continue doing research to try to improve on their methods, though it seems clear that the finite-difference methods will continue for quite a while to be the mainstay of reservoir simulation. As long as that is the case, there needs to be more research on finite-difference methods, to understand them better and to improve on them.

I have tried to do my own little part in the study of finite-difference methods used in reservoir simulation. Three papers illustrate what I have tried to do. The first [15] is a detailed study of the stability of difference equations that use semi-implicit relative permeability. The last two [16,17] discuss how to relate the finite-difference solution for the pressure of a grid block containing a well to the actual pressure at the well itself.

In conclusion, I hope I have conveyed some of the excitement of the early days of reservoir simulation, when we had to fight against the limitations of primitive computing equipment as well as overcome our naiveness about numerical methods. There are still plenty of challenges left today, and I think they can be just as exciting.

References

[1] M. Muskat, *The Flow of Homogeneous Fluids Through Porous Media* (New York: McGraw-Hill, 1937). Reprint edition (Boston: International Human Resources Development, 1982).

[2] W. Hurst, "Unsteady Flow of Fluids in Oil Reservoirs," *Physics* 5 (1934): 20–30.

[3] W. Hurst, "Water Influx into a Reservoir and its Application to the Equation of Volumetric Balance," *Trans AIME* 151 (1943): 57–72.

[4] A. F. Van Everdingen and W. Hurst, "The Application of the Laplace Transformation to Flow Problems in Reservoirs," *Trans AIME* 186 (1949): 305–24.

[5] G. G. O'Brien, M. A. Hyman, and S. Kaplan, "A Study of the Numerical Solution of Partial Differential Equations," *J. Math. Phys.* 29 (1951): 223–51.

[6] G. H. Bruce, D. W. Peaceman, H. H. Rachford, Jr., and J. D. Rice, "Calculation of Unsteady State Gas Flow through Porous Media," *Trans. AIME* 198 (1953): 79–92.

[7] Jim Douglas, Jr., "On the Numerical Integration of $u_{xx} + u_{yy} = u_t$ by Implicit Methods," *SIAM J.* 3 (1955): 42–65.

[8] D. W. Peaceman and H. H. Rachford, Jr., "The Numerical Solution of Parabolic and Elliptic Differential Equations," *SIAM J.* 3 (1955): 28–41.

[9] Jim Douglas, Jr., and D. W. Peaceman, "Numerical Solution of Two-Dimensional Heat Flow Problems," *AIChE J.* 1 (1955): 505–12.

[10] Jim Douglas, Jr., D. W. Peaceman, and H. H. Rachford, Jr., "A Method for Calculating Multi-Dimensional Immiscible Displacement," *Trans. AIME* 216 (1959): 297–308.

[11] J. P. Letkeman and R. L. Ridings, "A Numerical Coning Model," *Soc. Petr. Eng. J.* 10 (1970): 418–24; *Trans AIME* 249 (1970): 418–24.

[12] R. C. MacDonald and K. H. Coats, "Methods for the Numerical Solution of Water and Gas Coning," *Soc. Petr. Eng. J.* 10 (1970): 425–36; *Trans. AIME* 249 (1970): 425–36.

[13] J. S. Nolen and D. W. Berry, "Tests of the Stability and Time-Step Sensitivity of Semi-implicit Reservoir Simulation Techniques," *Soc. Petr. Eng. J.* 12 (1972): 253–66; *Trans. AIME* 253 (1972): 253–66.

[14] H. L. Stone, "Iterative Solution of Implicit Approximations of Multidimensional Partial Differential Equations," *SIAM J. Numer. Anal.* 5 (1968): 530–58.

[15] D. W. Peaceman, "A Nonlinear Stability Analysis for Difference Equations Using Semi-implicit Mobility," *Soc. Petr. Eng. J.* 17 (1977): 79–91; *Trans. AIME* 263 (1977): 79–91.

[16] D. W. Peaceman, "Interpretation of Well-block Pressures in Numerical Reservoir Simulation," *Soc. Petr. Eng. J.* 18 (1978): 183–94; *Trans. AIME* 265 (1978): 183–94.

[17] D. W. Peaceman, "Interpretation of Well-block Pressures in Numerical Reservoir Simulation with Nonsquare Grid Blocks and Anisotropic Permeability," *Soc. Petr. Eng. J.* 23 (1983): 531–43; *Trans. AIME* 275 (1983): 531–43.

Operation of the ENIAC.

METHODS

Particular algorithms have sometimes proven so effective that they redefine what we consider to be a soluble problem and offer us a new set of tools in computational analysis. Such algorithms become research topics in themselves in an attempt to exploit their capabilities in every possible application.

One such algorithm is the fast Fourier transform, discussed by James Cooley. Although known for many years—in fact, known to Gauss—its power became widely apparent only when implemented on a computer. Its uses have spread beyond signal processing to the development of "fast" algorithms in other areas of numerical analysis.

George Dantzig describes his work on the simplex method and the intuition behind its invention and wide applicability. The development of the simplex method is almost synonymous with the development of linear programming, because until recently it was the only effective algorithm for this problem—a problem barely examined before the invention of the computer, and now one of the world's most important computing applications.

Tinsley Oden gives his perspective on finite-element methods for solving partial differential equations. These methods have become a fundamental tool in engineering, allowing us to model both natural and synthetic objects with great flexibility.

Finally, Magnus Hestenes and David Young discuss iterative methods for solving linear equations. Both these researchers have played an essential role in developing these techniques, techniques that have allowed the efficient solution of large linear systems, and which in turn have allowed the solution of complex problems in science and engineering. Hestenes' work has been motivated by problems in control theory and optimization, and his essay includes descriptions of his activities in these areas. Young's work began when he was a student of Garrett Birkhoff and was inspired by computational problems in differential equations. It has resulted in a theoretical understanding of relaxation methods for solving linear systems.

How the FFT Gained Acceptance

James W. Cooley

1. Introduction

The fast Fourier transform (FFT) has had a fascinating history, filled with ironies and enigmas. Even more appropriate for this meeting and its sponsoring professional society, it speaks not only of numerical analysis but also of the importance of the functions performed by professional societies.

2. The Role of Richard Garwin

My involvement with the FFT algorithm, or algorithms, as we should probably say, started when Dick Garwin* came to the computing center of the new IBM Watson Research Center sometime in 1963 with a few lines of notes he made while he was with John Tukey at a meeting of President Kennedy's Scientific Advisory Committee, of which they were both members. John Tukey showed that if N, the number of terms in a Fourier series, is a composite, $N = ab$, then the series can be expressed as an a-term series of subseries of b terms each. If one were computing all values of the series, this would reduce the number of operations from N^2 to $N(a + b)$. Tukey also said that if this were iterated, the number of operations could be reduced from N^2 to $N \log N$. Garwin not only had the insight to see the importance of this idea, but also had the drive to pursue its development and publication.

 Dick told me that he had an important problem of determining the periodicities of the spin orientations in a 3-D crystal of He^3. I found out later that he was also trying to find ways of improving the ability to do remote seismic monitoring in order to facilitate agreement with Russia on a nuclear test ban and to improve our capability for long-range acoustic detection of submarines. Like many others, I did not see the significance in this improvement and put the job on a back burner while I continued some research I considered more important. However, I was told of Dick Garwin's reputation, and, prodded by his occasional telephone calls (some of them to my manager), I produced

---

* At that time, Garwin was a staff member of the Watson Scientific Laboratory at Columbia University. He is presently at IBM Watson Research Center, Yorktown Hts., NY.

a three-dimensional FFT program. I put some effort into designing the algorithm so as to save storage and addressing by overwriting data, and I spent some time working out a three-dimensional indexing scheme that was combined with the indexing within the algorithm.

3. The Decision to Publish

Garwin publicized the program at first by personal contacts, producing a small but increasing stream of requests for copies. I did a write-up and a version for a program library, but did not plan to publish right away. I gave a talk on the algorithm in one of a series of seminars in our mathematics department. Ken Iverson and Adin Falkoff, the developers of APL, participated, and Howard Smith, a member of the APL group, put the algorithm in APL when it was only a language for defining processes and before it was implemented on any machine. This gave the algorithm a thorough working-over at the seminar.

Another participant was Frank Thomas, a mathematically inclined patent attorney, who kept good contacts in the mathematics department. He suggested that there were patent possibilities and a meeting was called to decide what to do with it. It was decided that the algorithm should be put in the public domain and that this should be done by having Sam Winograd and Ray Miller design a device that could carry out the computation. My part of the strategy was to publish a paper with a footnote mentioning Miller and Winograd and their device. I sent my draft copy to John Tukey, asking him to be coauthor. He made some changes and emendations and added a few references to F. Yates, G. E. P. Box, and I. J. Good. Next came the task of getting it published as quickly as possible. I offered it to *Mathematics of Computation* by sending it to Eugene Isaacson at the Courant Institute of Mathematical Sciences, where I had worked before coming to IBM. I do not know how important my acquaintance with Eugene was or what effect it had on getting the paper published quickly. In any case, it appeared eight months after submission, in the April 1965 issue [1].

I found out later about an excellent paper by Gordon Sande, a bright statistics student of Tukey, who was exposed to the factorization idea in one of Tukey's courses. He carried the subject further, showing how it could be used to reduce computation in covariance calculations. After hearing about our paper going out to *Mathematics of Computation*, he did not publish his in its original form. However, he published several other excellent papers [2], one of which showed that the new algorithm was not only faster but more accurate than older techniques. His form of the FFT is now known as the Sande-Tukey algorithm.

Another result of Dick Garwin's efforts was a seminar run at the IBM Watson Research Center to publicize the algorithm and familiarize IBMers with it. For this, two capable statisticians, Peter D. Welch and

Peter A. W. Lewis, joined me in writing a thick research report describing the algorithm and developing some theory and applications. The three of us then published a series of papers on applications of the FFT. These papers elaborated on the theory of the discrete Fourier transform and showed how standard numerical methods should be revised as a result of the economy in the use of the FFT. These included methods for digital filtering and spectral analysis [3].

4. The IEEE ASSP Digital Signal Processing Committee

The next level of activity came with contact with the speech and signal processing people at MIT—notably Thomas Stockham, Charles Rader, Alan Oppenheim, Charles Rabiner—all of whom have gone on to become highly renowned people in digital signal processing. They had developed digital methods for processing speech, music, and images. The great obstacle to making their methods feasible was the amount of computing required. This was the first really impressive evidence to me of the importance of the FFT. I was invited to join them and others on the Digital Signal Processing Committee of the IEEE Acoustics Speech and Signal Processing Society.

This committee ran the now famous Arden House Workshops on the FFT in 1968 [4] and in 1970 [5]. These were unique in several respects. One was that they collected people from many different disciplines: There were heart surgeons, statisticians, geologists, university professors, and oceanographers, just to name a few. The common interest was in the use of the FFT algorithms and every one of the approximately 100 attending had something useful to say in his or her presentation. People got together to formulate and work out solutions to problems. As an example, Norman Brenner, then of MIT, designed a program that computed the FFT of a sequence of interferometer data of 512,000 elements, which was larger than available high-speed storage. He did this for Mme. Connes of the University of Paris, who returned home to perform a monumental calculation of the infrared spectra of the planets, which has become a standard reference book [6]. Others worked out algorithms for data with special symmetries.

5. Early History of the FFT

Meanwhile, back at the research center, I started learning the history of the FFT. Dick Garwin questioned his colleague, Professor L. H. Thomas of the Watson Scientific Laboratory of Columbia University, who had an office next to his. Thomas responded by showing a paper he published in 1963 [7]. His paper describes a large Fourier series calculation he did in 1948 on IBM punched card machines: a tabulator and a multiplying punch. He said that he simply went to the library and looked up a method. He found a book by Karl Stumpff [8] that was a cookbook of methods for Fourier transforms of various sizes. Most of these used the symmetries and trigonometric function identities to reduce computations by a constant factor. In a few places, Stumpff showed how to obtain larger transforms from smaller ones, and then left it to the reader to generalize. Thomas made a generalization that used mutually prime factors and got an efficient algorithm for his calculation.

The previouly mentioned algorithms of Good and Thomas have some favorable properties, but the constraint that the factors are mutually prime does not give a number of operations proportional to or as low as $N \log N$. Tukey's form of the algorithm, with repeated factors, has the great advantage that a computer program need only contain instructions for the algorithm for the common factor. Indexed loops repeat this basic calculation and permit one to iterate up to an arbitrarily high N, limited only by time and storage.

The credit for what I would consider the first FFT—a computer program implementing this iterative procedure and really giving the $N \log N$ timing—should go to Philip Rudnick of the Scripps Institution of Oceanography in San Diego, California. He wrote to me right after the publication of the 1965 paper to say that he had programmed the radix 2 algorithm using a method published by Danielson and Lanczos in 1942 in the *Journal of the Frankin Insitute* [9], a journal of great repute that publishes articles in all areas of science, but which did not enjoy a wide circulation among numerical analysts. Rudnick published some improvements in the algorithm [10] in 1966. I had the pleasure of meeting him and asked why he did not publish sooner. He said that his field was not numerical analysis and that he was only interested in getting a computer program to do his data analysis. Thus, we see another communication failure and lost opportunity, the primary point of Dick Garwin's 1969 Arden House keynote address [11].

Before continuing further with the discussion of the old literature on the FFT, I would like to point out two important concepts in numerical algorithms that had been stated long ago but did not have very much impact until they were demonstrated by the implementation of the FFT on electronic computers. The first is the divide-and-conquer approach. If a large N-size problem requires effort that increases like N^2, then it pays to break the problem into smaller pieces of the same structure. The second important concept is the asymptotic behavior of the number of operations. Obviously this was not significant for small N, and by habit of thought, people failed to see the importance of early forms of the FFT algorithms even where they would have been useful.

I can illustrate this point by going back to the Danielson and Lanczos paper [9]. The authors describe the numerical problem of computing Fourier coefficients from a set of equally spaced samples of a continuous function. One is faced not only with a long, laborious calculation, but also with the problem of verifying accuracy. Errors can arise from mistakes in computing or from undersampling the data. Lanczos pointed out that although his use of the symmetries of the trigonometric functions, as described by Runge, reduced computation by a significant factor, one still had an N^2 algorithm. In a previous reading of this paper, I obtained and published [12] the mistaken notion that Lanczos got the doubling idea from Runge. In fact, he only attributes the use of symmetries to Runge, citing papers published in 1903 and 1905 that I could not find. The Stumpff paper [8] gave a reference to Runge and König [13] that does contain the doubling algorithm and that appears to have been a standard textbook in numerical analysis. Thus, it appears that Lanczos independently discovered the clever doubling algorithm and used it to solve the problems of computational economy and error control. He says, in the introduction to [9] on page 366, "We shall show that, by a certain transformation process, it is possible to double the number of ordinates with only slightly more than double the labor." He goes on to say:

> In the technique of numerical analysis the following improvements suggested by Lanczos were used: (1) a simple matrix scheme for any even number of ordinates can be used in place of available standard forms; (2) a transposition of odd ordinates into even ordinates reduces an analysis for $2n$ coefficients to two analyses for n coefficients; (3) by using intermediate ordinates it is possible to estimate, before calculating any coefficients, the probable accuracy of the analysis; (4) any intermediate value of the Fourier integral can be determined from the calculated coefficients by interpolation. The first two improvements reduce the time spent in calculation and the probability of making errors, the third tests the accuracy of the analysis, and the fourth improvement allows the transform curve to be constructed with arbitrary exactness. Adopting these improvements the approximation times for Fourier analyses are: 10 minutes for 8 coefficients, 25 minutes for 16 coefficients, 60 minutes for 32 coefficients, and 140 minutes for 64 coefficients [9].

The matrix scheme in (1) in the preceding quotation reduces the data to even and odd components so that real cosine and sine transforms are computed. The rest of the process makes use of the symmetries of the sines and cosines, similar to the methods of Runge. After this, Lanczos uses the doubling algorithm. In step (2) he uses what we have been calling the twiddle factor multiplication, and in step (3) he does the butterfly calculation but observes accuracy by comparing the two inputs: the Fourier coefficients of the sub-series. Thus, it appears that Lanczos had the FFT algorithm; and if he had had an electronic computer, he would have been ready to write a program permitting him to go to arbitrarily high N. It may seem strange to us, then, to see his remark on page 376, "If desired, this reduction process can be applied twice or three times."

This is an outstanding example of the difference in point of view between different generations of numerical analysts. Here was the doubling algorithm, capable of doing Fourier transforms in $N \log N$ operations, described in detail. It seems to be appreciated as much as a method for checking accuracy as for reducing computing. The authors did not foresee the possibility of automating the procedure. In fact, in the beginning of the Danielson and Lanczos paper, it is presented as an economical way of doing the computation without using a mechanical analyzer available at the time. Then they published it in the *Journal of the Franklin Institute,* where it was unnoticed until Philip Rudnick, who was not a numerical analyst, revived it but ignored the opportunity to show it to the world. Lanczos later published his *Applied Analysis* in 1956 [14] with only a few words and a footnote (page 239) referring to the Danielson and Lanczos paper. I find no references to it at all in his later books, including his 1966 book, *Discourse on Fourier Series* [15].

6. Gauss and the FFT

After learning of the above early papers, I wrote what I thought to be the very early history of the FFT algorithm [12], going back to Runge and König. Some years later, while working on his book [16], Herman Goldstine told me of a paper by Gauss [17] that contained the FFT algorithm. I got a copy of the paper, which was in a neoclassic Latin that I could not read. The formulas and a slight recognition of parts of words indicated he was doing a kind of Lagrangian interpolation that leads to the basic FFT algorithm. I put this aside as an interesting post-retirement activity.

A few years later, some old signal processing friends, Don Johnson and Sidney Burrus at Rice University, told me that they put a bright, energetic graduate student, Michael Heideman, on the trail of Gauss and the FFT. He not only translated the Gauss article but found and described many others who wrote of FFT methods after Gauss and before my early references [18].

7. Conclusion

This story of the FFT can be used to help us appreciate the important functions of professional societies such as the ACM and SIAM. The following are some recommendations:

- □ Prompt publication of significant achievements is essential.
- □ Reviews of old literature can be rewarding.

□ Communication among mathematicians, numerical analysts, and workers in a wide range of applications can be fruitful.

□ Do not publish papers in neoclassic Latin.

References

[1] J. W. Cooley and J. W. Tukey, "An Algorithm for the Machine Calculation of Complex Fourier Series," *Math. Comp.* 19 (1965): 297.

[2] W. M. Gentleman and G. Sande, "Fast Fourier Transforms for Fun and Profit," in *1966 Fall Joint Computer Conf.,* AFIPS Proc. Vol 29 (Washington, DC: Spartan Press, 1966): 563–78.

[3] J. W. Cooley, P. A. W. Lewis, and P. D. Welch, "The Application of the Fast Fourier Transform Algorithm to the Estimation of Spectra and Cross-Spectra," *J. Sound Vibration* 12(3) (1970): 339–52.

[4] Various authors, "Special Issue on Fast Fourier Transform and Its Application to Digital Filtering and Spectral Analysis," *IEEE Trans. Audio and Electroacoustics* AU–15 (1967): 43–117.

[5] Various authors, "Special Issue on Fast Fourier Transform," *IEEE Trans. Audio and Electroacoustics* AU–17 (1969): 65–186.

[6] J. Connes, P. Connes, and J. P. Maillard, "Atlas des Spectres dans le Proch Infrarouge de Vénus, Mars, Jupiter et Saturne," *Éditions du Centre de la Recherche Scientifique* 15, quai Anatole France Paris VIIe (1969).

[7] L. H. Thomas, "Using a Computer to Solve Problems in Physics," in *Applications of Digital Computers,* W. F. Freiberger and W. Prager (eds.) (Boston: Ginn and Company, 1963).

[8] Karl Stumpff, *Grundlagen und Methoden der Periodenforschung* (Berlin: Springer, 1937); *Tafeln und Aufgaben zur Harmonischen Analyse und Periodogrammrechnung* (Berlin: Springer, 1939).

[9] G. C. Danielson and C. Lanczos, "Some Improvements in Practical Fourier Analysis and Their Application to X-ray Scattering From Liquids," *J. Franklin Inst.* 233, Pergamon Journals, Ltd. (1942): 365–80, 435–52.

[10] Philip Rudnick, "Note on the Calculation of Fourier Series," *Math. Comp.* 20 (1966): 429–30.

[11] R. L. Garwin, "The Fast Fourier Transform as an Example of the Difficulty in Gaining Wide Use for a New Technique," Special Issue on Fast Fourier Transform, *IEEE Trans. Audio and Electroacoustics,* AU–17 (1969): 69–72.

[12] J. W. Cooley, P. A. W. Lewis, and P. D. Welch, "Historical Notes on the Fast Fourier Transform," *IEEE Trans. Audio and Electroacoustics,* AU–15 (1967): 76–79.

[13] C. Runge and H. König, "Band XI, Vorlesungen Über Numerisches Rechnen," *Grundlehren Math. Wiss.* (Berlin: Verlag von Julius Springer, 1924).

[14] C. Lanczos, *Applied Analysis* (Englewood Cliffs, NJ: Prentice Hall, 1956).

[15] C. Lanczos, *Discourse on Fourier Series* (Edinburgh and London: Oliver and Boyd, 1966).

[16] H. H. Goldstine, *A History of Numerical Analysis from the 16th Through the 19th Century* (New York: Springer-Verlag, 1977), 249–53.

[17] C. F. Gauss, "Nachlass: Theoria interpolationis methodo nova tractata," in *Carl Friedrich Gauss, Werke*, Band 3 (Gottingen: Koniglichen Gesellschaft der Wissenschaften, 1866), 265–303.

[18] M. T. Heideman, D. H. Johnson, and C. S. Burrus, "Gauss and the History of the Fast Fourier Transform," *The IEEE ASSP Magazine* 1 (1984): 14–21.

Origins of the Simplex Method

George B. Dantzig

1. Introduction

In the summer of 1947, when I began to work on the simplex method for solving linear programs, the first idea that occurred to me is one that would occur to any trained mathematician, namely the idea of step-by-step descent (with respect to the objective function) along edges of the convex polyhedral set from one vertex to an adjacent one. I rejected this algorithm outright on intuitive grounds—it had to be inefficient because it proposed to solve the problem by wandering along some path of outside edges until the optimal vertex was reached. I therefore began to look for other methods that gave more promise of being efficient, such as those that went directly through the interior [4].

Today we know that before 1947, four isolated papers had been published on special cases of the linear programming problem: papers by Fourier (1824) [10], de la Vallée Poussin (1911) [9], Kantorovich (1939) [13], and Hitchcock (1941) [11]. All except Kantorovich's paper proposed, as a solution method, descent along the outside edges of the polyhedral set, which is the way we describe the simplex method today. There is no evidence that these papers had any influence on each other. Evidently they sparked zero interest on the part of other mathematicians and were unknown to me when I first proposed the simplex method. As we shall see, the simplex algorithm evolved from a very different geometry, one in which it appeared to be very efficient.

The linear programming problem is to find

$$\min z, x \geq 0 \text{ such that } Ax = b, \ cx = z(\min)$$

where $x = (x_1, \ldots, x_n)$, A is an m by n matrix, and b and c are column and row vectors.

Curiously, up to 1947 when I first proposed that a model based on linear inequalities be used for planning activities of large-scale enterprises, linear inequality theory had produced only 40 or so papers, in contrast to linear equation theory and the related subjects of linear algebra and approximation, which had produced a vast literature [16]. Perhaps this disproportionate interest in linear equation theory was motivated more than mathematicians care to admit by its practical use as an important tool in engineering and physics, and by the belief that linear inequality systems would not be practical to solve unless they had three or fewer variables [10].

My proposal served as a kind of trigger—ideas that had been brewing all through World War II but had never found expression burst forth like an explosion. Almost two years to the day after I first proposed that linear programming (LP) be used for planning, Koopmans organized the 1949 conference (now referred to as *The Zero-th Symposium on Mathematical Programming*) at the University of Chicago. There mathematicians, economists, and statisticians presented their research and produced a remarkable proceedings [15]. LP soon became part of the newly developing professional fields of Operations Research and Management Science. Today thousands of linear programs are solved daily throughout the world to schedule industry. These involve many hundreds, thousands, and sometimes tens of thousands of equations and variables. Some mathematicians rank LP as "the newest yet most potent of mathematical tools" [1].

John von Neumann, Tjalling Koopmans, Albert Tucker, and others well known today, some just starting their careers back in the late 1940s, played important roles in LP's early development. A group of young economists associated with Koopmans (R. Dorfman, K. Arrow, P. Samuelson, H. Simon, and others) became active contributors to the field. Their research on LP had a profound effect on economic theory and led to Nobel Prizes. Another group led by Tucker, notably including D. Gale and H. Kuhn, began the development of the mathematical theory.

This outpouring between the years of 1947 and 1950 coincided with the first building of digital computers. The computer became the tool that made the application of linear programming possible. Everywhere we looked, we found practical applications that no one earlier could have posed seriously as optimization problems because solving them by hand computation would have been out of the question. By good luck, clever algorithms in conjunction with computer development gave early promise that linear programming would become a practical science. The intense interest by the Defense Department in the linear programming application also had an important impact on the early construction of computers [5]. The U.S. National Bureau of Standards, with Pentagon funding, became a focal point for computer development under Sam Alexander; its Mathematics Group under John Curtis began the first experiments on techniques for solving linear programs, primarily by Alan Hoffman, Theodore Motzkin, and others [12].

Since we could see possible applications of linear programs everywhere we looked, it seemed only natural to suppose that there was an extensive literature on the subject. To my surprise, I found in my search of the contemporary literature of 1947 only a few references on linear inequality systems and none on solving an optimization problem subject to linear inequality constraints.

T. S. Motzkin, in his definitive 1936 Ph.D. thesis on linear inequalities [16], makes no mention of optimizing a function subject to a system of linear inequalities. However, 15 years later at the First Symposium on Linear Programming (June 1951), Motzkin declared: "There have been numerous rediscoveries [of LP] partly because of the confusingly many different geometric interpretations which these problems admit." He went on to say that different geometric interpretations allow one "to better understand and sometimes to better solve cases of these problems as they appeared and developed from a first occurrence in Newton's *Methodus Fluxionim* to right now."

The "numerous rediscoveries" that Motzkin referred to were probably the two or three papers we have already cited concerned with finding the least sum of absolute deviations, minimizing the maximum deviation of linear systems, or determining whether a solution to a system of linear inequalities exists. Fourier pointed out as early as 1824 that these were all equivalent problems [10]. Linear programs, however, had also appeared in other guises. In 1928, von Neumann [20] formulated the zero-sum matrix game and proved the mini-max theorem, a forerunner of the duality theorem of linear programming (for which he is also due credit) [3]. In 1936, Neyman and Pearson considered the problem of finding an optimal critical region for testing a statistical hypothesis. Their Neyman-Pearson Lemma is a statement about the Lagrange Multipliers associated with an optimal solution to a linear program [18].

After I had searched the contemporary literature of 1947 and found nothing, I made a special trip to Chicago in June 1947 to visit T. J. Koopmans to see what economists knew about the problem. As a result of that meeting, Leonid Hurwicz, a young colleague of Koopmans, visited me in the Pentagon in the summer and collaborated with me on my early work on the simplex algorithm, a method which we described at the time as "climbing up the bean pole": We were maximizing the objective.

Later I made another special trip, this one to Princeton in the fall of 1947, to visit the great mathematician Johnny von Neumann to learn what mathematicians knew about the subject. This was after I had proposed the simplex method, but before I realized how efficient it was going to be [4].

The origins of the simplex method go back to one of two famous unsolved problems in mathematical statistics proposed by Jerzy Neyman, which I mistakenly solved as a homework problem; it later became part of my Ph.D. thesis at Berkeley [8]. Today we would describe this problem as proving the existence of optimal Lagrange multipliers for a semi-infinite linear program with bounded variables.

Methods

Given a sample space Ω whose sample points u have a known probability distribution $dP(u)$ in Ω, the problem I considered was to prove the existence of a critical region ω in Ω that satisfied the conditions of the Neyman-Pearson Lemma. More precisely, the problem concerned finding a region ω in Ω that minimized the Lebesgue-Stieltjes integral defined by (3) below, subject to (1) and (2):

$$\int_\omega dP(u) = \alpha \tag{1}$$

$$\alpha^{-1} \int_\omega f(u)dP(u) = b \tag{2}$$

$$\alpha^{-1} \int_\omega g(u)dP(u) = z(\min) \tag{3}$$

where $0 < \alpha < 1$ is the specified "size" of the region; $f(u)$ is a given vector function of u with $m - 1$ components whose expected value z over ω is specified by the vector b; and $g(u)$ is a given scalar function of u whose unknown expected value z over ω is to be minimized.

Instead of finding a critical region, we can try to find the characteristic function $\phi(u)$ with the property that $\phi(u) = 1$ if $u \in \omega$ and $\phi(u) = 0$ if $u \notin \omega$. The original problem can then be restated as:

Find $\min z$ and a function $\phi(u)$ for $u \in \Omega$ such that:

$$\int_{u \in \Omega} \phi(u)dP(u) = \alpha \qquad 0 \le \phi(u) \le 1$$

$$\alpha^{-1} \int_{u \in \Omega} f(u)\phi(u)dP(u) = b$$

$$\alpha^{-1} \int_{u \in \Omega} g(u)\phi(u)dP(u) = z(\min)$$

A discrete analog of this semi-infinite linear program can be obtained by selecting n representative sample points $u^1, \ldots, u^j, \ldots, u^n$ in Ω and replacing $dP(u^j)$ by discrete point probabilities $\Delta_j > 0$, where n may be finite or infinite. Setting

$$x_j = (\Delta_j/\alpha) \cdot \phi(u^j) \qquad 0 \le x_j \le \Delta_j/\alpha$$

the approximation problem becomes the bounded variable LP:

Find $\min z$, $0 \le x_j \le \Delta_j/\alpha_j$:
$$\sum_1^n x_j = 1$$

$$\sum_1^n A_{.j} x_j = b \tag{4}$$

$$\sum_{1}^{n} c_j x_j = z(\text{min})$$

where $f(u^j) = A_{.j}$ are $m - 1$ component column vectors, and $g(u^j) = c_j$.

Since n, the number of discrete j, could be infinite, I found it more convenient to analyze the LP problem in the geometry of the finite $(m + 1)$ dimensional space associated with the coefficients in a column. I did so initially with the convexity constraint (4) but with no explicit upper bound on the non-negative variables x_j [2,3,15]. The first coefficient in a column (the one corresponding to (4)) is always 1, so my analysis omitted the initial 1 coordinate. Each column $(A_{.j}, c_j)$ becomes a point (y, z) in R^m where $y = (y_1, \ldots, y_{m-1})$ has $m - 1$ coordinates.

The problem can now be interpreted geometrically as one of assigning weights $x_j \geq 0$ to the n points $(y^j, z^j) = (A_{.j}, c_j)$ in R^m so that the "center of gravity" of these points (see Figure 1) lies on the

FIGURE 1.
The m-dimensional simplex.

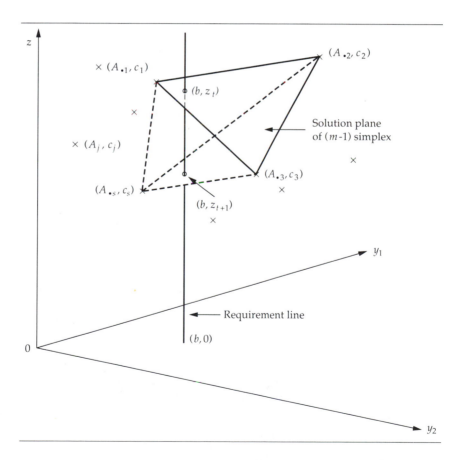

vertical "requirement" line (b, z) and such that its z coordinate is as small as possible.

2. Simplex Algorithm

Step t of the algorithm begins with an $(m - 1)$-simplex, as shown in Figure 1, defined by some m points $(A_{\cdot j_i}, c_{j_i})$ for $i = (1, \ldots, m)$ and m weights $x^0_{j_i} > 0$ (in the nondegenerate case), such that $\sum A_{\cdot j_i} x_{j_i} = b$. In the figure, the vertices of the $m - 1 = 2$ dimensional simplex correspond to $j_1 = 1, j_2 = 2, j_3 = 3$. The line (b, z) intersects the plane of the simplex (the triangle in the figure) in an interior point (b, z_t). A point $(A_{\cdot s}, c_s)$ is then determined whose vertical distance below this "solution" plane of the simplex is maximal.

Algebraically, the equation $z = \pi y + \pi_0$ of the plane associated with the simplex is found by solving the system of m equations $\pi A_{\cdot j_i} + \pi_0 = c_{j_i}, j_i = (j_1, \ldots, j_m)$. Next, let $j = s$ be the index of $(A_{\cdot s}, c_s)$, the point most below this plane, namely

$$s = \arg \min_j [c_j - (\pi A_{\cdot j} + \pi_0)]$$

If $[c_s - (\pi A_{\cdot s} + \pi_0)]$ turns out to be non-negative, the iterative process stops. Otherwise, the m-simplex, the tetrahedron in Figure 1, is formed as the convex combination of the point $(A_{\cdot s}, c_s)$ and points lying in the $(m - 1)$-simplex. The requirement line (b, z) intersects this m-simplex in a segment $(b, z_{t+1}), (b, z_t)$ where $z_{t+1} < z_t$. The face containing (b, z_{t+1}) is then selected as the new $(m - 1)$-simplex. Operationally the point $(A_{\cdot s}, c_s)$ replaces $(A_{\cdot j_r}, c_{j_r})$ for some r. The index r is not difficult to determine algebraically.

Geometrical insight as to why the simplex method is efficient can be gained by viewing the algorithm in two dimensions (see Figure 2). Suppose a piecewise linear function $z = f(y)$ is defined as the underbelly of the convex hull of the points $(y^j, z^j) = (A_{\cdot j}, c_j)$. We wish to determine $z = f(b)$ and to find two points $(y^j, z^j), (y^k, z^k)$ and weights $(\lambda, \mu) \geq 0$ on these two points such that $\lambda y^j + \mu y^k = b, \lambda + \mu = 1, \lambda z^j + \mu z^k = f(b)$. In this two-dimensional case, the simplex method resembles a kind of secant method in which, given any slope σ, it is cheap to find a point (y^s, z^s) of the underbelly such that the slope (actually the slope of a support) at y^s is σ, but in which it is not possible, given b, to find easily the two points (y^t, z^t) and (y^k, z^k) and corresponding weights (λ, μ) for determining $z = f(b)$.

In Figure 2, the algorithm is initiated (in phase II of the simplex method) by two points, say (y^1, z^1) and (y^6, z^6), on opposite sides of the requirement line. The slope of the "solution" line joining them is σ_1. Next, one determines that the point (y^5, z^5) is the one most below the line joining (y^1, z^1) to (y^6, z^6) with slope σ_1. This is done

FIGURE 2.
The underbelly of
the convex hull,
$z = f(y)$.

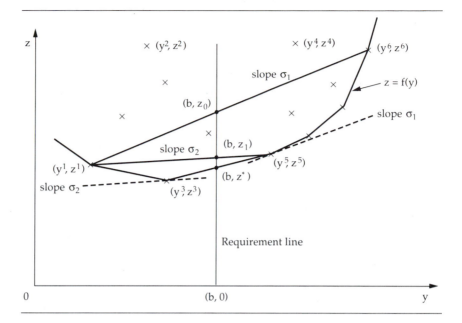

algebraically by simply substituting the coordinates (y^j, z^j) into the equation of the solution line $z - z^6 = \sigma_1(y - y^6)$ and finding the point $j = s$ such that $\sigma_1(y^j - y^6) - (z^j - z^6)$ is maximal. For the preceding example, $s = 5$ and thus (y^5, z^5) replaces (y^6, z^6). The steps are then repeated with (y^1, z^1) and (y^5, z^5). The algorithm finds the optimum point (b, z^*) in two iterations with the pair (y^3, z^3), (y^5, z^5).

In practical applications, one would expect that most of the points $(A_{.j}, c_j)$ would lie above the underbelly of their convex hull. We would therefore expect that very few j would be extreme points of the underbelly. Because the algorithm only chooses $(A_{.s}, c_s)$ from among the latter, and because these typically would be rare, I conjectured that the algorithm would have very few choices and would take about m steps in practice.

It is not difficult, of course, to construct cases that take more than m iterations, so let me make some remarks about the rate of convergence of z_t to z^*, the minimum value of z, in the event that the method takes more than m iterations.

3. Convergence Rate of the Simplex Method

Assume there exists a constant $1 \geq \overline{\theta} > 0$ such that for every iteration τ, the values of all basic variables $x_{j_i}^\tau$ satisfy

$$1 \geq x_{j_i}^\tau \geq \overline{\theta} > 0 \quad \text{for all } j_i$$

At the start of iteration t, by eliminating the basic variables from the objective equation, we obtain

$$z_{t-1} - z = \sum (-\bar{c}_j^t)x_j$$

where $\bar{c}_{j_{j_i}}^t = 0$ for all basic $j = j_i$. If $(-\bar{c}_s^t) = \max(-\bar{c}_j^t) \leq 0$, the iterative process stops with the current basic feasible solution optimal. Otherwise, we increase nonbasic x_s to $x_s = \theta_t \geq \bar{\theta}$ and adjust basic variables to obtain the basic feasible solution to start iteration $t + 1$.

Let $z^* = \min z$ and $x_j = x_j^* \geq 0$ be the corresponding optimal x_j. We define Δ_t as $z_t - z^*$.

Theorem 1. *Independent of the number of variables n,*

$$(\Delta_t/\Delta_0) \leq (1 - \theta_1)(1 - \theta_2) \cdots (1 - \theta_t) \leq e^{-\Sigma \theta_\tau} \leq e^{-\bar{\theta} \cdot t}$$

where $\theta_t \geq \bar{\theta} > 0$ is the value of the incoming basic variable x_s on iteration t.

Proof.

$$\Delta_{t-1} = z_{t-1} - z^* = \sum (-\bar{c}_j^t)x_j^* \leq (-\bar{c}_s^t) \sum x_j^* = (-\bar{c}_s^t)$$

$$\Delta_{t-1} - \Delta_t = z_{t-1} - z_t = (-\bar{c}_s^t)x_s = (-\bar{c}_s^t)\theta_t \geq \Delta_{t-1} \cdot \theta_t$$

where the inequality between the last two terms is obtained by applying the preceding inequality. Rearranging terms and applying t iteratively for $t = 2, 3, \ldots$

$$\Delta_t \leq (1 - \theta_t)\Delta_{t-1} < e^{-\theta_t}\Delta_{t-1} \leq e^{-\bar{\theta}}\Delta_{t-1}$$
$$\leq e^{-\bar{\theta}}(e^{-\bar{\theta}}\Delta_{t-2}) \cdots \leq e^{-\bar{\theta} \cdot t}\Delta_1$$

Corollary 2. *Assuming θ_τ has "on the average" the same average value as any other $x_{j_i}^\tau$, namely $(1/m)$, then the expected number of iterations t required to affect an e^{-k}-fold decrease in Δ_0 will be less than km iterations, that is,*

$$(\Delta_t/\Delta_0) < e^{-\Sigma \theta_\tau} \doteq e^{-t/m}$$

Thus, under the assumption that the value of the incoming variable is $1/m$ on the average, a thousand-fold decrease in $\Delta_t = z_t - z^*$ could be expected to be obtained in less than $7m$ iterations because $e^{-7} < .001$.

It was considerations such as these back in 1947 that led me to believe that the simplex method would be very efficient.

It is fortunate that when the simplex algorithm for solving linear programs was first being developed back in 1947, the column geometry, and not the row geometry, was used. As we have seen, the column geometry suggested a different algorithm, one that promised to be very efficient. Accordingly, I developed a variant of the algorithm without the convexity constraint (4) and arranged in the fall of 1947 to have the Bureau of Standards test it on George Stiegler's nutrition problem [19]. Of course, I soon observed that what appeared in the column geometry to be a new algorithm was, in the row geometry, the vertex descending algorithm that I had rejected earlier.

It is my opinion that any well-trained mathematician viewing the linear programming problem in the row geometry of the variables would have immediately come up with the idea of solving it by a vertex descending algorithm, as did Fourier, de la Vallée Poussin, and Hitchcock before me—each of us proposing it independently of the other. I believe, however, that if anyone had to consider it as a practical method, as I had to, he or she would have quickly rejected it on intuitive grounds as a stupid idea without merit. My own contributions towards the discovery of the simplex method were (1) independently proposing the algorithm, (2) initiating the development of the software necessary for its practical use, and (3) observing (by viewing the problem in the geometry of the columns rather than the rows) that contrary to geometric intuition, following a path on the outside of the convex polyhedron might be an efficient procedure.

4. The Role of Sparsity in the Simplex Method

To determine $s = \arg\min_j[c_j - (\pi A_{.j} + \pi_0)]$ requires forming the scalar product of two vectors π and $A_{.j}$ for each j. This "pricing out" operation, as it is called, is usually cheap because the vectors $A_{.j}$ are sparse; that is, they typically have few nonzero coefficients (perhaps, on the average, four or five nonzeros). Nevertheless, if the number of columns n is large, say several thousand, pricing can use up a lot of time. (Parallel processors could be used very effectively for pricing by assigning subsets of the columns to different processors [6].)

In single processors, various *partial pricing* schemes are used. One scheme, used in the MINOS software system, is to partition the columns into subsets of some k columns each [17]. The choice of s is restricted to columns that price out negative among the first k until there are none, and then moving on to the next k, and so forth. Another scheme used is to price out all the columns and rank them according to how negative they price out. A subset of j, say the 50 most negative in rank, are then used to iteratively select s until this subset no longer has a column that prices out negative. A new subset is then generated for selecting s, and the process is repeated. Partial pricing schemes are very effective when n is large, especially for matrix structures that contain so-called "GUB" (Generalized Upper Bound) rows [7].

Besides the pricing-out of the columns, the simplex method requires that the current basis B, that is, the columns $(j., \ldots, j_m)$ used to form the simplex in Figure 1, be maintained from iteration t to $t + 1$ in a form that makes it easy to compute two vectors v and π, where

$Bv = A._s$ and $\pi B = (c_{j_1}, \ldots, c_{j_m})$. The matrix B is typically sparse. In problems where the number of rows m is greater than 1000, the percent of nonzeros may be less than $\frac{1}{2}$ of 1 percent. Even for such B, it is not practical to maintain B^{-1} explicitly, because it could turn out to be 100 percent dense. Instead, B is often represented as the product of a lower and upper triangular matrix in which each is maintained as a product of elementary matrices, with every effort being made to keep the nonunit column of each elementary matrix as sparse as possible. Maintaining this sparsity is important, because otherwise, for the case of $m = 1000$ the algorithm would have to manipulate data sets with millions of nonzero numbers. Solving systems $Bv = A._s$ in order to determine which variable leaves the basis would become too costly.

5. The Role of Near-Triangularity of the Basis

The success of the simplex method in solving very large problems encountered in practice depends on two properties found in almost every practical problem. First, the basis is usually sparse. Second, one can usually rearrange the rows and columns of the various bases encountered in the course of solution so that they are nearly triangular. Near-triangularity makes it relatively inexpensive to represent it as a product of a lower and upper triangular matrix and to preserve much of the original sparsity.

Even if the bases were sparse but not nearly triangular, solving systems $Bv = A._s$ could be too costly to perform.

The success of solving linear programming therefore depends on a number of factors: (1) the power of computers, (2) extremely clever algorithms, and most of all (3) a lot of good luck that the matrices of practical problems will be sparse and that their bases, after rearrangement, will be nearly triangular.

For over 40 years the simplex method has reigned supreme as the preferred method for solving linear programs. Its efficiency is the historical reason for the practical success of the field. As of this writing, however, the algorithm is being challenged by new interior methods proposed by N. Karmarkar [14] and others and by methods that exploit special structure. If these new methods turn out to be more successful than the simplex method for solving practical linear programs, it will be not because of any theoretical reasons having to do with polynomial time for solving worst-case general linear programs, but because they can more effectively exploit the sparsity and near triangularity of practical problems than the simplex method is able to do.

References

[1] R. Coughlin and D. E. Zitarelli, *The Ascent of Mathematics* (New York: McGraw-Hill, 1984).

[2] G. B. Dantzig, "Linear Programming," in *Problems for the Numerical Analysis of the Future*, Proceedings of the Symposium on Modern Calculating Machinery and Numerical Methods, UCLA (July 29–31, 1948); *Appl. Math.* 15, National Bureau of Standards (1951): 18–21.

[3] G. B. Dantzig, *Linear Programming and Extensions* (Princeton University Press, 1963).

[4] G. B. Dantzig, "Reminiscences about the Origins of Linear Programming," in *Math. Programming*, R. W. Cottle, M.L. Kelmanson, and B. Korte (eds.), Proceedings of the International Congress on Mathematical Programming, Rio de Janeiro (1984): 105–12.

[5] G. B. Dantzig, "Impact of Linear Programming on Computer Development," *OR/MS Today* 14 (1988): 12–17.

[6] G. B. Dantzig, "Planning Under Uncertainty Using Parallel Computing," *Ann. Oper. Res.* 14 (1988): 1–16.

[7] G. B. Dantzig and R. M. Van Slyke, "Generalized Upper Bounding Techniques," *J. Comp. System Sci.* 1 (1967): 213–26.

[8] G. B. Dantzig and A. Wald, "On the Fundamental Lemma of Neyman and Pearson," *Ann. Math. Stat.* 22 (1951): 87–93.

[9] Ch. de la Vallée Poussin, "Sur la Methode de l'Approximation Minimum," *Ann Soc. Sci. Bruxelles Ser. I* 35 (1910–1911): 1–16.

[10] J. B. J. Fourier, "Solution d'une question particuliere du calcul des inegalities," original 1826 paper with an abstract of an 1824 paper reprinted in *Oeuvres de Fourier*, Tome II (Olms: Hildesheim, 1970), 317–19.

[11] F. L. Hitchcock, "The Distribution of a Product from Several Sources to Numerous Localities," *J. Math. Phys.* 20 (1941): 224–30.

[12] A. J. Hoffman, M. Mannos, D. Sokolousky, and N. Wiegmann, "Computational Experience in Solving Linear Programs," *SIAM J.* 1 (1953): 17–33.

[13] L. V. Kantorovich, *Mathematical Methods in the Organization and Planning of Production* (Publication House of the Leningrad State University, 1939). Translated in *Management Sci.* 6 (1960): 366–422.

[14] N. Karmarkar, "A New Polynomial-Time Algorithm for Linear Programming," *Combinatorica* 4 (1984): 373–95.

[15] T. C. Koopmans (ed.), *Activity Analysis of Production and Allocation* (New York: John Wiley & Sons, 1951).

[16] T. S. Motzkin, "Beitrage zur Theorie der Linearen Ungleichungen" (Jerusalem: Doctoral Thesis, University of Zurich, 1936).

[17] B. A. Murtagh and M. A. Saunders, "MINOS 5.0 User's Guide," Technical Report SOL 83–20, Systems Optimization Laboratory, Department of Operations Research, Stanford University (1983).

[18] J. Neyman and F. S. Pearson, "Contributions to the Theory of Testing Statistical Hypotheses," *Statist. Res. Mem.*, I and II (1936, 1938).

[19] G. J. Stigler, "The Cost of Subsistence," *J. of Farm Econ.* 27 (1945): 303–14.

[20] J. von Neumann, "Zur Theorie de Gesellschaftsspiele," *Math. Ann.* 100 (1928): 295–320. Translated by Sonya Bargmann in *Contributions to the Theory of Games*, Vol IV, A.W. Tucker and R.D. Luce (eds.), *Ann. of Math. Stud.* 40 (Princeton University Press, (1959): 13–42.

Historical Comments on Finite Elements

J. Tinsley Oden

1. Introduction

Finite elements: Perhaps no other family of approximation methods has had a greater impact on the theory and practice of numerical methods during the twentieth century. Finite element methods have now been used in virtually every area of engineering that can make use of models of nature characterized by partial differential equations.

Why have finite element methods been so popular in both the engineering and mathematical community? I believe that a principal reason for the success and popularity of these methods is that they are based on the weak, variational formulation of boundary and initial value problems. This is a critical property, not only because it provides a proper setting for the existence of very irregular solutions to differential equations (such as distributions), but also because the solution appears in the integral of a quantity over a domain. The simple fact that the integral of a measurable function over an arbitrary domain can be broken up into the sum of integrals over an arbitrary collection of almost disjoint subdomains whose union is the original domain is a vital property. Because of it, the analysis of a problem can literally be made locally, over a typical subdomain. Also, by making the subdomain sufficiently small, one can argue that polynomial functions of various degrees are adequate for representing the local behavior of the solution. This summability of integrals is exploited in every finite element program. It allows the analysts to focus their attention on a typical finite element domain and to develop an approximation independent of the ultimate location of that element in the final mesh.

The simple integral property also has important implications in physics and in most problems in continuum mechanics. Indeed, the classical balance laws of mechanics are global in the sense that they are integral laws applying to a given mass of material, a fluid, or solid. The only mathematical requirement is that the primitive variables be sufficiently regular for these integrals to be well-defined. Moreover, since these laws are supposed to be fundamental axioms of physics, they must hold over every finite portion of the material: every finite element of the continuum. Thus, once again, one is encouraged to think of approximate methods defined by integral formulations over typical pieces of the continuum under consideration.

2. The Origin of Finite Elements

When did finite elements begin? It is difficult to trace the origins of finite element methods because of a basic problem in defining precisely what constitutes a "finite element method." To most mathematicians, it is a method of piecewise polynomial approximation, and its origins, therefore, are frequently traced to the appendix of a paper by Courant [24] that discusses piecewise linear approximations of the Dirichlet problem over a network of triangles. Also, the "interpretation of finite differences" by Polya [58] is regarded as embodying piecewise polynomial approximation aspects of finite elements.

On the other hand, the approximation of variational problems on a mesh of triangles goes back as many as 92 years. In 1851, Schellbach [64] proposed a finite-element–like solution to Plateau's problem of determining the surface S of minimum area enclosed by a given closed curve. Schellbach used an approximation S_h of S by a mesh of triangles over which the surface was represented by piecewise linear functions, and he then obtained an approximation of the solution to Plateau's problem by minimizing S_h with respect to the coordinates of hexagons formed by six elements [74]. This is not quite the conventional finite-element approach, but certainly as much a finite-element technique as that of Courant.

Some say that there is even an earlier work that uses some of the ideas underlying finite-element methods: Leibniz himself employed a piecewise linear approximation of the Brachistochrone problem proposed by Bernoulli in 1696 [39]. With the help of his newly developed calculus tools, Leibniz derived the governing differential equation for the problem, the solution of which is a cycloid. However, most would agree that to credit this work as a finite element approximation is stretching the point. Leibniz had no intention of approximating a differential equation; rather, his purpose was to derive one. Two and a half centuries later it was realized that useful approximations of differential equations could be determined by keeping the elements finite in size, not necessarily by taking infinitesimal elements, as in the calculus. This idea is, in fact, the basis of the term "finite element."

There is also some difference in the process of laying a mesh of triangles over a domain, on the one hand, and generating the domain of approximation by piecing together triangles, on the other. Although these processes may look the same in some cases, they may differ dramatically in how the boundary conditions are imposed. Thus, neither Schellbach nor Courant—nor for that matter Synge, who used triangular meshes many years later—was particularly careful as to how boundary conditions were to be imposed or as to how the boundary of the domain was to be modeled by elements, issues that are now recognized as important features of finite-element methodologies. If a finite-element method is one in which a global approximation of a partial differential equation is built up from a sequence of local approximations over subdomains, then credit must go back to the early papers of Hrennikoff [32], and perhaps beyond. Hrennikoff chose to solve plane elasticity problems by breaking up the domain of the displacements into little finite pieces, over which the stiffnesses were approximated using bars, beams, and spring elements. McHenry used a similar "lattice analogy" [42]. While these works are draped in the most primitive physical terms, it is nevertheless clear that the methods involve some sort of crude, piecewise linear or piecewise cubic approximation over rectangular cells. Miraculously, the methods also seem to be convergent.

To the average practitioner, finite elements are much more than a method of piecewise polynomial approximation. Partitioning a domain, assembling elements, and applying loads and boundary conditions, and, of course, local polynomial approximation, are all components of the finite-element method.

If this is so, then one must acknowledge the early papers of Gabriel Kron. Kron developed his "tensor analysis of networks" in 1939 and applied his "method of tearing" and "network analysis" to the generation of global systems from large numbers of individual components in the 1940s and 1950s [37,38]. Of course, Kron never necessarily regarded his method as one of approximating partial differential equations; rather, the properties of each component were regarded as exactly specified, and the issue was an algebraic one of connecting them all appropriately together.

In the early 1950s, Argyris [1,2] began to put these ideas together into what some call a primitive finite-element method: He extended and generalized the combinatoric method of Kron and other ideas that were being developed in the literature on system theory at the time and added variational methods of approximation to them. This was a fundamental step toward true finite-element methodology.

Around the same time, Synge [69] described his "method of the hypercircle," in which he also spoke of piecewise linear approximations on triangular meshes, but not in a rich variational setting and not in a way in which approximations were built by either partitioning a domain into triangles or assembling triangles to approximate a domain. (Indeed, Synge's treatment of boundary conditions was clearly not in the spirit of finite elements, even though he was keenly aware of the importance of convergence criteria and of the "angle condition" for triangles, later studied in some depth by others.)

It must be noted that during the mid-1950s, there were a number of independent studies underway that made use of "matrix methods" for the analysis of aircraft structures. A principal contributor to this methodology was Levy [40], who introduced the "direct stiffness method" wherein he approximated the structural behavior of aircraft wings using assemblies of box beams, torsion boxes, rods, and shear panels. These assuredly represent some sort of crude local polynomial approximation in the same spirit as the Hrennikoff and McHenry approaches. The direct stiffness method of Levy had a great impact on the structural analysis of aircraft, and aircraft companies throughout the United States began to adopt and apply some variant of this method or of the methods of Argyris to complex aircraft structural analyses. During this same period, similar structural analysis methods were being developed and used in Europe, particularly in England. One must mention in this regard the work of Taig [70], in which shear lag in aircraft wing panels was approximated using basically a bilinear finite-element method of approximation. Similar element-like approximations were used in many aircraft industries as components in various matrix methods of structural analyses. Thus, the precedent for piecewise approximations of some kind was established by the mid-1950s.

To a large segment of the engineering community, the work representing the beginning of finite elements was the paper by Turner and colleagues [71], in which a genuine attempt was made at both a local approximation (of the partial differential equations of linear elasticity) and the use of assembly strategies essential to finite-element methodology. It is interesting that in this paper, local element properties were derived without the use of variational principles. It was not until 1960 that Clough [23] actually dubbed these techniques as "finite-element methods" in a landmark paper on the analysis of linear plane elasticity problems.

The 1960s were the formative years of finite-element methods. Once it was perceived by the engineering community that useful finite-element methods could be derived from variational principles, variationally based methods significantly dominated all the literature for almost a decade. If an operator was unsymmetric, it was thought that the solution of the associated problem was beyond the scope of finite elements because it did not lend itself to a traditional extremum variational approximation in the spirit of Rayleigh and Ritz.

From 1960 to 1965, a variety of finite-element methods were proposed. Many were primitive and unorthodox; some were innovative and successful. During this time, numerous attempts at solving the biharmonic equation for plate-bending problems were proposed that employed piecewise polynomial approximations but did not provide the essentials for convergence. This led to the concern of some as to whether the method was indeed applicable to such problems. On the other hand, it was clear that classical Fourier series solutions of plate problems were, under appropriate conditions, convergent and could be fit together in an assemblage of rectangular components [46]. Thus, a form of "spectral finite element methods" was introduced early in the study of such problems. However, such high-order schemes never received serious attention in this period, as it was thought that piecewise polynomial approximations could be developed that did give satisfactory results. It was not until the mid- to late 1960s that papers on bicubic spline approximations [13,14] provided successful polynomial finite-element approximations for these classes of problems.

Many workers in the field believe that the famous Dayton conferences on finite elements (at the Air Force Flight Dynamics Laboratory in Dayton, Ohio) represented landmarks in the development of the field [59]. Held in 1965, 1968, and 1970, these meetings brought specialists from all over the world to discuss their latest triumphs and failures. The pages of the proceedings, particularly the earlier volumes, were filled with remarkable and innovative accomplishments from a technical community just beginning to learn the richness and power of this new collection of ideas. In these volumes, one can find many of the premier papers of now well-known methods. In the first volume alone one can find mixed finite element methods [31], Hermite approximations [56], C^1-bicubic approximations [14], hybrid methods [57], methods for highly nonlinear elliptic systems [3], and other contributions. In later volumes, further assaults on nonlinear problems and special element formulations can be found.

In the late 1960s and early 1970s, there finally emerged the realization that the method could be applied to unsymmetric operators without difficulty, and thus, problems in fluid mechanics were brought within the realm of application of finite-element methods. In particular, finite element models of the full Navier-Stokes equations were first presented during this period [47,48,52].

The early textbook by Zienkiewicz and Cheung [75] did much to popularize the method with the practicing engineering community. However, the most important factor leading to the rise in popularity during the late 1960s and early 1970s was not purely the publication of special formulations and algorithms, but the fact that the method was being successfully used to solve difficult engineering problems. Much of the technology used during this period was the work of Bruce Irons, who with his colleagues and students developed a multitude of techniques for the successful implementation of finite elements. These included the frontal solution technique [34], the patch test [35], isoparametric elements [28], and numerical integration schemes [33]. The scope of finite element applications in the 1970s would have been significantly diminished without these contributions.

3. The Mathematical Theory

The mathematical theory of finite elements was slow to emerge from this caldron of activity. The beginning works on this theory were understandably concerned with one-dimensional elliptic problems and used many of the tools and jargon of Ritz methods, interpolation, and variational differences. Early works in this line include Varga's study of "Hermite interpolation-type Ritz methods" for two-point boundary value problems [72] and the contribution of Birkhoff, de Boor, Schwartz, and Wendroff on "Rayleigh-Ritz Approximation by Piecewise Cubic Polynomials" [12]. The latter is certainly one of the first papers to deal with the issue of convergence of finite-element methods, although some papers on variational differences yielded similar results though they did not focus on the piecewise polynomial features of finite elements. The work of Feng Kang [30], published in Chinese (a copy of which I have not been able to acquire for review), may fall into this category and is sometimes noted as relevant to the convergence of finite-element methods.

The mathematical theory of finite elements for two-dimensional and higher-dimensional problems began in 1968, and several papers were published that year on the subject. One of the first papers in this period to address the problem of convergence of a finite method in a rigorous way and in which a priori error estimates for bilinear approximations of a problem in a plane elasticity are obtained is the often-overlooked paper of Johnson and McClay [36]. This paper correctly developed error estimates in energy norms, and it even attempted to characterize the deterioration of convergence rates owing to corner singularities. In the same year there appeared the first of two papers by Ogenesjan and Ruchovec [53,54], in which "variational difference schemes" were proposed for linear second-order elliptic problems in two-dimensional domains. These works dealt with the estimates of the rate of convergence of variational difference schemes.

Also in 1968, there appeared the paper of Zlamal [76] discussing in detail the interpolation properties of a class of triangular elements and their application to second-order and fourth-order linear elliptic boundary-value problems. This paper attracted the interest of a large segment of the numerical analysis community, and several very good mathematicians began to work on finite-element methodologies. Zlamal's paper represented a departure from studies of tensor products of polynomials on rectangular domains and provided an approach toward approximation in general polygonal domains. In the same year, Ciarlet [18] published a rigorous proof of convergence of piecewise linear finite-element approximation of a class of linear two-point boundary-value problems and proved L^∞ estimates using a discrete maximum principle. Oliveira's work [55] on convergence finite-element methods established correct rates-of-convergence of certain problems in appropriate energy norms. In subsequent years, Schultz presented error estimates for "Rayleigh-Ritz-Galerkin methods" for multidimensional problems [65] and L^2-error bounds for these methods [66].

By 1972, finite-element methods had emerged as an important new area of numerical analysis in applied mathematics. Mathematical conferences were held on the subject on a regular basis, and there began to emerge a rich volume of literature on mathematical aspects of the method applied to elliptic problems, eigenvalue problems, and parabolic problems. A conference of special significance in this period was held at the University of Maryland in 1972. It featured a penetrating series of lectures by Ivo Babuška [8] and several important mathematical papers by leading specialists in the mathematics of finite elements, all collected in the volume edited by Aziz [5].

One unfamiliar with aspects of the history of finite elements may be led to the erroneous conclusion that the method of finite elements emerged from the growing wealth of information on partial differential equations, weak solutions of boundary-value problems, Sobolev spaces, and the associated approximation theory for elliptic variational boundary-value problems. This is a natural mistake, because the seeds for the modern theory of partial differential equations were sown about the same time as those for the development of modern finite-element methods, but in an entirely different garden.

In the late 1940s, Laurent Schwartz was putting together his theory of distributions, around a decade after the notion of generalized functions and their use in partial differential equations appeared in the pioneering work of Sobolev. Many other names could be added to the list of contributors to the modern theory of partial differential equations, but that is not our purpose here. Rather, we must note only that the rich mathematical theory of partial differential equations that began in the 1940s and 1950s, blossomed in the 1960s, and is now an integral part of the foundations of not only partial differential equations but also approximation theory, grew independently and parallel to the development of finite-element methods for almost two decades. There was important work during this period on the foundations of variational methods of approximation, typified by the early work of Lions [41] and by the French school in the early 1960s; but, although this work did concern itself with the systematic development of mathematical results that would ultimately prove to be vital to the development of finite-element methods, it did not focus on the specific aspects of existing and already successful finite-element concepts. It was, perhaps, an unavoidable occurrence that in the late 1960s these two independent subjects, finite-element methodology and the theory of approximation of partial differential equations via functional analysis methods, united in an inseparable way. So firmly were they united that it is difficult to appreciate the fact that they were ever separate.

The 1970s must mark the decade of the mathematics of finite elements. During this period, great strides were made in determining a priori error estimates for a variety of finite element methods, for linear elliptic boundary-value problems, for eigenvalue problems, and for certain classes of linear and nonlinear parabolic problems; also, some preliminary work on finite-element applications to hyperbolic equations was done. It is both inappropriate and perhaps impossible to provide an adequate survey of this large volume of literature, but it is possible to present a reference, albeit biased, to some of the major works along the way.

An important component in the theory of finite elements is an interpolation theory: How well can a given finite-element method approximate functions of a given class locally over a typical finite element? A great deal was known about this subject from the literature on approximation theory and spline analysis, but its particularization to finite elements involves technical difficulties. One can find results on finite-element interpolation in a number of early papers [6,7,8,11,15,65,76]. But the elegant work on Lagrange and Hermite interpolations of finite elements by Ciarlet and Raviart [20] must stand as an important contribution to this aspect of finite-element theory. The 1972 memoir of Babuška and Aziz [8] on the mathematical foundations of finite-element methods interweaves the theory of Sobolev spaces and elliptic problems with general results on approximation theory that have a direct bearing on finite-element methods.

It was known that Cea's lemma [17] established that the approximation error in a Galerkin approximation of a variational boundary-value problem is bounded by the so-called interpolation error; that is, by the distance in an appropriate energy norm from the solution of the problem to the subspace of approximations. Indeed, it was this fact that made the results on interpolation theory using piecewise polynomials particularly interesting to finite-element methods. The introduction of the "Inf-Sup" condition by Babuška [6] and Babuška and Aziz [8] dramatically enlarged this framework. The condition is encountered in the characterization of coerciveness of bilinear forms occurring in elliptic boundary-value problems. The characterization of this "Inf-Sup" condition for the discrete finite-element approximation embodies the essential elements for studying the stability in convergence of finite-element methods. Brezzi [16] developed an equivalent condition for studying constrained elliptic problems, and these conditions provide for a unified approach to the study of qualitative properties, including rates of convergence, of broad classes of finite-element methods.

The work of Nitsche [44] on L^{∞} estimates for general classes of linear elliptic problems must stand out as one of the most important contributions of the 1970s. Strang [68] pointed out "variational crimes" inherent in many finite-element methods, such as improper numerical quadrature, the use of nonconforming elements, and improper satisfaction of boundary conditions. All of these are common practices in applications, but all frequently lead to acceptable numerical schemes. In the same year, Ciarlet and Raviart [21,22] also studied these issues. Many of the advances of the 1970s drew upon earlier results on variational methods of approximation based on the Ritz method and finite differences; for example, the Aubin-Nitsche method for lifting the order of convergence to lower Sobolev norms [4,43,54] used such results. In 1974, Brezzi [16] used such earlier results on saddle-point problems and laid the groundwork for a multitude of papers on problems with constraints and on the stability of various finite-element procedures. Although convergence of special types of finite-element strategies such as mixed methods and hybrid methods had been attempted in the early 1970s [49], the Brezzi results and the methods of Babuška for constrained problems provided a general framework for studying virtually all mixed and hybrid finite elements [9,60,61].

The first textbook on mathematical properties of finite-element methods was the popular book of Strang and Fix [68]. An introduction to the mathematical theory of finite elements was published soon after by Oden and Reddy [51], and the treatise on the finite-element method for elliptic problems by Ciarlet [19] appeared two years later.

The work of Nitsche and Schatz [45] on interior estimates and of Schatz and Wahlbin [62,63] on L^∞ estimates and singular problems represented notable contributions to the growing mathematical theory of finite elements. Progress was also made on finite-element methods for parabolic problems and hyperbolic problems [25,26,27] and on the use of elliptic projections for deriving error bounds for time-dependent problems [73].

The 1970s was also a decade in which the generality of finite-element methods began to be appreciated over a large portion of the mathematics and scientific community, and it was during this period that significant applications to highly nonlinear problems were made. The fact that very general nonlinear phenomena in continuum mechanics, including problems of finite deformation of solids and of flow of viscous fluids, could be modeled by finite elements and solved on existing computers was demonstrated in the early seventies [49]. By the end of that decade, several "general purpose" finite-element programs were being used by engineers to treat broad classes of nonlinear problems in solid mechanics and heat transfer. The mathematical theory for nonlinear problems also was advanced in this period, in particular by Falk's work [29] on finite-element approximations of variational inequalities.

It is not too inaccurate to say that by 1980, a solid foundation for the mathematical theory of finite elements for linear problems had been established and that significant advances in both theory and application into nonlinear problems existed. The open questions that remain are difficult ones, and solving them will require a good understanding of the mathematical properties of the method.

4. Personal Reflections

The organizers of the meeting for which this discourse was prepared asked the invited authors to include "personal reflections" if possible. With such an invitation to relax customary standards of modesty and humility, I offer these closing comments on my own early introductions to the subject.

I remember very well my own introduction to finite elements. I had read thoroughly the work of Agyris and others on "matrix methods in structural mechanics" and had developed notes on the subject while teaching graduate courses in solid mechanics in the early 1960s, but none of the literature of the day had much impact on my university research at the time, or seemingly on the research of anyone in the university community. The aircraft industry was actively developing the subject during this period and was far ahead of universities in studying and implementing these methods.

Then, in 1963, I had the good fortune to enter the aerospace industry for a brief period and to meet and begin joint work with Gilbert Best, who had been charged with the responsibility of developing a large general-purpose finite-element code for use in aircraft structural analysis. Only the two of us worked on the project, but by fall 1963 we had produced some quite general results and one of the early working codes on finite elements. This code had features in it that were not fully duplicated for more than a decade. I still have copies of our elaborate report on that work [10].

It was Best who demonstrated to me the strength and versatility of the method. In our work we developed mixed methods, assumed-stress methods, and hybrid methods; explored algorithms for optimization problems, nonlinear problems, bifurcation, and vibration problems; and did detailed tests on stability and convergence of various methods by numerical experimentation. We developed finite elements for beams, plates, and shells; for composite materials; for three-dimensional problems in elasticity; for thermal analysis; and for linear dynamic analysis. Some of our methods were failures; most were effective and useful. Since convergence properties and criteria were not to come for another decade, our only way to test many of the more complex algorithms was to code them and compute solutions for test problems.

I returned to academia in 1964, and one of my first chores was to develop a graduate course on finite-element methods. At the same time, I taught mathematics and continuum mechanics, and it became clear to me that finite elements and digital computing offered hope of transforming nonlinear continuum mechanics from a qualitative and academic subject into something useful in modern scientific computing and engineering. Toward this end, I began work with graduate students in 1965 that led to successful numerical analyses of problems in finite-strain elasticity (1965, 1966), elastoplasticity (1967), thermoelasticity (1967), thermoviscoelasticity (1969), and incompressible and compressible viscous fluid flow (1968, 1969). These works, many summarized in [49], include early (perhaps the first) uses of Discrete-Kirchhoff elements, incremental elastoplastic algorithms, conjugate-gradient methods for nonlinear finite-element systems, continuation methods, dynamic relaxation schemes, Taylor-Galerkin algorithms (then called "finite-element based Lax-Wendroff schemes"), primitive-variable formulations in incompressible flow, curvilinear elements, and penalty formulations; all these subjects have been resurrected in more recent times and have been studied in far more detail and better style and depth than was possible in the 1960s.

Although my later work, work in the 1970s and 1980s, was influenced by the competent mathematicians (and friends) who developed the subject during the period (Babuška, Ciarlet, Strang, Douglas, Nitsche, and many others), the work and guidance of G. Best was basic to my interest in this subject, and I dedicate this note to him.

5. Acknowledgments

Portions of this paper are excerpts from an article to appear in the *Handbook of Numerical Analysis*, edited by J. L. Lions and P. G. Ciarlet, North Holland Publishing Co., Amsterdam. I am grateful to North Holland for granting permission to use this material in the present volume.

References

[1] J. H. Argyris, "Energy Theorems and Structural Analysis," *Aircr. Eng.* 26 (1954): 347–56, 383–87, 394.

[2] J. H. Argyris, "Energy Theorems and Structural Analysis," *Aircr. Eng.* 27 (1955): 42–58, 80–94, 125–34, 145–58.

[3] J. H. Argyris, "Continua and Discontinua," in *Matrix Methods in Structural Mechanics*, J. S. Prziemiencki, R. M. Bader, W. F. Bozich, J. R. Johnson, and W. J. Mykytow (eds.), AFFDL–TR–66–80, October 26–28, 1965, Wright-Patterson AFB, Ohio (1966): 11–190.

[4] J. P. Aubin, "Behavior of the Error of the Approximate Solutions of Boundary-Value Problems for Linear Elliptic Operators by Galerkin's Method and Finite Differences," *Ann. Scuola Norm. Pisa*, 3 21 (1967): 599–637.

[5] A. K. Aziz (ed.), *The Mathematical Foundations of the Finite Element Method with Applications to Partial Differential Equations* (New York: Academic Press, 1972).

[6] I. Babuška, "Error Bounds for the Finite Element Method," *Numer. Math.* 16 (1971): 322–33.

[7] I. Babuška, "Finite Element Methods for Domains with Corners," *Computing* 6 (1976): 264–73.

[8] I. Babuška and A. K. Aziz, "Survey Lectures on the Mathematical Foundation of the Finite Element Method" in *The Mathematical Foundation of the Finite Element Method with Applications to Partial Differential Equations*, A. K. Aziz (ed.) (New York: Academic Press, 1972), 5–359.

[9] I. Babuška, J. T. Oden, and J. K. Lee, "Mixed-Hybrid Finite Element Approximations of Second-Order Elliptic Boundary-Value Problems," *Comput. Methods Appl. Mech. Engrg.* 11 (1977): 175–206.

[10] G. Best and J. T. Oden, "Stiffness Matrices for Shell-Type Structures," Engineering Research Report No. 233, General Dynamics, Ft. Worth, Texas (1963).

[11] G. Birkhoff, "Piecewise Bicubic Interpolation and Approximation," in *Polygons, Approximations with Special Emphasis on Spline Functions*, I. J. Schoenberg (ed.) (New York: Academic Press, 1969), 85–121.

[12] G. Birkhoff, C. de Boor, M. H. Schultz, and B. Wendroff, "Rayleigh-Ritz Approximation by Piecewise Cubic Polynomials," *SIAM J. Num. Anal.* 3 (1966): 188–203.

[13] G. Birkhoff, M. H. Schultz, and R. S. Varga, "Piecewise Hermite Interpolation in One- and Two-Variables with Applications to Partial Differential Equations," *Numer. Math.* 11 (1968): 232–56.

[14] F. K. Bogner, R. L. Fox, and L. A. Schmit, Jr., "The Generation of Interelement, Compatible Stiffness and Mass Matrices by the Use of Interpolation Formulas," in *Proceedings of the Conference on Matrix Methods in Structural Mechanics*, Przemieniecki et al. (eds.) (1966): 397–444.

[15] J. H. Bramble and M. Zlamal, "Triangular Elements in the Finite Element Method," *Math. Comp.* 24 (1970): 809–20.

[16] F. Brezzi, "On the Existence, Uniqueness, and Approximation of Saddle-Point Problems Arising from Lagrange Multipliers," *Rev. Fran. d'Aut. Inf. Rech. Op.* 8–R2 (1974): 129–51.

[17] J. Cea, "Approximation Variationnelle des problems aux Limites," *Ann. Inst. Fourier (Grenoble)* 14 (1964): 345–444.

[18] P. G. Ciarlet, "An $O(h^2)$ Method for a Non-Smooth Boundary-Value Problem," *Aequationes Math.* 2 (1968): 39–49.

[19] P. G. Ciarlet, *The Finite Element Method for Elliptic Problems* (Amsterdam: North Holland, 1978).

[20] P. G. Ciarlet and P. A. Raviart, "General Lagrange and Hermite Interpolation in R^n with Applications to the Finite Element Method," *Arch. Rational Mech. Anal.* 46 (1972): 177–99.

[21] P. G. Ciarlet and P. A. Raviart, "Interpolation Theory over Curved Elements with Applications to Finite Element Methods," *Comput. Methods Appl. Mech. Engrg.* 1 (1972): 217–49.

[22] P. G. Ciarlet and P. A. Raviart, "The Combined Effect of Curved Boundaries and Numerical Integration in Isoparametric Finite Element Methods" in *The Mathematical Foundations of the Finite Element Method with Applications to Partial Differential Equations*, A. K. Aziz (ed.) (New York: Academic Press, 1972), 409–74.

[23] R. W. Clough, "The Finite Element Method in Plane Stress Analysis," in *Proceedings of the Second ASCE Conference on Electronic Computation* (1960).

[24] R. Courant, "Variational Methods for the Solution of Problems of Equilibrium and Vibration," *Bull. Amer. Math. Soc.* 49 (1943): 1–23.

[25] J. Douglas and T. Dupont, "Galerkin Methods for Parabolic Problems," *SIAM J. Numer. Anal.* 7 (1970): 575–626.

[26] J. Douglas and T. Dupont, "Superconvergence for Galerkin Methods for the Two-Point Boundary Problem via Local Projections," *Numer. Math.* 21 (1973): 220–28.

[27] T. Dupont, "L^2-Estimates for Galerkin Methods for Second-Order Hyperbolic Equations," *SIAM J. Numer. Anal.* 10 (1973): 880–89.

[28] I. Ergatoudis, B. M. Irons, and O. C. Zienkiewicz, "Curved Isoparametric Quadrilateral Finite Elements," *Internat. J. Solids and Structures* 4 (1966): 31–42.

[29] S. R. Falk, "Error Estimates for the Approximation of a Class of Variational Inequalities," *Math. Comp.* 28 (1974): 963–71.

[30] Feng Kang, "A Difference Formulation Based on the Variational Principle," in Chinese, *Appl. Math. and Comput. Math.* 2 (1965): 238–62.

[31] L. R. Herrmann, "A Bending Analysis for Plates" in *Matrix Methods in Structural Mechanics*, Przemieniecki et al. (eds.) (1966), 577.

[32] H. Hrennikoff, "Solutions of Problems in Elasticity by the Framework Method," *J. Appl. Mech.* A (1941): 169–75.

[33] B. Irons, "Engineering Applications of Numerical Integration in Stiffness Methods," *AIAA J.* 4 (1966): 2035–3037.

[34] B. Irons, "A Frontal Solution Program for Finite Element Analysis," *Internat. J. Numer. Methods Engrg.* 2 (1970): 5–32.

[35] B. Irons and A. Razzaque, "Experience with the Patch Test for Convergence of Finite Elements," in *The Mathematical Foundations of the Finite Element Method with Applications to Partial Differential Equations*, A. K. Aziz (ed.) (New York: Academic Press, 1972), 557-87.

[36] M. W. Johnson, Jr., and R. W. McLay, "Convergence of the Finite Element Method in the Theory of Elasticity," *J. Appl. Mech.* E 3, 5 (1968): 274–78.

[37] G. Kron, *Tensor Analysis of Networks* (New York: John Wiley & Sons, 1939).

[38] G. Kron, "A Set of Principles to Interconnect the Solutions of Physical Systems," *J. Appl. Phys.* 24 (1953): 965–80.

[39] G. W. Leibniz, "Leibnizens Mathematische Schriften," C. Gerhardt (ed.), *G. Olms Verlagsbuchhandlung* (1962): 290–93.

[40] S. Levy, "Structural Analysis and Influence Coefficients for Delta Wings," *J. Aeronaut. Sci.* 20 (1953): 449–54.

[41] J. Lions, "Problemes Aux Limites en Theorie des Distributions," *Acta Math.* 94 (1955): 13–153.

[42] D. McHenry, "A Lattice Analogy for the Solution of Plane Stress Problems," *J. Inst. Civ. Eng.* 21 (1943): 59–82.

[43] J. A. Nitsche, "Ein Kriterium für die Quasi-Optimalität des Ritzschen Verfahrens," *Numer. Math.* 11 (1963): 346–48.

[44] J. A. Nitsche, "Lineare Spline-Funktionen und die Methoden von Ritz für Elliptische Randwertprobleme," *Arch. Rational Mech. Anal.* 36 (1970): 348–55.

[45] J. A. Nitsche and A. H. Schatz, "Interior Estimates for Ritz-Galerkin Methods," *Math. Comp.* 28 (1974): 937–58.

[46] J. T. Oden, "Plate Beam Structures" (Stillwater, OK: Dissertation, Oklahoma State University, 1962).

[47] J. T. Oden, "A General Theory of Finite Elements; II. Applications," *Internat. J. Numer. Methods Engrg.* 1 (1969): 247–59.

[48] J. T. Oden, "A Finite Element Analogue of the Navier-Stokes Equations," *J. Engrg. Mech. Div., Proc. ASCE* 96 (1970): 529–34.

[49] J. T. Oden, "Some Contributions to the Mathematical Theory of Mixed Finite Element Approximations," in *Theory and Practice in Finite Element Structural Analysis,* Y. Yamada et al. (ed.) (University of Tokyo Press, 1972), 3–23.

[50] J. T. Oden, *Finite Elements of Nonlinear Continua* (New York: McGraw-Hill, 1976).

[51] J. T. Oden and J. N. Reddy, *An Introduction to the Mathematical Theory of Finite Elements* (New York: Wiley Interscience, 1976).

[52] J. T. Oden and D. Somogyi, "Finite Element Applications in Fluid Dynamics," *J. Engrg. Mech. Div., Proc. ASCE* 95 (1968): 821–26.

[53] L. A. Ogenesjan and L. A. Ruchovec, "Variational-Difference Schemes for Linear Second-Order Elliptic Equations in a Two-Dimensional Region with Piecewise Smooth Boundary," *U. S. S. R. Comput. Math. and Math. Phys.* 8 (1968): 129–52.

[54] L. A. Ogenesjan and L. A. Ruchovec, "Study of the Rate of Convergence of Variational Difference Schemes for Second-Order Elliptic Equations in a Two-Dimensional Field With a Smooth Boundary," *U.S.S.R Comput. Math. and Math. Phys.* 9 (1969): 158–83.

[55] Arantes E. Oliveira, "Theoretical Foundation of the Finite Element Method," *Internat. J. Solids and Structures* 4 (1968): 926–52.

[56] E. Pestel, "Dynamic Stiffness Matrix Formulation by Means of Hermitian Polynomials," in *Matrix Methods in Structural Mechanics*, Przemieniecki et. al. (eds.) (1966), 479–502.

[57] T. H. H. Pian, "Element Stiffness Matrices for Boundary Compatibility and for Prescribed Stresses," in *Matrix Methods in Structural Mechanics*, Przemieniecki et. al. (eds.) (1966): 455–78.

[58] G. Polya, "Sur une Interprétation de la Méthode des Différences Finies qui Peut Fournir des Bornes Supérieures ou Inférieures," *Compt. Rend.* 235 (1952): 995.

[59] J. S. Przemieniecki et. al. (eds.), *Matrix Methods in Structural Mechanics*, Report AFFDL–TR–66–80 (1966).

[60] P. A. Raviart, "Hybrid Methods for Solving 2nd-Order Elliptic Problems," in *Topics in Numerical Analysis*, J. H. H. Miller (ed.) (New York: Academic Press, 1975), 141–55.

[61] P. A. Raviart and J. M. Thomas, "A Mixed Finite Element Method for 2nd-Order Elliptic Problems," in *Proceedings of the Symposium on the Mathematical Aspects of the Finite Element Methods* (1977).

[62] A. H. Schatz and L. B. Wahlbin, "Interior Maximum Norm Estimates for Finite Element Methods," *Math. Comp.* 31 (1977): 414–42.

[63] A. H. Schatz and L. B. Wahlbin, "Maximum Norm Estimates in the Finite Element Method on Polygonal Domains, Part 1," *Math. Comp.* 32 (1978): 73–109.

[64] K. Schellbach, "Probleme der Variationsrechnung," *J. Reine Angew. Math.* 41 (1851): 293–363.

[65] M. H. Schultz, "Rayleigh-Ritz-Galerkin Methods for Multi-dimensional Problems," *SIAM J. Numer. Anal.* 6 (1969): 523–38.

[66] M. H. Schultz, "L^2-Error Bounds for the Rayleigh-Ritz-Galerkin Method," *SIAM J. Numer. Anal.* 8 (1971): 737–48.

[67] G. Strang, "Variational Crimes in the Finite Element Method," in *The Mathematical Foundations of the Finite Element Method with Applications to Partial Differential Equations*, A. K. Aziz (ed.) (New York: Academic Press, 1972).

[68] G. Strang and G. Fix, *An Analysis of the Finite Element Method* (New York: Prentice-Hall, 1973).

[69] J. L. Synge, *The Hypercircle Method in Mathematical Physics* (Cambridge University Press, 1957).

[70] I. C. Taig, "Structural Analysis by the Matrix Displacement Method," *English Electrical Aviation Ltd. Report*, S–O–17 (1961).

[71] M. J. Turner, R. W. Clough, H. C. Martin, and L. J. Topp, "Stiffness and Deflection Analysis of Complex Structures," *J. Aeronaut. Sci.* 23 (1956): 805–23.

[72] R. S. Varga, "Hermite Interpolation-type Ritz Methods for Two-Point Boundary Value Problems," in *Numerical Solution of Partial Differential Equations*, J. H. Bramble (ed.) (New York: Academic Press, 1966).

[73] M. F. Wheeler, "A Priori L^2-Error Estimates for Galerkin Approximations to Parabolic Partial Differential Equations," *SIAM J. Numer. Anal.* 11 (1973): 723–59.

[74] F. Williamson, "A Historical Note on the Finite Element Method," *Internat. J. Numer. Methods. Engr.* 15 (1980): 930–34.

[75] O. C. Zienkiewicz and Y. K. Cheung, *The Finite Element Method in Structural and Continuum Mechanics* (New York: McGraw-Hill, 1967).

[76] M. Zlamal, "On the Finite Element Method," *Numer. Math.* 12 (1968): 394–409.

Conjugacy and Gradients

Magnus R. Hestenes

I would like to describe my experiences in the field of numerical analysis and to illustrate how these experiences influenced me in my studies of mathematics. In particular, I will tell the story of the development of the conjugate-gradient method for solving linear systems. I was one of the originators of this method.

At the invitation of the Mathematical Association of America, John Todd and I wrote a short history of the Institute for Numerical Analysis [11] located on the campus of UCLA. This Institute, called INA, was a section of the National Applied Mathematical Laboratories, which formed the Applied Mathematics Division of the National Bureau of Standards (a part of the Department of Commerce). In this brief history we were concerned mainly with the mathematical aspects of this program. In particular, we considered who participated in the project, what they did, and which Universities they represented. It is not my intention to repeat the material presented in that history, except, perhaps, for some special items of interest.

My specialities in mathematics are variational theory and optimal control theory. My experiences in these fields have greatly influenced my approach to problems in numerical analysis. I shall describe certain aspects of variational theory, which are of interest in themselves and which led to a method of attack on certain computational problems.

I received my doctorate at the University of Chicago in 1932. After remaining at Chicago for a year, I left for Harvard as a National Research Fellow to work with Marston Morse. Inspired by the works of George D. Birkhoff, his mentor, Morse had become famous for his development of the calculus of variations in the large. Early in 1934, Birkhoff invited me to join him in writing a chapter on the calculus of variations. He wished to develop a new approach to the calculus of variations in the large. His idea was simple. It came from the observation that every critical point x of a function $F(x)$ satisfies constraints of the form of

$$F'(x, h) = 0$$

where h is held fast and x is allowed to vary. Here $F'(x, h)$ is the first variation of F, the differential of F. Unfortunately, in the general case, this procedure introduced too many singularities to be effective. However, it was effective in the quadratic case. In this case the condition $F'(x, h) = 0$ is a "conjugacy" condition, although we did not use the term. As a result, I wrote a long paper with Birkhoff on this subject [1], developing these ideas for calculus of variations in the small. I later wrote an extensive paper on the theory of "Quadratic Forms in Hilbert Space with Applications to the calculus of variations" [2]. In this paper the concept of conjugacy played a dominant role. I used the term "Q-orthogonality" instead of the term "conjugacy" in my writings. To see what conjugacy means in this context, may I remark that the extremals, the solutions of the Euler-Lagrange equations, are the elements that are conjugate to those that vanish on the boundary. Thus, I was familiar with the concept and use of conjugacy early in my career.

It is interesting to recall that in 1936, I developed an algorithm for constructing a set of mutually conjugate directions in Euclidean space for the purpose of studying quadric surfaces. I showed my results to Professor Graustein, a geometer at Harvard University. His reaction was that it was too obvious to merit publication. This shows that geometers were well-versed in the concept of conjugacy. It suggests that perhaps hidden in the literature on geometry there is a method for finding the center of an ellipsoid that is equivalent to the method of conjugate gradients.

During the latter years of World War II, I was a member of the Applied Mathematics Group at Columbia University. There I was concerned with the mathematical theory of aerial gunnery. We tested our theory with numerical computations. In one project, L. W. Cohen flew fighter planes on paper, duplicating with remarkable accuracy the results obtained by photography of actual paths of fighter planes flying under certain gunnery rules for attacking bombers. Cohen succeeded where others had failed. He succeeded because he wrote his algorithm in a manner so as to decrease the errors that one encounters in computations.

When World War II ended, I returned to the University of Chicago. Shortly thereafter I accepted a professorship at UCLA. There I was approached by E. Paxson of the Rand Corporation to study the problem of steering a fighter plane so that it reached a prescribed position and direction in minimum time. This was a complicated variational problem involving differential constraints. Such problems had various names, such as the Problem of Bolza, the Problem of Lagrange, or the Problem of Mayer. I found that the classical formulation of these problems did not fit this time-optimal problem in a natural manner. Accordingly, I reformulated the variational problem to make it more easily applicable to this minimum time problem. In doing so I had formulated a variational problem that is now known as an optimal control problem. I translated the known results to fit this new formulation. The results were written up in 1949 as a Rand report and were not published in a standard journal at that time. Later in 1965 I published a book [4] that included the theoretical basis for this time-optimal control problem. Pontryagin, too, was invited by his government to study the problem of aerial combat. This led to his formulation of optimal control theory and differential games. His first necessary condition for an optimal control problem is now called "Pontryagin's Maximum Principle." It is an extension of the standard conditions of Euler, Lagrange, and Weierstrass. He established his results under weaker hypotheses than had been used heretofore. Thus, the study of the theory of aerial combat led to the development of modern theory of optimal control both here and in Russia.

Let me return to the time-optimal problem proposed by Paxson. We obtained the equation of motion for our fighter plane and attempted to solve these equations numerically on a REAC. The REAC was an electrical analog computer with about 3 percent accuracy. We tried to solve our problem as an initial value problem, hoping to obtain the prescribed terminal conditions by a suitable choice of initial conditions. The results were disastrous. It turned out that our equations were unstable in the forward direction. They were also unstable in the backward direction. However, by making many trials, we did obtain some notion of the nature of optimal paths. But this did not give us a sought after "rule of thumb" method for flying a plane in an optimal manner. Because of this experience, I became convinced that we should look for an alternative approach to numerical solutions of variational problems of this type. In my considerations I restricted myself to simple variational problems. In particular, I chose to study the classical problem of finding the surface of revolution of least area having prescribed circular boundary curves. The Euler equations to this problem normally have more than one solution satisfying prescribed boundary conditions. Only one of these solutions is minimizing. I tried two iterative methods, namely Newton's method and an optimal gradient method. Our numerical experiments with these two methods were highly successful. In order to preserve these computations for future use, I wrote a second Rand report in 1949, describing what we did [3]. This report received a wide circulation among engineers, and I received undue credit for devising these methods.

Incidentally, with regard to the gradient method, I had to formulate an adequate definition of the concept of the gradient of an integral. To do so, I introduced an inner product $\langle g, h \rangle$ on the space of variations. The gradient of $F(x)$ at a point x is a variation g such that

$$F'(x, h) = \langle g, h \rangle$$

for all admissible variations h. I found that the inner product normally used was unsatisfactory because elements of the form $x + ag$ were not admissible elements. However, I also found that there was a large class of inner products that were suitable for the problem at hand. These inner products need not be fixed, but can vary with the element x concerned. One such inner product is the inner product $F''(x;g,h)$, induced by the second variation of F. When this inner product is used, our gradient method becomes a version of Newton's method. Thus, Newton's method can be viewed as a gradient method determined by a "preferred" inner product that varies at each step.

I also tried one other method, later called a penalty function method. In the simple case in which we minimize $f(x)$ subject to a constraint $g(x) = 0$, it proceeds as follows. Select a sequence $\{c_n\}$ converging to infinity. Obtain the minimizer x_n of the penalty function

$$F_n = f + c_n g^2$$

Then, under favorable conditions, the sequence $\{x_n\}$ will converge to the minimizer x_0 of f subject to $g = 0$. Moreover, the sequence $\{2c_n g(x_n)\}$ converges to the Lagrange multiplier λ. In theory, this method is excellent and can be used effectively for theoretical purposes. Unfortunately, when I tried to solve a simple problem numerically by this method, I found that it had poor convergence properties owing to roundoff errors, and so I abandoned it for the time being. Besides, for variational problems with differential constraints, I knew that I would need to consider what is now known as relaxed controls and that this would lead to a more complicated theory than I was willing to accept in that time. Later, in about 1969, I was invited to give a talk on computational procedures for solving optimization problems. It occurred to me at that time that a result in the folklore of variational theory could be used for this purpose. This result states that if x_0 minimizes $f(x)$ subject to $g(x) = 0$, then normally there is a multiplier λ and a constant c such that x_0 minimizes the function

$$F(x) = f(x) + \lambda g(x) + cg(x)^2$$

for all x near x_0, even when the constraint $g(x) = 0$ is not satisfied. Usually a relatively small value of c is effective. Having chosen c, a suitable value of the multiplier λ can be found by an iterative procedure. The iteration that we shall use is obtained by observing that the gradient of F is given by the formula

$$F'(x) = f'(x) + [\lambda + 2cg(x)]g'(x)$$

This formula suggests the following iteration:

Select an initial point x_1, an initial multiplier λ_1, and a suitable constant c.

Having obtained x_i and λ_i, find a minimizer x_{i+1} of the function

$$F_i(x) = f(x) + \lambda_i g(x) + cg(x)^2$$

Then set

$$\lambda_{i+1} = \lambda_i + \alpha g(x_{i+1}) \qquad (\text{say } \alpha = 2c)$$

and repeat.

To obtain an initial estimate for x_1 and c, one can begin with the penalty function method. I called this method "a method of multipliers." This algorithm with some modifications proved to be an effective method for solving constrained minimum problems. An equivalent algorithm was also suggested by M. J. D. Powell at about the same time.

Returning to the summer of 1949: At that time I was invited to join the Institute for Numerical Analysis (INA) on a part-time basis. In accepting this invitation, I expected to pursue my studies of numerical methods in variational theory. However, I was diverted by Barkley Rosser, who was the new director of INA. Rosser initiated a program of studying methods for solving linear equations and for finding eigenvalues and eigenvectors of matrices. He organized a seminar on this subject. The principal participants of this seminar were Barkley Rosser, George Forsythe, Cornelius Lanczos, Gertrude Blanch, William Karush, Marvin Stein, and I. Rosser and Forsythe specialized in finding solutions of linear equations. Forsythe, in particular, proceeded to classify known methods for such solutions. Karush, Stein, and I were chiefly responsible for the study of methods for finding eigenvalues and eigenvectors of matrices. Lanczos continued to refine his methods for solving eigenvalue problems. Blanch, who was in charge of numerical computations, acted as an advisor on numerical procedures. Of course, we did not limit ourselves to our specialties and participated actively in all the topics taken up in the seminar.

With regard to the study on solving linear equations, we specialized on iterative methods for solving linear equations. We did so in part because it appeared that they required less high-speed storage than other methods. Besides, we found them interesting. We surveyed the known methods from both a theoretical point of view and a numerical point of view. In preparing the short history of INA [11], I found a manuscript written by Rosser and myself developing a unified theory for a large class of methods. I had forgotten that we had written this article. A summary of the contents of this article is given in [11]. In this paper, we discussed various algorithms for solving a linear equation

$$Ax = h$$

where A is a nonsingular $n \times n$ matrix and h is a prescribed n-dimensional vector. We used the size of the residual

$$r = h - Ax = A(x_0 - x)$$

as a measure of the closeness of x to the solution x_0 of our equation. To measure the size of r, we sometimes used the largest component of r. At other times, with $*$ denoting transpose, we used a function of the form

$$f(x) = \tfrac{1}{2}r^*Kr = \tfrac{1}{2}x^*Bx - k^*x + c$$

where K is a positive definite symmetric matrix and

$$B = A^*KA \qquad k = A^*Kh \qquad c = \tfrac{1}{2}h^*Kh$$

The solution x_0 of $Ax = h$ minimizes f and solves the equation $Bx = k$. When A is a positive definite symmetric matrix, we can choose $K = A^{-1}$. Then $B = A$, $k = h$, and

$$f(x) = \tfrac{1}{2}x^*Ax - h^*x + c$$

where c is an unknown constant that plays no role in our considerations. It should be noted that the minimizer x_0 of $f(x)$ is the center of the ellipsoid, $f(x)$ = constant. Thus, the problem of solving $Ax = h$ is equivalent to that of finding the center of an ellipsoid. We observed further that the minimum point x_2 of $f(x)$ on a line

$$x = x_1 + tp$$

was the midpoint of the chord in which this line intersected the ellipsoid $f(x) = f(x_1)$.

Although it was not immediately obvious, we found that the algorithms that we studied were equivalent to one of the following type

$$x_{i+1} = x_i - H_i(Ax_i - h) = x_i + H_ir_i \tag{1}$$

where r_i is the residual

$$r_i = h - Ax_i$$

From this fact we concluded that if

$$\mu = \limsup_{i \to \infty} \|I - H_iA\| < 1$$

then the sequence $\{x_i\}$ converges linearly to the solution x_0 at the rate μ. In many cases, the matrix H_i need not be constructed explicitly by the algorithm. For example, we can obtain x_{i+1} from x_i by a subroutine of the following type:

Choose m vectors $u_1, u_2, \ldots, u_m$ that span our space and select vectors $v_1, v_2, \ldots, v_m$ such that $d_j = v_j^*Au_j$ is not zero for $j = 1, \ldots, m$. Select $y_1 = x_i$. Then, for $j = 1, \ldots, m$, set

$$y_{j+1} = y_j + d_ju_j \qquad d_j = v_j^*(k - Ay_j)/d_j$$

Finally set $x_{i+1} = y_{m+1}$.

It can be shown that when x_{i+1} is obtained from x_i in this manner, then there is a matrix H_i such that equation (1) holds. In view of this result, the Gauss-Seidel method and a large number of other standard methods can be studied simultaneously by considering an algorithm of the form (1). A discussion of our considerations of this nature can be found in [11]. I omit these considerations here. However, I would like to remark that in most of the numerical cases we considered, convergence was very slow. We were therefore on the lookout for more rapidly convergent algorithms. We also considered the introduction of a relaxation constant β in our algorithm, but did not develop an adequate theory for this case.

One of the algorithms that we tried was a gradient method for minimizing the error function

$$f(x) = \tfrac{1}{2}x^*Ax - h^*x$$

for the case when A is positive definite. The negative gradient of f is the residual $r = h - Ax$. Accordingly, the gradient algorithm is of the form

$$x_{i+1} = x_i + a_i r_i \qquad a_i = |r_i|^2/r_i^*Ar_i$$

where $r_i = h - Ax_i$ and $t = a_i$ is chosen to minimize $f(x_i + tr_i)$. We called this method the optimal gradient method. Forsythe constructed a positive definite 6×6 matrix in a random fashion and proceeded to test the optimal gradient method numerically. He found that the method "bogged down" and that the solution could not be obtained using a reasonable number of steps. Accordingly, he tried two different acceleration techniques. The first one used the relaxed equation

$$x_{i+1} = x_i + \beta a_i r_i$$

where β is some number between 0 and 2. Values of β such as 0.7, 0.8, and 1.2 were effective. Even $\beta = 0.2$ was better than $\beta = 1$. Forsythe also tried the following acceleration scheme suggested by Motzkin. When the algorithm bogged down, he added an additional step of minimizing f along the line through x_{i-2} and x_i to obtain a new estimate x_{i+1}. This method was equally effective, but somewhat more complicated to use. We discovered that Aitken had used the second scheme earlier. Incidentally, this acceleration scheme yields one step of the conjugate-gradient method described in the following section.

Rosser went to Cornell in the fall of 1950 but returned to INA in the summer of 1951 to pursue his studies of solutions of linear equations and to attend a conference on "Solutions of Linear Equations and the Determination of Eigenvalues" to be held at INA in August 1951. In June or July 1951, after almost two years of studying algorithms for solving systems of linear equations, we finally "hit" upon a conjugate-gradient method. I had the privilege of first formulating this new method. However, it was an outgrowth of my discussions with my colleagues at INA. In particular, my conversations with George Forsythe had a great influence on me. During the month of July 1951, I wrote an INA report on this new development. When E. Stiefel arrived at INA in August to attend the conference on solutions of linear equations, he was given a copy of my paper. Shortly thereafter he came to my office and said about the paper, "This is my talk." He too had invented the conjugate-gradient algorithm and had carried out successful experiments using this algorithm. Accordingly, I invited Stiefel to remain at UCLA and INA for one semester so that we could write an extensive paper on this subject. In the meantime, Lanczos observed that the conjugate-gradient method could be derived from his algorithm for finding eigenvalues of matrices. In view of these remarks, we see that there are three persons who are credited for inventing the conjugate-gradient method, namely Stiefel, Lanczos, and myself. However, as remarked earlier, this algorithm was an outgrowth of the program at INA on solutions of linear equations that was originated by Rosser and participated in by various members of INA, such as Forsythe, Karush, Motzkin, Paige, and Stein. Of these researchers, Forsythe was the most active in supplying numerical experiments for the algorithms discussed by the group. It was my privilege to invent the name "conjugate-gradient routine" for the new algorithm we had constructed.

The conjugate-gradient algorithm is based on the following property of ellipsoids:

The midpoints of parallel chords of an $(n - 1)$-dimensional ellipsoid E_{n-1} lie on a $(n - 1)$ plane π_{n-1} passing through the center x_0 of E_{n-1}. The $(n - 1)$ plane π_{n-1} and the vectors in π_{n-1} are said to be conjugate to these chords.

Analytically, an ellipsoid E_{n-1} is the set of points x satisfying an equation of the form

$$f(x) = \tfrac{1}{2}x^*Ax - h^*x = \text{constant} \qquad (A^* = A > 0)$$

The minimizer x_0 of f is the center of E_{n-1} and solves the equation

$$Ax = h$$

Parallel chords of E_{n-1} have a common direction vector p. A midpoint x of one of these chords minimizes f along this chord. It follows that the negative gradient

$$r = h - Ax = A(x_0 - x)$$

at such a midpoint x is orthogonal to p. That is,

$$p^*r = p^*(h - Ax) = p^*A(x_0 - x) = 0$$

or, equivalently,

$$p^*Ax = p^*h$$

This equation represents an $(n-1)$ plane π_{n-1} through the center x_0 of E_{n-1}. Its normal is the vector Ap. Every vector q in π_{n-1} is orthogonal to Ap and is conjugate to p. The relation

$$p^*Aq = 0$$

therefore expresses the conjugacy of two vectors p and q.

Let us apply this result to the two-dimensional case. We seek to find the center of an ellipse. Referring to Figure 1, let x be a point on an ellipse E. Let p be a vector tangent to E at x and let r be an inner normal of E at x. Through the tip y of r, draw a chord uv perpendicular to r. Let $z = y + bp = 1/2(u + v)$ be the midpoint of this chord. Denote the vector joining x to z by p_c. Then $p_c = z - x = r + bp$. The vector p_c is conjugate to p. The midpoint x_c of the chord eminating from x in the direction p_c is the center the ellipse E. The point x_c also minimizes the function

$$f(x) = \tfrac{1}{2}x^*Ax - h^*x \qquad (A^* = A > 0)$$

on this two-dimensional space, where $f(x) = $ constant is an analytical representation of E. The geometric construction of the minimizer x_c of f can be carried out analytically as follows:

Choose a point x and compute $r = h - Ax$. Let p be a vector orthogonal to r. Compute

$$p_c = r + bp \qquad b = -p^*Ar/p^*Ap \qquad (2a)$$
$$x_c = x + ap_c \qquad a = p_c^*Ar/p_c^*Ap_c \qquad (2b)$$

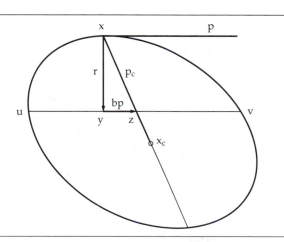

FIGURE 1.
Two-dimensional case.

Methods

The point x_c minimizes $f(x)$ on our 2-plane.

This result leads us to the conjugate-gradient routine.

We shall describe the conjugate-gradient algorithm (cg-algorithm) for solving the equation

$$Ax = h$$

where A is a positive definite symmetric matrix. This is the formulation given independently by Stiefel and Hestenes. It proceeds as follows.

Cg-algorithm I

Initial step. Select a point x_1 and compute

$$p_1 = r_1 = h - Ax_1 \tag{3a}$$

$$c_1 = p_1^* r_1 \qquad d_1 = p_1^* A p_1 \qquad a_1 = c_1/d_1 \tag{3b}$$

$$x_2 = x_1 + a_1 p_1 \qquad r_2 = h - Ax_2 = r_1 - a_1 A p_1 \tag{3c}$$

Iterative steps. Having obtained $p_{i-1}, d_{i-1}, x_i,$ and r_i compute

$$p_i = r_i + b_{i-1}p_{i-1} \quad \text{with} \quad b_{i-1} = -p_{i-1}^* A r_i / d_{i-1} \tag{3d}$$

$$c_i = p_i^* r_i \qquad d_i = p_i^* A p_i \qquad a_i = c_i/d_i \tag{3e}$$

$$x_{i+1} = x_i + a_i p_i \qquad r_{i+1} = h - Ax_{i+1} = r_i - a_i A p_i \tag{3f}$$

Terminate when $r_{m+1} = 0$. Then $x_0 = x_{m+1}$ solves $Ax = h$.

In this algorithm the length of the vector p_i is not important. We can therefore introduce, if we wish, a scale factor σ_i for p_i. When this is done our formulas for these vectors take the form

$$p_i = \sigma_i r_i \qquad p_{i+1} = \sigma_{i+1}(r_{i+1} + b_i p_i)$$

The scaling $\sigma_i = 1$, $\sigma_{i+1} = (1 + b_i)^{-1}$ is particularly useful because then $p_{i+1} = h - Ay_{i+1}$ at a point y_{i+1} on the line segment joining x_i to x_{i+1}. Alternatively, we can use generalized gradients in which we have the formulas

$$p_1 = Hr_1 \qquad p_{i+1} = Hr_{i+1} + b_i p_i \qquad b_i = -p_i^* H r_{i+1}/d_i$$

where H is a positive definite symmetric matrix. When these equations are used, we call our algorithm a generalized cg-algorithm. A discussion of these and other variants of the cg-algorithm can be found in my book [10].

The conjugate-gradient algorithm can be described as a minimization procedure of $f(x)$ on 2-planes, except for the initial step. In the first step we minimize $f(x)$ in the direction of steepest descent. Thereafter, we minimize $f(x)$ successively on 2-planes $\pi_1, \pi_2, \ldots$. The 2-plane π_{i-1} is determined by the points $x_{i-1}, x_i, x_i + r_i$, where r_i is the negative gradient of $f(x)$. The next 2-plane π_i is obtained from π_{i-1} by a $90°$

rotation about the line $x_i x_{i+1}$ in the 3-space determined by the points x_{i-1}, x_i, x_{i+1}, and $x_{i+1} + r_{i+1}$ as indicated schematically in Figure 2. Thus, after initialization, a cg-algorithm consists of a minimization of $f(x)$ on a 2-plane followed by a suitable $90°$ rotation of this 2-plane. The minimization of $f(x)$ in the 2-plane π_{i-1} described earlier can be carried out by the given conjugate algorithm or equivalently by the following two minimizations along lines:

(a) Obtain the minimizer z_{i+1} of $f(x)$ on the line $x = x_i + sr_i$.

(b) Then, obtain the minimizer x_{i+1} of $f(x)$ on the line through x_{i-1} and z_{i+1}.

It is also of interest to note that the conjugate-gradient algorithm can be put in the form (1) with H_i replaced by $a_i H_i$. We then have the iteration

$$x_{i+1} = x_i + a_i H_i r_i \qquad r_i = h - Ax_i$$

where H_i is a positive definite symmetric matrix. We adjoin to this an updating procedure for the matrix H_i. It has the property that $H_{n+1} = A^{-1}$. This form of the conjugate-gradient algorithm is due to Davidon, who fashioned it so as to be applicable to nonlinear equations. It was modified later by Fletcher and Powell. It is now called the Davidon-Fletcher-Powell method, or the variable metric method. There are several versions of this algorithm.

In the application of the cg-algorithm, it is often desirable to precondition the matrix A before applying the cg-algorithm. Also, the cg-algorithm is sometimes used in conjunction with other algorithms for solving linear equations.

FIGURE 2.
Minimization on
2-planes.

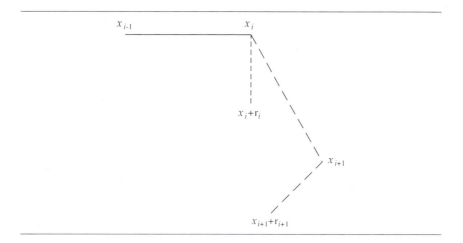

Cg-algorithm I has within it an algorithm for computing the characteristic polynomial of A. One needs only replace A by λ. This algorithm is equivalent to one developed earlier by Lanczos. It follows that the algorithm of Lanczos for finding eigenvalues implicitly contains the cg-algorithm, although none of us recognized this fact in the seminar we conducted. When Lanczos became aware of this feature of his algorithm, he formulated an alternative version of the cg-algorithm which he called a "Method of Minimized Iterations." The connections between his algorithm and the original cg-algorithm can be found in [11].

The cg-algorithm has some useful properties. At each step, the value of the error function $f(x)$ is diminished. So also is the distance of our estimate x_i from the solution x_0. This latter property may fail when generalized gradients are used. If A has multiple eigenvalues, the algorithm will terminate in fewer than n steps. It follows that if A has clustered eigenvalues, a good estimate of the solution is obtained early. Discussions of these and other properties of the cg-algorithm can be found in [8] and [10]. We also discussed the problem of finding least-square solutions for a general equation $Ax = h$, in which A may be nonsymmetric and singular. There is a vast literature on cg-algorithms and Lanczos' algorithms. References can be found in [8] and [12].

As I remarked earlier, in our seminar I was responsible for studies of methods for obtaining eigenvalues of a matrix A. We developed a gradient method for finding the eigenvalues of a symmetric matrix. It turned out that this method could be viewed as a generalization of the power method. Of course, we studied the power method and the inverse power method. We also considered the Jacobi method, but we did not have the computing facilities for a serious study of this method numerically. In addition, we considered the problem of finding singular values of matrices. Our studies complemented the studies of Lanczos for finding eigenvalues of matrices.

References

The following papers and books of mine are referred to in the text. Further references can be found in these papers and books.

[1] With G. D. Birkhoff, "Natural Isoperimetric Conditions in the Calculus of Variations," *Duke Math. J.* 1 (1935): 198–226.

[2] "Applications of the Theory of Quadratic Forms to the Calculus of Variations," *Pacific J. Math.* 1 (1951): 525–81.

[3] "A General Problem in the Calculus of Variations with Applications to the Paths of Least Time," The RAND Corporation, research memorandum (1949).

[4] *Calculus of Variations and Optimal Control Theory* (New York: John Wiley & Sons, 1966).

[5] "Numerical Methods for Obtaining Solutions of Fixed Endpoint Problems in the Calculus of Variations," The RAND Corporation, research memorandum 102 (1949).

[6] "Multiplier and Gradient Methods," *J. Optim. Theory Appl.* 4 (1969): 303–20.

[7] "Iterative Methods for Solving Linear Equations." This was my original paper on the conjugate-gradient method. It appeared as NAML Report 52–9 (1951). It was later published as a historical paper in *J. of Optim. Theory Appl.* 11 (1973): 323–34.

[8] With E. Stiefel, "Method of Conjugate Gradients for Solving Linear Systems," *J. Res. Nat. Bur. Standards* 49 (1952): 409–38.

[9] "The Conjugate Gradient Method for Solving Linear Systems," in J. H. Curtiss (ed.), *Proc. Sympos. in Appl. Math.,* 6 (1956).

[10] *Conjugate Direction Methods in Optimization* (New York: Springer-Verlag, 1980).

[11] With J. Todd, *NBS INA, The Institute for Numerical Analysis, UCLA 1947–1954*, U.S. National Bureau of Standards Special Publication, (Washington, DC: Mathematical Association of America, 1989).

The following work was also cited in the text.

[12] G. H. Golub and D. P. O'Leary, "Some History of the Conjugate Gradient and Lanczos Methods," *SIAM Rev.* 31 (1989): 50–100.

A Historical Review of Iterative Methods

David M. Young

1. Introduction

Originally, as suggested by the title, it was intended that this paper would give a broad historical review of iterative methods. However, it soon became apparent that in the available time and space it would be necessary to focus on a much narrower topic, namely, the history of the development of the successive overrelaxation method (SOR method) and of polynomial acceleration techniques for speeding up the convergence of basic iterative methods.

To begin the discussion, a brief summary of the highlights of the SOR theory will be given in Section 2. This will be followed in Section 3 by a description, from my perspective as a graduate student at Harvard working under the direction of Garrett Birkhoff, of the development and analysis of the SOR method. Section 4 is devoted to polynomial acceleration techniques including Richardson's method, Chebyshev acceleration, and second-degree methods. The close relation which sometimes holds between these methods and certain forms of the SOR method is described. This in some sense "rounds out" the theory of both types of methods.

2. Review of SOR Theory

In this section we review some of the highlights of the theory of the SOR method. For a more complete coverage of the SOR theory see [24].

Let us consider the problem of solving the linear system

$$Au = b \tag{1}$$

where A is a given real nonsingular $N \times N$ matrix and b is a given column vector. We assume that the diagonal elements of A do not vanish. Letting D be the diagonal matrix whose diagonal elements are the same as those of A, we can rewrite (1) in the form

$$u = Bu + c$$

where

$$\begin{cases} B = I - D^{-1}A \\ c = D^{-1}b \end{cases}$$

FIGURE 1.
Mesh for equation
(2).

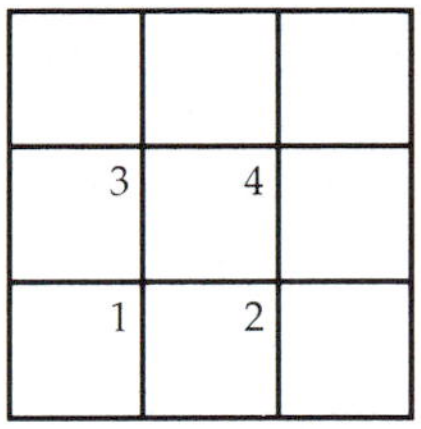

The Jacobi method is defined by

$$u^{(n+1)} = Bu^{(n)} + c$$

To define the successive overrelaxation method (SOR method) we define the strictly lower triangular matrix L and the strictly upper triangular matrix U, such that $B = L + U$. The SOR method is defined by

$$u^{(n+1)} = \omega\{Lu^{(n+1)} + Uu^{(n)} + c\} + (1 - \omega)u^{(n)}$$

or, equivalently by

$$u^{(n+1)} = L_\omega u^{(n)} + k_\omega$$

where

$$k_\omega = \omega(I - \omega L)^{-1}c$$
$$L_\omega = (I - \omega L)^{-1}[\omega U + (1 - \omega)I]$$

The main result of the SOR theory is a relation between the eigenvalues $\{\lambda_i\}$ of L_ω and the eigenvalues $\{\mu_i\}$ of B. This relation holds if A is consistently ordered (CO). We give a definition of a CO matrix in terms of graph theory. To do this, we construct an *undirected graph* of A. This graph consists of points $P_1, P_2, \ldots, P_N$, where N is the order of A, and edges $\overline{P_iP_j}$. The edge $\overline{P_iP_j}$, which is a line joining P_i and P_j, belongs to the graph if $a_{i,j} \neq 0$ or $a_{j,i} \neq 0$.

A matrix is said to have *Property A* if every simple closed path has an even number of edges. A matrix is CO if for every simple closed path, there are as many edges $\overline{P_iP_j}$ with $i < j$ as there are with $i > j$. It can be shown that for any matrix with Property A, we can permute the rows and corresponding columns of A to obtain a CO matrix. Evidently, if A is CO, then A has Property A.

As an example, consider the model problem involving Poisson's equation

$$u_{xx} + u_{yy} = -1 \tag{2}$$

on the unit square $[0, 1] \times [0, 1]$ with zero boundary values. Using the standard 5-point difference equation with $h = 1/3$, we get the mesh

FIGURE 2.
Graph for 4 by 4
matrix.

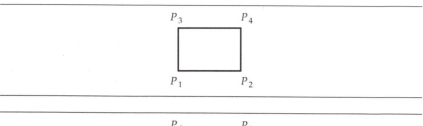

FIGURE 3.
Graph with red-black
ordering.

in Figure 1 and, with the indicated ordering of the mesh points, the linear system

$$\begin{bmatrix} 4 & -1 & -1 & 0 \\ -1 & 4 & 0 & -1 \\ -1 & 0 & 4 & -1 \\ 0 & -1 & -1 & 4 \end{bmatrix} \begin{bmatrix} u_1 \\ u_2 \\ u_3 \\ u_4 \end{bmatrix} = \begin{bmatrix} 1/9 \\ 1/9 \\ 1/9 \\ 1/9 \end{bmatrix}$$

In this example the matrix has Property A and is consistently ordered, as seen from its graph (shown in Figure 2). With the "red-black" ordering, we obtain the graph shown in Figure 3, and the matrix is CO. However, the matrix corresponding to the "to-and-fro" ordering has property A but is not CO, as is seen from its graph (shown in Figure 4). Finally we note that for the matrix

$$A = \begin{bmatrix} 1 & 1 & 1 \\ 1 & 1 & 1 \\ 1 & 1 & 1 \end{bmatrix}$$

we obtain the graph shown in Figure 5. This matrix does not have Property A.

The key eigenvalue relation for the SOR theory is given by

$$\lambda + \omega - 1 = \omega \mu_\backslash \overline{\lambda} \tag{3}$$

Here λ is an eigenvalue of L_ω, and μ is an eigenvalue of B. If A is also symmetric and positive definite (SPD), then a bound on the spectral

FIGURE 4.
Graph for to-and-
fro ordering.

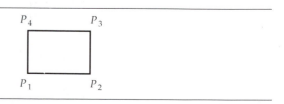

FIGURE 5.
Graph for 3 by 3 matrix.

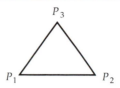

radius $S(L_\omega)$ can be found by solving (3) for each eigenvalue μ of B. (Actually, the eigenvalues of B are real, $S(B) < 1$, and the largest value of $|\lambda|$ corresponds to the eigenvalue $S(B)$ of B.) We can minimize $S(L_\omega)$ by letting $\omega = \omega_b$, where

$$\omega_b = \frac{2}{1 + \sqrt{1 - S(B)^2}}$$

The value of $S(L_{\omega_b})$ is given by

$$S(L_{\omega_b}) = \omega_b - 1 = r$$

For the preceding model problem, we have $S(B) = \cos(\pi h) \sim 1 - \frac{1}{2}\pi^2 h^2$ and

$$\omega_b = \frac{2}{1 - \sin(\pi h)} \qquad S(L_{\omega_b}) = \frac{1 - \sin(\pi h)}{1 + \sin(\pi h)} \sim 1 - 2\pi h$$

The number of iterations needed for convergence with the Jacobi method is $O(h^{-2})$; with the SOR method with $\omega = \omega_b$, it is $O(h^{-1})$. Thus, there is an order-of-magnitude improvement.

Suppose now that A is a "red-black" matrix of the form

$$A = \begin{bmatrix} D_R & H \\ K & D_B \end{bmatrix}$$

where D_R and D_B are square diagonal matrices. It can be shown that

$$\|L_{\omega_b}^n\|_{D^{1/2}} = r^n\{n(r^{1/2} + r^{-1/2}) + [n^2(r^{1/2} + r^{-1/2})^2 + 1]^{1/2}\} \qquad (4)$$
$$\approx 5nr^n$$

where $r = \omega_b - 1$. Normally one would expect r^n instead of $5nr^n$. The presence of the factor of n slows the convergence of the SOR method somewhat and is caused by the existence of a principal vector of grade 2 for L_{ω_b} for the eigenvalue r. The derivation of (4) was made possible by the availability of formulas for the eigenvectors and principal vectors of L_{ω_b} in terms of the eigenvectors of B; see [24].

3. Early Work on the SOR Method

In 1948, when I was a graduate student at Harvard in search of a thesis topic, I sought advice from Garrett Birkhoff. I had originally thought

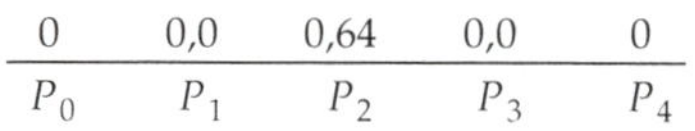

Methods

FIGURE 6.
Mesh for one-
dimensional
problem.

0	0,0	0,64	0,0	0
P_0	P_1	P_2	P_3	P_4

that I might work on Lie groups, but Birkhoff suggested that instead I work on "relaxation methods." He gave me several references, including the book by Sir Richard Southwell [16] and the report by Shortley, Weller, and Fried [14].

3.1. RELAXATION METHODS

I found the book by Southwell rather hard to understand, but after studying it and some other papers, I was able to get some idea what relaxation methods were all about. Actually, the term "relaxation methods" in the broad sense referred to a procedure for obtaining an approximate numerical solution to a problem involving a partial differential equation, usually elliptic. This procedure includes both the replacement of the given problem by a discretized problem involving a partial difference equation and also the solution of the discretized problem as a system of linear algebraic equations. In the narrower sense of the term, and the sense in which I believe it is now understood, "relaxation methods" simply refer to an iteration procedure for solving a system of linear algebraic equations.

I will now give my perception of relaxation methods. Consider the problem of solving the linear system

$$\begin{bmatrix} 2 & -1 & 0 \\ -1 & 2 & -1 \\ 0 & -1 & 2 \end{bmatrix} \begin{bmatrix} u_1 \\ u_2 \\ u_3 \end{bmatrix} = \begin{bmatrix} 0 \\ 64 \\ 0 \end{bmatrix}$$

We relate this to a one-dimensional problem involving 5 mesh points with 3 interior points as indicated in Figure 6. Letting the boundary values and the initial solution guesses be zero, compute the residuals $r_i = (b - Au)_i$ for each interior point, obtaining $r_1 = 0$, $r_2 = 64$, $r_3 = 0$. Mark the initial guesses to the left of each interior point and the initial residuals to the right.

We now are ready to carry out the relaxation process. Increments are indicated to the left of each point, and cumulative residuals are shown to the right. In the example shown in Figure 7, on Step 1 we add an increment of 32 to u_2, reducing r_2 to 0 but increasing r_1 and r_3 to 32. On Step 2 we add an increment of 16 to u_1, reducing r_1 to 0 but increasing r_2 to 32. The process can be continued until all r_i are negligible. At that point we accumulate the increments and get final values of the u_i. Then comes the heartbreak step—checking whether the actual residuals based on the u_i are correct! If there is an

FIGURE 7.
Relaxation process—
no overrelaxation.

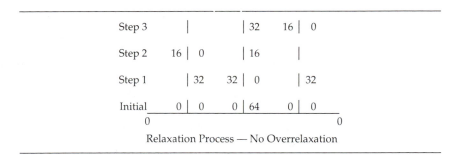

```
Step 3      |               | 32    16 | 0

Step 2   16 | 0            | 16         |

Step 1      | 32    32 | 0            | 32

Initial      0 | 0      0 | 64      0 | 0
          0                                    0
```
Relaxation Process — No Overrelaxation

error, it probably means that all the work to date has been wasted. I must confess that this happened all too frequently when I tried to use relaxation methods.

The convergence of the relaxation process can often be sped up by "overrelaxing." We suppose we overrelax at u_2 by 50 percent but do not overrelax at u_1 and u_3. We get the results shown in Figure 8.

Note that in some sense, the residuals tend to cancel out. After three steps we are much better off than we were when no overrelaxation was used.

3.2. SYSTEMATIC RELAXATION PROCEDURES

Partly because of my lack of success in getting the relaxation process to converge before the occurrence of numerical errors, I was interested in the possibility of more systematic procedures that could be adapted to the then-emerging high-speed computers. The paper "Numerical Solution of Laplace's and Poisson's Equations" [14] was concerned with the Liebmann method [10], an iterative method for solving the discrete analogue of Laplace's equation. The Liebmann method is a special case of the Gauss-Seidel method. The method can be regarded as a systematic form of relaxation in which one chooses a fixed ordering of the equations and relaxes the residuals (without overrelaxation) one at a time, repeatedly sweeping through the region. The same is

FIGURE 8.
Relaxation process
with overrelaxation.

```
Step 3      |               | 16    24 | 0

Step 2   24 | 0            | -8         |

Step 1      | 48    48 | -32         | 48

Initial      0 | 0      0 | 64      0 | 0
          0                                    0
```
Relaxation Process With Overrelaxation

done in the SOR method, except that one overrelaxes at each step by the factor ω.

The paper [14] gave an analysis of the convergence properties of the Liebmann method in terms of the eigenvalues and eigenvectors of certain matrices. There was also a discussion of the role of principal vectors of the iterative matrix that were not eigenvectors. Several very interesting conjectures were presented that stimulated my interest. Besides this, estimates for the rate of convergence of the Liebmann method were given.

Not too long after I began my work, Sir Richard Southwell visited Birkhoff at Harvard. One day when he, Birkhoff, and I were together, I told him what I was trying to do. As near as I can recall, his words were, "Any attempt to mechanize relaxation methods would be a waste of time." This was somewhat discouraging, but my propensity for making numerical errors was so strong that I knew that I would never be able to solve significant problems except by machines. Thus, though discouraged, I continued to work.

3.3. RICHARDSON'S METHOD

Besides the Liebmann method, I also studied a method of L. R. Richardson [12], which can be written in the form

$$u^{(n+1)} = u^{(n)} + \gamma_{n+1}(b - Au^{(n)}) \tag{5}$$

Here the parameters γ_1, γ_2, ... are to be chosen to speed up the convergence. One approach for choosing the $\{\gamma_i\}$ would be to choose an integer m and use the parameters in a cyclic order $\gamma_1, \gamma_2, \ldots, \gamma_m, \gamma_1, \gamma_2, \ldots$. If A is SPD, then the problem of choosing the best values of the $\{\gamma_i\}$ is equivalent to that of minimizing Δ where

$$\Delta = \max \prod_{i=1}^{m} |1 - \gamma_i \nu|$$

with the maximum being taken over the interval $m(A) \le \nu \le M(A)$. Here $m(A)$ and $M(A)$ are the smallest and largest eigenvalues of A, respectively. It is now well-known that the optimum values of the $\{\gamma_i\}$ can be found by the use of Chebyshev polynomials; this is discussed in Section 4. Unfortunately, I was not acquainted with Chebyshev polynomials, nor was I able to find "good" $\{\gamma_i\}$ that would have resulted in substantially more rapid convergence than the Liebmann method.

Besides considering the Liebmann method, I also considered a variant of Richardson's method where $\gamma_1 = \gamma_2 = \cdots = \gamma$ for some fixed γ and where new values are used as soon as available. I called this method the "Richardson-Liebmann method." If $a_{11} = a_{22} = \cdots = a_{N,N} = c$, and if $\gamma = \omega/c$, then the Richardson-Liebmann method reduces to the SOR method with relaxation factor ω.

A key breakthrough was the observation that for certain small linear systems derived from the model problem, the eigenvalues of the Gauss-Seidel method are the squares of those of the Jacobi method. A proof was then developed for a general region, assuming that the mesh points were numbered in a "consistent" ordering. The relation was also found to be true for more general elliptic equations. The same methods were used to show that a relation could also be obtained between the eigenvalues of the SOR method and the eigenvalues of the Jacobi method.

Garrett Birkhoff had previously called my attention to a paper of Hilda Geiringer [4]. This paper was concerned with iterative methods for solving general linear systems—not merely those arising from the solution of partial differential equations. This more general point of view motivated an attempt to define as general a class of matrices as possible, so that the basic SOR eigenvalue relation holds. As a result, the concepts of consistently ordered matrices and matrices with Property A were developed.

Another paper that proved to be most useful to me was that of Temple [17]. In this paper, it was shown that the problem of solving the linear system $Au = b$ with A SPD was the same as that of minimizing the quadratic for $Q(u) = \frac{1}{2}(u, Au) - (b, u)$. This quadratic form was used to show that for many problems, the spectral radius $S(B)$ of the Jacobi method is a monotone function of the size of the region. This is often useful in estimating the optimum value of ω for a nonrectangular region.

In 1949, a paper by Snyder and Livingston appeared in *Mathematical Tables and Other Aids to Computation* (MTAC), one of the few outlets for numerical analysis research results at that time. This paper described a procedure written in Univac machine language for solving Laplace's equation on a rectangle using the Liebmann method. I modified the program to handle Richardson's method and the Richardson-Liebmann method. A couple of years later, when I went to the Aberdeen Proving Ground, I was finally able to collaborate in writing a computer program based on the SOR method [28]. It was truly exciting to see the machine carry out the iterative process and also to see that the observed convergence properties of the SOR method were close to those predicted by the SOR theory.

Garrett Birkhoff was extremely helpful to me in my research efforts, especially in providing guidance and encouragement, pointing out references, and, of course, reading numerous drafts of the thesis. The name "successive overrelaxation method" was suggested by him and I believe it was an excellent choice.

After leaving Harvard I often returned during summers to work with Birkhoff and, on occasion, with Dick Varga, Bob Lynch, and others. Other years we would often work at the Argonne National Laboratory.

I would like to recall one anecdote. As mentioned earlier, when the optimum value of ω is used with the SOR method, there is a principal vector of grade 2 associated with the largest eigenvalue. This slows the convergence. I was able to actually find the principal vector and use it to obtain a bound on the 2-norm of the error as a function of the iteration number n. However, I was not able to find such a bound for the ∞-norm. I was afraid that when I mentioned this to Birkhoff, he would insist that I find a bound for the ∞-norm. I was also concerned that if he were to decide this, it might not be too easy to convince him to change his mind. However, when I saw him, I didn't explain the situation very well. He may have thought I was arguing *for* the ∞-norm. In any case, he appeared to be somewhat irritated and told me in no uncertain terms that the ∞-norm was old-fashioned and that I definitely should use the 2-norm. I made a silent sigh of relief and did not mention the subject again.

Almost simultaneous with the completion of my thesis was the appearance of the paper by Stanley Frankel [3] in MTAC (now *Mathematics of Computation* (MOC)). Frankel carried out a complete analysis of the SOR method, which he referred to as the "extrapolated Liebmann method," for the Laplace equation on the rectangle. He also gave an analysis of the second-order Richardson method—see the discussion in Section 4.

I had considerable difficulty in getting my thesis [20] published. This was due in part to the scarcity of periodicals that would even consider numerical analysis papers. Another reason was the difficulty I had in condensing it. It was very painful to be required to throw out some of the results that I thought were interesting.

The original thesis was 150 pages long. (Incidentally, because photocopying was unknown, all formulas had to be filled in by hand on all three copies.) By May 1951, the paper had been condensed to 75 pages and submitted to the *Transactions of the American Mathematical Society*. The referee, Hilda Geiringer, correctly pointed out that the paper was "far from ready for publication." She made a number of very useful criticisms and suggestions. After much agony and discarding of material, the paper was reduced to 15 pages and resubmitted. Some time later, I was told that I had cut out too much and that some expansion was needed to make the paper intelligible. A final iteration increased the length to 20 pages, and the paper [21] finally appeared in 1954—four years after the thesis was written. It can truly be said that without Garrett Birkhoff's continued interest and encouragement, the paper would never have seen the light of day!

4. Polynomial Acceleration

In this section we give a brief history of polynomial acceleration procedures for speeding up the convergence of certain basic iterative methods. By a *basic iterative method* we mean a one-step method of the form

$$u^{(n+1)} = Gu^{(n)} + k \tag{6}$$

where for some nonsingular matrix Q we have $G = I - Q^{-1}A$ and $k = Q^{-1}b$. Examples of basic iterative methods are the Richardson basic iterative method, in which $Q = I$, and the Jacobi method, in which $Q = D$. We assume throughout this discussion that $I - G$ is similar to an SPD matrix and, hence, that all eigenvalues of G are real and less than unity.

A procedure for accelerating the convergence of the basic iterative method (6) is a *polynomial acceleration procedure* if for some sequence of polynomials $P_0(x)$, $P_1(x)$, . . . , $P_n(x)$, . . . such that $P_n(1) = 1$ for all n, we have

$$u^{(n)} - \bar{u} = P_n(G)(u^{(0)} - \bar{u}) \tag{7}$$

Here $\bar{u}$ is the true solution of (1). The acceleration is linear if $P_0(x)$, $P_1(x)$, . . . do not depend on $u^{(0)}$, $u^{(1)}$, ... Richardson's method, discussed in Section 3, is a polynomial acceleration procedure for the Richardson basic iterative method

$$u^{(n+1)} = (I - A)u^{(n)} + b \tag{8}$$

Given a set of polynomials $P_0(x)$, $P_1(x)$, . . . such that $P_n(1) = 1$ for all n, we can easily show from (7) that

$$u^{(n)} = u^{(0)} + Q_{n-1}(G)\delta^{(0)}$$

where

$$\delta^{(0)} = Gu^{(0)} + k - u^{(0)} \quad \text{and} \quad Q_{n-1}(x) = (x - 1)^{-1}(P_n(x) - 1)$$

We can compute $u^{(1)}$, $u^{(2)}$, . . . given $u^{(0)}$ if we are given the coefficients $\{\alpha_{n,k}\}$ of the $\{P_n(x)\}$. Also, if we are given the roots of the $\{P_n(x)\}$ for each, we can compute $u^{(1)}$, $u^{(2)}$, . . . by a variable extrapolation procedure similar to Richardson's method (5). However, if the polynomials $\{P_n(x)\}$ satisfy a recurrence relation, it is often best to use a related recurrence relation for the $\{u^{(n)}\}$.

The "optimum" polynomials $\{P_n(G)\}$ are scaled Chebyshev polynomials and can be shown to satisfy a three-term recurrence relation [1,6,18]. We can use this relation to derive the following form [7]:

$$u^{(n+1)} = \rho_{n+1}\{\gamma(Gu^{(n)} + k) + (1 - \gamma)u^{(n)}\} + (1 - \rho_{n+1})u^{(n-1)} \tag{9}$$

where γ, ρ_1, ρ_2, . . . are given functions of the smallest eigenvalue and the largest eigenvalue of G. We say that (9) defines a (nonstationary) *second-degree procedure*.

Frankel [3] considered a procedure for accelerating the convergence of the Richardson basic iterative method (8). This procedure, which he called the "second-order Richardson method," can be regarded as a *stationary second-degree method* applied to the basic iterative method. By a stationary second-degree method applied to the basic iterative method (6), we mean a method of the form

$$u^{(1)} = \hat{\gamma}(Gu^{(0)} + k) + (1 - \hat{\gamma})u^{(0)}$$

$$u^{(n+1)} = \rho\{\gamma(Gu^{(n)} + k) + (1 - \gamma)u^{(n)}\} + (1 - \hat{\gamma})u^{(n-1)} \tag{10}$$

$$n = 1, 2, \ldots$$

where $\hat{\gamma}$, ρ, and γ are fixed. It can be shown that for any choice of $\hat{\gamma}$, the optimum values of ρ and γ are related to the optimum values of γ and ρ_1, ρ_2, ... for the Chebyshev procedure (9). Thus, γ is the same for both cases, and $\rho_\infty = \lim_{n\to\infty} \rho_n$. Moreover, the asymptotic convergence rate is the same for (10) as it is for (9). These results are given by Frankel [3] for Richardson's method. For the more general case see [5,6,8,25,27].

In some cases there is a close relation between second-degree methods applied to the Jacobi method and certain generalizations of the SOR method. Thus, let us assume that the linear system (1) is "red-black," that is, that it can be written in the form

$$\begin{bmatrix} D_R & H \\ K & D_B \end{bmatrix} \begin{bmatrix} u_R \\ u_B \end{bmatrix} = \begin{bmatrix} b_R \\ b_B \end{bmatrix}$$

where D_R and D_B are square diagonal matrices. We refer to the equations corresponding to D_R and D_B as the "red" equations and the "black" equations, respectively. The modified SOR method (MSOR method) involves using the SOR method with relaxation factors ω_1, ω_1', ω_2, ω_2', ... where ω_1 is used for the red equations on the first iteration, ω_1' is used for the black equations on the first iteration, and so on.

Frequently-used choices of the $\{\omega_1\}$ and $\{\omega_i'\}$ for the MSOR method (see [24, Chapter 10]) are the following:

(1) *The ordinary SOR method:*

$$\omega_1 = \omega_1' = \omega_2 = \omega_2' = \cdots = \omega_b \qquad \text{where} \qquad \omega_b = \frac{2}{1 + \sqrt{1 - S(B)^2}}$$

(2) *The Golub method [5]:*

$$\omega_1 = 1, \omega_1' = \omega_2 = \omega_2' = \cdots = \omega_b$$

(3) *The Cyclic Chebyshev Semi-Iterative Method (see [6,19]):*

$$\omega_1 = 1 \qquad \omega_1' = 2(2 - S(B)^2)^{-1}$$

$$\omega_{k+1} = \left(1 - \frac{S(B)^2}{4}\omega_k'\right)^{-1} \qquad \omega_{k+1}' = \left(1 - \frac{S(B)^2}{4}\omega_{k+1}\right)^{-1}$$

$$(k = 1, 2, \dots)$$

If the second degree methods (9) and (10) are applied to the Jacobi method, one obtains the sequence shown in Figure 9. The subvectors in the boxes do not depend on the subvectors not in boxes. Moreover, the vectors $(u_R^{(1)}, u_B^{(2)})^T$, $(u_R^{(3)}, u_B^{(4)})^T$, ... correspond to the MSOR method. In particular, Chebyshev acceleration corresponds to the Cyclic Chebyshev Semi-Iterative method, the case $\hat{\gamma} = \gamma$ corresponds to the Golub method, and the case $\hat{\gamma} = \rho_\infty \gamma$ corresponds to the ordinary SOR method.

It is relatively easy to analyze the convergence properties of the second-degree method by the use of the appropriate polynomials (see [27]). Such an analysis shows that Chebyshev acceleration is considerably faster than the stationary second-degree method, with $\hat{\gamma} = \rho_\infty \gamma$. This helps explain why the Cyclic Chebyshev Semi-Iterative method is faster, as measured by the reduction of the norm of the error, than the ordinary SOR method. On the other hand, it should be noted that the spectral radius of the matrix corresponding to the ordinary SOR method is smaller than that of the Cyclic Chebyshev Semi-Iterative method.

The relations between the second-degree methods and the given SOR method in some sense round out the theory. Such relations could have been, and probably were, suspected by some researchers in the early 1950s. I must confess to suspecting some such relation when working on Richardson's method and noting the similarity between its asymptotic rate of convergence and the SOR method's. I cannot remember when I received confirmation of these suspicions or from whom—it could have been when I heard a talk given in 1959 by Abe Taub, based on [1], when I read Golub's thesis [5], or later when I read the paper by Golub and Varga [6].

FIGURE 9.
Block matrix
diagram.

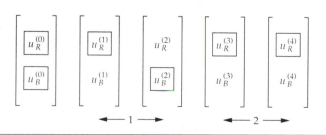

5. Extensions and Recent Developments

As stated earlier, I had originally planned to cover a great deal more of the history of iterative methods. A number of topics that might have been included, given unlimited time and space, are listed below. Some of these topics are covered in another paper of mine [26].

Extensions of the SOR method and theory
    block SOR; SOR for p-cyclic matrices; generalized consistently ordered matrices; Kahan's generalization of the theory to the case in which A is a Stieltjes matrix; the SSOR method

Other basic iterative methods
    ADI methods; methods based on approximate factorization of matrices (PDE-oriented and matrix-oriented)

Conjugate-gradient acceleration
    the conjugate-gradient method and the preconditioned conjugate-gradient method

Adaptive parameter determination
    automatic procedures for estimating upper and lower bounds for the eigenvalues of the basic iteration matrix and splitting parameters such as ω for the SSOR method

Methods for nonsymmetric systems
    complex Chebyshev; generalized conjugate-gradient methods such as OROTHODIR, ORTHOMIN, and ORTHORES; Lanczos methods; normal equations and generalized normal equations

General purpose software packages
    the ITPACK, ELLPACK, and PCG packages

Other methods
    multigrid methods, methods for vector and parallel systems

6. Acknowledgments

The preparation of this paper was supported in part by The National Science Foundation through Grant DCR–8518722, by the Department of Energy through Grant A505–81ER10954, and the U.S. Air Force Office of Scientific Research and Development through Grant AF–85–0052. The U.S. Government retains a nonexclusive, royalty-free license to publish or reproduce the published form of this contribution or to allow others to do so for U.S. Government purposes.

References

[1] A. Blair, N. Metropolis, J. von Neumann, A. H. Taub, and M. Tsingori, "A Study of a Numerical Solution of a Two-Dimensional Hydrodynamical Problem," *MTAC* 13 (1959): 145–84.

[2] D. Flanders and G. Shortley, "Numerical Determination of Fundamental Modes," *J. Appl. Phys.* 21 (1950): 1326–1332.

[3] S. P. Frankel, "Convergence Rates of Iterative Treatments of Partial Differential Equations," *MTAC* 4 (1950): 65–75.

[4] H. Geiringer, "On the Solution of Systems of Linear Equations by Certain Iterative Methods," in *Reissner Anniversary Volume, Contributions to Applied Mechanics* (Ann Arbor, MI: Edwards, 1949), 365–93.

[5] G. H. Golub, "The Use of Chebyshev Matrix Polynomials in the Iterative Solution of Linear Systems Compared with the Method of Successive Overrelaxation," (Urbana, IL: Doctoral Thesis, University of Illinois, 1959).

[6] G. H. Golub and R. S. Varga, "Chebyshev Semi-Iterative Methods, and Second-Order Richardson Iterative Methods," *Numer. Math.* 3 (1961): 147–68.

[7] L. A. Hageman and D. M. Young, *Applied Iterative Methods* (New York: Academic Press, 1981).

[8] D. R. Kincaid, "On Complex Second-Degree Iterative Methods," *SIAM J. Numer. Anal.* 11 (1974): 211–18.

[9] C. Lanczos, "Solution of Systems of Linear Equations by Minimized Iterations," *J. Res. Nat. Bur. Standards* 49 (1952): 33–53.

[10] H. Liebmann, "Die Angenahrte Ermittlung harmonischer Functionen und Konformer Abbildungen," *Sitzungsber. Akad. Wiss. Math.-Phys. Kl.* 47 (1918): 385–416.

[11] W. Markoff, "Uber Polynome, die in einem gegeben Intervallie moglichst wenig von Null abweichen," *Math. Ann.* 77 (1916): 213–258 (translation and condensation by J. Grossman of Russian article published in 1892).

[12] L. F. Richardson, "The Approximate Arithmetical Solution by Finite Differences of Physical Problems Involving Differential Equations with an Application to the Stresses in a Masonry Dam," *Philos. Trans. Roy. Soc. London Ser. A* 210 (1910): 307–57.

[13] G. Shortley, "Use of Tschebyscheff Polynomial Operators in the Numerical Solution of Boundary Value Problems," *J. Appl. Phys.* 24 (1953): 392–96.

[14] G. H. Shortley, Royal Weller, and Bernard Fried, "Numerical Solution of Laplace's and Poisson's Equations," in *The Engineering Experiment Station Bulletin* 107, vol. IX, No. 5 (1940). Revised January 1942.

[15] F. Snyder and H. Livingston, "Coding of a Laplace Boundary Value Problem for the UNIVAC," *MTAC* 3 (1949): 141–350.

[16] R. V. Southwell, *Relaxation Methods in Theoretical Physics* (Oxford University Press, 1946).

[17] G. Temple, "The General Theory of Relaxation Methods Applied to Linear Systems," *Proc. Roy. Soc. London Ser. A* 169 (1938): 476–500.

[18] R. S. Varga, "A Comparison of the Successive Overrelaxation Method and Semi-Iterative Methods Using Chebyshev Polynomials," *SIAM J.* 5 (1957): 39–46.

[19] R. S. Varga, *Matrix Iterative Analysis* (Englewood Cliffs, NJ: Prentice Hall, 1962).

[20] D. M. Young, "Iterative Methods for Solving Partial Difference Equations of Elliptic Type," (Cambridge, MA: Doctoral Thesis, Harvard University, 1950).

[21] D. M. Young, "Iterative Methods for Solving Partial Difference Equations of Elliptic Type," *Trans. Amer. Math. Soc.* 76 (1954): 92–111.

[22] D. M. Young, "On Richardson's Method for Solving Linear Systems with Positive Definite Matrices," *J. Math. Phys.* 32 (1954a): 243–55.

[23] D. M. Young, "On the Solution of Linear Systems by Iteration," in *Numerical Analysis,* Proc. Symp. Appl. Math. Amer. Math. Soc. VI (New York: McGraw-Hill, 1956), 238–98.

[24] D. M. Young, *Iterative Solution of Large Linear Systems* (New York: Academic Press, 1971).

[25] D. M. Young, "Second-Degree Iterative Methods for the Solution of Large Linear Systems," *J. Approx. Theory* 5 (1972): 137–48.

[26] D. M. Young, "A Historical Overview of Iterative Methods," to appear in *Computer Physics Communications* (New York: North Holland, 1989).

[27] David M. Young and David R. Kincaid, "Linear Stationary Second-Degree Methods for the Solution of Large Linear Systems," Report CNA–52 (Center for Numerical Analysis, Austin: The University of Texas, 1972).

[28] David M. Young and Francis Lerch, "The Numerical Solution of Laplace's Equation on ORDVAC," Ballistic Research Laboratories Memorandum Report No. 708 (Aberdeen Proving Grounds, MD, 1953).

[29] D. M. Young and C. H. Warlick, "On the Use of Richardson's Method for the Numerical Solution of Laplace's Equation on the ORDVAC," Ballistic Research Laboratories Memorandum Report No. 707 (Aberdeen Proving Grounds, MD, 1953).

Journal

für die

reine und angewandte Mathematik.

In zwanglosen Heften.

Herausgegeben

von

A. L. Crelle.

Mit thätiger Beförderung hoher Königlich-Preufsischer Behörden.

Dreifsigster Band.

In vier Heften.

Mit sechs lithographirten Tafeln.

Berlin, 1846.

Bei G. Reimer.

Et se trouve à PARIS chez Mr. Bachelier (successeur de Mme Ve Courcier),
Libraire pour les Mathématiques etc. Quai des Augustins No. 55.

Title page of Crelle's Journal, volume 30.

JOURNALS & MEETINGS

$\mathbf{A}$s the field of scientific computing has developed, so too have journals and meetings developed to publicize ideas and foster personal contacts. From a time a few decades ago when computational research had few outlets, we are now in a period in which professional societies and publications devoted to computational techniques are standard. Some of these developments are examined in this chapter.

Edward Block discusses SIAM and its many activities. SIAM has grown from a small society and a single journal in the early 1950s to a large organization sponsoring many conferences and publishing many journals, including five devoted to numerical analysis and computing. It has also played a role in some of the other developments discussed in this chapter. For example, it was a sponsor of the first Gatlinburg meeting and was considered as a sponsor for the journals *Mathematics of Computation* and *Transactions on Mathematical Software*.

Richard Varga's essay gives three viewpoints on this topic. It begins with the University of Michigan summer schools, goes on to discuss the series of Gatlinburg meetings on numerical linear algebra, and concludes with a history of the journal *Numerische Mathematik*.

Eugene Isaacson performs a similar service for the journal *Mathematics of Computation*, formerly known as *Mathematical Tables and Other Aids to Computation*. This journal's life straddles the invention of the electronic computer, and hence its early issues illuminate the special problems of hand calculation. Isaacson's essay also includes some personal recollections, in particular mentioning his experiences using Aiken's Mark I machine (see the essay in this volume by Cohen).

John Rice discusses the ACM, another society that has grown immensely as the need for computing has grown. He focuses on a particular journal, the *Transactions on Mathematical Software*, and on its activities in reviewing and distributing software.

The chapter concludes with Carl-Erik Fröberg's essay on *BIT,* the Scandinavian computer journal, and its role in the development of numerical mathematics in Europe.

Shaping the Evolution of Numerical Analysis in the Computer Age: The SIAM Thrust

I. Edward Block

1. Introduction

SIAM was conceived on 30 November 1951 at a meeting of the Servomechanisms Section of the Institute of Electrical Engineers in Atlantic City. Its first organizational meeting took place at the Drexel Institute of Technology (now Drexel University), Philadelphia, in December 1951.

The new society was created to fill the need of the unprecedented number of academic mathematicians and mathematical engineers working in industry at the time. During the war, many companies realized that mathematics was an essential tool for solving technical problems, and as a result they had hired mathematicians for basic research, engineering design, and computer programming. Many of those mathematicians, who had eyed industry as a career opportunity, missed the traditional academic dialogue to which they had become accustomed in the universities.

The young society had three objectives—to promote the applications of mathematics, to promote research in mathematics that could lead to useful techniques and methods, and to provide media for exchanging information and ideas between mathematicians and other technical and scientific professionals. These goals supported industry's idea that mathematics could be used to solve meaningful problems, improve design, and increase productivity.

Its first three meetings took place in the spring of 1952 at Drexel Institute of Technology, with the following three presentations, respectively:

- William F. G. Swann, then director of the Bartol Foundation of the Franklin Institute, "Mathematics in Science."
- Mina Rees, then director of the mathematics division of the office of Naval research, "The Role of Mathematics in Government Research."
- William E. Bradley, Jr., then director of research for Philco Corporation, "Is It Mathematics?"

The three speakers examined the role of mathematics in government, industry, and science and set the stage for what was to become a "reaching" out by SIAM into all areas where mathematics could play a role in solving problems of the real world.

During the following academic year, SIAM sponsored a series of eight lectures on operations research, computer programming, and electrical engineering. Among the speakers were David Blackwell, Grace Hopper, and L. A. Zadeh.

In that same year, the SIAM membership, mostly local to Philadelphia, elected its first officers, board, and council. Among those elected were John Mauchly as a board member, Grace Hopper as vice president for planning, and William Bradley, Jr., as president.

2. The First Step Toward Growth

Early in its first full year, SIAM leadership decided SIAM should have a quarterly journal and a newsletter. The first issue of the newsletter appeared in February 1953, and the first issue of the journal came out in September 1953. The journal was the vehicle that would eventually take SIAM into numerical analysis and other computer-related areas of mathematics.

Mailings in late 1952 and 1953 to promote SIAM activities also elicited inquiries about establishing sections of SIAM. The first section was established in Boston-Cambridge in 1953. Solicitations in the newsletter led within a few years to the formation of 14 sections from the east coast to the west.

Many of the sections sponsored computer-oriented meetings. Some of the computer topics addressed were autocorrelation on Whirlwind, integration of differential equations by difference methods, advances in automatic coding, a survey of linear programming, and polynomial approximation with least maximum error.

3. Involvement in Computers

SIAM developed an interest in computers early in its "career." It was forced to do so by the people who joined SIAM. In the early days of the computer, engineers were using the machines in antenna design, optical and electromagnetic ray tracing, cam design, structural analysis, vibration studies, and analyses of flows over wings. Statisticians were learning to do linear regression on the new computers. Mathematicians were developing ways to invert matrices, find eigenvalues and eigenvectors, and integrate nonlinear systems of ordinary differential equations. Physicists were developing ways to find numerical solutions to the wave equation and the diffusion equation. Even biomathematicians were using computers.

For many years, the sections organized local meetings focusing on their own interests. Topics dealing with numerical methods were interspersed with topics on virtually everything else, including serial correlation in communications, network calculations, mathematics in weather forecasting, and so forth. There were no dominant themes.

In 1955, SIAM, with the cosponsorship of the Institute of Radio Engineers and the Institute of Electrical Engineers, conducted a series of eight meetings on the use of mathematics in solving problems on digital computers. The first meeting, in the auditorium of the Drexel Institute of Technology, featured Franz Edelman of RCA speaking on programming a digital computer. Using closed-circuit television provided by Philco Corporation, he demonstrated the writing and debugging of a program on a new IBM 650 located in Drexel's basement. There were no corporate allegiances here, notwithstanding the computer enterprises at Philco and RCA. Another meeting featured E. E. David, then at Bell Laboratories, on digital analysis and synthesis of voice. These meetings were typical of early SIAM, when there was a strong mix of engineering mathematics and computers.

4. The Turn to Numerical Analysis

Except for the section meetings, all SIAM meetings until the early 1960s were held jointly with the summer meetings of the American Mathematical Society and the Mathematical Association of America. It was the first of these joint meetings, held at Pennsylvania State University in August 1957, that sparked SIAM's growth as a major publisher of journals in applied mathematics, and in particular, numerical and computer-related mathematics.

SIAM had been publishing its *Journal of the Society for Industrial Applied Mathematics* since 1953. It appeared on time, faithfully, every March, June, September, and December, with four or five papers per issue. There was a healthy mix of applied mathematics papers, including some fundamental papers on numerical analysis and computer-related mathematics. Papers on numerical mathematics in the early issues included the following:

- □ "Computational Experience in Solving Linear Programs," by A. J. Hoffman, M. Mannos, D. Sokolowsky, and N. Wiegmann (in the first issue).
- □ "The Automatic Analysis and Control of Computing Errors," by Saul Gorn.
- □ "On the Order of Convergence of Solutions of a Difference Equation," by M. L. Juncosa and D. M. Young.
- □ "The Numerical Solution of Parabolic and Elliptic Equations," by D. Peaceman and H. H. Rachford.
- □ "On the Numerical Integration of $u_{xx} + u_{yy} = u_t$ by Implicit Methods," by J. Douglas, Jr.

□ "Computing Constrained Minima with Lagrange Multipliers,"
   by George Forsythe.

□ "Terminating and Nonterminating Iterations for Solving Linear
   Systems," by A. S. Householder.

The December 1956 issue of the journal contained a paper by Irene
A. Stegun and Milton Abramowitz entitled "Pitfalls in Computation."
It was apropos of the time when SIAM was beginning to develop its
initiative in numerical analysis. The paper opened with a quote from
Bertrand Russell: "Mathematics may be defined as the subject in which
we never know what we are talking about, nor whether what we are
saying is true." The authors followed with the statement:

> The numerical analyst of today often finds himself in a position in
> which he does not know what he is doing, and worries whether what
> he says is true. This undesirable state of affairs is caused, to a large
> extent, by present day methods of computation on high-speed electronic
> computers. For, most frequently, only the final result of a computation
> is read out from the computer's memory and most if not all intermediate
> computations are performed more or less blindly. Thus, the numerical
> analyst may only become aware of a pathological situation that has
> developed if it renders the final result obviously incorrect.

The paper focused attention on some of the more frequent basic pitfalls
in computation and pointed out ways that would often prevent the
numerical analyst from falling prey to them. The authors received
more than 2000 requests for reprints in the months that followed.

During those early years, SIAM received numerous papers in
numerical analysis for publication in its journal, but it also received
papers in both traditional applied mathematics and engineering
mathematics. Although submissions were steady, they were not
increasing, and there was some concern that the journal might not
survive.

At the meeting at Penn State in August 1957, the idea was hatched
to invite the participants in the Wayne State University Conference on
Matrix Computations, September 3–6, 1957, to submit their papers for
publication in SIAM's journal. D. L. Thomsen, Jr., who was a member of the editorial board of the journal and was going to the conference, agreed to carry the invitation to the conference participants. The
response to that invitation was the turning point for SIAM's journal
as an outlet for papers in numerical analysis. In the two years that
followed the Wayne State conference, SIAM published many of the
conference papers in its journal:

□ "Computation of Plane Unitary Rotations Transforming a
   General Matrix to Triangular Form," by Wallace Givens.

□ "Inversion of Matrices by Biothogonalization and Related
   Results," by Magnus Hestenes.

- ☐ "Iterative Solution of Large-Scale Linear Systems," by C. Lanczos.

- ☐ "A New Method for Developing Simple Formulae for the Eigenvalues of Linear Ordinary Self-Adjoint Differential Equations," by H. Wittmeyer.

- ☐ "Determination of Eigenvalues of Matrices of Polynomial Elements," by Ivan Tarnove.

- ☐ "Computing Eigenvalues of Non-Hermitian Matrices by Methods of Jacobi Type," by Robert L. Causey.

- ☐ "Results Using Lanczos' Method for Finding Eigenvalues of Arbitrary Matrices," by Robert T. Gregory.

- ☐ "On Acceleration and Matrix Deflation Processes Used with the Power Method," by Elmer E. Osborne.

- ☐ "Computing Eigenvalues of Complex Matrices by Determinant Evaluation and by Methods of Danilewski and Wielandt," by Werner Frank.

- ☐ "The Evaluation of Matrix Inversion Programs," by Morris Newman and John Todd.

A new breed of applied mathematician—the numerical analyst—had suddenly come to SIAM's attention. These mathematicians were developing computer algorithms to find the zeros of functions, to invert matrices, and to integrate ordinary and partial differential equations. However, unlike many engineers and others, they dedicated their research to the estimation of truncation and rounding errors and rates of convergence and to finding ways to control the errors automatically while computations were underway. Analyses of the algorithms to estimate accuracy and the number of arithmetic operations were often main themes of their investigations. Jargon such as "iterating to a tolerance" and "automatic error control" became commonplace.

At the same time, another breed of mathematician was developing computational approaches for solving linear programs. The development of various implementations of the simplex method dominated most of their work, but relaxation methods and game-theoretic approaches were also being studied. The editors of the SIAM journal accepted papers reporting on this work, but there was no special effort to support it. Such work is now, of course, a part of the much larger field called "discrete mathematics."

In the years following the Wayne State submissions, there was a dramatic upsurge in interest in the SIAM journal, evidenced by the increase in submissions, both in traditional applied mathematics and in numerical analysis. During the period 1958 to 1960, most issues of the journal consisted largely of papers in numerical analysis. The publication of those papers in the journal should have established once and for all SIAM's interest in promoting research in numerical analysis. However, although the high rate of submissions continued, submissions in numerical analysis began to wane. In 1960, Harry Polachek, then editor of *Mathematical Tables and Aids to Computation*, asked SIAM if it would be interested in taking over the publication of that journal from the National Research Council.

The proposal was presented to the SIAM Council in early 1961. To compound the difficulty of declining submissions in numerical analysis, the council decided to table the matter until a later date. Subsequently, the American Mathematical Society took on the responsibility. About that time, the name was changed to *Mathematics of Computation*.

However, all was not lost. At about the same time, Alston Householder proposed that SIAM sponsor a symposium on matrix theory at Gatlinburg, Tennessee. It was to be a workshop of approximately 60 participants and would be supported by the U.S. Atomic Energy Commission and the National Science Foundation. SIAM did accept the proposal and in April 1961 conducted the first SIAM-Gatlinburg conference. SIAM continued in that role throughout the 1960s.

5. The New Journal in Numerical Analysis

In 1963, SIAM decided to introduce a separate special series of its journal devoted to numerical analysis. It was to be a quarterly periodical called the *Journal of the Society for Industrial and Applied Mathematics. Series B: Numerical Analysis*. SIAM had already begun publication of *Series A: Control* in 1962.

The first issue of *Series B* was published as a single volume in 1964. The papers in it were taken largely from submissions to the original journal. The journal was an immediate success with more than 1200 library subscriptions received on the first promotional mailing.

In 1966, SIAM changed the names of its journals. *Series B* became the *SIAM Journal on Numerical Analysis*, which continues today to be one of SIAM's most popular journals.

6. Other SIAM Journals in Computational Mathematics

SIAM currently publishes nine journals. Recently it announced two new journals—one on matrix analysis and one on discrete mathematics. The dominating theme of the matrix analysis journal will be applications, but it will include papers on numerical analysis in context with the applications. The journal on discrete mathematics, to some extent, will provide an outlet for those researchers and their successors who started out in the 1950s developing algorithms to solve linear programs.

By 1988, SIAM will have five journals devoted entirely or in part to numerical and computer-related mathematics:

- □ *SIAM Journal on Numerical Analysis*
- □ *SIAM Journal on Computing*
- □ *SIAM Journal on Scientific and Statistical Computing*
- □ *SIAM Journal on Matrix Analysis and Applications*
- □ *SIAM Journal on Discrete Mathematics*

In addition, from time to time, *SIAM Review* contains a survey paper on a topic of numerical analysis.

7. Other SIAM Activities in Numerical Analysis

Numerical analysts form a large component of SIAM membership— approximately 20 percent. A larger proportion have demonstrated some interest in numerical analysis.

Since the mid-1960s, SIAM has been conducting national meetings and, more recently, conferences devoted entirely or in part to numerical and computer-related mathematics and applications.

SIAM now has special interest groups called SIAM Activity Groups. One of these groups focuses on the mathematics of large-scale high-performance scientific computing. Three others focus on linear algebra, discrete mathematics, and optimization. To date, their primary activities have been the organization of conferences every two or three years.

Surely, the editors of SIAM's first journal who were engaged in numerical analysis research and its applications in those early years did much to influence the directions of SIAM's journals. Many of them also contributed substantially to the development of the field. Among those editors were H. H. Bottenbruch, Stephen H. Crandall, John H. Curtiss, Philip Davis, H. H. Goldstine, T. N. E. Greville, Alan J. Hoffman, Alston S. Householder, Herbert B. Keller, Harold W. Kuhn, Mervin E. Muller, Ward C. Sangren, Richard S. Varga, Herbert S. Wilf, and David M. Young.

Tom Greville became the first managing editor of SIAM's numerical analysis journal. Ward Cheney, Jim Douglas, Jr., Peter Henrici, Thomas E. Hull, Herb Keller, Frank W. J. Olver, Seymour V. Parter, William Prager, and Herb Wilf were the first members of the editorial board.

SIAM's impact on the evolution of numerical mathematics will need to be determined by the historians. But whether that impact was large or small, SIAM is greatly indebted to all its editors, authors, meeting participants, and active volunteers for the success it has had.

Reminiscences on the University of Michigan Summer Schools, the Gatlinburg Symposia, and *Numerische Mathematik*

Richard S. Varga

1. The University of Michigan Summer Schools

These summer schools were ably directed in the early 1960s by Professor Robert Bartels (emeritus) of the University of Michigan. Bartels brought in people such as Golub, Henrici, Householder, Taussky, Todd, Varga, Young, and Wilkinson to give intensive lectures of one or two weeks in duration at the University of Michigan. This gave interested people from both industrial and academic life the possibility to come and learn firsthand about the new (and flowering) area of numerical analysis from leading experts in the field. There are several things worth mentioning about this summer school experience:

- There was the learning experience of hearing, firsthand, lectures on material that would become the well-known books in numerical analysis. This was, in a certain sense, a proving ground for the books of Henrici, Householder, Varga, Todd, and Wilkinson.

- There was the fellowship of eating with the gang at the Old German Restaurant in Ann Arbor. Here the indentations of pitchers of dark beer produced interesting Gerschgorin circles on table cloths! It was a friendly group, and it has remained over the years a very friendly group.

- There were evening seminars in which the day's lecturers presented seminars, just for this select group, on their current research. For example, there were many fine lectures by Jim Wilkinson, and participants could see on a first hand basis the development of his research on eigenvalue problems.

It is important to note that this was an exciting learning process for *all* of us, in that we were filling in necessary mathematical backgrounds and learning new tools. This should come as no surprise, since none of the lecturers (save Gene Golub and David Young) actually wrote theses in numerical analysis. We were, in fact, being converted, via these lectures and seminars, to practitioners in numerical analysis, even though we had come from training in analysis (such as my own training) or linear algebra. It was indeed a wonderful way to learn more about this new field of numerical analysis, and we sincerely thank Bob Bartels for this great opportunity to learn from the masters.

2. The Gatlinburg Symposia on Numerical Linear Algebra

It is impossible to give a truly unbiased and unemotional description of the impact of one's first Gatlinburg meeting. This is because the meetings were specialized, current, and attended by the world's leaders. Because these meetings were relatively small (usually fewer than 100 people), it meant that one could talk shop with the greats in the field. My first Gatlinburg Symposium was in 1961, and I can recall with pleasure meeting so many European numerical analysts for the first time.

Initially these symposia were structured so that there were *no* invited lecturers. All came with the idea of sharing new ideas, results, tools, references, and so forth. As the spirit so moved us, talks somehow materialized. (There was a committee, however, to help "prompt" people to offer to give "spontaneous" lectures.)

I won't speak for others, but my first Gatlinburg Symposium, in 1961, had to be one of the best conferences I ever attended. There was a magic feeling of a "happening" at this meeting, with so many provocative and stimulating lectures and open research problems.

One aspect to these Gatlinburg Symposia certainly has changed, at least for me. Because numerical analysis was in its infancy when these Gatlinburg Symposia began, I believe I was personally able to understand *all* the lectures that were given, from linear algebra, O.D.E.s, P.D.E.s, to graph theory. This, alas, is no longer the case, and I don't think this has to do with my declining abilities. Numerical analysis has grown rapidly, and in many diffuse directions; it is a maturing discipline, after all. It now takes a local expert to understand lectures on the cutting edge of research in many subdivisions of numerical analysis. For example, the last few Gatlinburg Symposia have had great lectures on robust software construction (such as EISPACK) at one end of the numerical analysis spectrum and on deep problems in what has to be called applied functional analysis dealing with Sobolev spaces and application to finite elements at the other end. This growth in numerical analysis makes it increasingly difficult to be a "renaissance man" today in all areas of numerical analysis, and this means, unavoidably, that certain subgroups of numerical analysts have greater difficulty in communicating with each other.

It is important to remark that these Gatlinburg Symposia were first-rate meetings, with first-rate people in attendance and first-rate lectures. I believe we owe a special vote of thanks to Alston Householder for creating these meetings and for organizing and executing the first few meetings. The structure of these meetings was such that there was always plenty of time for in-depth informal discussions between interested parties. Also, there was a fever-pitch level of stimulation about these meetings. I can vividly recall sitting in the back seat of a VW Beetle owned and driven by W. Kahan. On one outing to the Smoky Mountains, Fy Fan and Kahan were seated in front, and Mrs. Kahan and I were in the rear. On the way back to our hotel, on a winding and particularly steep road, the two gentlemen in the front began to argue loudly and almost physically about some fine point in mathematics. I really didn't enter the fray—I was too worried about an accident! But I do recall Mrs. Kahan saying to me, after Velvel (Kahan) had given a rather long rebuttal, "Isn't he just brilliant?" Yes, he *is* brilliant.

It should also be mentioned that the Gatlinburg Symposia were originally designed to be "closed" meetings but that there has been growning concern and dislike by many about this particular nature of these Gatlinburg Symposia. The reason for closed meetings was simply to limit the number of participants to about 100, so as to ensure that participants really could interact with one another. (This is still the way that the Oberwolfach meetings in the Black Forest of Germany are carried out, for example, even after 40 years.) This is in contrast with the large, open, annual meetings of the American Mathematical Society and the SIAM meetings, which attract thousands of participants.

The Gatlinburg 10 Symposium was held 19–23 October 1987 at the Fairfield Glade in Tennessee. The idea was to bring these Gatlinburg Symposia back to the United States, where they started. It would have

TABLE 1
The Gatlinburg Symposia

Year	Number	Place Held	Organizer
1951	−1	Los Angeles	O. Taussky
1957	0	Detroit	W. Givens
1959	1	Gatlinburg	A. S. Householder
1961	2	"	"
1965	3	"	"
1969	4	"	"
1972	5	Los Alamos	R. S. Varga
1974	6	Hopfen am See	F. L. Bauer
1977	7	Monterey	G. H. Golub
1981	8	Oxford	J. Wilkinson/ L. Fox
1984	9	Waterloo	Alan George
1987	10	Fairfield Glade	G. W. Stewart

been nice to have gone back to the original site of Gatlinburg, but Gatlinburg, once a quiet and peaceful resort area, is now reported to be loud and commercial. The Gatlinburg 10 meeting was an open meeting, but each person wishing to participate was requested to submit a short abstract of his or her research and interests. Things *do* change.

In Table 1, we list all the Gatlinburg Symposia, along with the persons responsible for organizing and executing them. We remark that the Gatlinburg Symposia were influenced in part by the existence of two earlier and similar symposia, the first organized by Olga Taussky in 1951 and the second by Wallace Givens in 1957. These earlier symposia have often been referred to as Gatlinburg Symposia -1 and 0.

3. The *Numerische Mathematik* Connection

The first volume of *Numerische Mathematik* (*NM*) was published by Springer-Verlag in 1959, with founding editors A. S. Householder, R. Sauer, E. Stiefel, J. Todd, and A. Walter. (You may know that we celebrated the 25th anniversary with a meeting in Munich in 1984.) Since this first volume, there have been 35 volumes of *NM* through 1981 (roughly $1\frac{1}{2}$ volumes per year), with each volume having approximately 450 pages of research.

Each issue of *NM* has contained the following unchanging description of the role to be played by this journal:

> The journal "Numerische Mathematik" provides for the international dissemination of contributions dealing with the general problems of digital computation. Such contributions may include discussions of existing numerical techniques as well as the development of new ones, but preferably with reference to the application of these techniques to programming for automatic computation.

But the truth of the matter is that *NM* has had a much more selective and specific role as a technical journal, as its self-description might have read:

> The journal "Numerische Mathematik" is dedicated to the international dissemination of outstanding contributions dealing with the theory and applications of numerical mathematics. Such theory and applications are included in finite elements and their applications, iterative and direct methods for matrix equations, spline functions and their applications, linear and nonlinear optimization methods, linear algebra, and numerical methods for ODEs and PDEs.

The rejection rate for papers submitted to *Numerische Mathematik* has remained over the years at about $\frac{1}{3}$. As George Forsythe in his infinite wisdom once said, "A journal is only about as good as the manuscripts it receives!" This remains true today for all journals.

It might be a good idea to recall the original main editors of *NM*, to show the changes over the years. These were the founding editors:

1959–1966: Householder, Sauer, Stiefel, Todd, Walter

Then, K. Samelson, F. L. Bauer, and J.H. Wilkinson were added as main editors in 1967, with the death of Professor R. Sauer and with the resignation of Professor A. Walter.

1967–1971: Bauer, Householder, Samelson, Stiefel, Todd, Wilkinson

R. S. Varga was added in 1972:

1972–1976: Bauer, Householder, Samelson, Stiefel, Todd, Varga, Wilkinson

Then, G. H. Golub was added in 1977:

1977–1979: Bauer, Golub, Householder, Samelson, Stiefel, Todd, Varga, Wilkinson

J. Stoer replaced E. Stiefel in 1979 after Stiefel's death:

1980: Bauer, Golub, Householder, Samelson, Stoer, Todd, Varga, Wilkinson

Then, K. Samelson died in 1980:

1981: Bauer, Golub, Householder, Stoer, Todd, Varga, Wilkinson

A quantum change came in 1981 with the addition of R. Bulirsch, H. B. Keller, G. W. Stewart, and C. Zenger:

1981–1986: Bauer, Bulirsch, Golub, Householder, Keller, Stewart, Stoer, Todd, Varga, Wilkinson, Zenger

With the untimely death in 1986 of J. H. Wilkinson, the main editors of *Numerische Mathematik* numbered 10. Finally in 1988, I. Babuška, P. Ciarlet, and B. Parlett were added:

1981–1986: Babuška, Bauer, Bulirsch, Ciarlet, Golub, Householder, Keller, Parlett, Stewart, Stoer, Todd, Varga, Zenger

Although I have dwelt on the main editors of *NM*, who were perhaps the guiding spirit behind *NM*, there are now 30 associate editors also, many of them in the audience. Without a doubt, they too have contributed very much to the success and vitality of *NM*.

The Origin of *Mathematics of Computation* and Some Personal Recollections

Eugene Isaacson

1. *Mathematics of Computation*

The American Mathematical Society (AMS) currently publishes *Mathematics of Computation* quarterly. This journal was started in January 1943 as *Mathematical Tables and Aids to Computation* (*MTAC*) and was edited initially by Raymond Clare Archibald on behalf of the Committee for MTAC of The National Research Council (NRC) of the National Academy of Sciences (NAS) of the United States. This committee was established in 1939 with Archibald as chairman. He continued as chairman and editor until his retirement from the committee at the end of 1949. The following excerpts from the "Introductory" in vol. I (1943) explain the purpose of the journal and the committee:

> This Quarterly Journal, a new publication of the National Research Council, is to serve as a clearing-house for information concerning mathematical tables and other aids to computation. . . .
>
> Up to the present the chief duty of the Committee has been to prepare a series of comprehensive Reports on mathematical tables, valuable for various types of research in different fields. D. H. Lehmer's *Guide to Tables in the Theory of Numbers* was published in February, 1941. It is expected that a more elaborate Report, in another field, may be ready for publication during 1943. Since most members of the Committee are at the present time deeply involved in national service, the completion of still further Reports in the near future is likely to be very difficult to achieve.
>
> Meanwhile, it is hoped this new periodical may render notable current service, and that in years to come it, and the Reports, may be regarded as the standard sources to which one may naturally turn for guidance in connection with all mathematical tables of importance in contemporary research.
>
> On behalf of the Committee,
>
> R. C. A.

> R. C. A. greatly regrets the apparent necessity for numerous personal contributions in this issue as well as in the second. It seems certain that elimination in this regard shall be noticeably operative in the third and later issues.

It was primarily the efforts of Archibald that resulted in the establishment of *MTAC*. Archibald was born on 7 October 1875. One of

211

his scholarly pursuits involved the collection and study of mathematical tables and the collection of mathematics books. In fact, he developed the excellent Brown University mathematics library as well as the library of the American Mathematical Society. Archibald appreciated the importance of disseminating information about mathematical tables for widespread applications in the basic sciences, engineering, navigation, astronomy, insurance, and so on. He retired from teaching and became a professor emeritus at Brown University in 1943, the year that the first issue of *MTAC* was published with Archibald as editor. The dedication and thoroughness that Archibald devoted to his editorship of *MTAC* has set an unattainable level for his successors.

His Committee on MTAC (in 1943) contained 23 younger experts covering the spectrum of the subject—including two from England and one from Japan. D. H. Lehmer was the expert in number theory, and he joined Archibald as editor in 1944. The unique tradition of publishing papers on algebra and number theory in the journal has been continued ever since. Incidentally, the name *Mathematical Tables and Other Aids to Computation* seems to have been chosen without comment by the editors, beginning with the October 1943 issue.

During the mid-1940s, the large, Harvard–IBM electromechanical computer Mark I was built and shortly superseded by electronic computers. This was the beginning of a new era. In just a few years, the table-making industry was engulfed by the algorithm-making industry, and "numerical analysis" became the subject matter of most of the papers in *MTAC*.

Thus, in 1959 the editorial committee decided that it was appropriate to change the name from *MTAC* to *Mathematics of Computation* (*MOC*). The name change became effective with the January 1960 issue and is explained in a preface by Harry Polachek.

During 1960, the National Academy of Sciences NRC requested Polachek, the chairman of the editorial committee of *MOC*, to seek another publisher for the journal. A proposal was received from the American Mathematical Society (AMS) to assume publication of *MOC*. The AMS stated that it would permit the journal to be managed as it had been in the past by the editorial committee of *MOC* (which had been chosen by the NAS-NRC). The *MOC* editors recommended that the change of publisher be made. The January 1962 issue of *MOC* was published by the AMS, under the editorial control of the NAS-NRC, signalling the beginning of a four-year trial period for changing publishers. The AMS assumed both editorial and publication control of *MOC* beginning with the July 1965 issue.

It is a worthwhile experience to browse through the early issues of *MTAC*. Some of their flavor can be discerned from parts of the contents of volume 1, number 1, January 1943:

Recent Mathematical Tables. This is an index of 74 reviews of tables that Archibald authored previously in *Scripta Mathematica*. In addition, this section contains 13 reviews by Archibald and one review by Lehmer of recent mathematical tables.

Mechanical Aids to Computation. This contains a brief history of seventeenth century calculating machines. It was written by Archibald and refers to articles that appeared in *Nature* on the occasion of a tercentenary celebration in London of B. Pascal's invention of a calculating machine.

Notes. Archibald wrote this section. The first two of these three notes are brief biographical sketches of two table makers. The third note is quoted here in order to shed some light on the state of computing in 1942:

> In *Science* . . . there is an account by R. C. Archibald of the set-up and remarkable achievements of "The New York Mathematical Tables Project" . . . as part of the Government's Works Projects Administration Program. . . . A year ago 350 computers were working, in two shifts, in order fully to utilize 150 computing machines. By August the number of computers had been reduced to 250. Since the WPA is to be liquidated on 1 February 1943 the New York Mathematical Tables Project is also to be terminated by that date. Had all the computers in the Project been dispersed, the loss to scientific research would have been irreparable. We learn, however, that 47 members of the group have been taken over by the U. S. Bureau of Standards and by the Hydrographic Office.
>   Unless a much more adequate nucleus of the present Project is preserved, with calculating machines, a large number of mathematical tables now in process may never come to publication.

Queries. Archibald rhetorically asks where and why is it desirable to have tables with "from 15 to 60 or more places of decimals."

Queries–Replies. Lehmer responds with some number theory applications of such special tables.

Archibald and Lehmer continued as the editors of *MTAC* with the cooperation of L. J. Comrie and S. A. Joffe from 1944 until Archibald retired at the end of 1949. For the one issue of January 1946, Harry Bateman was listed along with Archibald and Lehmer as editor. Unfortunately, Bateman died on 21 January 1946 (see *MTAC* 2 [1946]: 79).

Beginning with the January 1950 issue, the journal was managed by the chairman of the editorial committee. Lehmer continued as the first chairman. The following are the names of the chairmen and the years they served:

D. H. Lehmer	1950–1954
C. B. Tompkins	1955–1958
Harry Polachek	1959–1965
Eugene Isaacson	1966–1974
James H. Bramble	1975–1983
Walter Gautschi	1984–present

The chairman of the editorial committee received the additional descriptive title "Managing Editor" beginning with the issue of January 1979. The editorial board for the January 1987 issue consisted of 24 members.

For information about Archibald and Lehmer see [1–7].

2. Personal Recollections

I was employed as a computer by the U. S. National Bureau of Standards at the Mathematical Tables Project (MTP) in New York from April through December of 1943 (see note 3 in *MTAC* 1 [1943]: 29–30, for Archibald's description of the prehistory of this activity). My prior training in computing consisted of a semester course at the City College of New York in Ordinary Differential Equations using L. R. Ford's book. The text contained a chapter on differences, interpolation, numerical integration, and numerical methods for solving ordinary differential equations. The scientific leader and manager of the computers at MTP was Gertrude Blanch, who reported to Arnold Lowan, the director of the project. I learned about using the mechanical calculators and about computing from this fine team. Among the staff of about 25, I recall most clearly Blanch, Abraham Hillman, Sidney Horenstein, Ida Rhodes, and Herbert Salzer. In fact, Salzer asked me to help him find some errors in an 1883 *Acta Mathematica* table by J. P. L. Bourguet that had been reprinted in a 1933 book by H. T. Davis. Subsequently, Salzer arranged for the errata to be published under both of our names in *MTAC* (1 [1943]: 124). At some time during the nine months that I spent at the project, Cornelius Lanczos joined the group and worked with a mechanical calculator. I regret that I did not get to know him better then. Some years later, I was to read some of his books and papers.

In January 1944, I was hired by Richard Courant as a research assistant (computer) for the mathematics group at New York University. Marie Johnson was the other part-time computer there. Later, while still a graduate student, I became the manager of the hand computer group for the mathematics institute, with a staff of about eight graduate students. During the war, Nina Courant, the wife of Richard and daughter of C. Runge, voluntarily assisted as a part-time computer for me. This mechanical calculator group persisted until the mid-1950s, even though our institute at New York University housed the Univac Model 1 in 1952 and managed the Northeastern Computing Facility of the U. S. Atomic Energy Commission in a renovated hat factory building at 25 Waverly Place in the Greenwich Village area of Manhattan, New York. I had the "pleasure" of being the acting chief of this facility for the first five months. This required that (a) I hire some former NYU graduate students to be trained as programmers, (b) I hire an engineer and technicians to be trained at the Philadelphia factory to maintain the Univac, (c) I hire operators to be trained, (d) I commute irregularly to Philadelphia to check on the operation for the first few months, (e) I arrange for the University to buy and alter the building in Manhattan, and (f) I arrange for the move and installation of the Univac 1 so that it could operate continuously on behalf of the various AEC laboratories. Among the first people I hired was Herbert B. Keller, who later coauthored our book. The "pleasure" came from the excitement of learning numerical analysis with the graduate students, some faculty, and post docs.

In connection with the essay on Howard Aiken by I. B. Cohen in this volume, let me add that sometime in 1947 I was asked by Richard Courant to prepare a calculation for the Harvard-IBM Mark I calculator. He said that Howard Aiken had requested that we solve a large and significant problem so that Aiken could decide how to design the Harvard Mark II. The problem I chose to solve was a three-dimensional, time dependent, heat conduction problem with axial symmetry, suggested by J. K. L. MacDonald. MacDonald and Samuel Schaaf contributed to simplifying the formulation of the problem. J. Orten Gadd and Theodore Singer of Aiken's Computation Laboratory of Harvard University visited me in New York, and I gave them a complete description of the problem and of the explicit finite-difference scheme that was to be used to find the solution. After several months, they informed me that the problem was solved and invited me to visit Harvard to obtain the computer results. When I arrived at their office in Aiken's new Crufts Laboratory building, they closed the door and spoke in hushed tones as they explained to me that the problem ran continuously and alone for 30 days. Sometime during the first two days, they had discovered a bug in the program, but were fearful of what would happen if they destroyed the first two days of calculated and printed results. So, they simply corrected the instructions, but continued with the data that had been obtained (with the wrong code) at 48 hours. I laughed and told them that they were fortunate that they were solving a heat conduction problem. This is the first time that I have written about this event.

On that day, I met Aiken (who was referred to as Commander Aiken by his staff). He told me that he was most pleased that after the construction was completed, Harvard received a 10 percent reduction in the cost of his new computer laboratory building. The construction contract stipulated that when no change was requested during the course of the construction, a 10 percent reduction would be made by the contractor.

Aiken's electronic computers produced a number of tables and also heralded the demise of table making. The heat conduction problem is described in [8].

References

[1] C. R. Adams with Otto Neugebauer, "Obituary. Raymond Clare Archibald," *Amer. Math. Monthly* 62 (1955): 743–45.

[2] R. C. Archibald, "Mathematical Table Makers. Portraits, Paintings, Busts, Monuments, Bio-Bibliographical Notes," Scripta Mathematica Studies 3, *Scripta Mathematica* (1948).

[3] Albert A. Bennett, "Raymond Clare Archibald," *MTAC* 4 (1950): 1–2.

[4] R. C. Gibbs, "Note of Appreciation," *MTAC* 4 (1950): 1–2.

[5] D. H. Lehmer, "Guide to Tables in the Theory of Numbers," Bulletin of the National Research Council, 105, National Research Council, Washington, DC (1941).

[6] D. H. Lehmer, "Raymond Clare Archibald, 1875–1955," *MTAC* 10 (1956): 112–13.

[7] Various authors, "Dedicated to D. H. L. on his Seventieth Birthday," *MOC* 29 (1975): 1–341.

[8] Eugene Isaacson, J. Orten Gadd, and Theodore Singer, "Mathematical Determination of Transient Temperatures in Solids," IMM-NYU 164, CL–HU 29 (1948).

Mathematical Software and ACM Publications

John R. Rice

1. Introduction

Mathematical software started as a scientific activity almost as early as serious scientific computing. The field was brought into focus at the symposium "Mathematical Software" held at Purdue University on 1–3 April 1970. The symposium's organizing committee consisted of John Rice (chairman), Robert Ashenhurst, Charles Lawson, M. Stuart Lynn, and Joseph Traub. It was sponsored by ACM and SIGNUM (Special Interest Group on Numerical Mathematics) and financially supported by the Office of Naval Research. Mathematical software was defined then as *the set of algorithms in the area of mathematics* and it was noted that this definition is much broader than the traditional definition of numerical analysis. Even today there are large areas of mathematical software that are relatively undeveloped (e.g., geometric algorithms).

The first chapter of the symposium proceedings [4] presents a brief history of the field up to that point. It is noted there that the first mathematical software published was an EDVAC machine language program to convert base 10 integers to binary; it was in *Mathematical Tables and Aids to Computations*, now called *Mathematics of Computation* (3 [1949]: 427–31). Note that the book [8] contains a thorough discussion of the mathematical software (subroutine library) for the EDSAC. The second chapter of *Mathematical Software*, "The Distribution and Sources of Mathematical Software," summarizes the state of the field as of 1970. See also [1].

Chapter 3 of *Mathematical Software* is "The Challenge for Mathematical Software," which raises many points still completely unresolved. It concludes with recommendations for the establishment of two items:

☐ A journal of mathematical software
☐ A center or focal point for mathematical software

The implementation of the first recommendation is the main theme of this article, but the other recommendation has yet to be carried out. Perhaps mathematical software is now too big for a "center" to cover the whole field, but a focal point would still serve a very important scientific function.

2. Establishment of the ACM TOMS

The Software Certification Workshop was held at Granby, Colorado, in August 1972, sponsored by the National Science Foundation. Thirty-one people attended, and one short session was devoted to a discussion of a journal of mathematical software. As a result, John Rice organized a one-day meeting at Argonne National Laboratory with Tom Hull, M. Stuart Lynn, and Joseph Traub to explore the possibility seriously.

The meeting was held on 3 November 1972 with Wayne Cowell as host. By that time, discussions of interest had been held with Academic Press, ACM, SIAM, and SIGNUM. All aspects of the journal were discussed at Argonne, and the following points of agreement were reached:

□ Establishment of a journal of mathematical software should be pursued even though there were 10 journals identified that claimed they would publish mathematical software papers. None of these seemed serious (now, 15 years later, we see that most of them were not serious).

□ Lloyd Fosdick would be invited to join the group (he was then editor of the Algorithms section of the *Communication of the ACM*).

□ A professional society publisher would be preferable to a commercial publisher.

Attention was thus focused on ACM and SIAM as potential publishers. The new journal would be coordinated with the ACM *Journal of Collected Algorithms (CALGO)* in a formal way, which might mean a cooperative arrangement between ACM and SIAM. In the next months, obstacles at both ACM and SIAM became clear. First, ACM was in the midst of a financial crisis, and one small faction within ACM claimed that the crisis was due to subsidizing technical journals. Even though it was well known in other societies that journals generally (and often handsomely) support other society activities, ACM's accounting system at that time could not provide any reliable information on the profitability of ACM publications. Thus, there was some opposition to a new journal, and many who were in favor in principle were cautious because of the financial implications.

At SIAM, there was concern by the editors of two existing journals (*Journal of Computing* and *Journal of Numerical Analysis*) about overlapping areas. The editors of both journals thought it would be appropriate for each to simply expand and include the mathematical software area. There was also the tricky problem of dividing expenses and control with ACM's *CALGO* publication. Finally, there was some reluctance within SIAM to become so involved with computing.

During the spring of 1973, the definition of the proposed journal was polished (a complete "sample" issue was constructed, for example) and many operational issues decided. Most importantly, John Pasta at the National Science Foundation reacted favorably to the idea of sponsoring a conference on mathematical software whose proceedings would be the first issue or two of the new journal. This would greatly reduce financial risk.

By the summer of 1973 it became clear that the obstacles at SIAM would be very difficult to overcome. SIAM wanted to move toward mathematical software without becoming tainted with computer programs, and no one could see how to do this effectively. The National Science Foundation funding for the conference "Mathematical Software II" seemed assured, so the efforts were focused on convincing ACM that their financial risk was tolerable.

There were two other factors within ACM that supported establishing a new journal, the *ACM Transactions on Mathematical Software* (*TOMS*). First, it would remove the Algorithms section from the *Communications of the ACM*, and this appealed to many for both financial and aesthetic reasons. Second, it would set a pattern for other specialty journals that many thought that ACM should be publishing. For example, the *ACM Transactions on Computer Systems and Programming* was included abstractly in ACM discussion documents in the summer of 1973.

During the winter of 1973–74, many financial analyses were made, all of which indicated that the National Science Foundation support would reduce the first year cost of the new journal to a very small amount for ACM, even with pessimistic assumptions ($5300 was the "final" figure), and that the journal would thereafter be profitable (making a profit of over $15,000 in the third year). These figures were based on first-year assumptions of 333 individual subscribers and 200 institutional subscribers. The actual numbers of first-year subscribers were 1242 individuals and 351 institutional, so *TOMS* made a substantial profit, even in its first year. Figure 1 shows the circulation figures of *TOMS* for its first 10 years, but the counts are not exactly on a calendar year (or volume) basis. The category "others" includes institutional, corporate members of ACM and back issues. The launch of the *ACM Transactions on Mathematical Software* was formally recommended by the ACM Publications Board on 8 May 1974 and approved by the ACM Council the same week.

The conference "Mathematical Software II" was held at Purdue on 29–31 May 1974. SIGSAM people, as well as SIGNUM people, were heavily involved in organizing this conference. This set the precedent for various SIGs to have an official role in *TOMS* operations. There were over 225 attendees with 82 papers presented, including 22 invited presentations. All were considered for publication in *TOMS*,

FIGURE 1.
Circulation of TOMS for 1975–86. No separate data for "others" and ACM "members" is available for 1975. The "projected" values were used for the final assessment of the financial feasibility of the journal.

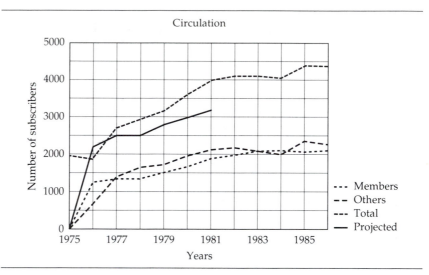

and most went through the normal refereeing procedure (a number of the papers were submitted to other journals). The conference received $31,000 in support from the National Science Foundation, of which over $16,000 went to help support the publication of 22 papers in the first issues of *TOMS*. The proceedings of Mathematical Software II had 324 pages and was strictly limited to conference attendees (only 250 copies were printed). It was not made available otherwise. This was to prevent double publication of papers in the proceedings and *TOMS*. It has led to recurring confusion, because there are books *Mathematical Software* [4] and *Mathematical Software III* [6], so people assume there is a *Mathematical Software II* (which there is [5]), and that they should be able to obtain it (which they cannot).

3. Algorithms

The publication of algorithms is one of the main functions of *TOMS*. The biggest challenge faced by the editors of *TOMS* is to apply normal, scientific refereeing procedures to algorithms and to make them available in a reasonable way. The difficulty faced by the editors is seen right at the outset: There is wide disagreement about the definition of an algorithm. The traditional mathematical definition defines an algorithm as *an unambiguous set of instructions for a machine*. That, it turns out, is a quite ambiguous definition, and there are three colloquial definitions in widespread use:

□ **Method:** This is a general approach or strategy used in computing, something not defined in complete detail. Examples are divide and conquer, steepest descent, predictor-corrector, and finite differences.

☐ **Algorithm:** This is a set of mathematical steps for an abstract computation. Examples are the Euclidean algorithm, bubble sort, Gauss elimination (no scaling or pivoting), and the formula for the roots of a quadratic polynomial. Algorithms are thought of as short and restricted to a single "purpose."

☐ **Computer Program:** This is something written in Algol, Ada, Fortran, Assembler, and so forth.

A little thought shows that the computer program definition is the closest to being an algorithm in the precise mathematical sense. However, the colloquial definition of algorithm is so widespread that there is continual confusion about what it means to publish "algorithms."

In this section we discuss two aspects of publishing programs that the editors of *TOMS* have found difficult: evaluating the performance of algorithms and distributing the algorithms. After 12 years of publication, *TOMS* (and *CALGO*) are the only journals that handle these aspects with a high quality of scientific publication.

The ACM algorithms started in the *Communications of the ACM* as short Algol programs. Thus, they originated as algorithms both in the precise and colloquial senses. The first 225 ACM algorithms were not refereed at all, and many were trivial in nature.

In the 1970s two significant editorial policies were adopted. First, algorithms to be published had to have significant utilitarian value, and second, algorithms had to meet high standards. Establishing standards and enforcing them has created a large burden on the editors, the referees, and the authors. The acceptance rate for algorithms is less than half that of regular papers. It takes two or three times as much effort to process an algorithm, and, unfortunately, it also usually takes twice as long. As one might guess, it takes relentless effort by the editors to enforce standards of style and documentation. Some authors cannot believe it when their otherwise great software is rejected because the documentation is inadequate. The result is, however, worth the effort; most (alas, we are still striving for perfection) ACM algorithms perform a worthwhile task in a reliable, efficient manner and are easily used. These algorithms are truly valuable. At today's cost of software development, the algorithms in *TOMS* for a given year are worth almost $1 million. The subscribers to the *ACM Collected Algorithms* certainly get a bargain! The algorithms have become much longer, so long that some people say they are "programs" and not "algorithms." These words are nearly synonymous to me, but others see a large distinction. The *TOMS* algorithms range from 48 to 55,560 lines of code. The longest ACM algorithm (algorithm 607: "Text Exchange

System" by W. V. Snyder and R. I. Hanson) would have a listing of about 925 pages. Of the TOMS algorithms, 84 (out of 148) have over 1000 lines, and 8 have over 10,000 lines. Needless to say, few algorithms are printed in full in *TOMS*, and even in *CALGO* the longer ones are given on microfiche.

Figures 2 and 3 show the distribution of algorithms over the various fields of mathematics. Totals are given for 12 areas and 3 periods: 1960–74, 1975–80, and 1981–86. The 12 areas, in order of frequency in the first period, are *functions* (computation of special and elementary functions), *linear algebra* (matrices, linear equations, etc.), *statistics*, *approximation/optimization* (curve fitting, least squares, minimization), *polynomials* (root finding, factoring, manipulation), *operations research/graph theory* (linear programming, spanning, trees, shortest paths, etc.), *differential equations* (ordinary and partial), *miscellaneous*, *sorting*, *others* (categories other than miscellaneous that have few algorithms), *arithmetic* (multiple precision, modular, exact), *calculus* (integration and differentiation). One sees that the size of the functions category has dropped substantially, from 20 percent in the first period to 10 percent in the most recent. Similarly, sorting has almost disappeared. I attribute this to the fact many of the early algorithms were translations of formulas or single methods into Algol; that type of algorithm has disappeared from *TOMS*. Linear algebra

FIGURE 2. Number of ACM algorithms published in three time periods for the six most frequent categories of the first period.

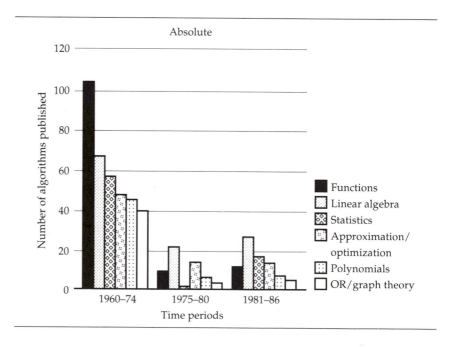

FIGURE 3.
Number of ACM algorithms published in three time periods for the six least frequent categories of the first period. "Miscellaneous" is a separate category, and "others" is a collection of categories with very few algorithms.

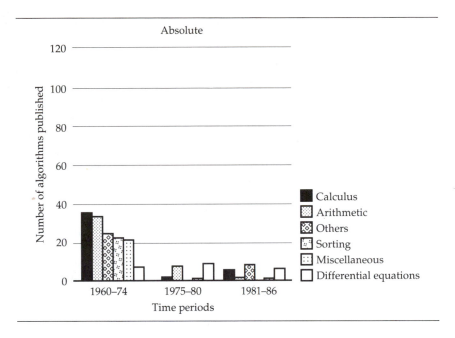

has become the most significant area, rising from 13 percent in the first period to 28 percent in the second and 25 percent in the third period. Differential equations and approximation/optimization have both increased significantly in frequency since algorithm publication started.

4. Algorithm Performance

The standards for refereeing algorithms include the criterion of performance. Algorithms that perform significantly better than any previously known algorithm (for an interesting problem) are clearly valuable scientific contributions. In many instances, the sole objective of a program is to be able to solve a particular class of problems. There are no alternatives, so no efficiency comparisons are made and less-than-high reliability might be acceptable for some difficult classes of problems. It is common, however, that competing algorithms do exist; and then the *TOMS* referees must judge the relative performance of the algorithms. Here, all qualities come into consideration, from efficiency to accuracy to robustness to long-term maintenance.

Once one gets away from elementary or simple problem areas, it becomes very difficult to say which problems a particular algorithm should solve correctly. Most of the algorithms considered in *TOMS* are applicable to unsolvable problem classes. The term "unsolvable" is used here in its strong, technical sense; that is, one can show that no algorithm exists that can solve all the problems in the class under consideration. As a result, given an algorithm, one can usually construct problems in which it fails miserably. In principle, mathematics provides a mechanism to exclude such problems. For example, one might specify that an algorithm is to be applied only to differential equations whose solution has its fourth derivative bounded by 1000. One can then hope to prove theorems about the algorithm's performance. Such an assumption is an *unverifiable hypothesis*: There is no algorithm to determine whether the assumption is satisfied. Most mathematical analysis assumptions are of this type and are useless in practice.

The result of this uncomfortable situation is the development of batteries of test problems that are hoped to represent the spectrum of problems that occur in real applications. One recent paper in *TOMS* [7] is devoted to a detailed critique of the test problem sets that are currently being used to evaluate programs for solving stiff ordinary differential equations (a particularly difficult and important class of problems). The need for care in choosing test problem sets is illustrated by the example of solving linear equations; the early practice of generating test matrices at random led to completely misleading results about the robustness and reliability of algorithms.

A consequence of the fact that most algorithms in *TOMS* apply to unsolvable problems is that they contain heuristics in certain key places. For example, programs that involve the convergence of something use a heuristic test; the robustness of such software is often directly related to the quality of the heuristic used. The presence of heuristics in the programs makes the usual "software validation" or "program proving" techniques partially inapplicable, as there is no concept of correctness of a heuristic. Only performance is meaningful to discuss.

There is a large contrast in the material in *TOMS* and in the June 1982 issue of ACM *Computing Surveys* (*CSUR*), which is devoted to the validation and testing of software. Even the *CSUR* article entitled "Validation of Scientific Programs" has almost no overlap with the material in *TOMS* or the principle issues discussed by *TOMS'* algorithm authors. The *CSUR* paper concentrates on topics such as requirements analysis, design analysis, source code analysis, and code auditing. One might say it discusses the large-scale application of good programming practices. In the performance evaluation papers and algorithm refereeing for *TOMS*, it is assumed as a matter of course that programs are developed with good programming practices. One reason for the high rejection rate for algorithms submitted to *TOMS* is that, alas, this assumption is often false. However, once evidence of poor code is seen, a program is summarily excluded from further consideration—either as a *TOMS* algorithm or as a candidate for serious performance evaluation.

Two recent *TOMS* papers evaluate software in truly difficult problem areas, optimization and nonlinear equations, and the results illustrate the nature of many of the problem areas involved in *TOMS'* papers. Both studies involved 8 algorithms (programs) regarded as being among the best available for the problem areas. In the first study [2], all but one of the programs solved the "standard" set of 36 test problems. No program could solve all, or even almost all, of the more difficult set of test problems, even though every problem could be solved by some program. The second study [3] used 57 problems, mostly difficult, each in three versions (according to the scaling of the problems). The two best performing programs were able to solve only 98 of the 171 test problems (not the same 98). As one has learned to expect in such difficult problem areas, no single program is best, and one needs a set of programs either to apply or to "tune" one of the programs for the particular problem at hand. Some of the test problems were not solved by any of the programs.

5. Algorithm Distribution

Even before *TOMS* was conceived, Lloyd Fosdick had started to explore better ways of distributing algorithms to the scientific community. The practice in the *Communications of the ACM* of printing hundreds of lines of code was clearly inadequate. Serious study of an algorithm includes using it, and it is both tedious and error-prone to copy code from the printed page. Further, pages of codes are particularly dull if one does not have a serious interest in the algorithm. Fosdick initiated a distribution service of machine-readable forms of algorithms. He selected some algorithms for distribution and then distributed them using the ad hoc resources of his department at the University of Colorado. His experience showed that such a service was feasible, that there was a real demand for it, and that there were substantial operational hurdles to face.

One of the original objectives of launching the *TOMS* was to establish a systematic, reliable distribution service for the ACM algorithms. There were serious obstacles. First, the ACM publication staff did not have any experience with software distribution, was unhappy to contract such an important function to an outside organization, and had inadequate facilities to do it internally. Second, the volume of distribution would be low enough that the service would not be an attractive commercial venture.

After some time, Ed Battiste, President of IMSL, Inc., agreed to handle the distribution service as a "public service," charging only enough to recover approximately the direct costs of the service. It then took several months of negotiation to get the ACM publications staff to agree to this arrangement. The mathematical software community owes a large debt to IMSL for their service, because they have distributed the algorithms with a high level of professionalism, and they surely lose money every year in this service. The success and changing nature of this service is seen from Table 1, in which the volume of the service is given for the first full year (1976) and the past six years. Algorithm distribution on microfiche was initiated and then dropped after several years, because of a lack of interest. The *netlib* entry, which is for ACM algorithms obtained through the mathematical software distribution service via networks, is operated by Oak Ridge National Laboratory and AT&T Bell Laboratories.

The ACM Algorithm Distribution Service is designed to remove artificial limits on length caused by printing costs. The first step when *TOMS* was started was to publish only excerpts in *TOMS* itself, and to publish full text in *CALGO*. This allowed algorithms of 10, 20, or 30 pages in length to be published in *TOMS*, but printed in full in *CALGO*. In the late 1970s, microfiche supplements to *CALGO* were initiated so that a "small" segment of an algorithm would be printed in *CALGO* and the remainder printed on microfiche. Thus, algorithm 607 with 55,560 lines can be published even though it takes four microfiche sheets to print. Keep in mind that the *primary* publication medium for such an algorithm is not the printed version, but the machine readable version available from the ACM Algorithms Distribution Service. Even so, the printed distribution of ACM algorithms via *CALGO* has continued to grow, as seen in Figure 4.

TABLE 1
Volume of algorithms ACM distributed, by type of distribution. See *TOMS* for detailed definitions of the types. The total algorithms number is only an estimate.

	1976	1981	1982	1983	1984	1985	1986
Single algorithms							
listing	5	106	89	111	114	71	–
cards	17	37	30	20	14	7	–
diskettes	–	–	–	–	–	75	102
netlib	–	–	–	–	–	475	1839
Quarterly issues	22	57	113	95	96	41	12
Volume issues	–	38	73	140	153	96	41
5-year tapes	–	48	38	32	46	96	97
5-year subscription						37	
Total algorithms	132	6000	5900	6600	8300	12700	13300

FIGURE 4.
Circulation of the
ACM *Collected
Algorithms* (*CALGO*)
for the period 1973–
86. The breakdown
between members
and others is not
known before 1976.

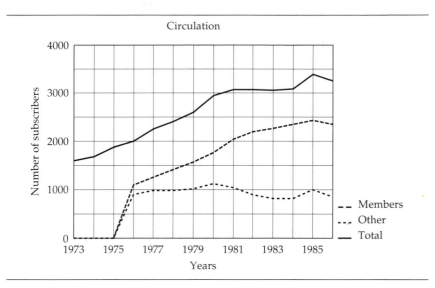

References

[1] Wayne R. Cowell, *Sources and Development of Mathematical Software* (Englewood Cliffs, NJ: Prentice Hall, 1984).

[2] K. L. Hiebert, "An Evaluation of Mathematical Software That Solves Nonlinear Least Squares Problems," *ACM Trans. Math. Software* 7 (1981): 1–16.

[3] K. L. Hiebert, "An Evaluation of Mathematical Software That Solves Systems of Nonlinear Equations," *ACM Trans. Math. Software* 8 (1982): 5–20.

[4] John R. Rice, *Mathematical Software* (New York: Academic Press, 1971).

[5] John R. Rice, *Mathematical Software II*, an informal conference proceedings, Purdue University (1974).

[6] John R. Rice, *Mathematical Software III* (New York: Academic Press, 1977).

[7] Lawrence F. Shampine, "Evaluation of a Test Set for Stiff ODE Solvers," *ACM Trans. Math. Software* 7 (1981): 409–20.

[8] M. V. Wilkes, P. J. Wheeler, and S. Gill, *The Preparation of Programs for an Electronic Digital Computer* (Reading, MA: Addison-Wesley, 1951).

BIT—A Child of the Computer

Carl-Erik Fröberg

The 19th century could perhaps be characterized as a period of preparation for the advent of the computer. It so happened that quite a few Swedish inventors played a role in this development. Scheutz, father and son, as well as Wiberg, constructed mechanical devices that solved simple arithmetic problems somewhat automatically by performing a series of predetermined operations. In fact, Wiberg was able to compute a logarithm table that even appeared in print (Figure 1). Later, Odhner built a robust, mechanical, hand-driven calculator that was followed around 1930 by electromechanical calculators. All lengthy calculations had to be performed manually at this time. A few examples from Sweden will illustrate the situation.

A hydrodynamical problem of great interest was to find periods of so-called internal waves in the sea. These waves are huge in size, 20 to 30 meters, but are nevertheless invisible. They are generated by the moon and observed as sharp changes in the salinity. The method used was numerical autoanalysis, a kind of Fourier analysis of the function with itself.

During the war there was a great need for ballistic tables, and a special group was formed to compute bomb tables for the Swedish Air Force. The classical Runge-Kutta method was used with air resistance represented graphically and with normal assumptions concerning the air density. From a basic set of orbits, the desired tables could be produced by interpolation. It is a sad fact that all these tables could probably have been computed in a couple of minutes on a fast modern computer.

In 1946 some people in the Swedish Navy and in the Academy for Engineering Sciences got interested in the progress in automatic computation in the United States, and after visiting the key projects they reported back home with great enthusiasm. It was quickly decided to offer scholarships to four young students, who were selected in the spring of 1947. They arrived in August or September; two of them went to Harvard and MIT, and two, including myself, went to Princeton. All of us were received with great hospitality and complete sincerity. Back home in 1948, some of us got involved in the construction of a relay computer, BARK, that was completed in 1950. However, it was soon understood that there was a need for more computer facilities, and the construction of BESK under Erik Stemme was initiated.

FIGURE 1.
Front page of
Wiberg's logarithm
table.

LOGARITHMIC-TABLES

COMPUTED AND PRINTED

BY MEANS OF HIS CALCULATING-MACHINE

BY

D" M. WIBERG.

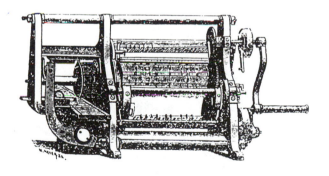

STOCKHOLM.

THE PRINTING COMPANY FORSETE,

1876.

It was completed in 1953, and for a short time it was considered to be one of the most powerful computers in the world. Its structure was much the same as the Princeton computer.

In 1956 a simplified copy of BESK, called SMIL, was completed at Lund University, built with a minimal budget of some $20,000. This computer was used for a large variety of problems in nuclear physics (particularly eigenvalue problems), spectroscopy, mathematics (number theory and table making), and also social sciences (geographical simulations). Several problems from research organizations and industry were also treated.

The actual and potential use of computers created a natural interest in conferences, because the literature on the subject was scarce at this time. The first Scandinavian conference on computers was held in May 1959 in Karlskrona. We chose this site because the Swedish Navy played an important role in the development of the computer, and also because the Baltic was especially lovely in the spring. Preliminary and informal discussions were held on the need for a Nordic journal on computer-related problems. At the next conference, in Copenhagen, 1960, a more formal meeting was arranged, and it was unanimously decided to start a Nordic journal within the computer area, to appear quarterly. The journal was intended to be international with papers published in English, German, or the Scandinavian languages. As it turned out, only four or five papers have been published in German, and papers in the Scandinavian languages gradually disappeared. Nowadays it is required that all papers be written in English.

The name of the journal is a long one, *Nordisk Tidskrift for Informationsbehandling*, but by playing around with the initials in a clever way, we were able to form the name *BIT*. All members of the editorial board come from the Nordic countries, but referees, naturally, are chosen all over the world. Peter Naur of Copenhagen has been a member of the board since the beginning in 1961, and Germund Dahlquist of Stockholm since 1962. Further, I have served as editor all the time up till now. We got financial support from the Danish company Regnecentralen under Niels Ivar Bech and from several official sources including the Nordic Research Organisations for Natural Sciences. Finally, just a few years ago we managed to become self-supporting, with the help of favorable exchange rates.

During the first decade, *BIT* tried to meet the public demands to supply information on new developments within the computer area. It is natural that the growing crowds of people working with computer applications of different kinds felt an increasing difficulty in keeping up with the rapid progress in hardware and software. That left a gap that *BIT* tried to fill. Simultaneously we tried to accomodate scientific papers, particularly in numerical analysis and in computer languages. Very early we opened a special column for algorithms written in Algol 60. As a consequence of this policy, our subscribers during the first decade, to a large extent, were individual Scandinavians. Then the situation slowly started to change. The need for general information decreased because this information appeared in special new publications, such as *Datamation*, and also in ordinary newspapers and magazines. Simultaneously, the number of scientific contributions to *BIT* increased strongly, first in numerical mathematics, and later in computer science. As a consequence of this development, the number of Scandinavian subscribers decreased, and the number of non-Scandinavian subscribers, mostly universities, libraries, and research organisations, increased. The net result was slightly positive. In 1980 *BIT* was divided into two sections, one for computer science and one for numerical mathematics. In spite of obvious difficulties, we have been able to strike a reasonable balance between these two areas. At

FIGURE 2.
Distribution of authors (1961–1964) and of subscriptions (1984).

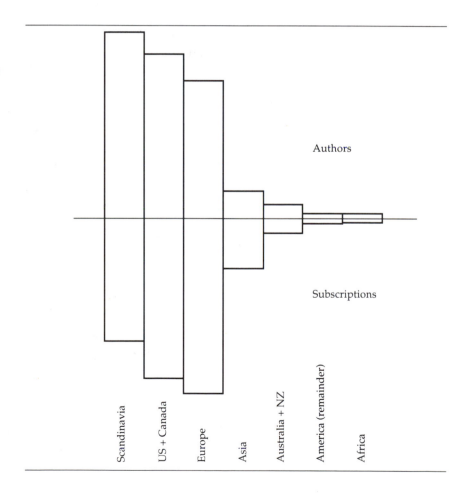

the same time, we appointed special area editors, Peter Naur for computer science and Åke Björck for numerical mathematics. The gradual development from a domestic magazine to an international scientific journal is illustrated clearly in Figures 2 and 3.

The first volume (1961) had 290 pages and was typewritten and photographed. By volume 2, we were already printing in the traditional way. *BIT* had obviously been observed abroad, because two contributions, one from the United States (Louis Fein) and one from the Netherlands (Peter Wynn), appeared in the first volume. Several "foreign" papers (among them, one by Gene Golub) were presented in volume 2. During the first years, there was a certain ambivalence with respect to papers on hardware. We did publish a few such papers in the beginning, but finally they disappeared.

It is, of course, hard to tell which papers have had an impact on the general development of the computer. Turning first to computer science, we can see an important subject that attracted considerable attention during the first 10 to 15 years, namely computer languages and compiler construction. The main focus was on Algol 60, because at that time, Fortran was only available for users, and the corresponding compilers were kept secret. However, different aspects of other programming languages, such as Cobol, Algol 68, Pascal, and Simula, have also been treated. In later years a great deal of attention has been given to data structures, searching, and sorting.

In numerical mathematics I think that papers on stability problems (by Dahlquist and others), on numerical methods for stiff systems (Enright, Hull, and Lindberg), and on Runge-Kutta methods (various authors) have had a considerable influence. I would also like to men-

FIGURE 3.
Percentage of non-Scandinavian printed pages. The drop in 1985 is due to a number of invited Scandinavian papers.

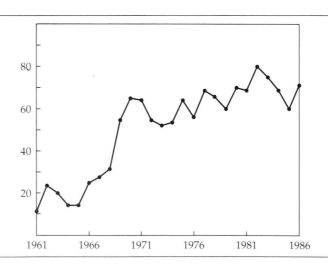

tion the special issue dedicated to Germund Dahlquist on his 60th birthday, 16 January 1985. It was followed by another special issue dedicated to *BIT* on its 25th birthday and by one dedicated to Peter Naur on his 60th birthday, 25 October 1988.

Concerning the geographical distribution of authors and subscribers, we can say roughly that the Nordic countries, the rest of Europe, and the United States plus Canada account for about one third each, for both authors and subscribers. One of the most striking features is the steep increase in contributions from Taiwan; we have also had quite a few from mainland China. In both cases the quality has been rather good. Also, some exotic countries are represented by authors: Nigeria, Singapore, Ecuador, Sudan, and the Fiji Islands, just to mention a few. Even if several papers must be rejected, we try to encourage the authors; and in many cases the papers can be published after some revision. The overall rejection rate is now about 40 percent, and the time between reception and publication of a paper is, on the average, about 12 months.

In order to encourage scientific work in computer science and numerical mathematics, a special prize of 50,000 DKr was created in 1985. It is awarded to the best contribution by a Nordic author, a restriction imposed in recognition of the support given to *BIT* during previous years from the Nordic governments. The first winner was Sigurd Meldal, a Norwegian computer scientist from Oslo University. He received the prize at a ceremony during the NordDATA conference in Trondheim, Norway, June 1987.

View of a part of the wartime Los Alamos Laboratory.

PLACES

In the United States, the federal government has long supported the development of scientific computing through its laboratories and funding agencies. In recent years, for instance, the Argonne National Laboratory has been a center for the production of high-quality software, such as the Linpack collection of subroutines. This tradition goes back to the first days of electronic computing.

In essays by N. Metropolis and John Todd we see examples of this support at the Los Alamos Laboratory and the National Bureau of Standards (now the National Institute of Standards and Technology). Los Alamos is, of course, famous for its work on atomic weapons during and after World War II, and from the start it has been stretching the limits of computing and computers. John von Neumann was much involved in its activities, in projects such as his development of the Monte Carlo method with Ulam. The National Bureau of Standards has had a broader mission, providing support for scientists and engineers in a great many disciplines. In earlier decades this led to the production of mathematical tables, and now it motivates the development and testing of computational methods for a wide array of technological applications. The computational work of both institutions straddles the invention of the computer, and both these essays discuss the changes brought about by the computer.

We cross the Atlantic Ocean with the essay by David Wheeler on his work at Illinois and Cambridge. He describes his experiences with early computers, such as the EDSAC and the ILLIAC, including the difficulties of debugging programs on machines with unreliable hardware and software. Leslie Fox discusses early numerical analysis in the United Kingdom, concentrating on the precomputer era. He continues the discussion of the relaxation method, describing its invention by Southwell and its use in hand calculations.

Martin Gutknecht takes us to Switzerland and writes of the algorithmic work of Eduard Stiefel and Heinz Rutishauser and of the use there of Konrad Zuse's computers.

Finally, we move to eastern Europe. Ivo Babuška discusses Czechoslovakia—the closing of the universities by Hitler in 1939 and the gradual reawakening of mathematical activities. V. N. Kublanovskaya describes the research on numerical linear algebra in Leningrad from 1950 to the present, particularly in the work of Faddeeva, Faddeev, and herself.

The Los Alamos Experience, 1943–1954

N. Metropolis

1. The Origins of Modern Computing

The time is World War II. A proposal is made by John Mauchly and Presper Eckert, Jr., to the Aberdeen Proving Ground to build the first electronic computer at the University of Pennsylvania. Construction is completed in 1945 just as the war is winding down in Europe and Asia—the ENIAC is born. The story has been told many times. What is perhaps less well-known is that all electronic tubes, resistors, and diodes used in the ENIAC were joint Army-Navy rejects, so that in principle the ENIAC could have been built before the war and could have made an even bigger impact! The technology was clearly in place; perhaps the compelling applications of commerce (and science?) were being satisfied by the good progress in electromechanical computers.

But the war was to change all that by demanding solutions to all kinds of nonlinear differential equations. At Los Alamos, from the very beginning in April 1943, it was clear that nonlinearities would come into their own—a new experience for the theorists who had learned to touch only linear phenomena and had a built-in shyness for anything beyond.

But the applications at hand were compelling and numerical methods the only recourse, so a lot of people became experts on desk calculators. The pounding these machines took soon took its toll. At first the machines would be shipped to the manufacturer for repair, but the delays were not tolerable, especially when the number of viable machines dwindled. So Richard Feynman took charge and set up a repair shop with me as his assistant. Applying the techniques of analysis by observing the sequence of mechanical linkages of a good desk calculator with that of a faulty one, we soon found the hang-ups and, with time, became pseudo-experts. We hung a sign outside the office door proclaiming our skills and services available. When the administration discovered this extracurricular activity, some critical eyebrows were raised and the service self-destructed. When the number of viable computers dwindled again, however, criticism turned to pleas to restore the status quo.

Before long a formal group doing hand calculations was formed under the aegis of mathematician Donald Flanders (an authority on transfinite numbers). Many wives of scientists were enlisted and indeed contributed nobly to this effort, but it was soon evident that much more help was needed. Dana Mitchell proposed the punched-card approach of IBM, based on the application of such machines in astronomy at Columbia University before the war. Stanley Frankel and Eldred Nelson were put in charge, aided and abetted by the ubiquitous Feynman. In due course, I joined that group. (The description of that effort is temporarily interrupted in order to set the stage for the modern development of computing.)

At Princeton University, a young Englishman named Alan Turing came to study with the logician Alonzo Church shortly before World War II. The concepts of computable numbers and computer universality were born. Nearby, at the Institute for Advanced Study, John von Neumann was concerned with similar problems in logic and mathematics. He offered Turing an assistantship at the Institute—a marvelous plum—but the war clouds were too distinct, and Turing's loyalty to his country prevailed. It was only in 1976 that Brian Randell, the British computer historian, secured permission from his government to describe the wartime development of the Colussus and Turing's contributions to that effort. Meanwhile, von Neumann was expanding his interest in computational methods, most certainly for the war effort, but like Turing for deeper reasons. Both realized that modern computers could have profound effects in nonlinear mathematics by virtue of observing the unfolding of mathematical solutions that could stimulate thoughts about models and structures in those very refractory areas.

Perhaps their greatest contribution to computer development was the fact that they took a serious interest in it; this attracted good scientists to the discipline on a much shorter time scale than might have been otherwise. It is not to say that their *other* contributions were not monumental.

It is sad to observe that a war seems to be essential to encourage and stimulate developments such as the computer. The example is not unique—nuclear energy is another instance; moreover, there was a synergistic relationship between the two disciplines. We shall try to describe this mutual development, as seen from Los Alamos.

2. Wartime Los Alamos

The theoretical problems at wartime Los Alamos that required large amounts of computing were hydrodynamical in nature. Numerical methods were invoked because of nonlinearities (owing to the equations of state). As previously mentioned, the available resources were electromechanical devices, mostly used for business applications at the time. The highly repetitive and simple arithmetic operations could be adapted to mechanization, however, and the devices indeed acquitted themselves well. Except for the occasional particle of dust that wreaked havoc with the basic component relays, they seemed tireless. The adjoined, more sophisticated aspects (fortunately a relatively small fraction of the total computing), such as the treatment of shock waves, were dealt with by desk calculators and introduced into each time step of the computation.

One learned about stability conditions in numerically integrating partial differential equations of various kinds, and that attention must be paid to the relation between space and time steps in the integration process. This is now old hat. Some photographs of the scene are shown in Figures 1 and 2.

One must be reminded of one unusual characteristic of that wartime situation: Various theoretical models could not be physically tested, and hence, great reliance was placed on numerical, nonlinear mathematics.

There were, of course, other challenging theoretical problems, such as critical mass calculations, based on integral-diffusion equations requiring numerical processing for *finite* boundary conditions. Another direction was the study of nuclear explosive effects, again *gedanken* experiments. So the desk calculators and the electro-mechanical com-

FIGURE 1.
The immediate postwar configuration of IBMs with some of the personnel.

FIGURE 2.
Close-up view of a
multiplier unit that
had been converted
to perform triple
products as a single
operation.

FIGURE 3.
John von Neumann,
1903–1957 (immediate
postwar photograph).

puters kept churning, and more scientists became conscious of numerical methods, along with their causes and cures.

It was John von Neumann (shown in Figure 3) who kept us informed about progress on other computer fronts. The composite electromechanical Mark I at Harvard was nearing completion under the aegis of Howard Aiken; there was also the relay calculator at Bell Laboratories with G. R. Stibitz and S. B. Williams. We learned about the brain research of W. S. McCulloch and W. Pitts that provided a neuronal model for the foundations of computer science. The most exciting development, however, was the ENIAC. We learned of this in January 1945, with the ongoing construction to be completed in some five or six months. The timing of the announcement was perfect. At the time, most of the theoretical studies of fission at Los Alamos were in hand; and Edward Teller and his group had begun to concentrate on thermonuclear ideas. It was von Neumann's thought that possibly the difference equations of some thermonuclear reactions might be initially studied using the ENIAC, a much more realistic prospect than the much less sophisticated electromechanical computers. He was a consultant to both Los Alamos and the Ballistics Research Laboratory (BRL) at Aberdeen; thus, he might persuade the latter that Los Alamos could provide a more comprehensive and exhaustive shakedown cruise than the firing tables that BRL primarily studied. (Score a point for the genius of Mauchly and Eckert, who looked beyond the then-current approach to BRL's needs.)

Von Neumann asked Stanley Frankel and me if we were interested; we leapt at the opportunity and remained committed to that pursuit of a new discipline forever more. Adele Goldstine was very helpful in the early acquaintance with the ENIAC, and that assistance was much appreciated. Because it was a shakedown cruise, bugs were no surprise; and we learned patience, as one should, especially with new experimental setups. The latter had its rewards: It provided many opportunities for discussions with Mauchly and Eckert, and we learned much about that recent past of ENIAC evolution and of the optimistic prospects beyond ENIAC. It was evident that a new discipline was born.

The testing program lasted several months. In the later phases, our colleague Anthony Turkevich joined us, and, as always, we benefited considerably by that association.

Owing to the general uncertainties with respect to the future of the Laboratory following the end of World War II, Edward Teller called a meeting early in 1946 to document the results of our ENIAC experience and to give a final report of the thermonuclear group. Among those present were N. Bradbury, E. Fermi, S. Frankel, D. Froman, E. Konopinski, R. Landshoff, N. Metropolis, A. Turkevich, S. Ulam, and J. von Neumann.

One reaction was quite clear. A short time ago we had learned about the refractory nature of nonlinear phenomena, that numerics were our only recourse. We had learned about the slow and arduous methods of desk calculators, then the primitive adaptations to electromechanical devices; finally, the dawn of electronic computing was emerging. Even scientists thought they were dreaming. Many of us were anxious to explore some of the new directions as we returned to peacetime academia.

There were perhaps two episodes worth describing that relate to the tenor of those times:

1. Before leaving for Chicago, Fermi wanted to learn some details about electromechanical computing. In a discussion about the various machines, he characteristically pulled out of his shirt pocket a small piece of paper on which he had written his semiempirical formula for atomic masses as a function of atomic number A and charge number Z. "How would you do this?" he

asked. And that was how he learned, in his typically thorough manner, to do every step with his own hands. He had sensed accurately the degree of complexity that the machines could handle. Later he was to repeat his performance to satisfy his curiosity of electronic computing, and once again he had a computational problem that was consistent with the new capabilities: the phase shift calculations of the scattering of negative pions by hydrogen.

2. Soon after our ENIAC experience, Frankel and I joined the physics faculty at the University of Chicago. We were anxious to attempt a second set of computational problems on the ENIAC before it was to be moved from Philadelphia to Aberdeen Proving Ground in Maryland. It seemed appropriate to consider calculations in the liquid-drop model of fission; this model had been proposed by Bohr and Wheeler just before the war.

We were no less amazed by the ENIAC capabilities the second time around; moreover, this time there were no classification restrictions. We also harbored the unexpressed concern that attempting to move the ENIAC from Philadelphia to Aberdeen could well be the last thing that happened to it; its size would fill an auditorium. Remember that those were the days of the vacuum tube and discrete components; transistors were unborn, and integrated circuits were not even a gleam.

The manuscript was submitted to the *Physical Review*. An associate editor hesitated about accepting it—there were too many computational overtones. An appeal was made to Charles Critchfield, one of his colleagues, and the associate editor was persuaded that he should recognize the inexorable harbingers of physics. (Many years later, that article was reprinted in a collection commemorating 40 years of nuclear fission.)

3. Postwar Los Alamos, 1948–54

During the period following Alamogordo and the end of World War II, computing expanded at Los Alamos. Plans were made to have two separate but interactive groups; one would provide computational capability for the Laboratory's needs, and the other would represent the research effort in this fledgling discipline. The latter was discussed in January 1948 and was started in 1949. Inasmuch as computer engineers had to be trained, not just hired, it seemed a good plan to follow in the footsteps of the group at the Institute for Advanced Study, where von Neumann had started his project in 1946. Work started on building a copy of the arithmetic unit and its controls. Copying proceeds faster than developing, and soon we had an operating unit.

Owing to the circumstance that J. H. Richardson had joined our staff from Toronto, where he had some preliminary experience with the Williams tube approach to a parallel memory, we explored some possibilities with two-inch cathode ray tubes while awaiting the completion of the Princeton effort using five-inch tubes. In the end, we opted for our own design for the memory unit and ventured out on our own to complete the computer. It ran the first real problem in early March 1952. At the baptism, MANIAC became its name; later a one (I) was added to it.

Briefly, MANIAC I had an auxiliary drum store of 10,000 40-bit words in parallel; and the input-output unit had a 5 (4 + 1) channel paper tape and a single channel magnetic tape drive. Finally, there was a commercial (Analex) line printer. That period was very exciting, and the original team that put it together, both hardware and software, was indeed a memorable one; the roster is shown in Table 1, and MANIAC I is seen in Figure 4. (The present account is interrupted so as to catch up with other developments, both at Los Alamos and at Aberdeen.)

3.1. MONTE CARLO

Sampling techniques were well known to statisticians but had not enjoyed much application because of the tedium of implementing the various concepts. Early in the postwar period, while listening to the

TABLE 1
The staff of MANIAC I. Men and women were equally divided on the programming staff; the latter have their married names in parentheses.

MANIAC I	
Hardware	**Software**
H. Demuth	R. Bivins
T. Gardiner	D. Bradford
E. Klein	L. Cook (Leurgans)
R. Merwin	V. Ellingson (Gardiner)
H. Parsons	E. Felix (Alei)
W. Orvedahl	J. Jackson
J. Richardson	M. Jones (Devaney)
	P. Stein
	M. Tsingou (Menzel)
	M. Wells

FIGURE 4.
MANIAC I at Los Alamos, 1952. Of the six panels, the end ones contain the controls, and the central four are the three arithmetic registers. Twenty of the 40 Williams' tubes (parallel, electrostatic memory) are packaged and reside above the arithmetic unit. The remaining 20 are on the obverse side. Two staff programmers are running a problem on a "hands-on" basis.

FIGURE 5.
Stanislaw Ulam (1909–1984).

first ENIAC experience, Stan Ulam (Figure 5) realized that the advent of the ENIAC had changed all that. If computations could be done with the speed implied by electronic switching times, then sampling could be trivialized and statistical techniques should be revived. Neutron diffusion and related chain reactions were natural applications.

His remarks to von Neumann were quickly appreciated, and just as quickly Johnny outlined a procedure to implement the notion. One of the key ingredients was a set of subroutines to provide random numbers reflecting various distribution functions (e.g., the exponential, logarithm, and cosine distributions). Such matters intrigued von Neumann, and he amused himself and others considering efficient algorithms to achieve these ends. Plans were made to test the method on various nuclear material configurations to determine criticality, spatial and velocity distributions of neutrons, and so forth using the ENIAC. (In one of my baptismal moods, it seemed to me that the name Monte Carlo was very appropriate.) But a hiatus developed—the ENIAC was indeed being moved to Aberdeen Proving Ground in Maryland—and many learned skeptics had the opinion that the ENIAC had performed its last arithmetic operation. However, they had not reckoned with the dedication, genius, and care exercised by two young electronics engineers, Josh Gray and Richard Merwin, two fearless uninitiates who acquitted themselves nobly.

In the interim, Richard Clippinger, an applied mathematician on the Aberdeen staff, suggested a more efficient method to program the ENIAC. Instead of viewing the computer as a giant plug board and setting up a problem by making all the jack plug connections to effect the appropriate sequence of arithmetic operations, he envisioned setting up, once and for all, a vocabulary, with each instruction specified by a pair of decimal digits. A given problem would then be sequenced on the so-called function tables, an already existing component of the ENIAC. The task to structure the controls was started by Adele Goldstine in Princeton. She soon realized that the background operations to implement the concept utilized the available facilities when only partially through the vocabulary, so she abandoned the project. On a visit to Aberdeen in preparation for the ambitious Monte Carlo problems in collaboration with Klari and John von Neumann, I was shown a partially constructed many-to-one matrix control panel planned to expand an original logical function (so-called master programmer). Clearly, such a device would simplify implementing the Clippinger idea and perhaps render it feasible. This project was achieved by Klari and me, and the new mode was used for the Monte Carlo problems. A photograph shows a close-up of the function tables in Figure 6.

3.2 STATISTICAL SAMPLING REVISITED AND THE FERMIAC

Because of the interruption caused by the ENIAC's move to Aberdeen, back in Los Alamos Fermi had proposed a simple analog device to

FIGURE 6.
The so-called function tables that were used to store sequences of two decimal digit instructions, six per line, 102 lines per table.

FIGURE 7.
The FERMIAC, a
simple analog device
to compute neutron
trajectories in various
media. Neutrons
could have one of
two energies.

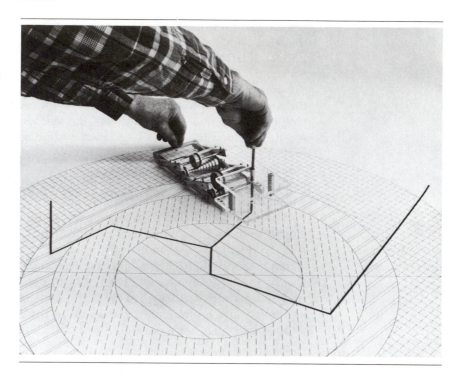

FIGURE 8.
Enrico Fermi
(1901–1954).

expedite modest but meaningful Monte Carlo calculations on neutron transport. The suggestion was made to a colleague, Perc King, on a bright Sunday morning hike in the nearby mountains. Figures 7 and 8 show the instrument and its master. This title episode is to introduce the role of Fermi in his sustained interest not only in computers in general, but also in the Monte Carlo method in particular. According to Emilio Segrè [3], his student and collaborator, "Fermi had invented, but of course not named, the present Monte Carlo method, when he was studying the moderation of neutrons at the University of Rome. He did not publish anything on the subject, but he used the method to solve many problems with whatever calculating facilities he had, chiefly a small mechanical adding machine." This was in the early 1930s.

In a more recent conversation with Segrè, I learned that Fermi took great delight in astonishing his Roman colleagues by his remarkably accurate, "too-good-to-believe" predictions of experimental results. After enjoying sufficient amusement, he revealed that his "guesses" were really derived from the statistical sampling techniques that he calculated whenever his insomnia prevailed in the wee morning hours!

We return to the story of MANIAC I and the excitement that continued in the postwar period. The ENIAC had been formally dedicated in Philadelphia, as was the Mark I in Cambridge. Among the participants in the latter affair, Turing was the most impressive. It was the only time I saw him.

Interest in electronic computers and computing was crystallizing rapidly—the word was spreading quickly. This was the period of ruggedized double triode vacuum tubes as well as cathode ray tubes, resistors and diodes of higher quality, and so on. Transistors were yet to come, and integrated circuits were not even imagined. Logical structures of computers were advancing rapidly; flow diagram concepts were developed by von Neumann; and assembly languages were emerging as precursors to more ambitious gleams. In the long run it was the applications, the problems solved by the computers, that would determine how the new discipline would be judged. Los Alamos, with its established tradition of interdisciplinary activities during the war, seemed like fertile ground. And so it was that in addition to working on Laboratory problems, the MANIAC was utilized for a wide variety of challenges so as to learn about possible lacunae in the logical structure of computers. We were still in the very earliest stage of the new discipline. Some of the earlier studies were the following:

1. *Fermi and phase shift analysis.* Fermi and Anderson had constructed the Chicago cyclotron for the production of the relatively new nuclear particles, the pions. Fermi came to Los Alamos the first summer of the MANIAC to learn firsthand how to prepare problems and how to run them—not in the abstract, but something real, of his phase shift analysis of pion scattering. During the course of that study, we learned a lot of physics, but we also learned more about how a great man works.

2. *Tellers and Rosenbluths and equations of state.* Like Fermi, Teller has always had a real interest in computers; also, his close friend was John von Neumann. The problem of interest was a Monte Carlo approach to two-space-dimensional equations of state [1]. The team included Mici Teller and Arianna and Marshall Rosenbluth. The work engendered some interest because of its novel statistical methods in general and its importance-sampling techniques.

3. *Turkevich and colleagues and intranuclear cascades.* A pioneer of the first ENIAC application, Anthony Turkevich, proposed the study, using statistical techniques, of nuclear cascades initiated by elementary particles on complex nuclei. Earlier R. Serber had suggested the approach. In addition to R. Bivins and M. Storm of the local group, J. M. Miller from Columbia and G. Friedlander of Brookhaven participated. A relativistic, three-dimensional model was adopted. Incident protons and neutrons of both low and high energies on a variety of target nuclei were studied in two stages: The first was an intranuclear cascade, followed by

a second, relatively slow stage of an evaporation mechanism. The comparison with experimental data was good.

4. *G. Gamow and early statistical studies of the genetic code.* It was Gamow who first suggested that the sequence of bases in the long polynucleotide chains of DNA or RNA dictates the order of some 20 amino acids in long polypeptide chains in proteins. Statistical studies were made to study the relationship between the frequency of occurrence of different amino acids and the number of different neighbors they possess in natural sequences and in artificial sequences generated by various coding procedures.

5. *Fermi-Pasta-Ulam problem.* Starting with the energy in a given normal mode, Fermi, Pasta, and Ulam studied the approach to thermodynamic equilibrium of a one-dimensional sequence of anharmonic oscillators. They supposed that the relaxation time would correspond to the dissipation of energy to the neighboring modes. By accident, they discovered the now well-known recurrence phenomena, which was a startling development. Later, J. L. Tuck and M. Menzel discovered super recurrence cycles. Also, M. Kruskal and N. Zabusky studied the continuous limit and arrived at solitons. Inverse scattering phenomena also became quite an industry.

6. *Anticlerical chess.* In 1949, with the advent of electronic computing, Claude Shannon at Bell Labs proposed the notion of computer chess. The first attempt at programming a strategy was made by Paul Stein and Mark Wells with a small group in late 1952. In those early days, a relatively modest effort was pursued by eliminating the bishops and reducing play to a six by six board. The strategy included decision tree pruning based on a minimax principle specified by von Neumann and Morgenstern. Computing time per move was about 20 minutes. Anthropomorphic allusions and illusions were in evidence.

4. Concluding Remarks

In conclusion I should like to make some brief remarks about some later computational developments concerning MANIAC II.

4.1 FINITE LIMIT SETS AND UNIVERSAL SEQUENCES

In the late sixties, Paul Stein, Myron Stein, and I became interested in function iteration—specifically, a quadratic function with a single parameter λ:

$$x_{n+1} = \lambda x_n (1 - x_n) \qquad n = 0, 1, \ldots \qquad 0 < x < 1 \qquad 3 \le \lambda \le 4 \qquad (1)$$

The numerical experiments were greatly aided by a display scope under computer control. As the parameter λ was varied, periodic solutions $\{x_0, x_1, x_2, \ldots, x_k\}$ were found, with $k = 1, 2, \ldots$. Some 4400 solutions were tabulated. The sequence of periodic solutions exhibited a curious property. If the particular function (1) was replaced by another function with the same general features as (1), such as unimodality, convexity, and symmetry (about $x = 1/2$), the same sequence of periodic patterns was found. We called the sequence universal.

Subsequences of these solutions corresponded to period doubling; that is, each point x_i in a periodic solution split into two points; higher values of λ resulted in a further splitting, and so forth. These so-called "harmonics" of a "fundamental" pattern converged in λ. Somewhat later, M. Feigenbaum at Los Alamos calculated the convergence rate of these harmonics and found a uniform rate. He then went on to describe a model for the onset of turbulence.

Still later came a lively study of strange attractors, various models of chaos, paradoxes of determinism vs. randomness, and so on. Some clarification is expected.

4.2 SIGNIFICANCE ARITHMETIC

The study of the propagation of inherent errors in initial data as the course of a calculation proceeds has been for the most part neglected. This is partly due to its refractory nature. More recently, there has been a small resurgence that has been called sensitivity of initial data.

The well-established tradition among experimentalists to express results accompanied by standard deviations seems to be taken less seriously by the computer practitioners. (Considerable attention has been focused on roundoff errors, a slightly different matter.)

With the increasing power of new computers and the stimulated interest in the foundations of computational methods, perhaps we shall see some resolution of the existence and uniqueness of mathematical solutions on the one hand, and of random character in the numerics on the other hand.

4.3 THE MIRACLE OF THE CHIP

Finally, a remark on the qualitative changes in computing. More than 40 years ago the electromechanical relay was replaced by the vacuum tube. The consequences of that transition continue to amaze us. However, the potential to broaden the whole activity owing to the miracle of the chip that enables us to shift from serial sequencing to massively parallel operation will dwarf the relay to vacuum tube transition.

For the first time we shall be able to study nature in full three-space dimensions for the physical sciences; to deal with some of the challenges in the softer sciences; and to explore some of the complexities that mock us today.

But we must not underestimate the enormous effort required to realize the potential of these new logical structures and of the physical implementation. New concepts in languages, operating systems, and algorithms must be achieved. The stimulus and pressure, as always, must come from worthy applications.

For further discussion of the preceding material, see [2].

References

[1] N. Metropolis et al., "Equations of State Calculations by Fast Computing Machines," *J. Chem. Phys.* 21 (1953): 1087–1092.

[2] R. D. Richtmyer and N. Metropolis, "Modern Computing," *Phys. Today* 2 (1949): 8–15.

[3] E. Segrè, *From X-Rays to Quarks (Modern Physicists and Their Discoveries)* (San Francisco: W.H. Freeman, 1980).

The Prehistory and Early History of Computation At the U.S. National Bureau of Standards

John Todd

1. Introduction

Our ancestors were the surveyors, navigators, astronomers, gunners, table makers, and electronic engineers. Speaking at Princeton, I would be remiss if I did not mention Otto Neugebauer and Herman Goldstine, who have covered, respectively, the earliest computations and computations in the sixteenth to nineteenth centuries; and A. W. Tucker, who, apart from his work in linear programming and game theory, resolved the identity of the Gauss in Gauss-Jordan [cf. 2].

In a conference on the history of computing, we must recognize the contributions of R. C. Archibald (1875–1955) as the founder in 1943 of *Mathematical Tables and Other Aids to Computation* (since 1960, *Mathematics of Computation*) and as its editor until 1949. For accounts of his work see [17,18]. His book [3] includes portraits of many scientists mentioned in the following sections (for example, L. J. Comrie, A. N. Lowan, J. C. P. Miller, and A. J. Thompson).

Magnus R. Hestenes and I, at the invitation of the Mathematical Association of America, have completed an extensive, illustrated history of the National Bureau of Standards (NBS) Institute for Numerical Analysis at the University of California at Los Angeles, 1947–1954 [15]. I have also written an account of numerical analysis at the NBS [39] and an obituary [40] of John H. Curtiss, the first chief of the Applied Mathematics Division of NBS (sometimes known as the National Applied Mathematics Laboratories, NAML). I have tried as far as possible to avoid repeating material from these papers here. I have also omitted details of the reports [5,19] on the work of the Mathematical Tables Project [1938–1947].

2. 1871–1929

I would like to begin in 1871, the year in which the British Association for the Advancement of Science (BAAS) Mathematical Tables Committee began operations, which lasted at varying intensity until 1948 when the Royal Society took over. In its final report [4], it is seen that some of the greatest British mathematicians, both pure and applied, were active in this project. The Royal Society Committee was

251

discharged in 1965, the chairmen having been Sir Charles Darwin, D. R. Hartree, and M. V. Wilkes.

The development of studies in numerical computation at universities, at government institutions, and in commercial enterprises requires our attention.

In Germany, the work of Carl Runge has been described in [29,31]. Runge, whose name will be familiar to everyone who has had to solve a differential equation numerically, was a professor of applied mathematics at Göttingen, 1904–1924, and published his *Vorlesungen über numerisches Rechnen*, one of the early texts on numerical analysis, with H. König. (This book appeared in 1924 as volume 11 of the Springer Yellowback series.)

When E. T. Whittaker (1873–1956) came to the University of Edinburgh in 1912 from the Royal Observatory in Ireland, he founded a Mathematical Laboratory. For an account of Whittaker's views about the importance of such organizations, see [8,21]. McCrea [21] writes "Dublin and Edinburgh probably offered greater play for his individuality and enabled him to give effect to his ideas such as that of a mathematical laboratory, in ways that would not have been possible elsewhere." Hans Schneider, to whom numerical algebraists are indebted for his work on the periodical "Linear Algebra and its Applications," recently told me that as a student at Edinburgh in 1948, he participated in the Mathematical Laboratory. Apparently this was still much as described in the preface to [44]. Schneider recalls that he

FIGURE 1.
A. J. Thompson's machine.

filled out by hand printed schedules for Fourier analysis, as included in [44], and also that he did not choose this course as one of the four out of six in which he was examined.

There were few textbooks available at that time (1914): The faculty at Edinburgh began to write some. Apart from the classical treatise of Whittaker and G. Robinson [44], a series of Edinburgh Mathematical Tracts [43] were edited by Whittaker. The influence of astronomy on the choice of titles is clear. It is interesting to note that later, Stiefel's first book was on descriptive geometry—it was, however, only in his last period that he worked in celestial mechanics.

Whittaker maintained an interest in numerical mathematics throughout his life and in 1938 presided over a BAAS Symposium, "From Function to Printed Table: Some Aspects of the Work of Preparing a Table of a Mathematical Function." His successor at Edinburgh, A. C. Aitken (1895–1967), made numerous contributions to numerical mathematics, as did one of his pupils, E. L. Ince (1891–1941). Ince's work on Mathieu functions brought them into the range of "standard" tabulated functions (see later work by G. Blanch and W. G. Bickley). Ince also contributed a volume of tables in algebraic number theory to the British Association Series—at least one mathematician I know "never leaves home without [it]."

A notable event took place in Naples in 1927 when Mauro Picone (1885–1976) established an Instituto Nazionale per le Applicazioni del Calcolo (INAC). He first characterized the Instituto as a "living table of functions," but later, in 1952, wrote, "It is the place where the marriage between functional topology and numerical calculation has taken place." The Instituto was transferred to Rome in 1932.

In 1928 Alwin Walther (1898–1967) began the development of Institut für praktische Mathematik at Darmstadt [6].

3. The 1930s

This was an important, if transitional, decade in the history of our subject. All I can do is to mention some of the events and publications that appear to be influential for later developments. Above all there is the 1936/37 paper of A. M. Turing [41]. Next there is a paper by A. M. Ostrowski [23] on the stability of computations (followed a decade later by one on symbolic integration [24]).

In view of the importance of graphics, it is worthwhile mentioning the books of tables of Jahnke-Emde and the work of Carl Størmer (1874–1957), which began early in the century and was surveyed in [34]. I had contacts with Størmer in the late 1940s about his early work on arctangent relations [AMS11].

FIGURE 2.
Carl Størmer.

S. A. Gerschgorin (1901–1933) made contributions in his short life to numerical mathematics in three areas: discretization errors in the

FIGURE 3.
Model of trajectories,
by C. Størmer.

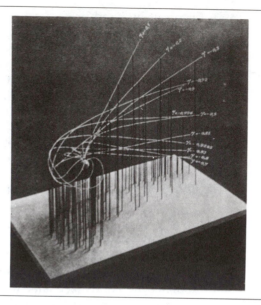

solution of partial differential equations [11], construction of conformal maps [13], and estimates for the characteristic values of matrices [12]. All of these were taken up decades later by NBS workers, including G. E. Forsythe, A. J. Hoffman, A. M. Ostrowski, Olga Taussky, John Todd, S. E. Warschawski, and W. R. Wasow. Actually the work on

FIGURE 4.
Olga Taussky and
Cornelius Lanczos.

FIGURE 5.
Twin Brunsviga.

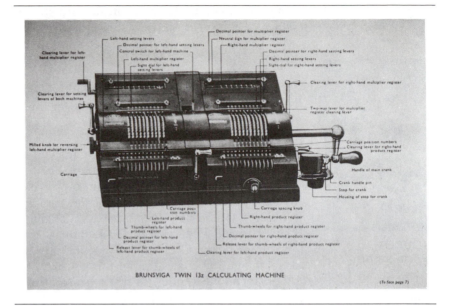

FIGURE 6.
D. H. Sadler.

Gerschgorin circles was begun earlier by Taussky, when she still was at the (British) National Physical Laboratory in World War II. She made topics in matrix theory (developing from Gerschgorin), a major theme of much work at NBS. Outside NBS there were contributions to this area from the schools of A. T. Brauer and R. S. Varga.

In 1936, Comrie (1893–1950) left his position as superintendent of the (British) Nautical Almanac Office to found the Scientific Computing Service in London. For an account of his work, see [20]. One of Comrie's contributions to our subject was the ingenious use (or misuse) of commercial equipment for scientific calculations, notably the NCR accounting machine. (This was the machine for which von Neumann probably wrote his first program, designed for a problem suggested by D. H. Sadler, who succeeded Comrie as superintendent of the Nautical Almanac Office [38].) Comrie also showed how to use the hand-operated Twin Brunsviga 13Z efficiently as a parallel machine, for example, to calculate $r \cos \theta$ and $r \sin \theta$ simultaneously. When this machine became unavailable in World War II, he showed how to couple two (electric) Marchant machines, available from the United States, for use in artillery calculations.

We mention here the work of A. J. Thompson, although it covered four decades beginning in the 1920s and culminating in his books [36], which give logarithms to 20 digits of the numbers from 10^4 to 10^5. Not only did he compute these numbers on a machine he built himself, coupling four (Triumphator) hand machines, but he set it all himself on a Monotype keyboard. All this was done in his spare time: He was a civil servant in the British General Register (Census) Office. Thompson acknowledges his debt to the Triumphator agent who passed on his entire stock of spare parts when he went out of business.

Another important event was the establishment in 1938 of the Works Progress Administration (WPA) Mathematical Tables Project in New York under the scientific control of the U.S. National Bureau of Standards. L. J. Briggs was director of this project from 1933 to 1945 [5,19].

FIGURE 7.
Lyman J. Briggs.

The contribution of Lyman J. Briggs (1874–1963), the third director of NBS, to our topic has been underestimated. Some of his admirers presented a series of papers to him on his eightieth birthday in 1955, which appeared in the *Journal of the Washington Academy of Sciences* (volumes 44 and 45). The paper of G. Blanch and I. Rhodes begins, "This paper is dedicated to Dr. Lyman J. Briggs, whose sympathetic encouragement and generosity of spirit gave the much needed impetus to mathematical computing in this country."

Blanch and Rhodes [5, p. 3] record "the most generous cooperation of that remarkable group of table makers (the BAAS Mathematical Tables Committee). Among the men who gave freely of their time were Bickley, Comrie, Miller, Milne-Thomson, Sadler to name a few."

4. World War II

During this period there was, of course, an intensification of the efforts in our subject. More mathematicians were drafted into it, and some remained with it.

FIGURE 8.
Ida Rhodes.

My own experience, briefly, was the following: After working in C. P. Snow's census of Scientists and Engineers in 1940, I saw to it that I was assigned as a Degaussing Range Officer. However, this was the time of acoustic mines, and my assignment was changed first to work in the Mine Design Department near Portsmouth. There I had my first encounter with NBS. We used the WPA tables of e^x to design delay circuits, which ensured that our magnetic mines, although triggered ahead of the bow of a target, would detonate under the engine room. We also had to make tables of the dip and drift of our contact mines. After observing this for some months, I convinced my superiors that I could organize more effective use of mathematicians and mathematics and was transferred to the Admiralty Department of Scientific Research and Experiment. There I had considerable freedom and support and education from my colleagues, especially Erdélyi and Sadler. The Admiralty Computing Service was organized. Accounts of its work are [9,32,33].

The wartime activities of mathematicians in the United States have been well documented [25,26,27,28,30]; in Germany there have also been comprehensive reports [35,42].

One of the successes of the Admiralty Computing Service was the discovery of the location from incomplete and imperfect data of an enemy transmitter in France that was guiding bombers to targets in 1940/41. This was acknowledged in the official History of British Intelligence. Comrie reports that a Spitfire found and photographed the camouflaged transmitter within 100 meters of his estimate.

Just after the end of World War II, the Service published its "Index of Mathematical Tables." An enlarged second edition appeared later [10]. These volumes remain a monument to Comrie and the Service, whose staff included H. O. Hartley and Miller. It is also appropriate to mention here the complementary guide [14].

I have a personal reminiscence of Comrie to tell. There was no love lost between him and the Admiralty, an enmity that I inherited although I was a very temporary scientific officer during the Admiralty Computing Service times. Comrie scolded me for misspelling Britannica, for instance. However, things improved and we arranged to have a friendly lunch in Soho, midway between our offices. We had just ordered, in a backroom under a skylight protected by glued-on linen, when a V1 landed close by us. We were enshrouded by the dirty linen. Dusty but undamaged, we gave up lunch and returned to his office. There we waited for the return of his computers, who were also lunching within range—fortunately unhurt—to be given some brandy and sent home.

5. Post World War II

In the early postwar years, local and national centers for applied mathematics, and in particular for computing, were organized in many countries.

FIGURE 9.
Burton Colvin.

I returned to King's College, London, and gave my first course in numerical mathematics in 1946. We had two Marchant ACT 10M machines for the class. In this course I introduced the Cholesky method as the preferred one for the solution of positive definite systems $Ax = b$. This was taken up by L. Fox, who analyzed it deeply with his National Physical Laboratory colleagues H. D. Huskey, J. H. Wilkinson, and Turing. It has indeed become one of the workhorses of numerical linear algebraists. In this course I also discussed the Rayleigh-quotient method for determining the characteristic values of A. This method was later thoroughly analyzed by Ostrowski.

I will now discuss briefly what happened at the NBS. What happened in the United Kingdom at the National Physical Laboratory is discussed by Fox elsewhere in this volume.

The U.S. NBS was constituted in 1901. The first formal recognition of mathematics in its program occurred in 1947 with the formation of an Applied Mathematics Division, known for some time as the National Applied Mathematics Laboratories. This division had

258   Places

four sections: Institute for Numerical Analysis, Computation Laboratory, Statistical Engineering Laboratory, and Machine Development Laboratory. An annual budget of $360,000 was contemplated, with a total complement of about 100 staff. An Applied Mathematics Series to include tables, symposium proceedings, and so on was set up in 1948. To date 63 volumes have been published, and these are listed in the Appendix, with some earlier publications of the Mathematical Tables Project. The activity in numerical mathematics continues to the present and reached a relative maximum in the early 1950s. The leaders were J. H. Curtiss (1947–1953), F. L. Alt (1953–1954), E. W. Cannon (1954–1972), B. W. Colvin (1972–1986), and F. E. Sullivan (1986–present).

As stated at the beginning of this paper, I will confine my attention to some general remarks and to some matters that were not sufficiently emphasized elsewhere.

The success of the Applied Mathematics Division had several reasons. First, the director of the NBS, E. U. Condon, was a distinguished mathematical physicist, as was his opposite number C. G. Darwin, director of the National Physical Laboratory. Second, the chief of the laboratories, J. H. Curtiss, was ideally suited for the job and well-trained in mathematics and statistics. He was a part of the U.S. mathematical establishment, as was his father, D. R. Curtiss, and his brother-in-law, A. W. Tucker. A third reason for success was the usually liberal policy of the U.S. Civil Service Commission on hiring noncitizens, such as Agmon, Fortet, Hartree, Kato, Ostrowski, Stiefel, Wielandt, Taussky, and myself, all of whom had previous experience in numerical mathematics. Also, the NBS provided many opportunities for career development at various levels, and that, at the postdoctoral level, was particularly successful (for example, this attracted J. R. Rice and Marvin Marcus). Finally, let me mention the experienced members of the WPA Group (Abramowitz, Blanch, Lanczos, Rhodes, Salzer, Stegun, Zucker) and the (sometimes) generous support from other agencies of the Federal Government.

The period 1947 to 1950 was also a transitional period from hand and punched-card equipment to the new automatic electronic computers SEAC and SWAC. These machines had to be designed and built, and then we had to learn to use them. We had to develop a philosophy for the solution of massive problems. It was, roughly, that of controlled computational experiments—that is, to compare the theoretical results of academic problems with the experimental results obtained by the use of appropriate algorithms on the academic problems. See [16,22].

After the actual completion of the machines, there was little time for experimentation, and it is surprising that much significant work was accomplished. We recall that the building of SEAC was funded

FIGURE 10.
E. W. Cannon.

FIGURE 11.
F. Alt.

FIGURE 12.
Milton Abramowitz.

FIGURE 13.
Irene Stegun.

by the U.S. Air Force when there were delays in the delivery of their UNIVAC. Consequently the Air Force wanted it for their linear programming problems, and the engineers who built it wanted continually to improve it. Things got worse when SEAC was commandeered by the AEC.

Alan J. Hoffman was responsible for the related activities in the Computation Laboratory. Apart from the solution of specific problems (some even going back to the WPA Group), a comparative study of algorithms for linear programming was made, which is still cited as a model of how computational experiments should be made and reported. Hoffman himself wrote a seminal report on the approximate solution of linear inequalities and pointed out the connections with combinatorial problems. This area was greatly advanced by J. Edmonds and was then developed into a specialty of its own.

During this time steady progress was made in fulfillment of the dream to publish a 'neuerer' Jahnke-Emde. With encouragement from P. M. Morse, among others, and financial support from the National Science Foundation, *Handbook of Mathematical Functions* [1] was published in 1964, unfortunately after the death of Abramowitz (1914–1958). It was a resounding success.

During the McCarthy era, the NBS and the mathematics group did not escape severe losses. Condon, for example, resigned in 1950. Condon's successor, A. V. Astin, was fired in 1953 because of the

FIGURE 14.
A demonstration of SEAC by Morris Newman.

FIGURE 15.
Alan J. Hoffman.

FIGURE 16.
Churchill Eisenhart.

ADX2 Battery Additive Affair (see, for example, [15, Chapter 7]). After public outcry he was reinstated, but despite a favorable report by the Kelly Committee, the size of the NBS operation was greatly reduced. In particular, the Institute for Numerical Analysis operation in Los Angeles was terminated in 1954, and there was a substantial reduction in force in the Computation Laboratory: about a third of its staff, then numbering about 100. Fortunately, there was quite a demand from industry and universities for people with actual computer experience.

A numerical analysis section (with a somewhat less ambitious program than the Institute for Numerical Analysis), of which I was chief, was separated off from the Computation Laboratory. Abramowitz became chief of the Computation Laboratory until his death in 1958.

It is important to recall that the NBS Applied Mathematics Division was, in its early days at any rate, not well funded. It operated as a small business on funds transferred from other government agencies for services rendered. For instance, in fiscal year 1953, out of a total budget of $1,546,200, only $128,400 came from NBS appropriations. Accordingly, the marketing of its services was an important aspect of the Division administration. Descriptions of the projects involved are given in the quarterly reports. Many were, properly, routine computations suitable for centralization, but some were major contributions to national needs: navigational tables, specification, and acceptance testing for the early commercial computers and computation for nuclear weapons.

Another important component of the work of NBS was the preparation of tables and handbooks for applied statistics. This was largely the work of the Statistical Engineering Laboratory under its first chief, Churchill Eisenhart, and his successors. Although some of the material was in traditional form, much more was of a combinatorial nature, and different methods of construction and checking had to be developed. Difference methods, for instance, are not relevant for tables of designs for experiments. The work in this area passed the investigations resulting from the ADX2 affair with flying colors. See the following volumes of the AMS listed in the Appendix: 6, 7, 21–24, 33, 44, 47–48, 50, 54, 58, 62–63.

The Division ran several training programs financed by other agencies. One, in 1957, supported by the National Science Foundation, was in Numerical Analysis for senior university staff. The proceedings of this program was published [37], and the program was repeated under the direction of P. J. Davis in 1959.

We had our failures, too. I recall an early problem about a nonlinear differential equation occurring in a biomedical context. A discontinuity was developing in our solution, and our local mathematician assured us that such things could occur. The sponsor was excited by the "threshold effect" and got new money for more computations in a new machine: These ultimately led us to find an overflow error in the first computations and required an embarrassing correction in the sponsor's publication.

6. Conclusion

In 1957 I received an invitation from Cal Tech to help build up its numerical analysis program, and I accepted it because of my interest in teaching and because of the impending move of NBS to suburban Maryland. I was replaced by Davis, and he, later, by Morris Newman. After this, I was no longer in direct contact with NBS, and there were many organizational and personnel changes.

7. Acknowledgments

I am grateful for comments on drafts of this paper from Churchill Eisenhart, D. H. Sadler, H. E. Salzer, Olga Taussky, and H. S. Tropp.

References

[1] M. Abramowitz and I. A. Stegun (eds.), "Handbook of Mathematical Functions," National Bureau of Standards, *Applied Mathematics Series* 55 (1964); (New York: Wiley, 1982).

[2] S. C. Althuen and Renate McLaughlin, "Gauss-Jordan Reduction: A Brief History," *Amer. Math. Monthly* 94 (1987): 130–42.

[3] R. C. Archibald, "Mathematical Table Makers," *Scripta Mathematica* (New York: Yeshiva University, 1948).

[4] BAASMTAC, "Final Report," *Adv. Science* 7, 3427. Reprinted in *MTAC* 3 (1948): 333–40.

[5] G. Blanch and Ida Rhodes, "Table Making at NBS, 16," in *Studies in Numerical Analysis: Papers in Honor of Cornelius Lanczos,* B. R. Scaife (ed.) (London: Academic Press, 1974).

[6] W. de Beauclair and Alwin Walther, "IPM and the Development of Calculator Computer Technology in Germany 1930–45," *Ann. Hist. Comput.* 8 (1986): 334–50.

[7] Jesse Douglas, "A Method of Numerical Solution of the Problem of Plateau," *Ann. of Math.* (2) 29 (1928): 180–88.

[8] A. Erdélyi, "E. T. Whittaker," *MTAC* 11 (1957): 53–54.

[9] A. Erdélyi and John Todd, "Advanced Instruction in Practical Mathematics," *Nature* 158 (1966): 690–92.

[10] A. Fletcher, J. C. P. Miller, L. Rosenhead, and L. J. Comrie, *An Index of Mathematical Tables,* two volumes (Reading, MA: Addison-Wesley, 1962).

[11] S. A. Gerschgorin, "Fehlerabschätzung für das Differenzenverfahren zur Lösung partieller Differentialgleichungen," *Z. Angew. Math. Mech.* 10 (1930): 373–82.

[12] S. A. Gerschgorin, "Über die Abgrenzung der Eigenwerte einer Matrix," *Akad. Nauk SSSR, Ser. fiz-mat.* 6 (1931): 749–54.

[13] S. A. Gerschgorin, "Über die konforme Abbildung eines einfach zusammenhängenden Bereich auf den Kreis," *Rec. Math.* 40 (1933): 48–58.

[14] J. A. Greenwood and H. O. Hartley, *Guide to Tables in Mathematical Statistics* (Princeton University Press, 1962).

[15] M. R. Hestenes and John Todd, *NBS INA, The Institute for Numerical Analysis, UCLA, 1947–1954*, U.S. National Bureau of Standards Special Publication (Washington, DC: Mathematical Associaton of America, 1989).

[16] A. J. Hoffman, M. Mannos, D. Sokolovsky, and N. Wiegmann, "Computational Experience in Solving Linear Programs," *SIAM J.* 1 (1953): 17–33.

[17] D. H. Lehmer, "Raymond Clare Archibald 1875–1955," *MTAC* 10 (1956): 112.

[18] A. A. Bennett, "Raymond Clare Archibald," *MTAC* 4 (1950): 12.

[19] A. N. Lowan, "The Computation Laboratory of the National Bureau of Standards," *Scripta Math.* 15 (1949): 33–63.

[20] H. S. W. Massey, "L. J. Comrie," *Obit. Notices Fellows Royal Soc. London* 8 (1952): 97–107.

[21] W. H. McCrea, "E. T. Whittaker," *J. London Math. Soc.* 32 (1957): 234–56.

[22] Morris Newman and John Todd, "The Evaluation of Matrix Inversion Programs," *SIAM J.* 6 (1958): 466–76.

[23] A. M. Ostrowski, "Über die Konvergenz und die Abründungsfestigkeit des Newtonschen Verfahren," *Rec. Math.* 2 (1937): 1073–1098.

[24] A. M. Ostrowski, "Sur l'intégrabilité élémentaire de quelque classes d'expressions," *Comment. Math. Helv.* 18 (1946): 283–305.

[25] Mina S. Rees, "The Federal Computing Machine Program," *Science* 112 (1950): 731–36; reproduced with new introduction, *Ann. Hist. Comput.* 7 (1985): 151–68.

[26] Mina S. Rees, "Mathematics and the Government: The Post-War Years as Augury of the Future," in *The Bicentennial Tribute to American Mathematics, 1776–1976*, Dalton Tarwater (ed.) (Washington, DC: Mathematical Association of America, 1977), 101–18.

[27] Mina S. Rees, "The Mathematical Sciences and World War II," *Amer. Math. Monthly* 87 (1980): 607–21.

[28] Mina S. Rees, "The Computing Program of ONR," *Ann. Hist. Comput.* 4 (1982): 102–20.

[29] G. Richenhagen and Carl Runge, *Von der reinem Mathematik zur Numerik* (Göttingen: Van den Hoeck & Ruprecht, 1985).

[30] J. Barkley Rosser, "Mathematics and Mathematicians in World War II," *Notices Amer. Math. Soc.* 29 (1982): 509–15.

[31] Iris Runge, "Carl Runge [1856–1927] und sein wissenschaftliches Werk," *Abh. Akad. Wiss. Göttingen Math-Phy. Kl. Folge 3* 23 (1949).

[32] D. H. Sadler and John Todd, "Admiralty Computing Service," *MTAC* 2 (1947): 289–97.

[33] D. H. Sadler and John Todd, "Mathematics in Government Service and Industry," *Natur. J.* 157 (1946): 571–73.

[34] C. Størmer, "Programme for the Quantitative Discussion of Electron Orbits in the Field of a Magnetic Dipole with Application to Cosmic Rays and Kindred Phenomena," in *Comptes Rendus du Congrès Internationale des Mathematiciens* (1936): 61–75. See also Viggo Brun, "Carl Størmer in Memoriam," *Acta Math.* 100 (1958): I–VII.

[35] W. Süss (ed.), *Field Information Agencies Technical, Review of German Science 1939–1946, Pure Mathematics*, two volumes (Wiesbaden, Germany: Dieterich'sche Verlagsbuchhandlung, 1948).

[36] A. J. Thompson, *Logarithmetica Britannica*, two volumes (Cambridge University Press, 1952).

[37] John Todd (ed.), *Survey of Numerical Analysis* (New York: McGraw-Hill, 1962).

[38] John Todd, "John von Neumann and the National Accounting Machine," *SIAM Rev.* 16 (1974): 526–30.

[39] John Todd, "Numerical Analysis at the National Bureau of Standards," *SIAM Rev.* 17 (1975): 361–70.

[40] John Todd, "John Hamilton Curtis, 1907–1977," *Ann. Hist. Comput.* 2 (1980): 106–10.

[41] A. M. Turing, "On Computable Numbers with an Application to the Entscheidungsproblem," *Proc. London Math. Soc. (2)* 42 (1936–37): 230–65.

[42] A. Walther (ed.), *Field Information Agencies Technical, Review of German Science 1939–1946, Applied Mathematics*, five volumes (Wiesbaden, Germany: Dieterich'sche Verlagsbuchhandlung, 1948).

[43] E. T. Whittaker (ed.), *Edinburgh Mathematical Tracts* (London, G. Bell and Sons, 1915). This series included the following monographs:

1. E. L. Ince, "A Course in Descriptive Geometry and Photogrammetry for the Mathematical Laboratory";

2. D. Gibb, "A Course in Interpolation and Numerical Integration for the Mathematical Laboratory";

4. G. A. Carse and G. Shearer, "A Course in Fourier Analysis and Periodogram Analysis for the Mathematical Laboratory";

5. Herbert Bell, "A Course in the Solution of Spherical Triangles for the Mathematical Laboratory";

[44] E. T. Whittaker and G. Robinson, *The Calculus of Observations, A Treatise on Numerical Mathematics (4)* (London, Glasgow: Blackie, 1948).

APPENDIX

There follows a listing of the books in the AMS series together with lists of books published in an earlier MT series and by the Columbia University Press.

American Mathematical Society

AMS1. "Tables of the Bessel Functions $Y_0(x)$, $Y_1(x)$, $K_0(x)$, $K_1(x)$, $0 \le x \le 1$." (1948): ix, 60 pp. (Reissued as AMS25).

AMS2. H. E. Salzer, "Table of Coefficients for Obtaining the First Derivative without Differences." (1948): 20 pp.

AMS3. "Tables of the Confluent Hypergeometric Function $F(n/2, 1/2; x)$ and Related Functions." (1949): xxii, 73 pp.

AMS4. "Tables of Scattering Functions for Spherical Particles." (1949): xii, 119 pp.

AMS5. "Tables of Sines and Cosines to Fifteen Decimal Places at Hundredths of a Degree." (1949): viii, 95 pp.

AMS6. "Tables of the Binomial Probability Distribution." (1950): x, 387 pp.

AMS7. "Tables to Facilitate Sequential t-Tests." (1951): xix, 82 pp. Introduction by K. J. Arnold.

AMS8. H. E. Salzer, "Tables of Powers of Complex Numbers." (1950): iv, 44 pp.

AMS9. "Tables of Chebyshev Polynomials $S_n(x)$ and $C_n(x)$." (1952): xxix, 161 pp.

AMS10. H. Swanson, "Tables for Conversion of X-Ray Diffraction Angles to Interplanar Spacing." (1950): iii, 159 pp.

AMS11. J. Todd, "Tables of Arctangents of Rational Numbers." (1951): xi, 105 pp.

AMS12. A. S. Householder (ed.), "Monte Carlo Method." Proceedings of a symposium held on June 29, 30, and July 1, 1949, at the NBS Institute for Numerical Analysis, Los Angeles, California. (1951): vii, 42 pp.

AMS13. "Tables for the Analysis of Beta Spectra." (1952): iii, 61 pp.

AMS14. "Tables of the Exponential Function e^x." (1951): x, 537 pp. (A reissue of MT2).

AMS15. "Problems for the Numerical Analysis of the Future." Four papers presented at the Symposia on Modern Calculating Machinery and Numerical Methods, held in July 1948, at the NBS Institute for Numerical Analysis, Los Angeles, California. (1951): iv, 21 pp. Foreword by J.H. Curtiss.

AMS16. H. E. Salzer, "Tables of $n!$ and $\Gamma(n + \frac{1}{2})$ for the First Thousand Values of n." (1951): iii, 10 pp.

AMS17. "Tables of Coulomb Wave Functions." Volume 1. (1952): xxvii, 141 pp. Introduction by M. Abramowitz; foreword by Gregory Breit.

AMS18. E. F. Beckenbach (ed.), "Construction and Applications of Conformal Maps." Proceedings of a symposium held on June 22–25, 1949, at the NBS Institute for Numerical Analysis, Los Angeles, California. (1952): vi, 280 pp. (See also AMS 42).

AMS19. C. Snow, "Hypergeometric and Legendre Functions with Applications to Integral Equations of Potential Theory." (1952): xi, 427 pp. (Supersedes MT15).

AMS20. S. Herrick, "Tables for Rocket and Comet Orbits." (1953): xxiv, 100 pp.

AMS21. "A Guide to Tables of the Normal Probability Integral." (1952): iv, 16 pp.

AMS22. "Probability Tables for the Analysis of Extreme-Value Data." (1953): iii, 32 pp. Introduction by E. J. Gumbel.

AMS23. "Tables of Normal Probability Functions." (1953): ix, 344 pp.

AMS24. H. B. Mann, "Introduction to the Theory of Stochastic Processes Depending on a Continuous Parameter." (1953): v, 45 pp.

AMS25. "Tables of the Bessel Functions $Y_0(x)$, $Y_1(x)$, $K_0(x)$, $K_1(x)$, $0 \le x \le 1$." (1952): ix, 60 pp. (A reissue of AMS1 with minor revisions in the introduction).

AMS26. "Tables of arctan x." (1953): xiii, 170 pp. (A reissue of MT16).

AMS27. "Tables of 10^x. (Antilogarithms to the Base 10)." (1953): vi, 543 pp. Introduction by H. E. Salzer.

AMS28. "Table of Bessel Clifford Functions of Orders Zero and One." (1953): ix, 72 pp. Introduction by M. Abramowitz.

AMS29. L. J. Paige and Olga Taussky (eds.), "Simultaneous Linear Equations and the Determination of Eigenvalues." Proceedings of a symposium held on August 23–25, 1951, at Los Angeles, California, under the sponsorship of the National Bureau of Standards and the Office of Naval Research. (1953): iv, 126 pp.

AMS30. H. E. Salzer, "Tables of Coefficients for the Numerical Calculation of Laplace Transforms." (1953): 36 pp.

AMS31. "Table of Natural Logarithms for Arguments between Zero and Five to Sixteen Decimal Places." (1953): x, 501 pp. (A reissue of MT10). Introduction by A. N. Lowan; foreword by H. B. Dwight.

AMS32. "Table of Sine and Cosine Integrals for Arguments from 10 to 100." (1954): xv, 187 pp. (A reissue of MT13). Introduction by A. N. Lowan; foreword by J. A. Stratton.

AMS33. E. J. Gumbel, "The Statistical Theory of Extreme Values and Some Practical Applications." Prepared for publication by J. Lieblein. (1954): viii, 51 pp.

AMS34. "Table of the Gamma Function for Complex Arguments." (1954): xvi, 105 pp. Introduction by H. E. Salzer.

AMS35. "Tables of Lagrangian Coefficients for Sexagesimal Interpolation." (1954): ix, 157 pp. Introduction by H. E. Salzer.

AMS36. "Tables of Circular and Hyperbolic Sines and Cosines of Radian Arguments." (1953): x, 407 pp. (A reissue of MT3.) Introduction by A. N. Lowan; foreword by C. E. Van Orstrand.

AMS37. "Tables of Functions and of Zeros of Functions." Collected Short Tables of the Computation Laboratory. (1954): ix, 211 pp. Introduction by A. N. Lowan.

AMS38. C. Snow, "Magnetic Field of Cylindrical Coils and of Annular Coils." (1953): 29 pp.

AMS39. Olga Taussky (ed.), "Contributions to the Solution of Systems of Linear Equations and the Determination of Eigenvalues." (ed.) (1954): 139 pp.

AMS40. "Table of Secants and Cosecants to Nine Significant Figures at Hundredths of a Degree." (1954): vi, 46 pp. Introduction by M. Abramowitz.

AMS41. "Tables of the Error Function and its Derivative." (1954): xi, 302 pp. (A reissue of MT8.) Introduction by A. N. Lowan; foreword by T. C. Fry.

AMS42. J. Todd. (ed.), "Experiments in the Computation of Conformal Maps." (1955): 61 pp.

AMS43. "Tables of Sines and Cosines for Radian Arguments." (1955): xi, 278 pp. (A reissue of MT4.)

AMS44. "Table of Salvo Kill Probabilities for Square Targets." (1955): ix, 33 pp.

AMS45. "Table of Hyperbolic Sines and Cosines, $x = 2$ to $x = 10$." (1955): v, 81 pp.

AMS46. "Tables of the Descending Exponential, $x = 2.5$ to $x = 10$." (1955): v, 76 pp.

AMS47. W. H. Clatworthy, "Contributions on Partially Balanced Incomplete Block Designs with Two Associate Classes," (1956): iv, 70 pp.

AMS48. "Fractional Factorial Experimental Designs for Factors at Two Levels." (1957): iv, 85 pp.

AMS49. "Further Contributions to the Solution of Simultaneous Linear Equations and the Determination of Eigenvalues." (1958): 81 pp.

AMS50. "Tables of the Bivariate Normal Distribution Function and Related Functions." (1959): xlv, 258 pp.

AMS51. "Table of the Exponential Integral for Complex Arguments." (1958): xiv, 634 pp.

AMS52. "Integrals of Airy Functions." (1958): 28 pp.

AMS53. "Table of Natural Logarithms for Arguments from Five to Ten to Sixteen Decimal Places." (1958): xiii, 506 pp. (A reissue of MT12.) Introduction by A. N. Lowan.

AMS54. W. S. Connor and M. Zelen, "Fractional Factorial Experiment Designs for Factors at Three Levels," (1959): v, 35 pp.

AMS55. M. Abramowitz and A. Stegun (eds.), "Handbook of Mathematical Functions." (1964): 1061 pp.

AMS56. H. E. Salzer, "Tables of Osculatory Interpolation Coefficients," (1959): 34 pp.

AMS57. Marvin Marcus, "Basic Theorems in Matrix Theory," (1960): iv, 27 pp.

AMS58. W. S. Connor and Shirley Young, "Fractional Factorial Designs for Experiments with Factors at Two and Three Levels," (1961): 65 pp.

AMS59. "Tables Relating to Mathieu Functions." (1967): xlviii, 311 pp. (A reissue with additions of CUP13.) Introduction by G. Blanch.

AMS60. Morris Newman, "Matrix Representations of Groups," (1968): 79 pp.

AMS61. Joseqh Lehner, "Lectures on Modular Forms," (1969): 77 pp.

AMS62. J. A. John (University of Southampton, England), F. W. Wolock (Southeastern Massachusetts University), and H. A. David (University of North Carolina), "Cyclic Designs." (1972): 79 pp. Appendix by J. M. Cameron and J. A. Speckman, National Bureau of Standards.

AMS63. W. H. Clatworthy (formerly NBS Statistical Engineering Laboratory), State University of New York at Buffalo, "Tables of Two-Associate-Class Partially Balanced Designs." (1973): 327 pp. Contributions by J. M. Cameron and J. A. Speckman, National Bureau of Standards.

Columbia University Press Series (CUP)

CUP1. "Table of Reciprocals of the Integers from 100,000 through 200,009." (1943): viii, 204 pp.

CUP2. "Table of the Bessel Functions $J_0(z)$ and $J_1(z)$ for Complex Arguments." (1943): xliv, 403 pp. Introduction by A. N. Lowan; foreword by H. Bateman.

CUP3. "Table of Circular and Hyperbolic Tangents and Cotangents for Radian Arguments." (1943): xxxviii, 412 pp.

CUP4. "Tables of Lagrangian Interpolation Coefficients." (1944; 2d printing 1948): xxxvi, 394 pp. Introduction by A. N. Lowan; foreword by J. Shohat.

CUP5. "Table of arcsin x." (1945): xix, 124 pp. Introduction by A. N. Lowan.

CUP6. "Table of Associated Legendre Functions." (1945): xlvi, 306 pp. Introduction by A. N. Lowan.

CUP7. "Tables of Fractional Powers." (1946): xxx, 488 pp. Introduction by A. N. Lowan.

CUP8. "Tables of Spherical Bessel Functions, Volume I." (1947): xxviii, 375 pp. Introduction by A. N. Lowan; foreword by P. M. Morse.

CUP9. "Tables of Spherical Bessel Functions, Volume II." (1947): xx, 328 pp. Introduction by A. N. Lowan.

CUP10. "Tables of Bessel Functions of Fractional Order, Volume I." (1948): xlii, 413 pp. Introduction by M. Abramowitz; foreword by S. A. Schelkunoff.

CUP11. "Tables of Bessel Functions of Fractional Order, Volume II." (1949): xviii, 365 pp. Introduction by M. Abramowitz; foreword by R. E. Langer.

CUP12. "Tables of the Bessel Function $Y_0(z)$ and $Y_1(z)$ for Complex Arguments." (1950): xl, 427 pp. Introduction by A. N. Lowan; foreword by R. von Mises.

Mathematical Table Series (MT)

MT1. "Table of the First Ten Powers of the Integers from 1 to 1000." (1939): viii, 80 pp.

MT5. "Tables of Sine, Cosine, and Exponential Integrals, Volume I." (1940): xxvi, 444 pp.

MT6. "Tables of Sine, Cosine, and Exponential Integrals, Volume II." (1940): xxxvii, 225 pp.

MT7. "Table of Natural Logarithms, Volume I." (1941): xviii, 501 pp.

MT9. "Table of Natural Logarithms, Volume II." (1941): xviii, 501 pp.

MT11. "Tables of the Moments of Inertia and Section Moduli of Ordinary Angles, Channels, and Bulb Angles with Certain Plate Combinations." (1941): xiii, 197 pp.

MT17. "Miscellaneous Physical Tables: Planck's Radiation Functions, and Electronic Functions." (1941): vi, 58 pp. This includes as Part I tables of "Planck's Radiation Functions," which were reprinted from the *Journal of the Optical Society of America* in February 1940. Part II on "Electronic Functions" is superseded by NBS Circular 571, "Electron Physics Tables," by L. Marton, C. Marton (NBS Electron Physics Section), and W. G. Hall. (1956): 83 pp.

Programmed Computing at the Universities of Cambridge and Illinois in the Early Fifties

David J. Wheeler, FRS

1. Introduction

The fifties were a time of transition from calculating using hand calculating machines to computing with the aid of digital computers. At that time the computers were slow and unreliable, but relatively fast compared with hand calculations. About one in a hundred calculations went wrong when computing by hand, but about one in a million when computing by automatic computers in the early fifties. Thus the type of checking changed. The programs were written by hand and errors occurred again at the rate of a few errors per hundred instructions written down. However, once the programs had been corrected, the errors did not recur, although everyone seems to know of exceptions! The effects of most errors were more obvious than those occuring in hand calculation. Infinite loops, early stopping, and totally spurious results were easy to detect. Removing the errors thus located left the more subtle ones to be found.

2. Early Calculations on the EDSAC

EDSAC was designed by M. V. Wilkes and W. Renwick after Wilkes had attended the lectures given at the Moore School of Electrical Engineering in July and August 1946.

The computer ran its first calculation about 40 years ago in May 1949 at the Mathematical Laboratory, Cambridge. It was a table of squares, printed in a reasonable layout. The major part of the program was for binary to decimal conversion and laying out the results. The calculation was totally automatic, requiring no human intervention apart from pressing the start button after loading the program tape in the paper tape reader. It was the first calculation done fully under program control in a programmable computer.

The main effort over the next few months was to make the computer more reliable and also to make it easy to use. After all, we were all nonprofessionals.

The design of the EDSAC was very convenient for the user. A start button activated a uniselector (stepping switch) that loaded a prewired program into the store and executed it. This starting program, known as the initial orders, then input the program from the paper tape in the paper tape reader to the store and started the program. The first version of the starting program was replaced in August 1949 to make it more versatile and able to cope with relocation of subroutines and their parameterization during input. They could thus be adapted to a calculation without wasting time or space during the running of the program.

The original design of the EDSAC was to hold numbers less than two in the two's-complement representation. When constructed, it turned out that all numbers were less than one— we rapidly convinced ourselves that this was better for calculations!

The rounding of results was done by an explicit order. The original aim was to force programmers to consider where and how to round. However, as rounding typically slowed a computation loop by about 10 percent, some effort was made to avoid the rounding operation. It was nominally needed after each multiplication and shift order.

The very early programs were monolithic and written without the aid of subroutines, as the library of subroutines was not yet written or organized. A few of these early programs were kept and used as demonstrations. I can remember a program that computed primes by means of subtraction and tests alone. It was quite a short demonstration program and had the property of visibly slowing as the potential primes became larger. I am not sure now why we thought this was an interesting property.

We then settled down to make the computer into a useful calculator. The first subroutines to go into the paper tape library were the input and output subroutines. Almost every program needed these. The methods chosen to implement functions and procedures were adapted from existing methods but with a different emphasis on speed and power. One of the defects of the EDSAC was that it had no division order. This distorted the available methods in an awkward way, favoring methods not needing division. Even if the program needed division, care was needed to select the appropriate division subroutine. To use such subroutines always took more orders than would be needed if the division had been included in the order code. Division was first implimented using the standard second-order iterative process as the basis for a subroutine. This was soon supplemented by one based on a repetitive process that was shorter and faster although slightly less accurate.

I believe the most significant library subroutine was Stan Gill's modification of the Runge-Kutta method of solving differential equations. This was a remarkable piece of programming design, and it appeared at just the right time. It was a small subroutine of 66 orders and handled the complete solution. It minimized the use of working space, taking only three storage locations per differential equation while effectively accumulating the step increments to extra precision. It used four derivative evaluations per step and was of the fourth order. The computer had only 35 bits in a word, and scaling considerations meant the available accuracy was much less, so full accuracy could be attained in about one hundred steps or so. Higher-order methods would not be very much faster if they had more complicated steps needing more evaluations.

There was no automatic adjustment of step length. However, it was easy to check the precision by repeating the calculation with a step of half the length. The extra precision algorithm of the library subroutine gave an extra bit to the intermediate results, so the algebraic truncation error and the rounding error both decreased, and no awkward estimates had to be made. In the early fifties, the computers did not run on long calculations without inspection of intermediate results, so probably the time had not come for the fully automatic methods.

Bit-by-bit calculations were a natural technique, particularly where speed was not important but the size of a program was. An example using this technique was a method of computing logarithms by repeated squaring and doubling. The extension of this method to computing the inverse cosine was natural, but I blundered. It was clear that the subroutine would be inaccurate for small angles, and it was tested over about one hundred random numbers. One might even say that because the program was derived using a loop invariant, it had been proven correct. Van A. Wijngaarden pointed out that the error function was spikey, losing up to half precision for certain angles. Thus, a few evaluations were not sufficient to test the subroutine. This taught me a lesson that has endured to this day.

Another process that had to be adapted for automatic calculation was finding the root of a function: given a computable function and two arguments whose values had different signs, finding the root in that range. Nearly all hand processes rely on the application of intelligence at some stage. The obvious automation is the repeated subdivision of the interval bracketing the root. This can be done by using linear interpolation to find an inside argument, evaluating the function at that argument, and replacing the limit value with the same sign by the new value. Thus, the automatic program has to check for a zero functional value and stop there, else hunt for two adjacent arguments of opposite sign in the overall range.

The simple method soon slows to a first-order method as the curvature, positive or negative, causes one end of the range to be nibbled away, rather than allowing the linear interpolation to be effective. The EDSAC library subroutine avoided this drastic slowdown by the following method. Although a functional value was not replaced, its value was halved, except for the first time. Thus, the error was roughly cubed every three evaluations. By paying close attention to rounding and other essential details, we could arrange that it would stop when the adjacent arguments were as close as possible and their functions had opposite signs.

Floating point subroutines were developed for problems in which programmed scaling was difficult or impossible. Interpretive subroutines were used for this purpose so that the sequence of calculations could be done more readily than by repeated calls to subroutines. These subroutines slowed the computer by an order of magnitude, so although they made the calculation programming easier, their use was restricted.

Sines, cosines, logarithms, exponentials, and so forth, were evaluated using economized power series rather than by the hand technique of tables and interpolation. An interpolation subroutine was available that used Neville's method, but this was rarely used.

3. Checking of Programs

How did we ensure the results were correct? Programs had the advantage that errors that were removed did not return. Computer errors usually gave rise to obvious disasters, such as looping forever, stopping, or printing crazy results. When such programs were rerun, one might get the correct results, as most computer errors were intermittent.

When a computer is unreliable, it has a disproportionate effect on the debugging process. It is human nature to blame the computer first, even if experience shows that program errors are much more likely. People often insist on a rerun to make sure no intermittent error has occurred before they will analyze the data to locate the remaining faults.

The errors were removed by trial and observation. A program was run and information was collected by various means. Some was obtained by observation of numbers changing in the store. This could be done very well on EDSAC, because rotary switch enabled the content of a mercury tank to be observed. Usually one noticed if it was changing or if a negative counter was approaching zero. It was not unusual to obtain the precise value of a number in this way. Many programmers arranged their variables in the 16 locations of a single tank so that they were easy to observe.

A loudspeaker gave the rhythm of a program, so discrepancies were noticed immediately, without conscious effort, for programs that had run before. When a program came to a premature end or was stopped because it was looping, a postmortem tape kept at the console was run, which enabled selected portions of the store to be printed as numbers or orders. A modification to the computer enabled a telephone dial to select the portion of store that needed printing.

A stronger method of locating program errors, a method created by Stan Gill, was a trace subroutine, which printed the sequence of orders obeyed by the program. Although it slowed the program down by a factor of about 20, it was very useful for otherwise hard-to-find faults. The program tape had to be augmented to use such a program, and usually a small extra tape called a jiffy tape was used for the purpose.

Checkpoint subroutines were developed that enabled printing of the accumulator or other variables at selected points of a program for selected numbers of times. They were not used much. I had thought originally that such methods would be used for proving programs, but because of human nature they tended to be used as a last resort.

4. Corrections

Paper tape is very slow to correct or adjust. It involves copying and making changes. The tape preparation room did have equipment for this, but the work was slow and tedious. It was usual for program tapes to have either a stop order, requiring a manual restart, or else an inch or two of blank tape so that the pressing of a stop button would have an equivalent effect before the starting directive at the end of a tape.

Thus, changing the tape in the paper tape reader to a jiffy or correction tape before the starting directive was obeyed made it easy to modify and correct the program without repunching the entire tape. Further corrections could then be incorporated in the jiffy tape by extending that short tape. Thus, the jiffy tape grew, and it became worthwhile changing the main program tape—often under the incorrect assumption that the last error had been found.

5. Computer Operation

The computer was rarely stepped through programs an order at a time as a means of locating program faults. Instead, we had testing periods when we could run a short program for a minute or two and get some information from it. Many people wished to make tests in a short time, so there was plenty of advice given if anyone was using wasteful methods.

Even when operators were provided to run the computer, test runs were usually run by the authors of the programs. Production runs tended to be longer and were usually handled by the operators. The maximum length of run allowed during the day was half an hour, but a more usual duration was 10 minutes.

At night the computer was handed over to various groups to use. Their competence had been assessed before they were allowed to do this. They were classified into fully and partially authorized users.

This determined whether they could be in sole charge of the computer and what adjustments they could make to the computer hardware. There was no night maintenance in the early fifties, so they worked until the computer broke down, and occasionally all through the night.

One of the night groups under the leadership of S. F. Boys, a theoretical chemist, did calculations of electronic wave functions lasting many tens of hours. Boys's approach was very professional, all runs being repeated with separate program tapes. The terms of the six dimensional integration were themselves derived by algebra in the program.

As the computer began to yield useful results, a priority committee was set up to determine which submitted calculations were suitable, how they might be programmed, and how much computer time they could use. Problems were submitted from most science and engineering faculties.

6. Computer Improvements

During the life of the computer, many improvements were made that enhanced its power and made it more reliable. The input speed rose from 7 characters per second up to 50 characters per second. The directly coupled teleprinter working at 7 characters per second was replaced by a laboratory constructed punch that went at 35 characters per second. A B register was added to speed up order modification, and magnetic tapes were connected to give an auxiliary store. A telephone dial was added to allow selective control while running. The output code was changed to a two-out-of-five code so that simple errors were obvious in the printed results, and it required two errors of opposite types to cause a decimal digit to be printed as another.

7. University of Illinois

I went to Urbana, Illinois in September 1951 and stayed there for two years. During the first year, the ORDVAC was finished, tested, and sent to the Ballistic Research Laboratory at Aberdeen Proving Ground some 700 miles away in Maryland in February 1952. It was based on the I.A.S. computer at Princeton, which was under construction at that time.

The ILLIAC, an improved copy of the ORDVAC, was not finished until about September 1952. For some time, then, we used the ORDVAC in Urbana by sending programs and receiving results by the Teletype network.

These were more powerful computers than the EDSAC, being parallel and using cathode tube stores rather than delay lines. The store had about 1000 words rather than about 500 words, but it suffered from a limitation in use—the read round ratio—which increased the programmer's burden slightly. The engineers improved the ratio until by mid-1953 almost no inconvenience was suffered.

The programming system was similar to and derived from that of the EDSAC, although each program tape had to have its own bootstrap starting program copied on its front. The larger store size enabled more matrix calculations to be done. In particular, a program was made, following a suggestion by H. H. Goldstine, based on the Jacobi method. This was used to find the eigenvalues and vectors of symmetric matrices. It was used a surprising amount, rather more for factor analysis than physical problems. It was a very apt program for the time.

It was a small program, so most of the program could be used to store the matrix or matrix and vectors. It simply gave the answers in all cases, with no special cases. Although it was slower than other methods for the small matrices that it could handle, the factor was nowhere near the asymptotic factor for large matrices. The program could handle matrices up to order 43 for eigenvalues and up to 25 for both eigenvalues and vectors.

Another matrix method was developed for solving linear equations. The equations were reduced as they were read in so that only a triangular matrix of reduced coefficients was stored, and larger matrices could be dealt with efficiently, up to about 43 equations.

The sizes that could be handled were small by present day standards. In those days, most matrices were generated by hand, and this tended to keep their size small.

The use of the ILLIAC was integrated into the teaching of undergraduates and became part of the curriculum in a way that was unique at the time. It became an accepted and effective research and teaching tool, but I will omit discussion of this because I had little firsthand knowledge beyond 1953.

8. Unsupervised Calculations

During the summers of 1952 and 1953, the ILLIAC tended to be underused. The staff and students were mostly elsewhere. This was an effect of nine-month staff contracts and lack of air conditioning in all but the computer room.

In the first of these summers, e was calculated to 60,000 decimal places; and in the second, the primality of $2^{8191} - 1$ was checked by the Lucas test. In both these cases, the program was completely checked for arithmetic, operator, punch, and reader errors. It had half-hour runs on a computer with mean free time between errors of about 6 to 10 hours. The calculations took about 50 hours. These programs being checked were part of a scheme to assess the performance of the computer—therein lay the justification for this type of calculation.

I was convinced that both of these programs were correct. It was pointed out to me later that the printed result claiming to be e was $e - 2$, the fractional part of e, so in this carefully checked program, about nine tenths of the printed decimal digits were wrong! This has subsequently affected my attitude to proven programs.

9. Preparation of Program Tapes

This continued to be a tedious affair. Each program tape was composed by copying subroutines and punching the rest of the program and data. Thus, users spent more time in preparing tapes than using them.

One episode I can remember in particular was when Joe Wagstein of the NBS visited us. We explained how easy our computer was to use, and he gave us a problem. The printed results were available in minutes. The two reasons for this speed, which was not typical, were that it was a Sunday, so we had full access to the computer, and that for teaching classes we had prepared a class tape that contained the bootstrap and the important library subroutines. This class tape and a rapidly prepared jiffy tape sufficed for the problem. It was the fastest I had ever done a complete calculation.

10. EDSAC 2

I returned to Cambridge in September 1953 and continued to develop the use of EDSAC. After the ORDVAC and ILLIAC, it seemed a slow and unreliable computer. There was a large amount of crystallographic and radio telescope work, some of which was done by the fast Fourier transform.

Rather than give more details about the first EDSAC, it is perhaps worth discussing the design of the EDSAC 2, which incorporated our experience to date and came into service in 1957.

This was a 40-bit word, parallel computer with two orders per word. It was made with tubes. The store used ferrite cores, the arithmetic unit was bit-sliced, and the total number types of pluggable units was about 18, with nearly all the computer being made of a few types. Thus, it was intended to be reliable and easily maintainable.

Floating-point was included to make calculations easier. The computer was microprogrammed and had a ferrite-core, read-only memory of 768 words. The user store was 1024 words.

The fixed memory enabled many useful subroutines to be permanently available. These included sine, cosine, polar conversion, logarithms, exponentials, and solutions of differential equations. Later on, matrix division was added to the list of permanently available subroutines. The fixed memory included an assembler and set of print subroutines that enabled input and output to be done elegantly and readily throughout the execution of a program. The microprogram and fixed store cooperated to make a trace, which enabled the flow of control in a program to be printed.

The microprogram allowed orders to be carefully designed, less dependent on accidents of hardware. For example, the fixed-point order to store the accumulator caused the rounded result to be placed in the store while the accumulator was left unchanged. The special case in which rounding would cause overflow was done by choosing the nearest number in range. Floating-point rounding was done equally carefully, although each operation caused a packed rounded result to be left in the accumulator, rather than the extra precision unpacked version.

The order code was orthogonal in the modern sense, and some orders used many micro-orders to produce correct results, as in the case of division with remainder.

Both fixed- and floating-point were provided, so there were two versions each of the functional subroutines. Because of the need for space economy, most of the calculations were done for the fixed-point and rounded for the floating-point version. Thus, the precision of the subroutines, particularly the floating-point subroutines, was almost the maximum possible. The floating-point representation used 32-bit fraction and 8-bit exponent. The range and precision sufficed for most calculations.

Convenience of use was one of the main objects, so in addition to producing well-designed orders and subroutines, error detection facilities were built in. All unused codes in the order code caused an immediate "report." This printed the location, offending order, and content of the accumulator and modifier registers and stopped the computer. Similar reports were caused by using nonstandardized floating-point numbers in floating-point orders, input syntax errors, untested overflows, and so forth. Before the input of a program tape, the store was normally cleared to a value—all ones—that would cause a report if used as an order or a floating-point operand.

11. Performance

The computer could do a simple instruction in about 20 microseconds, and multiplication needed about a quarter of a millisecond. The pair of paper tape readers read at the rate of 1000 characters per second, and the fastest output punch could do 300 characters per second. In the early years, the final output was still printed by teleprinter.

The computer was designed with ease of use as a primary design consideration. We believe we achieved this aim. The complete guide to programming and the reference guide together were 64 small pages.

Users were able to run simple problems after a few hours tuition. It was my favorite computer and the last one that could be designed as a whole without running into various compatability compromises. The ease of use of EDSAC 2 delayed the advent of programming languages in Cambridge for some years.

12. Teaching

Both at Urbana and Cambridge, the computer was used in an "open shop" manner. Users were expected to program their own calculations, assisted when necessary by the computer staff or their colleagues. Lectures were given to train newcomers, and the first summer school for training outsiders was held in Cambridge in 1950. The use of the computer spread rapidly as successful users infected their friends.

One way information spread rapidly in the early days was by the "grapevine." While users were waiting their turn to use the computer, information was exchanged about new procedures, machine weaknesses, successful ploys, and so on. This rapid "documentation" system contributed to the success of open shop policies. Closed shop policies of restricting the use of the machine to coders, who solved the problems of others, would have been a failure at these Universities.

13. Review of the Calculating Methods Used

Early calculations done on computers could have been done by those experienced in the use of hand calculators. There were not many with those qualifications.

The methods chosen were not particularly new, but they were selected for rather different properties than those needed for hand calculations. Thus, binary chopping was tedious to do by hand, but the large tables essential for many hand calculations were rarely used in programmed calculations. In fact, when there were few computers about, many thought the sole use of computers would be to generate tables suitable for hand calculation.

The methods that turned out well-suited for computers were Runge-Kutta methods for differential equations, Gaussian methods for quadrature, economized power series for functions, Jacobi for eigenvalues, and fast Fourier methods for transforms.

The problem of getting programs correct dominated the early use of computers, and users' views of their computers were determined by turn-around and the methods for removing errors from programs, rather than by the numerical analysis problems.

Another important factor was the size of program. Interesting problems tended to be near the limits of the computer, so program space as well as running efficiency was of importance.

Later on, reliability became more important than space, and extra facilities could be incorporated. A good example is the square root. Early subroutines failed on zero, usually looping forever. Later versions incorporated tests so that zero was dealt with correctly and negative arguments were detected, but they were longer programs.

A factor of significance was the reliability of the library routines. In the very early days, there was a tendency to accept all for the library. This soon ran into problems. Many programs were developed under problem-specialized limitations. This meant they did not work under general circumstances. Until a strong discipline was established with thorough testing and the rejection of many submissions, the useful subroutines were hard for users to find. This discipline had to be rediscovered many times at many locations. Nowadays, well-constructed software libraries are available for serious computation.

Nevertheless, the early computers did calculations that would not have been possible otherwise. The early work at Cambridge contributed directly to three Nobel prizes.

Related Readings

[1] R. A. Brooker and D. J. Wheeler, "Floating Operations on the EDSAC," *MTAC* 7 (1953): 37–47.

[2] A. Burks, H. H. Goldstine, and J. von Neumann, "Preliminary Discusion of the Logical Design of an Electronic Computing Instrument," Institute for Advanced Study report, Princeton (1946).

[3] S. Gill, "A Process for the Step by Step Integration of Differential Equations in an Automatic Digital Computing Machine," *Proc. Camb. Philos. Soc.* 47 (1951): 96–108.

[4] S. Gill, "The Diagnosis of Mistakes in Programs on the EDSAC," *Proc. Roy. Soc. London Ser. A* 206 (1951): 538–54.

[5] "Theory and Techniques for Design of Electronic Digital Computers," Lectures given to a special course at the Moore School of Electrical Engineering 8 July to 31 August 1946. University of Pennsylvania, Philadelphia. Four volumes (1947–8).

[6] R. E. Meagher and J. P. Nash, "The ORDVAC," *Proc. of the Joint AIEE–IRE Computer Conference* (New York: AIEE, 1952), 37–43.

[7] D. J. Wheeler and J. E. Robertson, "Diagnostic Programs for the ILLIAC," *Proc. IRE 41–10* (1953): 1320–1325.

[8] D. J. Wheeler, "Programme Organization and Initial Orders for the EDSAC," *Proc. Roy. Soc. London Ser. A* 202 (1950): 573–89.

[9] M. V. Wilkes, "The EDSAC—An Electronic Calculating Machine," *J. Sci. Inst.* 26 (1949): 385–91.

[10] M. V. Wilkes, D. J. Wheeler, and S. Gill, *The Preparation of Programs for an Electronic Digital Computer with Special Reference to the EDSAC and the Use of a Library of Subroutines* (Cambridge, MA: Addison-Wesley, 1951).

[11] C. R. Williams, "A Review of ORDVAC Operating Experience," in *Proceedings of the Eastern Joint Computer Conference* (New York: IRE, 1953), 91–95.

Early Numerical Analysis in the United Kingdom

L. Fox

1. Introduction

Rumor has it that the term "numerical analysis" was coined or perhaps resurrected sometime in the late 1940s by the numerical statistician J. H. Curtiss at the National Bureau of Standards in Washington, DC (the NBS being effectively the American National Physical Laboratory, the English version of which I shall mention in the following sections). That date makes numerical analysis a rather new subject, and in fact I lived through a lot of the early history in the United Kingdom. But in some respects, the subject has a long history, and this I shall mention briefly.

Throughout history individuals have wanted numerical solutions for simple problems like the volume of a rectangular solid with given sides and for complicated problems like the determination of the position in space at a particular time of a vehicle launched from a specified point on earth. Such individuals are not really numerical analysts, and I think of them as engineers or scientists. But then there are others, perhaps of a more mathematical bent, who decide that they can help the scientists in general rather than in particular numerical contexts. These are the people I do think of as numerical analysts, and indeed, in the early days, before numerical analysis became a topic in a mathematics degree, assistance to the scientists was an important motivation for their work. One of the earliest such operations, which continued for many years, was the construction and publication of mathematical tables.

2. Table Making

When all arithmetic was done with pencil and paper, multiplication and division, at least, were tedious and time-consuming operations. To ease this, some early mathematical tables were produced that gave the results of multiplying any number, say up to four figures, by any other such number. Allied tables of reciprocals helped with a corresponding division operation to a certain level of accuracy that respectable tables would discuss in a suitable introduction. The invention of logarithms more or less eliminated the need for multiplication and division, and many tables of logarithms were produced by numerical analysts, tables differing mainly in the selected arguments and the number of figures given.

Other functions of integers were found to be useful, and one of the first books of such tables was published in 1814 by Barlow [8] and recast in two more modern editions in 1930 and 1941 by the famous table-maker L. J. Comrie. The last edition gave n^2, n^3, $n^{1/2}$, $(10n)^{1/2}$, $n^{1/3}$, and n^{-1} for $n = 1(1)12500$. It gave extra attention to reasonably small n for n^4, $n!$, and $n^{-1/2}$; integer powers up to n^{10} for $n = 1(1)100$ and up to n^{20} for $n = 1(1)10$; binomial coefficients for $n = 1(1)12$; and a list of useful constants. The nonexact numbers have 7, 8, or 9 significant figures, with some facilities for interpolation and a relevant description thereof in the introduction.

Barlow's 1814 preface makes interesting reading—the following being part of it—with address of The Royal Military Academy, Woolwich (1 July 1814).

> In presenting the following Mathematical Tables to the attention of the public, the far greater part of which are the result of laborious calculation, little need be said to prove that I have not had in view the accomplishment of any pecuniary object, as the time employed in the computation, the expense of publication, and the limited number of purchases which from the nature of the subject is to be apprehended, preclude any idea of adequate remuneration. And as little is to be expected of mathematical reputation, nothing more being requisite for the execution of such an undertaking than a moderate skill in computation and a persevering industry and attention; which are not precisely the qualifications a mathematician is most anxious to be thought to possess.
>
> In fact the only motive which prompted me to engage in this unprofitable task was the utility I conceived might result from my labor; and if I have succeeded in facilitating any of the more abstruse arithmetical calculations, and thereby rendered mathematical investigations more pleasant and easy, I have obtained the principle object I had in view.

As applied mathematicians developed their skills, their computational problems became increasingly complex, and more advanced mathematical tables were needed and indeed produced. The first group included the trigonometric functions and their inverses, the corresponding treatment of hyperbolic functions, and the increasing and decreasing exponentials and the logarithmic functions. Common logarithms of these elementary functions were also frequently tabulated for obvious purposes.

The next group included the so-called higher functions of mathematical physics, commonly occurring, for example, in certain methods of solving partial differential equations. For this and other purposes, they included the functions of Bessel, Legendre, and so on, gamma and allied functions, Weber parabolic cylinder functions, exponential and logarithmic integrals, elliptic functions, elliptic integrals, and many others.

More and more, numerical analysis was now needed because the calculation of relevant tabular values was no longer trivial. Moreover, close preliminary attention was needed to the question of what auxiliary function or functions should be tabulated, particularly for the simplification of interpolation in difficult regions. As a simple example, consider the tabulation of the exponential integral

$$-Ei(-x) = \int_x^\infty t^{-1}e^{-t}dt$$

For small x we have the series expansion

$$-Ei(-x) = -\gamma - \ln(x) + \sum_1^\infty (-1)^{n-1}(x^n/n \cdot n!) \qquad (1)$$

but the singularity at $x = 0$ makes it desirable to tabulate the function $-Ei(-x) + \ln(x)$, which is not singular and interpolates nicely. For large x there is the asymptotic expansion

$$-Ei(-x) \sim \frac{e^{-x}}{x}\left(1 - \frac{1!}{x} + \frac{2!}{x^2} - \cdots\right) \equiv \frac{e^{-x}}{x}S(x) \qquad (2)$$

Here S can be tabulated nicely and conveniently with argument $z = x^{-1}$, and the required quantity is easily recovered.

Of course, the ascending series may not be economic for good accuracy for medium-sized x, and the asymptotic series may not give the required accuracy for too small an x. There may be a middle range in which other methods are desirable if not completely necessary. For example, for the function

$$f(x) = \int_0^\infty (u + x)^{-1}e^{-u^2}du$$

there are two series corresponding respectively to (1) and (2), but in a middle range of x it is more convenient to integrate by numerical methods the ordinary differential equation

$$f' + 2xf = \pi^{1/2} - x^{-1}$$

Other frequent computations involved recurrence relations. For example, the Bessel function $J_r(x)$, for fixed argument x and variable order r, satisfies the recurrence relation

$$J_{r+1}(x) = \frac{2r}{x}J_r(x) - J_{r-1}(x) \qquad (3)$$

For all intents and purposes, this can be used to compute successive $J_r(x)$ for integer r, starting, say, with known values of $J_0(x)$ and $J_1(x)$.

The other obvious task was the direct evaluation of definite integrals, and all these various operations had to be performed on desk calculating machines, sometimes with high accuracy and always as economically as possible.

The final important topic in table making was the systematic use of finite-difference formulas for checking computed values by inspecting differences, for subtabulating them as mechanically as possible to obtain other tabular values easily, and then for providing accurate and reasonably economic methods for interpolation in the published tables. The subtabulation, which is systematic interpolation at a constant fraction of the original interval (usually one-fifth or one-tenth thereof), was performed mechanically by machines like the Hollerith punched-card machine or the National Accounting Machine.

The interpolation by the user was based on finite-difference formulas typified by the Everett formula

$$f_p = (1 - p)f_0 + pf_1 + E_2\delta^2 f_0 + F_2\delta^2 f_1 + E_4\delta^4 f_0 + F_4\delta^4 f_1 + \cdots \qquad (4)$$

where the δ^2 and δ^4 are central-difference symbols and the E and F functions are simple polynomials in p, the fraction of the (constant) distance between tabular points. Comrie found that the fourth difference could be "thrown back" into the second difference, with the explicit part of (4) replaced by

$$f_p = (1 - p)f_0 + pf_1 + E_2\delta_m^2 f_0 + F_2\delta_m^2 f_1 \qquad \delta_m^2 f = \delta^2 f - 0.184\delta^4 f \qquad (5)$$

to make (5) only slightly less accurate than (4) and clearly much more convenient.

The construction of the more advanced mathematical tables and relevant publishing continued until the 1960s. The main table-making activities were originally organized by the British Association Mathematical Tables Committee, and from 1948 onwards by the Royal Society.

Other early publications included [57] on the accuracy of finite-difference interpolation, [9,10] on formulas for numerical integration and differentiation, [19] on "throwback interpolation," [20] on mechanical operations with the National Accounting Machine, and [3, 11] on the summation of slowly convergent series. Fletcher, Miller, and Rosenhead [23] published the comprehensive Index of Mathematical Tables. Miller [44] wrote about table making in general and about his solution of ordinary differential equations in particular. This he performed with the Taylor series method, not too difficult when, as often occurred, the relevant differential equations were linear. However, Miller thought nothing of using up to twelfth derivatives with a large interval of tabulation.

Miller was probably the dominant member of the relevant British Association and Royal Society committees, and much of his work appeared for the first time in the introductions to the various tables that were written singly or jointly by members of the committees and which included important numerical analysis. Prominent in this respect is the introduction to [12], which includes the famous Miller algorithm in connection with the recurrence relation (3). Miller quickly realized that the forward recurrence produced increasing inaccuracy as r increased beyond x. He solved this problem by *backward recurrence* with a replacement of (3) given by

$$\bar{J}_{r-1}(x) = \frac{2r}{x}\bar{J}_r(x) - \bar{J}_{r+1}(x) \quad \bar{J}_N(x) = 0 \quad \bar{J}_{N-1}(x) = 1$$

and then by scaling the computed $\bar{J}_r(x)$ to give, for example,

$$J_r(x) = k\bar{J}_r(x) \quad k = J_0(x)/\bar{J}_0(x)$$

For sufficiently large N this gives good results, accuracy increasing as r decreases.

Perhaps the final useful publication was the booklet "Interpolation and Allied Tables," developed at H. M. Nautical Almanac Office. It first appeared in 1936 [48] when Comrie was superintendent. It was reissued at frequent intervals and with amendments and additions until the last appearance in 1956, when D. H. Sadler was superintendent. The original booklet contains finite-difference formulas of all kinds, and the 1942 edition also gave a method for solving ordinary differential equations that actually used central differences with estimation and subsequent correction, in the spirit of more modern predictor-corrector methods. A companion booklet "Subtabulation" [49], published in 1958, gives a comprehensive version of the relevant methods developed over many years in H. M. Nautical Almanac Office.

3. Other Early Numerical Analysis

Apart from table making and the much-earlier contributions by Gauss, Newton, Runge and Kutta, and Bashforth and Adams, a few other workers, particularly astronomers and theoretical scientists, suggested numerical methods for both ordinary and partial differential equations and a few other topics. But by 1939, the start of World War II, there was little in the way of numerical literature, and numerical analysis was hardly a mathematical topic. In the United Kingdom, there were only a few books published with a numerical content, such as [13,43,45,54,59].

Scattered in the journal literature of this period were papers such as Aitken's [4, 5] on Bernoulli's method for solving algebraic equations and on his own δ^2 method for accelerating the convergence of such iterations, [41] on mathematical and mechanical (differential analyzer) methods for the solution of parabolic partial differential equations, and [53] on "the deferred approach to the limit" for accelerating the convergence of finer-net approximations to the numerical solution of ordinary differential equations.

The last mentioned method is still in common use, and Richardson, a major figure in this field, also wrote important papers on the solution of partial differential equations. Perhaps the most famous of these is [51], and [52] gives a short summary of this and other work. In [51] he discussed finite-difference methods for what he called "jury" problems given by

$$\Delta^2\Phi = 0 \quad (\Delta^2 + k^2)\Phi = 0 \quad \Delta^4\Phi = 0 \quad (\Delta^4 - k^4)\Phi = 0 \quad (6)$$

with suitable boundary conditions and an extension of the "deferred approach to the limit" to improve the accuracy of the eigenvalues in addition to that of the eigenfunctions. He solved the finite-difference equations by direct methods if their number was small enough; otherwise, he used an iterative method.

The following example appears in the 1925 paper. The equations

$$Ax = b \quad A = \begin{bmatrix} -4 & 1 & 0 & 1 \\ 1 & -4 & 1 & 0 \\ 0 & 1 & -4 & 1 \\ 1 & 0 & 1 & -4 \end{bmatrix} \quad b = \begin{bmatrix} -3 \\ -7 \\ 0 \\ 0 \end{bmatrix} \quad (7)$$

obviously relate to a particular member of the first of (6), with boundary values on a unit square and with interval $h = 1/3$ in both directions. He uses the iteration

$$x^{(r+1)} = x^{(r)} + a_r^{-1}(Ax^{(r)} - b) \quad (8)$$

showing in this example that if $x^{(1)} = (1, 2, 0.3, 0.2)^T$, then with $a_1 = 4$, $a_2 = 2$, $a_3 = 6$, the computed $x^{(4)}$ is the exact solution of (7). This, of course, follows from the fact that the eigenvalues of A are -4, -4, -2, and -6, but Richardson was aware that the eigenvalues are not usually available. He observed that the largest and smallest can be obtained with rough accuracy, that a single $a_r > 1/2|\lambda_{max}|$ in (8) will produce ultimate convergence, but that "it saves time to spread out the values of the a_r over the range covered by the eigenvalues."

This was a remarkable piece of work, on which David Young, Gene Golub, Richard Varga and others did more research in the 1950s. The paper has many other interesting sections that suggest other things about finite differences (what to do, for example, near boundaries that are not rectangular) and about the importance of a nondimensional treatment of the problem prior to computation. He also considered the parabolic problem

$$\frac{\partial\Phi}{\partial t} = \frac{\partial^2\Phi}{\partial x^2}$$

with appropriate boundary conditions, but his suggested

$$\Phi_{r,s+1} = \Phi_{r,s-1} + 2\frac{\Delta t}{(\Delta x)^2}(\Phi_{r+1,s} - 2\Phi_{r,s} + \Phi_{r-1,s})$$

is now known to be unstable.

It was with some pleasure that I found the following in the 1954 Royal Society Biographical Memoir of Lewis Fry Richardson [36]. "He was, I believe, pleased by the reference to 'his useful simple method' as one appropriate for use by workers in the field of differential equations who may wish to obtain more accurate solutions than the simple relaxation process can provide without becoming involved in finite-difference theory, in L. Fox's 1950 paper on 'The numerical solution of elliptical differential equations when the boundary conditions involve a derivative'; and by the inclusion of his method to a 'jury problem,' the solution of $y'' + x^{-1}y' + y = 0$ with boundary values specified at both ends of the range of x; approximate values were obtained to eight significant figures, the maximum error being 20 in the last two figures."

In passing it is interesting to note that it was this prewar numerical analysis that was mainly examined in postgraduate courses in the subject, courses that did not start seriously until the early 1950s. They were usually organized by the Computing Laboratory rather than by the Mathematics Department, and one of the first was the Cambridge diploma in Numerical Analysis and Automatic Computing. At the start this had one theoretical paper and one practical paper on numerical analysis and one paper on the hardware and software of the new stored-program computers. The two numerical papers of the first examination in 1954 reveal that the material so far discussed is well represented. This is, perhaps, not surprising since Miller was the dominant force in this part of the diploma, but later diplomas had little more variety. Even by 1959, the theoretical paper at Cambridge had three questions on interpolation, two on quadrature, and one on the Taylor-series method for a particular (nonlinear) ordinary differential equation. It also had one on Richardson's method for elliptic equations, one on Aitken and other iteration topics, and one on three methods for the eigenvalues of symmetric matrices of small and large order with comparison of desk machines and automatic computation.

4. War-time Groups

4.1 RELAXATION AT OXFORD

In 1939 I had just started my D.Phil. research at Oxford with R. V. Southwell, who had told my tutor that he needed a mathematician to work on extensions of his "relaxation method." In the early thirties, he had invented what was originally called the method of "systematic relaxation of constraints" for solving problems of loaded frameworks; and in the decade 1932 to 1942 he had a regular group of research students at Oxford working on these and somewhat similar problems in the finite-difference solution of elliptic partial differential equations. From 1939 onwards, arrangements in World War II caused applied and even pure mathematicians to work on military problems with whatever techniques they had available. The Oxford group was one of the first of these and, in particular, the name "relaxation," if not the original method, has carried over to modern techniques for relevant problems.

Two papers by Southwell in 1935 described the method for frameworks. Basically, this used iteration to solve the linear equation

$$Ax = b$$

where x is the vector of displacements and b of the forces at the joints of the framework. The matrix A was sparse and generally diagonally dominant. Southwell considered in an engineering sense not only the problem, but also its method of solution. He postulated a system of "constraints" at the joints that could bear the forces without allowing any displacements. Then, usually selecting the joint with the currently largest force, he permitted a displacement at this point by "relaxing the constraint," wholly or partially at this stage, so that at this joint, the framework was now bearing all or at least some of its force. This also changed the forces at other joints in an easily calculable manner, and by systematically "relaxing the constraints" (the word "systematically" originally meaning "in descending order of magnitude of forces still borne by the constraints"), he expected on engineering principles that the process would converge. In other words, the *residual* forces still borne by the constraints, components of the residual vector

$$r^{(n)} = Ax^{(n)} - b \tag{9}$$

at stage n of the iteration, would systematically be reduced to zero or to very small quantities as n increases. In fact Southwell contemplated the acceptance of any solution for which the residual forces were less than some "engineering fraction" of the original forces, because the latter are unlikely to be known accurately.

Now, if at joint s the residual force r_s is reduced temporarily to zero by a change in the displacement x_s at that joint, then this is one step of Gauss-Seidel iteration, and indeed for some problems this method had already been used by other workers. But Southwell concentrated on the residuals, which were actually recorded at every joint, and he and his research students used a variety of methods to reduce them sensibly to zero. The following simple examples illustrate some of these methods.

FIGURE 1.
One-dimensional
calculation: stage 1.

First we solve a one-dimensional problem with equations

$$f_{r+1} - 2f_r + f_{r-1} = b_r \qquad f_0 = 100 \qquad f_5 = -1000$$
$$b_1 = 20 \qquad b_2 = 80 \qquad b_3 = -40 \qquad b_4 = 600 \tag{10}$$

where the selected values of b_r and f_0 and f_5 are effectively arbitrary numbers. Suppose that we start with the guess $f_1 = f_2 = f_3 = f_4 = 0$, so that the first relevant picture is that of Figure 1, in which the current f values are to the left and the current residuals to the right of the "nodal lines." The first residuals are just the $-b_r$ at $r = 2$ and 3 and $-b_1$ and $-b_4$ plus the respective contributions from the specified boundary values at the two nodes next to the boundaries.

In the relaxation process, we use the same diagram throughout, recording *additions* to the displacements on the left of the nodal lines and the *current* residual on the right. In the first step we "liquidate" the residual of largest magnitude, but the form of the equations (10) shows that a *group displacement* of a multiple -320 of displacements 1, 2, 3, and 4 at the successive nodal points will eliminate the -1600 residual without altering any others. The current state is then shown in Figure 2.

Next we eliminate the -80 residual with a single joint relaxation, a displacement of -40 at that joint changing the residual by 80 at that joint and -40 at the adjacent joints on each side. This leaves a residual of 40 at the first joint and zero at all other joints. Finally, the multiple 8 of the group displacement 4, 3, 2, 1, the reverse of the first group displacement, produces zero residuals everywhere (the picture of Figure 3) and values of -288, -656, -944, and -1272 at

FIGURE 2.
One-dimensional
calculation: stage 2.

		−320			−640			−960			−1280	0	
100			0	80		0	−80		0	40		0	−1600	−1000

FIGURE 3.
One-dimensional
calculation: stage 3.

		32	0		24								
		−320	40		−40	0		16	0		8	0	
100			0	80	−640	−80		−960	40		−1280	−1600	−1000
		(−288)			(−656)			(−944)			(−1272)		

the successive points. A check calculation of the residuals from (9) confirms that all the residuals have zero values.

In a group displacement, several constraints are relaxed simultaneously; and when the displacement changes are the same at the relevant set of joints, it is called a block displacement. This, as well as the joint displacement, is useful in the treatment of differential equations by finite-difference methods. Equation (10) might approximate to the solution of a simple ordinary differential problem like

$$\frac{d^2f}{dx^2} = g(x) \qquad f(x_0) = \alpha \qquad f(x_n) = \beta$$

with $g(x)$ and α and β specified and with the chosen interval taken to be $h = \frac{1}{5}(x_n - x_0)$.

Similarly, for the simple elliptic partial differential equation

$$\frac{\partial^2 f}{\partial x^2} + \frac{\partial^2 f}{\partial y^2} = g(x, y)$$

with f having specified values on a closed boundary and with $g(x, y)$ also specified for all x, y within the region, the equation corresponding to (10) is

$$f_{r,s+1} + f_{r,s-1} + f_{r+1,s} + f_{r-1,s} - 4f_{r,s} = h^2 g_{r,s} \qquad (11)$$

in obvious notation and with constant interval h in both directions. We present a solution of this (there are, of course, many other possibilities) with $f = 0$ on the boundary of a unit square, $h = 0.2$, and $g = -2500$ so that with an initial guess of $f = 0$ everywhere, the first picture corresponding to that of Figure 1 is given in Figure 4. The boundary lines and all zero displacements are omitted for convenience.

FIGURE 4.
Two-dimensional calculation.

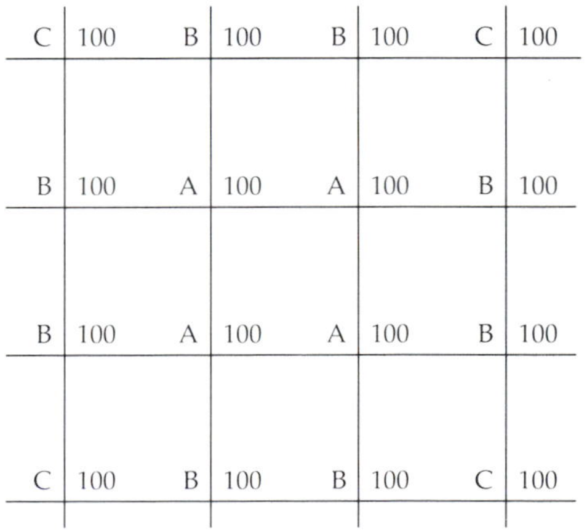

C	100	B	100	B	100	C	100
B	100	A	100	A	100	B	100
B	100	A	100	A	100	B	100
C	100	B	100	B	100	C	100

We now use the word "point" instead of "joint," since in South-well's language, the framework had become a tensioned net. "Net point" became the accepted terminology. Other useful words were "overrelax," deliberately to change the sign of the relevant residual(s) when adjacent points have residuals of the same sign and have a "wash-back" effect, and "underrelax," in regions in which the signs of residuals alternate. These words are still used in modern methods, but have rather different applications. We also note with respect to (11) (and indeed also with respect to (10))—that the algebraic sum of residuals is unchanged unless a displacement is made at one or more points next to the boundary. Residuals, then, should be "swept" from the center of the region towards the boundaries, rather than in the reverse direction. A useful first step is to use a complete block operation, which reduces the algebraic sum of residuals virtually to zero.

There is much symmetry in Figure 4, and indeed there are only three independent values, respectively at points marked A, B, and C. Table 1 gives a list of operations and the resulting residuals. A displacement at A means the same displacement at all A points in Figure 4, and the same goes for B and C.

Operation (i) reduces the sum of residuals to zero, and the remaining operations would be understood easily by any competent and experienced operator. Notice that simple numbers are used throughout, with no useless early attempts to make any residuals exactly zero. The fact that at the end of Table 1 there are only zero or negative residuals tells us immediately that all the values are too large, that of C perhaps especially. But a complete extra block of -1 would leave residuals of 0, 1, and 0 for A, B, and C, so that every value would then be slightly too small. Table 1 gives $A = 167$, $B = 117$, $C = 84$, the exact values being $166\frac{2}{3}$, $116\frac{2}{3}$, $83\frac{1}{3}$. This table, of course, would nowhere be recorded, and all the operations would be performed on a single sheet of paper, with perhaps only one eighth of Figure 4, by an experienced operator who takes the symmetries in his or her stride. Figure 5 shows all that is needed.

TABLE 1
Operations and residuals

Operation	Displacement Changes			Current Residuals		
	A	B	C	A	B	C
(i)	100	100	100	100	0	-100
(ii)	70			-40	70	-100
(iii)		20		0	10	-60
(iv)			-16	0	-6	4
(v)	-3	-3		0	0	-2

FIGURE 5.
Requirements for calculation.

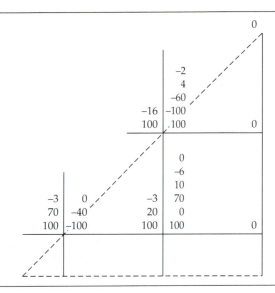

We learned a lot about the "condition" of various problems, measured by the size of the displacements needed to liquidate sets of residuals. The condition, of course, worsens as the interval is reduced, but more to the point is the fact that the Laplace equations are much better-conditioned than the biharmonic equations. As the condition worsens, the need for significant overrelaxation increases. A good starting approximation helped considerably with the convergence, and in an engineering background some workers could envisage geometrically and really accurately the nature of the correct solution. We simplified the use of a finer mesh, first by interpolating accurately (or, when possible, by using the differential equation to get a good start at the finer net points), and then by a process that now has the name "multi-grid." Unlike modern multigrid methods, we never used more than one coarser mesh for this purpose.

The latter technique did not obtain written publicity, but most of the useful devices appear in [7]. This, together with Southwell's last books [55,56], also gives a full account of the problems solved by relaxation—some nonlinear, some involving eigenvalues, some with boundaries of initially unknown position, some in three dimensions, and some with parabolic and hyperbolic systems. The eigenvalue techniques were rather interesting. Normally a guess at the eigenfunction gave a starting estimate of the eigenvalue with the use of Rayleigh's principle, and some relaxation was then performed. This cannot proceed too far because the equations do not have a solution at this stage, and a favorite trick was to try to arrange for displacements that made the residual at each point reasonably proportional to its displacement. The computation of a new eigenvalue estimate then gives better results and a good start for further operations. When this was difficult, a method called *intensification* was used, which turns out to be just the method of inverse iteration for

$$(A - \lambda I)x = 0$$

given by

$$Ax^{(r+1)} = x^{(r)} \tag{12}$$

Occasionally the operator $A - kI$ might be used in (12), not so much to increase the rate of convergence as to simplify the relaxation solution of the linear equations.

One final comment on the relaxation method is essential. The success of the method (and it was successful even with the meager computing equipment then available) depended significantly on the ability of the human eye and brain to pick out quickly the largest of a sequence of numbers or a cluster of such numbers, to recognize patterns of numbers, and to forecast the overall effects of relaxation operations. In fact, it was rather like a game of chess, and I return briefly to this point a little later.

4.2 ADMIRALTY COMPUTING SERVICE

In 1943 I joined the new Admiralty Computing Service at Bath, probably the first group with the words "Computing Service" in its title. It was headed by John Todd, with consultants J. C. P. Miller and A. Erdelyi. Workers included E. T. Goodwin, F. W. J. Olver, and H. H. Robertson, names well known in the literature of numerical analysis. Important additional help came from D. H. Sadler, who was Comrie's successor as Superintendent of the Nautical Almanac Office, in which department the Admiralty Computing Service was located. We solved a fair number of problems for the Admiralty and learned a lot about the numerical methods of Miller and Sadler, and I extended my knowledge of and capabilities with the relaxation method. Some problems were written up as reports for "Department of Scientific Research and Experiment—Admiralty Computing Service," mainly in 1945, and listed in the references are two of the problems [1,2] that have particular interest for me.

The first is the evaluation of the two-variable function

$$f(x,y) = \int_0^x e^{-k}[J_0(kx) \cosh (ky) - 1] \operatorname{cosech} (k) \, dk \tag{13}$$

at the points $x = 0(0.1)5.0$, $y = 0(0.1)1.0$. This is how the problem was presented, but we discovered that $f(x,y)$ satisfies the elliptic equation

$$\frac{\partial^2 f}{\partial x^2} + \frac{1}{x}\frac{\partial f}{\partial x} + \frac{\partial^2 f}{\partial y^2} = 0 \tag{14}$$

and that boundary values can be calculated with some interesting numerical analysis, giving quite rapid techniques. I then solved the problem by relaxation methods, and the first point of interest is that this is the first publication of my use of the "difference correction" for correcting a first approximate solution on the same finite-difference mesh. (The year in which these computations were performed was either 1943 or 1944.) The second interesting point is that in this early problem, equation (14) was known originally, but a mathematician deduced (13) cleverly, without knowing that a direct treatment of (14) here is computationally preferable. Just how much early mathematics is valuable in numerical work has always been a matter of some speculation and dispute!

The other interesting problem was the solution by Goodwin and myself of a Volterra integral equation of the first kind, with a mixture of Laplace transforms, Taylor's series, and direct numerical solution of a corresponding second-order equation in which the trapezoidal rule had attached to it several correcting expressions from Gregory's quadrature formula. Here Sadler was a source of great strength, with a wealth of finite-difference knowledge of the kind contained in *Interpolation and Allied Tables*. He published little himself, but he was always able and willing (if not determined) to make suggestions about methods that were almost always exceedingly useful, and he had a genius for spotting errors in our computation. He insisted that all this should be done on good paper, in ink, and he delighted to peer frequently over our shoulders and triumphantly note an error before we had wasted too much sequential time!

5. Mathematics Division, National Physical Laboratory

The Admiralty Computing Service was successful, and its success was one of the main reasons for setting up the Mathematics Division in 1945, a new division of the National Physical Laboratory. Goodwin, Fox, Olver, and Robertson went in 1945 from Bath to the NPL at Teddington. J. H. Wilkinson joined in the following year, and roughly at that time we also recruited Clenshaw, Gill, Hayes, and a number of others with perhaps less well-known names. The famous Turing came to contemplate building his version of the new idea of stored-program computers, and we had a number of junior workers on desk machines and punched-card machines. We also acquired from Germany a large differential analyzer. Our duties were to help other divisions of NPL with their "mathematical and computational" problems, to do the same for other stations of the current version of the Department of Scientific and Industrial Research (and indeed for many other government or government-type laboratories), and above all to engage in research in the theory and practice of numerical computation.

About this time there were other small groups in government and government-type laboratories and at several universities, particularly Cambridge and Manchester, who were also working on computer construction and use. Comrie had formed the London Scientific Computing Service, which Miller joined, but as far as the mathematics of numerical analysis was concerned, the NPL group was by far the largest and the most experienced. There is no doubt that what you would call the more modern numerical analysis in the United Kingdom started with this group, which, indeed, was dominant in our numerical work for at least 30 years.

The history of the NPL work has two parts, the smaller for a decade or so until the mid-fifties, in a period in which the new computer was not generally available, and the larger after the appearance of the lusty Pilot ACE computer in a form from which useful computations could be obtained. My history virtually ends with the first of these parts, in which much useful research was still performed. I mention in what follows a few of the topics and resulting publications.

Table making continued, and NPL started its own series of mathematical tables, a project for which Fox [29] wrote a lengthy volume that extended much of the Chebyshev theory of Lanczos and Miller for interpolation and other relevant formulas. Work on ordinary differential equations produced papers by Fox [24,25], Fox and Goodwin [31], Gill [35] (in which the effect of the new computer was already foreshadowed), and Clenshaw and Olver [17]. Clenshaw [14,15,16] started important work on Chebyshev methods for ordinary differential equations, and Olver, after a comprehensive paper on computing the zeros of polynomials [50], collaborated with Clenshaw [18] on the use of economized polynomials in mathematical tables. Fox and Goodwin [32] continued their ACS work on integral equations with a comprehensive account of finite-difference methods for both Volterra and Fredholm equations, and Goodwin and Staton [39] and Goodwin [37] added to earlier work on methods for evaluating particular integrals. There was some curve fitting [42] and a little linear algebra [34,38,33,26,28], but the main papers for the stimulation of future work in this area came from Turing [58] and Wilkinson [60,61]. We did little on partial differential equations except papers on further relaxation by Fox [24,27], including the difference-correction method. Some independent workers, however, contributed significantly in this field, including (of course) Crank [21] and Crank and Nicolson [22], who produced one of the very useful stable methods for parabolic equations. Motz [46] and Woods [63] did useful work on singularities in elliptic problems. Singularities in some integral equations were also treated by Young [64].

The NPL group joined together to produce the book *Modern Computing Methods* [47] and its second edition (1961), which includes an extensive bibliography. This was one of the first modern books on numerical analysis, somewhat more up-to-date at that time than the very readable one by Hartree [40]. My book [30] on *The Numerical Solution of Two-point Boundary Problems in Ordinary Differential Equations* put into print the work started some 15 years earlier on relaxation methods and the "difference-correction" method. This, again, must be one of the earliest books on this topic.

And that is really the end of the "Early Numerical Analysis" story. In the mid-1950s and onwards, there was a flood of books and papers on numerical analysis of all kinds and from many places, largely stimulated by the development of the stored-program computer. The NPL contribution to this feast was supplied largely by J. H. Wilkinson. His third relevant paper [62] was merely the first of a series that for the next 30 years transformed both the theory and the practice of virtually all problems in numerical linear algebra.

But that is another story. I end the current story by making a few comments on the effect of the new computing machine on our earlier work. First, in 1958 at a meeting of the Royal Society Mathematical Tables Committee, chairman M. V. Wilkes raised the question of the committee's role in the new computer world. This led to considerable and lengthy debate, but the extent of table making decreased rapidly, and the committee virtually ceased to exist around 1965. Second, the old relaxation methods were never used in the same spirit with the new computers. The latter did not match the human eye and brain in picking out relatively quickly the largest of a sequence of numbers or in recognizing useful patterns, and the new relaxation method developed by David Young and others worked in a virtually completely systematic way. This, of course, led to some useful and interesting mathematical theories, but the modern method bears only slight relation to the original relaxation concept.

My "difference-correction" method for differential and integral equations of all kinds was also treated afresh by V. Pereyra and others. They also made some changes, though perhaps not so violent as those of the relaxation story. For example, for the two-point boundary problem

$$y'' + f(x)y' + g(x)y = k(x) \qquad y(a) = \alpha \qquad y(b) = \beta$$

I replaced the differential equation by the recurrence relation

$$(1 - \tfrac{1}{2}hf_r)y_{r-1} - (2 - h^2 g_r)y_r + (1 + \tfrac{1}{2}hf_r)y_{r+1} = h^2 k(x_r) + c(y_r)$$
$$y(a) = \alpha \qquad y(b) = \beta \tag{15}$$

where $c(y_r)$ is the difference-correction at mesh point x_r. I expressed this in terms of central differences, here involving third, fourth, and higher-order differences. I proposed to solve (15) iteratively in the form

$$(1 - \tfrac{1}{2}hf_r)y_{r-1}^{(n+1)} - (2 - h^2g_r)y_r^{(n+1)} + (1 + \tfrac{1}{2}hf_r)y_{r+1}^{(n+1)} = h^2k(x_r) + c(y_r^{(n)})$$

$$c(y_r^{(0)}) = 0$$

a device similar to the modern use of "iterative refinement" for simultaneous linear algebraic equations. I inspected the differences of $y_r^{(1)}$ to discover what orders of differences at this interval made contributions to $c(y_r^{(1)})$ for the required accuracy, whether from this point of view the interval length was satisfactory and, really accurately, how the interval should be changed for this purpose. All further calculations were performed at this "satisfactory" interval, starting with a new $y_r^{(1)}$ and continuing with the iterative sequence. Using only the differences at every stage that were expected to contribute to $c(y_r)$, I performed the iteration as many times as needed to reach consistency in the computed results. Some external values had to be computed and even "corrected" to produce the central differences near boundary points.

Pereyra, however, showed that whereas $y_r^{(1)}$ has global error $O(h^2)$, $y_r^{(2)}$ has global error $O(h^4)$ if $c(y_r^{(1)})$ uses only third and fourth differences, and $y_r^{(3)}$ has global error $O(h^6)$ if $c(y_r^{(2)})$ is computed using only up to sixth differences. Normally the number of differences to be used finally would be decided before the computation started, and if consistency had not been reached at this stage the process would be repeated at a smaller interval. I am not clear what the present position is, but in the early routines external values were not computed, and forward or backward differences were used for at least some y_r in $c(y_r)$. Again, this new theory is very important, but the method has undoubtedly changed, at least to some extent, including the fact that as with initial value problems, a second-order equation is now likely to be treated as simultaneous first-order equations with the trapezoidal rule.

Finally, the new computers were so powerful that they quickly put an effective end to the use of analogue equipment (like the differential analyzer for the solution of partial differential equations) and other pieces of equipment for various problems in which the data and answers were measured by physical quantities like length, voltage, current, and so on. Another analogue device was the construction of alignment nomograms, which up to this time had been a regular feature of problem solving of certain kinds and had developed quite a literature. At NPL my colleague J. G. L. Michel was our "analogue expert," both with the differential analyzer and with nomography, and he joined the others in producing the fourth edition of a very good book on the subject [6].

Since that time I have heard no more about nomography, but of course it is proper that old methods should be reviewed, readapted, and, if necessary, discarded when new equipment becomes available. This is one of the important ways in which numerical analysis continues to make good progress in its initial task of helping the scientists in their work.

References

[1] Admiralty Computing Service, "Tabulation of the function $f(x,y) = \int_0^\infty e^{-k}(J_0(kx) \cosh (ky) - 1) \operatorname{cosech} (k) \, dk$," Report SRE/ACS 47, (S. R. E. Department) (1945).

[2] Admiralty Computing Service, "Solution of Integral Equations Occurring in an Aerodynamical Problem," Report SRE/ACS 89, (S. R. E. Department) (1945).

[3] J. R. Airey, "The Converging Factor in Asymptotic Series and the Calculation of Bessel, Laguerre and Other Functions," *Philos. Mag.* 24 (1937): 521–52.

[4] A. C. Aitken, "On Bernoulli's Numerical Solution of Algebraic Equations," *Proc. Roy. Soc. Edinburgh Sect. A* 46 (1926): 289–305.

[5] A. C. Aitken, "Studies in Practical Mathematics II. The Evaluation of the Latent Roots and Latent Vectors of a Matrix," *Proc. Roy. Soc. Edinburgh Sect. A* 57 (1937): 269–304.

[6] H. J. Allcock, J. R Jones, and J. G. L. Michel, *The Nomogram* (London: Pitman, first edition 1932, 1950).

[7] D. N. de G. Allen, *Relaxation Methods* (New York: McGraw-Hill, 1954).

[8] P. Barlow (ed.), *Barlow's Tables* (London: Spon, 1814). L. J. Comrie (ed.), editions 1930, 1941.

[9] W. G. Bickley, "Formulae for Numerical Integration," *Math. Gaz.* 23 (1939): 352–59.

[10] W. G. Bickley, "Formulae for Numerical Differentiation," *Math. Gaz.* 25 (1941): 19–26.

[11] W. G. Bickley and J. C. P. Miller, "The Numerical Summation of Slowly Convergent Series of Positive Terms," *Philos. Mag.* 22 (1936): 754–67.

[12] *British Association Mathematical Tables, Volume X. Bessel Functions, Part II* (Cambridge University Press, 1952).

[13] D. Brunt, *The Combination of Observations* (Cambridge University Press, 1923).

[14] C. W. Clenshaw, "Polynomial Approximations to Elementary Functions," *MTAC* 8 (1954): 143–47.

[15] C. W. Clenshaw, "A Note on the Summation of Chebyshev Series," *MTAC* 9 (1955): 118–20.

[16] C. W. Clenshaw, "The Numerical Solution of Linear Differential Equations in Chebyshev Series," *Proc. Camb. Philos. Soc.* 53 (1957): 134–49.

[17] C. W. Clenshaw and F. W. J. Olver, "Solution of Differential Equations by Recurrence Relations," *MTAC* 5 (1951): 34–39.

[18] C. W. Clenshaw and F. W. J. Olver, "The Use of Economized Polynomials in Mathematical Tables," *Proc. Camb. Philos. Soc.* 51 (1955): 614–28.

[19] L. J. Comrie, *British Association Mathematical Tables Volume I* (Cambridge University Press, 1931).

[20] L. J. Comrie, "Inverse Interpolation and Scientific Applications of the National Accounting Machine," *J. Roy. Statist. Soc. Supplement* 3 (1936): 87–114.

[21] J. Crank, *The Mathematics of Diffusion* (Oxford University Press, 1956).

[22] J. Crank and P. Nicolson, "A Practical Method for Numerical Evaluation of Solutions of Partial Differential Equations of the Heat-Conduction Type," *Proc. Camb. Philos. Soc.* 43 (1947): 50–67.

[23] A. Fletcher, J. C. P. Miller, and L. Rosenhead, *An Index of Mathematical Tables* (London: Scientific Computing Service, 1946, 1962).

[24] L. Fox, "Some Improvements in the Use of Relaxation Methods for the Solution of Ordinary and Partial Differential Equations," *Proc. Roy. Soc. London Ser. A* 190 (1947): 31–59.

[25] L. Fox, "The Solution by Relaxation Methods of Ordinary Differential Equations," *Proc. Camb. Philos. Soc.* 45 (1949): 50–68.

[26] L. Fox, "Practical Methods for the Solution of Linear Equations and the Inversion of Matrices," *J. Roy. Statist. Soc. Ser. B* 12 (1950a): 120–36.

[27] L. Fox, "The Numerical Solution of Elliptic Differential Equations When the Boundary Conditions Involve a Derivative," *Philos. Trans. A* 242 (1950b): 345–78.

[28] L. Fox, "Practical Methods for the Solution of Linear Equations and the Inversion of Matrices," *Appl. Math. Ser. U.S. Nat'l. Bur. Stand.* 39 (1954): 1–54.

[29] L. Fox, *The Use and Construction of Mathematical Tables.* NPL series volume I (London: H. M. Stationery Office, 1956).

[30] L. Fox, *The Numerical Solution of Two-point Boundary Problems in Ordinary Differential Equations* (Oxford University Press, 1957).

[31] L. Fox and E. T. Goodwin, "Some New Methods for the Numerical Integration of Ordinary Differential Equations," *Proc. Camb. Philos. Soc.* 45 (1949): 373–88.

[32] L. Fox and E.T. Goodwin, "The Numerical Solution of Non-Singular Linear Integral Equations," *Phil. Trans. A* 245 (1953): 501–34.

[33] L. Fox and J. G. Hayes, "More Practical Methods for the Inversion of Matrices," *J. Roy. Statist. Soc. Ser. B* 13 (1951): 83–91.

[34] L. Fox, H. D. Huskey, and J. H. Wilkinson, "Notes on the Solution of Algebraic Linear Simultaneous Equations," *Quart. J. Mech. Appl. Math.* 1 (1948): 149–73.

[35] S. Gill, "A Process for the Step-by-step Integration of Differential Equations in an Automatic Digital Computing Machine," *Proc. Camb. Philos. Soc.* 47 (1951): 96–108.

[36] E. Gold, "Lewis Fry Richardson," *Biographical Mem. Fellows Royal Soc.* 9 (1954): 217–35.

[37] E. T. Goodwin, "The Evaluation of Integrals of the Form $\int_{-\infty}^{\infty} f(x) \cdot e^{-x^2} dx$," *Proc. Camb. Philos. Soc.* 45 (1949): 241–45.

[38] E. T. Goodwin, "Note on the Evaluation of Complex Determinants," *Proc. Camb. Philos. Soc.* 46 (1950): 450–52.

[39] E. T. Goodwin and J. Staton, "Table of $\int_0^\infty (u + x)^{-1} e^{-u^2} du$," *Quart. J. Mech.* 1 (1948): 319–26.

[40] D. R. Hartree, *Numerical Analysis* (Oxford University Press, 1952, 1957).

[41] D. R. Hartree and J. R. Womersley, "A Method for the Numerical or Mechanical Solution of Certain Types of Partial Differential Equations," *Proc. Roy. Soc. London Ser. A* 161 (1937): 353–66.

[42] J. G. Hayes and T. Vickers, "The Fitting of Polynomials to Unequally Spaced Data," *Phil. Mag.* 42 (1951): 1387–1400.

[43] H. Levy and E. A. Baggott, *Numerical Studies in Differential Equations* (London: Watts, 1934).

[44] J. C. P. Miller, "The Construction of Mathematical Tables," *Sci. J. Roy. Coll. Sci. London* 20 (1949): 1–11.

[45] L. Milne-Thomson, *The Calculus of Finite Differences* (London: Macmillan, 1933, 1951).

[46] H. Motz, "The Treatment of Singularities of Partial Differential Equations by Relaxation Methods," *Quart. J. Appl. Math.* 4 (1946): 371–77.

[47] National Physical Laboratory, *Modern Computing Methods* (London: H. M. Stationery Office, 1957, 1961).

[48] Nautical Almanac Office, *Interpolation and Allied Tables* (London: H. M. Stationery Office, 1936, 1956).

[49] Nautical Almanac Office, *Subtabulation* (London: H. M. Stationery Office, 1958).

[50] F. W. J. Olver, "The Evaluation of Zeros of High-Degree Polynomials," *Philos. Trans. A* 244 (1952): 385–415.

[51] L. F. Richardson, "The Approximate Arithmetical Solution by Finite Differences of Physical Problems Involving Differential Equations with an Application to the Stresses in a Masonry Dam," *Philos. Trans. A* 210 (1910): 307–57.

[52] L. F. Richardson, "How to Solve Differential Equations Approximately by Arithmetic," *Math. Gaz.* 12 (1925): 415–21.

[53] L. F. Richardson and J. A. Gaunt, "The Deferred Approach to the Limit," *Philos. Trans. A* 226 (1926): 299–361.

[54] J. B. Scarborough, *Numerical Mathematical Analysis* (Oxford University Press, 1930, 1950).

[55] R. V. Southwell, *Relaxation Methods in Theoretical Physics* (Oxford: Clarendon Press, 1946).

[56] R. V. Southwell, *Relaxation Methods in Theoretical Physics, Volume II* (Oxford: Clarendon Press, 1956).

[57] N. F. Sheppard, "On the Accuracy of Interpolation by Finite Differences," *Proc. London Math. Soc.* 4 (1906): 320–41.

[58] A. M. Turing, "Rounding-off Errors in Matrix Processes," *Quart. J. Mech.* 1 (1948): 287–308.

[59] E. T. Whittaker and G. Robinson, *The Calculus of Observations* (London: Blackie, 1924).

[60] J. H. Wilkinson, "Linear Algebra on the Pilot ACE," in *Proc. Symp. Autom. Dig. Comput. NPL* (London: H. M. Stationery Office, 1954a): 129–36.

[61] J. H. Wilkinson, "The Calculation of the Latent Roots and Vectors of Matrices on the Pilot Model of the ACE," *Proc. Camb. Philos. Soc.* 50 (1954b): 536–66.

[62] J. H. Wilkinson, "The Uses of Iterative Methods for Finding the Latent Roots and Vectors of Matrices," *MTAC* 9 (1955): 184–91.

[63] L. C. Woods, "The Relaxation Treatment of Singular Points in Poisson's Equation," *Quart. J. Mech.* 6 (1953): 163–85.

[64] A. Young, "The Application of Product-Integration to the Numerical Solution of Integral Equations," *Proc. Roy. Soc. London Ser. A* 224 (1954): 561–73.

The Pioneer Days of Scientific Computing in Switzerland

Martin H. Gutknecht

1. Getting Started: The Founding of the Institute

When looking for a date marking the beginning of computer science and scientific computing in Switzerland, one naturally thinks of January 1948 and the founding of the Institute for Applied Mathematics at the Swiss Federal Institute of Technology in Zurich (Eidgenössische Technische Hochschule, or ETH) under the directorship of Professor Eduard Stiefel (see Section 5 for Stiefel's biographical data). Before then, Stiefel was known in the scientific world as an excellent topologist who, in his thesis written under Heinz Hopf, had laid the basis for the theory of vector fields on manifolds. None of the seven papers he had published before 1948 were on numerical analysis, but in his regularly held courses in descriptive geometry, he came into contact with engineers and learned of their need for constructive and computational mathematics. Moreover, as an officer of the Swiss Army during World War II, Stiefel had, to some extent, worked on computational problems. After the war, when he became aware of the development of computers and algorithms in other countries, in particular the United States, he realized the scientific and economic importance of this research for a highly industrialized country. Through his personal initiative, the Institute for Applied Mathematics was founded. Its aim and purpose were the introduction of scientific computing on programmable machines in Switzerland. From the beginning Stiefel was backed up in his basic decisions by a Committee for the Development of Computers in Switzerland and by the Board of the ETH (Schweizerischer Schulrat).

At that time electronic computers were not yet on the market, but many research institutions around the world were designing and building their own machines. Some relay computers, such as Aiken's Mark I (1944), and at least one machine based on electron tubes, Eckert and Mauchly's ENIAC (1946), were already running. In the United States several groups of researchers competed to create the biggest and the fastest machine, and the costs of some of these projects exploded. There was no chance of receiving so much money in Switzerland, so it was clear that in relation to these American projects, a Swiss machine had to be at a Swiss scale. In fact, at the beginning Stiefel's budget was very limited, and the technical equipment of his institute consisted just of a Madas mechanical desk calculator and a Loga drum, a cylindrical instrument combining various slide rules.

But Stiefel was also a very successful administrator who was able to acquire grant money from public and private sources and to get contracts with private industry and even with the army. In contrast to the situation in the United States, military funding is quite unusual. But it is very likely that Stiefel's military career, which ended at the high rank of a colonel, was beneficial for his projects. Later, from 1958 to 1966, Stiefel also played a significant role in local politics: He was an important member of the (legislative) community council of Zurich. Thus, besides being a truly innovative and highly competent mathematician in various areas, Stiefel fits also into the image of the Swiss establishment as it is colorfully painted in McPhee's *Place de la Concorde Suisse* [9]. Clearly, being engaged and successful in so many disjoint activities required good organization, and Stiefel could in fact keep things running with seemingly very little effort.

When starting the institute, it was of course very important to find good collaborators. In this respect, Stiefel was again highly successful: As assistants he chose the mathematician Heinz Rutishauser (see Section 6 for Rutishauser's biographical data) and the electrical engineer Ambros P. Speiser,* both former students of the ETH. Rutishauser had left the ETH three years before and was working as a high school (Gymnasium) teacher while finishing his excellent dissertation in complex analysis in his spare time. Speiser was just getting his diploma in electrical engineering with a thesis related to computers.

2. Learning from Others: The Trips to the United States

Although prototype computers were being constructed in various countries, the United States was clearly ahead in computer technology. Hence, it was decided that Stiefel and his two assistants should visit the United States to acquire some of the American knowhow. The following is a brief summary of Stiefel's report [35] from the first trip, from 18 October 1948 until 12 March 1949. Rutishauser and Speiser stayed longer, until the end of 1949.

The first stopover was at the Mathematical Center in Amsterdam, where Dr. v. Wjingarden directed the construction of a relay computer and a mechanical integrator and also provided a scientific computing service to the Dutch industry. Next, Stiefel spent seven weeks in

---

* Ambros P. Speiser (born 13 November 1922; dipl. El.-Ing. Eidgenössischen Technischen Hochschule (ETH), 1948; Dr. sc. techn., 1950; Privatdozent at ETH, 1952; Professor, 1962) became in 1955 the first director of the IBM Research Laboratory in Zurich. He is now Director of Research of Brown Boveri & Cie., Baden (Switzerland). From 1965–1968 he was president of IFIP.

New York, mainly at the IBM Watson Laboratory for Scientific Computation at Columbia University (with Dr. Eckert and Dr. Thomas), where he had a chance to use a large selection of IBM computing equipment. In particular, he became familiar with IBM's Selective Sequence Electronic Calculator, a computer containing some 12,000 electron tubes. In New York, Stiefel visited the Institute for Mathematics and Mechanics at NYU (with Professor Courant and Professor Friedrichs) and the Computation Laboratory of the National Bureau of Standards (with Dr. Lowan and Dr. Salzer). Both institutions were still without electronic computers, though the NBS had already published some 30 volumes of mathematical tables. These were mostly produced on desk calculators and IBM punched card machines, which were widespread computing aids at that time.

In Washington Stiefel spent two weeks at the Office of Naval Research and the National Bureau of Standards. At the ONR, Dr. Mina Rees was then Head of the Mathematics Branch. Her continuing help in the organization of Stiefel's trip, and in particular, her importance for giving him access to various computers in laboratories of the Navy and the Army, are gratefully acknowledged in Stiefel's report.

It was, of course, a must to visit Boston, where Harvard University Professor H. Aiken was designing his Mark III, while Mark I was running "24 hours a day and 7 days a week." During Stiefel's three weeks' visit some of this computer time was consumed by a free boundary problem submitted by Professor G. Birkhoff. He and his student David Young informed Stiefel also of a new relaxation method for solving linear systems of equations. In addition, Stiefel had discussions with Professor S. Bergmann and his group on the use of kernel functions in conformal mapping. Certainly these discussions aroused Stiefel's interest in relaxation methods, which led on the one hand to cooperation with Professor M. R. Hestenes on the conjugate gradient method [4,37] and, on the other hand, to a series of papers by Stiefel, Rutishauser, Engeli, and Ginsburg on relaxation methods in general and their interrelations. See in particular [38,2].

Finally, Stiefel spent two weeks at the Institute of Advanced Study in Princeton, where he tried to learn from Professor J. von Neumann, who was at the leading edge of both theoretical computer science and hardware design. Rutishauser remained there, monitoring the work at von Neumann's computer project, while Speiser was left in Boston, working on Aiken's Mark III. In the middle of the year they exchanged their positions.

Besides the stops already mentioned, Stiefel visited briefly a number of other places, either for information about computers or for giving lectures. He also spent some time in Princeton and in Chicago working on his former research subjects, geometry and continuous groups.

Throughout his trip Stiefel was highly impressed by the widespread use of mathematical and numerical methods in scientific, industrial, and military research and the confidence of government and industry in this approach. He noted that this widespread use was not only due to the existence of large electric and electronic computers, but also to the different American attitude toward applied mathematics. Actually, many of the computations were still done on desk calculators, punched card machines, and analog computers.

Concerning the construction of computers, Stiefel had learned that many unexpected difficulties had appeared with large machines, in particular concerning their reliability. None of the six types of memory he had seen satisfied him. In his discussions with Professor Aiken, he was assured that a relatively small and slow but reliable machine could be built with a small budget and that such a machine could nevertheless become a useful and cost-effective tool for Swiss science and industry. A first tentative design of this machine called ERMETH (Elektronische Rechenmaschine der ETH) was worked out by Speiser in Boston and, after his return, in Zurich. It is documented in Speiser's doctoral thesis [28].

The computer science knowledge acquired by Stiefel, Rutishauser, and Speiser during their visit to the United States and the following year in Zurich was compiled in [10], which became a widespread standard work in the early computer science literature; it was even translated into Russian.

Some time later, from July 1951 until February 1952, Stiefel stayed once more in the United States, now mainly in Los Angeles at the Institute for Numerical Analysis of the National Bureau of Standards and at the UCLA. In his report [36] he again called attention to the great support for and confidence in scientific computing and to the different situation in Switzerland. There only a few mathematicians had a chance of finding a job in industry, so some of the best chose to emigrate to the United States. (Well-known examples are W. Gautschi, P. Henrici, H. J. Maehly.) Further remarks on the limited possibilities for applied mathematicians in Switzerland are found in some of Stiefel's later annual reports until 1956; afterwards the situation started to change.

Concerning Stiefel's research at NBS, it is well known that he was working with M. R. Hestenes on the conjugate gradient method [3, 4].

On this second trip Stiefel also got new information on some of the computer projects. He noted that quite a few had been abandoned and that only three of the "superfast" machines were working regularly on mathematical problems (namely, SEAC at the Computation Laboratory of the NBS in Washington, Mark III at Harvard University, and Whirlwind at MIT, which had been a secret project at the time of

Stiefel's first trip). In particular, von Neumann's EDVAC was still not working. (It became operational in 1952.) So, Stiefel was confirmed in his opinion that the ERMETH should be simple and reliable.

3. Computing on the Z4

When Stiefel came back from his first trip to the United States in the spring of 1949, he anticipated that the design and the construction of the ERMETH would take several years. In order to promote numerical computations with his institute he needed some other equipment that was immediately available. He first thought of renting IBM punched card machines [35]. But then he learned that the German Konrad Zuse had been able to save one of his relay computers, the Z4, through the devastating time at the end of World War II. Zuse had hidden it in a cow stable at Hopferau in the Allgu, close to the Austrian border. After inspecting the Z4 there on July 13, 1949, Stiefel and Zuse worked out a lease: ETH rented the Z4 for a period of five years for a total of SFr. 30,000. (It is worth noting that Aiken, when asked for advice, was opposed to this lease, because he considered the relay technology too old-fashioned.)

Konrad Zuse (born 22 June 1910) was a highly gifted civil engineer who had started to design and assemble a mechanical computer called Z1 in his parents' living room in Berlin in 1936. Its logical design was far ahead of the time. Zuse's basic concept, although not yet fully implemented in the Z1, included full programmability and remained the same up to the Z4. The basic number representation was already in binary floating-point. However, because of the limited accuracy of the mechanical parts, the Z1 was never fully operational. But after replacing the processor by one built from relays, Zuse had a working computer, the Z2, in 1939. Two years later Zuse finished the Z3, which contained in its processor and its memory some 2600 relays and which many experts consider as the first programmable computer worldwide. The next model, the Z4 rented by Stiefel, was under construction from 1942 until 1945. It contained some 2200 relays and worked with normalized 32-bit binary floating-point numbers with 22-bit mantissa. A multiplication took 2.5 to 3 seconds. The program was read from two switchable punched-tape readers. The Z4 was more powerful than the Z3, although it had again a mechanical memory (for 64 numbers). Old movie films were used as tapes, so there was a certain amount of entertainment for the people operating the machine (although they did not have a projector)!

After 1950 Zuse kept on designing computers, and some of them were fairly successful on the small German market. Zuse's work is well documented by his autobiography [46] and the references listed there. The Z4, which is now exhibited in the Institute of History of

Siemens in Munich, is also described in [1,27,29,31,32]. Among its many interesting features, we might mention the unique handling of the value infinity and the hardware square root based on Zuse's own ingenious algorithm (cf. Rutishauser et al. [10]). Zuse also made a seminal early contribution to programming by formulating algorithms in his "Plankalkül" [1,44,45].

Before its delivery to Zurich, the Z4 had to be repaired and overhauled. Also, on the proposal of Stiefel and his team, conditional instructions were included. After its installation in August 1950, which was followed by some further servicing work, the Z4 proved extremely reliable, except for some minor problems with mechanical parts—in particular, the memory. Typically the Z4 was running day and night at the ETH, often unattended when working on a long job. The list of 55 projects that were performed on it before its removal in April 1955 contains an amazing variety of subjects, such as a fourth-order PDE for the tensions in a dam; the eigenvalues of an 8×8 matrix from quantum chemistry determined by inverse iteration; a linear system with 106 unknowns, which came from a plate problem solved by the conjugate gradient method; ODEs modeling rocket trajectories; and so on. Some of these projects are described in the excellent survey by Schwarz [27], who together with Dr. U. Hochstrasser was doing some time-consuming computations related to the design of a Swiss supersonic military aircraft [5,26].

Of course, numerical experiments related to the basic numerical analysis research performed at the ETH at that time were also run on the Z4. For example, after Stiefel had returned from his second United States trip, Lanczos's eigenvalue method [13] and the conjugate gradient method of Hestenes and Stiefel [4] were coded. We must further mention Rutishauser's early investigations on the stability of numerical methods for initial value problems of ODEs [12], Rutishauser's qd algorithm and LR-transform [14], and H. J. Maehly's polynomial root finder [8].

For some sparse matrix problems, the code for the Z4 was extremely long (up to 6000 instructions) because there was no provision for address computation. Thus, the actual addresses of the nonzero elements in the matrix had to be used when calculating a sparse matrix-vector product. To simplify the preparation of such codes, Rutishauser developed a program for computing these addresses and for producing the corresponding section of the code. See Schwarz [27, Section 4] for more details. This, however, was just the beginning of his seminal work on "automatic coding" ("automatische Rechenplanfertigung"). The first peak of it was Rutishauser's habilitation thesis [11], in which he described in full detail a method for compiling the machine code for a certain problem by the computer itself from the mathematical formulas. He allowed for expressions with arbitrary levels of brackets and for loops with bounds, depending on the data. Moreover, he discussed loop unrolling (which nowadays receives much attention on vector computers). His examples included a program for solving a linear system by computing the LU decomposition column by column and then using forward and backward substitution. Except for the fact that the keywords are in German, the program already looks like the body of an ALGOL procedure.

4. Constructing the ERMETH

While all this basic research and all these computations on the Z4 were going on, Stiefel's gradually growing group was also working hard on the design and the construction of the ERMETH (Elektronische Rechenmaschine der ETH). Speiser, also a Privatdozent since 1952 (his habilitation thesis [30] was on analog computers), was the technical director leading a group of five engineers and three mechanics. On the other hand, Rutishauser worked on the logical organization and its relation to his "automatic coding." It was only in early 1953 that it was decided to use electron tube technology instead of relays. By the end of the same year, however, the year when Rutishauser also worked out the qd algorithm, the basic logical organization and the design of the arithmetical unit were close to being completed. Also nearing completion was a prototype magnetic drum memory, which was attached to the Z4 to test the operational reliability of this new technology. However, to work out all the details of the ERMETH, to have the electronic and some of the mechanical parts manufactured by private companies, and to actually assemble the machine took another two and a half years. In July 1956 it ran the first time, but still with a second prototype memory. In 1955 the Institute met with difficulties because Rutishauser had health problems and Speiser left to take over the IBM Research Laboratory in Zurich. The electrical engineer Alfred Schai became the new director of the technical group completing the ERMETH; he is still the director of the Computer Center at the ETH. In particular there were problems with the large magnetic drum memory, which finally was installed in 1957. At the end of 1958 the cost for the ERMETH had accumulated to one million Swiss francs.

The ERMETH worked with 16-digit decimal words, each of which contained two instructions, and one 14-digit fixed-point number or one floating-point number with 11-digit mantissa. A floating-point addition took 4 ms; a multiplication, 18 ms. The magnetic drum could store 10,000 words. Hence, for the time, the machine was not very fast, but it had a remarkably large memory. The machine contained some 1900 electron tubes and some 7000 germanium diodes. For more details see Schwarz [27], who also discusses some of the applications and numerical investigations that were run on the machine. Schwarz moreover describes the most important developments of the programming language Algol, in the basic design of which, I think it is fair to say, Rutishauser had a leading role. Schwarz himself wrote the Algol compiler for the ERMETH.

Among the contemporary articles on the ERMETH, we mention [24,25,31,32,33,41,42]. There exist also a few copies of a manual [43]. A recent article [34] describes briefly many of the basic considerations that influenced the design of the machine.

The ERMETH was in use at the ETH until 1963. The machine is now on display at the Technorama in Winterthur.

We conclude this article with short profiles of the two distinguished numerical analysts involved: Eduard Stiefel and Heinz Rutishauser.

5. Eduard Stiefel (1909–1978)

Biographical data: Born 21 April 1909 in Zurich. 1927–1931 student at ETH, 1931 diploma in mathematics, 1931–32 with fellowship at the universities of Hamburg and Göttingen, then assistant at ETH. 1935–36 Dr. sc. math., 1936 lecturer. 1939 marriage with Jeannette Beltrami. 1942 Privatdozent, 1943 full professor at ETH. From 1948 director of the new Institute for Applied Mathematics at ETH. 1956–57 president of the Swiss Mathematical Society, 1958–1966 community councilman, city of Zurich. 1970–1974 president of GAMM. 1971 Dr. h.c. of the University of Louvain, 1974 Dr. h.c. of the University of Würzburg and the University of Braunschweig. Died 25 November 1978.

Outline of his work: Stiefel's list of publications is published in a memorial issue of the *Zeitschrift für Angewandte Mathematik und Physik*, volume 30, number 2 (1979). This issue also contains Stiefel's own comments on the list and a profile written by J. Waldvogel, U. Kirchgraber, H. R. Schwarz, and P. Henrici. In his comments on the bibliography, Stiefel divides his work into five periods:

1. Topology
2. Group theory and representation of groups
3. Numerical linear algebra
4. Numerical methods in approximation
5. Analytical methods in mechanics, especially celestial mechanics

In all of these areas Stiefel made truly original and fundamental contributions. In fact, even as a newcomer to a field he was able to find a solution to some important basic problem, and in retrospect, Stiefel's solution was simple and surprising at the same time.

With respect to scientific computation, period 3 is the most important, but periods 4 and 5 must not be overlooked. The paramount contribution to numerical linear algebra is of course the conjugate gradient algorithm introduced in the joint paper with M. R. Hestenes [4] and further investigated in a series of papers (in particular [37,38]). However, one should also mention Stiefel's promotion of the use of variational principles for deriving the linear system from the physical problem [2]. With this approach he put difference methods on a common basis with the finite-element method.

Stiefel's period in approximation theory, although considered "less fruitful" by Stiefel himself, features the introduction of the single exchange version of the Remez algorithm and the proof of its equivalence with the simplex method, if the latter is applied to the discrete linear Chebyshev approximation problem [39,40]. The highlight of the fifth period is the introduction of the KS transform (jointly with P. Kustanheimo) for regularizing Kepler's differential equation of celestial mechanics [7].

6. Heinz Rutishauser (1918–1970)

Biographical data: Born 30 January 1918 in Weinfelden (Thurgau). 1936–1942 student at ETH, 1942 diploma in mathematics, 1942–1945 assistant at ETH, 1945–1947 Gymnasium teacher in Glarisegg and Trogen. 1948 marriage with Margrit Wirz. 1948–49 New York and Princeton, 1948–50 Dr. sc. math., 1949–1955 research associate at the new Institute of Applied Mathematics at ETH. 1951 Privatdozent, 1955 associate professor, 1962 full professor at ETH. From 1968 director of the computer science group at ETH. Died 10 November 1970.

Outline of his work: Rutishauser's list of publications is contained in Research Report 82–01 of the *Seminar für Angewandte Mathematik* at ETH.

Rutishauser has come up with several of the most important ideas in numerical analysis and programming. In his habilitation thesis [11] he described the automatic compilation of a suitably formulated algorithm and thus introduced the concept of what is now known as a compiler. Later his ideas on how to formulate algorithms left traces in the design of Algol, to which he committed himself strongly [19].

In numerical analysis Rutishauser's name is first of all linked with eigenvalue computations: The qd algorithm [14,18,22 (Appendix)] was meant for it, and so was its generalization, the LR transform, the basic principle of which reappeared later in the QR algorithm of Francis. This is also true with respect to spectral shifts, where Rutishauser found a cubically convergent variant of the LR transform [15]. Another truly original proposal was his algorithm, based on Jacobi rotations, for the reduction of band matrices to tridiagonal form [16].

But Rutishauser contributed also to a number of other areas of numerical analysis. We mention his early work on the instability of methods for solving ODEs [12]; his general definition and survey of "gradient methods" for linear equations [2] (in this paper he also introduced a preconditioned conjugate-gradient algorithm); his application of Romberg extrapolation to the notoriously difficult problem of numerical differentiation [17]; his thoughts on the regularization of the nearly rank-deficient least-squares problem [20]; his contribution to a survey of interpolation, quadrature, and approximation [23 (Chapters H and I.II)]; and his ideas on finding polynomial zeros [21]. (These ideas have been completed in Kellenberger's dissertation [6].) Finally, one should mention Rutishauser's unfinished pioneering work on axioms for a reasonable computer arithmetic [22 (Appendix)].

FIGURE 1.
The staff of the Institute of Applied Mathematics at ETH around 1953. Standing from left to right: Professor Stiefel; PD Dr. Rutishauser; Miss Hürlimann; Mr. Schäppi; PD Dr. Speiser; Mr. Läuchli; Mr. Stock; Mr. Schai; and Mr. Appenzeller. Seated are Mr. Sieberling, Mr. Walter, Mr. Engel, and Mr. Messerli.

7. Acknowledgment

This article was initially planned as joint work with Professor P. Henrici, who unfortunately was not able to pursue this project because of a severe illness that ultimately lead to his death in March 1987. The author is much indebted to Mrs. Rutishauser, Professor Schwarz, Professor Speiser, and Mrs. Stiefel for discussions that not only helped clarify some of the details, but also vividly recalled an era long passed.

References

[1] E. Engeler, E. Graf, R. Peikert, T. Fehlmann, Z. Lomecky, R. Mäder, H. P. Biland, and G. Schild, "Konrad Zuse und die Frühzeit des wissenschaftlichen Rechnens an der ETH," Dokumentation zur Ausstellung. *Mathematisches Seminar ETH Zürich* (1981).

[2] M. Engeli, Th. Ginsburg, H. Rutishauser, and E. Stiefel, "Refined Iterative Methods for Computation of the Solution and the Eigenvalues of Self-adjoint Boundary Value Problems," *Mitt. Inst. f. angew. Math. ETH Zürich* 8 (Basel, Stuttgart: Birkhäuser, 1959).

[3] M. Hestenes, "Conjugacy and Gradients," in this volume.

[4] M. Hestenes and E. Stiefel, "Methods of Conjugate Gradients for Solving Linear Systems," *J. Res. Nat. Bureau Standards* 49 (1952): 409–36.

[5] U. Hochstrasser, "Flatterrechnung mit Hilfe von programmgesteuerten Rechenmaschinen," *Z. Angew. Math. Phys* 6 (1955): 300–15.

[6] W. Kellenberger, "Ein konvergentes Iterationsverfahren zur Berechnung der Wurzeln eines Polynoms," Diss. ETH Nr. 4653, Zürich (1971).

[7] P. Kustaanheimo and E. Stiefel, "Perturbation Theory of Kepler Motion Based on Spinor Regularization," *J. Reine Angew. Math.* 218 (1965): 204–19.

[8] H. J. Maehly, "Zur iterativen Auflösung algebraischer Gleichungen," *Z. Angew. Math. Mech.* 5 (1954): 260–63.

[9] J. McPhee, *Place de la Concorde Suisse* (New York: Farrar, Straus & Giroux, 1984).

[10] H. Rutishauser, E. Speiser, and E. Stiefel, "Programmgesteuerte digitale Rechengeräte (elektronische Rechenmaschinen)," *Mitt. Inst. f. angew. Math. ETH Zürich* 2 (Basel, Stuttgart: Birkhäuser, 1951). Also in *Z. Angew. Math. Phys.* 1 (1950): 277–97, 339–62; 2 (1951): 1–25, 63–92.

[11] H. Rutishauser, "Automatische Rechenplanfertigung bei programmgesteuerten Rechenmaschinen," *Habilitationsschrift ETH Nr. 4. Mitt. Inst. f. angew. Math. ETH Zürich* 3 (Basel, Stuttgart: Birkhäuser, 1952).

[12] H. Rutishauser, "Ueber die Instabilität von Methoden zur Integration gewöhnlicher Differentialgleichungen," *Z. Angew. Math. Phys.* 3 (1952): 65–74. English translation: National Advisory Committee for Aeronautics (NACA), Technical Memorandum 1403 (1956).

[13] H. Rutishauser, "Beiträge zur Kenntnis des Biorthogonalisierungs-Algorithmus von Lanczos," *Z. Angew. Math. Phys* 4 (1953): 35–56.

[14] H. Rutishauser, "Der Quotienten-Differenzen-Algorithmus," *Mitt. Inst. f. angew. Math. ETH Zürich* 7 (Basel, Stuttgart: Birkhäuser, 1957). Contains revised versions of the papers in *Z. Angew. Math. Phys.* 5 (1954): 233–51, 496–508; 6 (1955): 387–401.

[15] H. Rutishauser, "Ueber eine kubisch konvergente Variante der *LR*-Transformation," *Z. Angew. Math. Mech.* 40 (1960): 49–54.

[16] H. Rutishauser, "On Jacobi Rotation Patterns," *Proc. Sympos. Appl. Math.* 15 (1963): 219–39.

[17] H. Rutishauser, "Ausdehnung des Rombergschen Prinzips," *Numer. Math.* 5 (1963): 48–54.

[18] H. Rutishauser, "Stabilie Sonderfälle des Quotienten-Differenzen-Algorithmus," *Numer. Math.* 5 (1963): 95–112.

[19] H. Rutishauser, *Description of ALGOL 60 (Handbook for Automatic Computation, Volume Ia)* (Berlin, Heidelberg, New York: Springer, 1967).

[20] H. Rutishauser, "Once Again: The Least Square Problem," *Linear Algebra Appl.* 1 (1968): 479–88.

[21] H. Rutishauser, "Zur Problematik der Nullstellenbestimmung bei Polynomen," in *Constructive Aspects of the Fundamental Theorem of Algebra*, B. Dejon and P. Henrici (eds.) (New York: Wiley Interscience, 1969), 281–94.

[22] H. Rutishauser, *Vorlesungen über numerische Mathematik*, 2 volumes. Ed. by M. Gutknecht in cooperation with P. Henrici, P. Läuchli, and H. R. Schwarz (Basel, Stuttgart: Birkhäuser, 1976).

[23] R. Sauer and I. Szabó (eds.), *Mathematische Hilfsmittel des. Ingenieurs, Teil III.* (Berlin, Heidelberg, New York: Springer, 1968).

[24] A. Schai, "Die elektronischen und magnetischen Schaltungen der ERMETH," *Scientia Electrica* 3 (1957): 127–40.

[25] H. Schlaeppi, "Entwicklung einer programmgesteuerten elektronischen Rechenmaschine am Institut für angewandte Mathematik der ETH," *Z. Angew. Math. Phys.* 5 (1954): 435–36.

[26] H. R. Schwarz, "Ein Verfahren zur Stabilitätsfrage bei Matrizen-Eigenwertproblemen," *Z. Angew. Math. Phys.* 7 (1956): 473–500.

[27] H. R. Schwarz, "The Early Years of Computing in Switzerland," *Ann. Hist. Comput.* 3 (1981): 121–32.

[28] A. P. Speiser, "Entwurf eines elektronischen Rechengerätes unter besonderer Berücksichtigung der Erfordernis eines minimalen Materialaufwandes bei gegebener mathematischer Leistungsfähigkeit," Diss. ETH Nr. 1933, Zürich (1950); *Mitt. Inst. angew. Math.* 1 (Basel, Stuttgart: Birkhäuser, 1950).

[29] A. P. Speiser, "Das programmgesteuerte Rechengerät an der Eidgenössischen Technischen Hochschule in Zürich," *Neue Zürcher Zeitung* 1796 (1950): 50.

[30] A. P. Speiser, "Ueber die Konstruktion von Rechengeräten mit linearen Potentiometern sowie die mathematischen Grundlagen der zugehörigen Kurvenanpassungen," Zürich (1951) (unpublished, available at ETH Main Library). Shortened version: "Rechengeräte mit linearen Potentiometern," *Z. Angew. Math. Phys.* 3 (1952): 449–59.

[31] A. P. Speiser, " 'ERMETH,' Projekt einer elektronischen Rechenmaschine an der Eidgenössischen Technischen Hochschule in Zürich und bisherige Entwicklungsergebnisse," *Neue Zürcher Zeitung* 1903 79 (1954): 4.

[32] A. P. Speiser, "Projekt einer elektronischen Rechenmaschine an der E.T.H. (ERMETH)," *Z. Angew. Math. Mech.* 34 (1954): 311–12.

[33] A. P. Speiser, "Eingangs- und Ausgangsorgane, sowie Schaltpulte der ERMETH," *Nachrichtentechn. Fachber. (NTF)* 4 (1956): 87–89.

[34] A. P. Speiser, "38 Jahre Informatik in der Schweiz," *Bull. SEV/VSE* 78 (1987): 3–7.

[35] E. Stiefel, "Bericht über eine Studienreise nach den Vereinigten Staaten von Amerika (18. Oktober 1948–12. März 1949)," Zürich (1949, unpublished).

[36] E. Stiefel, "Bericht über ein Semester als Gastprofessor an der Universität von Californien und über die mathematischen Organisationen des 'National Bureau of Standards' (22. Juli 1951–21. Februar 1952)," Zürich (1952, unpublished).

[37] E. Stiefel, "Über einige Methoden der Relaxationsrechnung," *Z. Angew. Math. Phys.* 3 (1952): 1–33.

[38] E. Stiefel, "Kernel Polynomials in Linear Algebra and their Numerical Applications," *Nat. Bureau Standards, Appl. Math. Ser.* 49 (1958): 1–22.

[39] E. Stiefel, "Über diskrete und lineare Tschebyscheff-Approximationen," *Numer. Math.* 1 (1959): 1–28.

[40] E. Stiefel, "Note on Jordan Elimination, Linear Programming and Chebyshev Approximation," *Numer. Math.* 2 (1960): 1–17.

[41] J. R. Stock, "An Arithmetic Unit for Automatic Digital Computers," *Z. Angew. Math. Phys.* 5 (1954): 168–72.

[42] J. R. Stock, "Die mathematischen Grundlagen für die Organisation der elektronischen Rechenmaschine der Eidgenössischen Technischen Hochschule," *Mitt. Inst. Angew. Math.* 6 (Basel, Stuttgart: Birkhäuser, 1956).

[43] H. Waldburger, "Gebrauchsanleitung für die ERMETH," *Inst. f. angew. Math. ETH Zürich* (1958).

[44] K. Zuse, "Über den allgemeinen Plankalkül als Mittel zur Formulierung schematisch-kombinativer Aufgaben," *Arch. Math.* 1 (1948–49): 441–49.

[45] K. Zuse, "Über den Plankalkül," *Elektron. Rechenanl.* 1 (1959): 68–71.

[46] K. Zuse, *Der Computer—Mein Lebenswerk* (München: Verlag Moderne Industrie, 1970); second edition (Berlin, Heidelberg, New York: Springer, 1986).

The Development of Computational Mathematics in Czechoslovakia and the USSR

*I. Babuška**

1. Introduction

I would like to share some of my observations and remembrances about the development of computational mathematics in Czechoslovakia and the USSR. My observations will be very subjective and broad in scope.

2. The Development in Czechoslovakia

2.1. EARLY DEVELOPMENTS

An essential milestone in the development of science in Central Europe was the foundation of the Charles University in Prague in 1348. To my knowledge, the first mathematical text at this University was *Algorismus Prosaycus* by Křištan from Prachatice (in Czechoslovakia), written in 1400. This text concentrates on arithmetic, and so I see it as the first text on computational mathematics in Central Europe.

Many outstanding mathematicians interested in computations were directly or indirectly, for shorter or longer periods, associated with the Charles University. Let me mention the astronomers Brahe (1546–1601), Kepler (1571–1630), and Bürgi (1552–1632), among others. The silver mining in Bohemia (the major mining site in Europe at this time) and the construction of a system of ponds in Southern Bohemia required significant effort and high accuracy in geodesic measurements and computations. This, together with the needs of astronomy, contributed to the development of computational mathematics. Computational methods of Brahe (how to multiply numbers by additions with help of tables of sin and cos) together with the logarithmic tables of Napier, Kepler, and Bürgi and the development of a mechanical computer based on Kepler's inspiration, by Schickard, from Tubingen in Germany (1592–1632), led to new developments in computational mathematics. The *Algebra* by Bürgi was edited by Kepler, because it contributed to computational techniques. Many other important developments happened in Prague, especially in connection with the University; nevertheless, I will not go into details except to emphasize

* Partially supported by NSF Grant DMS 8315216.

that this progress was closely related to the development of applied mathematics.

2.2. THE PERIOD 1918–1945

After World War I, Czechoslovakia was established as a democratic republic. The development of computational mathematics was closely related to applications, especially in engineering. Let me mention as an example the fields with which I am familiar: structural mechanics, elasticity, and strength of material. An outstanding scientist in these areas was Z. Bažant, professor of the Technical University in Prague. Traditionally, computational methods for the analysis of frame constructions were of great interest. Essentially, these techniques were related to direct and iterative methods for solving systems of linear algebraic equations. These usually sophisticated methods were based on physical and engineering intuition rather than on mathematical theories, because at this time maximal simplification was needed for any computation. Some of these methods could be described today as splitting methods, block iterations, and methods of dimensional reduction.

Approximate methods for analyzing plates and shells were based, for example, on Fourier and series methods, and were the typical approaches for solving partial differential equations. Various solution methods had the character of finite-difference methods but were derived on physical grounds by "spring analysis." Note that Cauchy's spring model of an elastic medium can be interpreted as a finite-difference scheme for the Lamé-Navier equations with Poisson ratio $\nu = 1/3$. Various methods for solving nonlinear problems and eigenvalue problems were developed in connection with buckling and stability considerations. In mechanical engineering, various methods were developed in connection with vibration problems.

The book [1], written in 1934 by two professors of mathematics at the Technical University in Prague, became a widely used text. This book covered the essentials of numerical analysis in a relatively accurate and detailed manner. Although this book did not break new ground or introduce new approaches, it became a major source of education in computational mathematics and in computational research in engineering applications in Czechoslovakia.

Czechoslovakia was a highly developed industrial country. The Skoda enterprises, an industrial concern, supported a theoretical department that was heavily involved in computations. Thanks to that, Czechoslovakia had a broad and firm tradition in applied mathematics and through this, in computational methods.

It is interesting to compare the scientific situation in Czechoslovakia and Poland. Without any doubt, Poland was a superpower in pure mathematics during this time; it was in the absolute forefront of world research in developing such mathematical fields as functional analysis, real analysis, topology, and so on. On the other hand, in my opinion, the level of applied mathematics was higher in Czechoslovakia than in Poland.

In the fall of 1938, Czechoslovakia was crippled by the Munich treaty; on 15 March 1939 Hitler occupied Bohemia and Moravia, the industrial western part of Czechoslovakia, and created the puppet state of Slovakia from the eastern part of Czechoslovakia. In other words, Czechoslovakia ceased to exist.

On 17 November 1939 Hitler closed all universities to prevent the higher education of the Czech population. Universities were closed until the end of the war and the collapse of Hitler's Germany. This, of course, had a profound effect on the development of science in general, and mathematics in particular. Although there were underground seminars, and although some elementary and research-level mathematical papers publications somehow appeared, an entire generation of scientists (six to eight years worth) was lost. Some effects of this will be discussed in the following sections.

2.3. THE EARLY POSTWAR PERIOD: PERIOD OF BASIC EDUCATION

Almost immediately after the end of the war, the universities were opened, and maximal efforts started to fill the gap created by the six-year closing of the schools. Shortened studies were designed to fill the gap as quickly as possible. Basic lectures were given in theaters for 1500 to 2000 students. This emergency education had surprisingly good effects because of the high motivation of the students and teachers. In three to four years, the major part of the educational gap was closed—especially in the education of engineers, teachers, and medical personnel—but was not and could not be completed in the field of science and in the education of scientists.

In February 1948, the Communist party took over the government. The pattern of Soviet organization was applied in Czechoslovakia, including scientific education and research. Already by 1949 the institution of "aspirants" was established. "Aspirantura" was an organization for graduate studies in and outside the universities. Aspirants were awarded fellowships. Almost at the same time, preparations for the foundation of the Academy of Sciences (Soviet style) were started.

In mathematics, the major responsibility for the education of aspirants was given to E. Čech, a professor at Charles University and a well-known topologist. He gathered about a dozen of the best and most promising young students, graduates from the universities, and led their scientific education. Let me mention a few names from this group, names that became well known in mathematics in and outside of Czechoslovakia: I. Babuška (numerical and applied mathematics), M. Fiedler (theory of matrices), J. Kurzweil (theory of ordinary differential equations), V. Pták (functional analysis), O. Vejvoda (differential equations), and M. Zlámal (finite element method). Under the leadership of Čech, the best Czechoslovak mathematicians participated in this program. I would like to mention especially V. Knichal, and V. Kořínek, professors at Charles University in Prague; F. Vyčichlo, Professor at Technical University; and O. Borůvka, Professor at the University in Brno. This group of students and their teachers was a congenial, dedicated group of the highest quality. I have not seen such a congenial group of students and teachers anywhere in the world since then.

Professor Čech, although a pure mathematician with basic interests in topology and geometry, had very broad views that he imposed on the group, together with his dedication, hard work, and interest in every aspirant (student). Čech insisted that all of his aspirants become familiar with numerical methods. To this end, he obtained from the Soviet Union an old copy of the book by Kantorovich and Krylov [2], which was well known in the Soviet Union and was translated later in the West. Because copying machines did not exist at that time in Czechoslovakia, with the exception of the ditto sheet machine, Čech translated the book and dictated it to his secretary, so that the entire book was typed and (by ditto technology) given to his aspirants. This and similar Čech acts were typical of his dedication. Nevertheless, it is necessary to say that Professor Čech was a highly demanding person—completely "obsessed" by mathematics in the best sense of the word—who constantly challenged his students, individually and as a group, in an almost dictatorial fashion. In retrospect, one has to admire more and more his mathematics, dedication, and wisdom, which he gave to "his" youngsters (with or without their consent).

Čech also insisted that the aspirants get basic education in computer technology and its use. He arranged for lectures by Professor A. Svoboda. Svoboda worked in the field of electronics in the United States during World War II. He returned to Czechoslovakia in 1946 and went back to the United States in 1966. Svoboda was the leader in the development of computers in Czechoslovakia. Under his leadership, a unique relay computer was designed and implemented (tubes were not available at this time). Svoboda's machine—called SAPO—was a triplet machine with three arithmetic units that "voted" after every operation (made simultaneously) and used the majority vote as the answer. The SAPO computer had many unique features. Unfortunately it was not completed until the next generation (tubes) was already in full swing.

During this period, work seminars were routine. Teachers as well as students were involved in these seminars. I remember, for example, the work in a paper by Goldstine and Neumann [3] that convinced us that there was no hope that the elimination method could and would be used in the future for matrices larger than 100 (what a wrong conclusion!). Another paper that had great impact was the one by Courant, Friedrich, and Levy [4], which was analyzed in every detail; Čech and others noted many connections with other fields of mathematics.

Čech, Kořínek, Knichal, and Vyčichlo were able to grow a new generation of active mathematicians and fill the gap created by Hitler in a relatively short period of time. Even with this extraordinary effort, it took 8 to 10 years to overcome the basic effects of the closing of the universities.

2.4. THE MATHEMATICAL INSTITUTE OF THE CZECHOSLOVAK ACADEMY OF SCIENCE

In the early fifties, the Mathematical Institute of the Czechoslovak Academy was established. Čech, Knichal, Novák, and Vyčichlo, together with some of the previous aspirants, played a prominent role in leading the Institute. New research groups were built and another generation of young researchers was educated.

In the fields of applied and numerical mathematics and partial differential equations, Babuška and Rektorys* became very active in collaboration with Professor Vyčichlo.

The main emphasis was the mechanics of solids and partial differential equations, especially of elliptic type. The main direction was the relation between modern exact mathematics and applications, with an emphasis on constructive approaches that could be used for the concrete solution of problems. One result of this effort was the book [6], based on the theory of analytic functions of complex variables in the spirit of the Muschelishvili theory. This philosophy of applied mathematics later led to the book [5] by Rektorys and his coworkers. In its purest form, and influenced by Bourbaki, this philosophy led to the efforts by Knichal and others to create a precise axiomatic system of applied mathematics. This effort did not accomplish much.

The early postwar period (I call it the "period of education") ended roughly in 1954 when the Mathematical Institute was firmly established.

2.5. THE ORLÍK PROJECT

The Orlík project was an important milestone in the development of computational and applied mathematics in Czechoslovakia. This project was mentioned as one of the principal achievements of the

---

* Rektorys is the author of [5,7], which are well known in the United States.

Czechoslovak Academy of Sciences on the thirtieth anniversary of its foundation, and in [8] on the occasion of 40 years of postwar mathematics.

The Orlík project was a large-scale computational project (although still performed on desk calculators) that could be considered the transition from the precomputer to the computer era in Czechoslovakia [9]. This project had a profound impact and was characterized by principles that after 30 years are still at the center of interest in computational and applied mathematics in the United States and elsewhere.

The Orlík research project was related to the proposed building of the largest dam in Czechoslovakia, located about 40 miles south of Prague on the river Vltava. The dam was of concrete gravitational type, about 400 feet high. The Orlík project was a complex integrated research project in mathematics, engineering, and material science (cement and concrete). The leader of the mathematical part was I. Babuška; of the engineering part L. Mejzlík (Professor of the Technical University Brno); and of the technological part, H. Jirsák. It was a team project and included a large staff of people working on desk calculators.

The main technical problem was that concrete releases a significant amount of heat during hardening. Simultaneously the hardening, which depends strongly on the temperature, significantly changes material properties such as elasticity, creep, and relaxation. This creates significant stress, which is "frozen in" during the hardening and later could lead to dangerous and serious cracks. The effects could be controlled by proper building technology. The large dams in the United States used a cooling-pipes system inserted in the dams.

The basic research questions were the following: (a) What are the effects of various building procedures on the possible cracks? Is it necessary to use pipe cooling? Could the cracks, if any, be predicted? (b) How do the properties of the concrete influence the undesirable effects of building and the later functions of the dam? Based on the research results, the dam was built without cooling in blocks about 12 feet high using a relatively quick building schedule. The dam behaved as predicted and serves its purpose well. Results of the analysis were presented at the world dam congress in 1958, and were included with distinction in the congress reporter's paper. Some technical conclusions can be found in [10,11].

The essential novelty was the emphasis on an integrated approach and on the reliability of the conclusions. The reliability aspects were divided into the following groups:

a. reliability of the mathematical model
b. reliability of the available input data

c. reliability of the numerical method and the principles of its selections

d. reliability of the arithmetic computations (roundoffs); it was essential to use a minimal number of digits for computations on desk calculators

These questions were directly and indirectly addressed in a series of theoretical and engineering papers and reports.

The problem was highly nonlinear and three-dimensional. Because three-dimensional solution was out of the question for obvious reasons, a series of two-dimensional problems were solved and combined approximately into three-dimensional ones by a sort of splitting approach. Let me explain now some of the problems in a simplified way.

(1) Thermoproblem with and without cooling. The basic equation considered was:

$$c(u, \delta)\frac{\partial u}{\partial t} = \frac{\partial}{\partial x}a(u, \delta)\frac{\partial u}{\partial x} + \frac{\partial}{\partial y}a(u, \delta)\frac{\partial u}{\partial y} + F(u, \delta) \qquad (1a)$$

$$\frac{d\delta}{dt} = G(u, \delta) \qquad (1b)$$

Here u is the temperature, F the intensity of the heat created by hydration, δ a fictive time (age) in which the same amount of heat was produced as when the temperature was fixed (at about 70° F). This fictive time characterizes the state of the chemical reaction. The coefficients $c(u, \delta)$ and $a(u, \delta)$ were found to be so mildly dependent on u and δ that average values were used. The characterization of $F(u, \delta)$ was essential. Special care was devoted to the laboratory experiments. Finally, the previously mentioned model, based on a chemical model of hydration, was accepted, and a differential equation (1a,b) was designed and used. The data were obtained by the measurement of the heat release in the period $(0, t)$ under constant temperatures and in an adiabatic state. The computation of the increments in F was organized so that the total heat was exactly preserved. This was essential for reliability.

The building technique consisted of quick production of blocks about 12 feet high with time intervals T in between. The scheme is shown in Figure 1. To simplify the problem, a periodic solution (in time and space) was analyzed. It was shown that the solution quickly approaches the state $u(t + T, x, y + d) = u(t, x, y)$, $0 \le t \le T$, and this state was numerically computed [12].

The numerical method was essentially a finite-difference method with the scheme derived by cell integration identity

FIGURE 1.
Schematic state of
progressed dam.

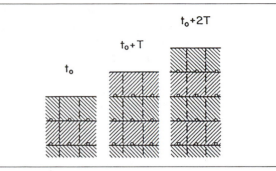

principles to guarantee the balance condition. This technique
was close to the technique of Marchuk's identity, elaborated
later in [13].

An essential feature that was introduced much later in the
finite-element method under the name 'special elements' was
used in the computations. In the presence of cooling pipes, there
was a significant heat sink. Hence, the solution was written in
the form

$$u(x, y, t) = v(x, y, t) + w(x, y, t)$$

where $w(x, y, t)$ was the linear solution of a point source (more
precisely a single circle source) with the intensity $c(t)$ which
was the computed intensity of cooling. The function v was
determined by a finite-difference method as previously explained,
and the hydration heat was included in this term. (The method
of special elements was obtained for the stationary solution.)

(2) The freezing problem. The building of the dam had to
continue during winter when freezing of the concrete in the
beginning phase of hardening could create serious damage. At
most the concrete was allowed to freeze for a short time at a
depth of 1 to 2 inches. The wooden siding for laying the concrete
served also as insulation, and the freezing occurred when the
siding was moved in the next building cycle. The main approach
was to solve a stochastic problem for equation (1) when the
boundary conditions were a stochastic function—the outside
temperature. The main value and dispersion for the desired
information were computed. The theoretical basis was described
in [14]. (Currently a large research project for solving this
problem with stochastic input data is in progress, sponsored
by NASA Lewis.)

(3) The elasticity problem. Given the temperature, the thermo-
stresses were computed. The essential problem was the

formulation of the problem with respect to material properties, including change of elasticity module and creep (relaxation) properties. A rheological model based on a description of the chemical process of hardening was designed and tested in the laboratory.

The numerical solution was based on a series of plane problems in the spirit of splitting methods. In this phase, Nečas contributed significantly to the research. Among others, the theoretical papers [15,16] are directly related to this work. The monograph [17] by Nečas is the only basic monograph which does not avoid nonsmooth domains. This monograph and other results of Nečas are well known in the West. Various iterative methods were used in connection with splitting the problem into two dimensional ones. Let us mention one of them, a type of Schwarz alternating algorithm. Mathematically, the main generalization used was based on the following functional analytical framework (which is today more or less standard), formulated here in the simplest form:

Let P_1, P_2 be projection operators on the subspaces $S_1, S_2 \subset H$. Then $(P_1 P_2)^n$ converges pointwise to the projection onto $S_1 \cap S_2$.

(4) Error control. The basic idea of error control in the numerical method was to interpret the numerical solution as the exact solution of a problem with slightly different input data. The mathematical models were verified by computation of some simple laboratory experiments. The roundoff error was analyzed in a way close to that explained later in [13] by α-sequences.

In the Orlík project, a team of researchers was involved. In addition to those already mentioned—Babuška, Mejzlík, Jirsák, Vitásek, and Nečas—other researchers participated, especially Rektorys, Práger, and Vyčichlo. Various publications and reports, which directly or indirectly were related to the project, were published during this time.

2.6. RESEARCH IN OPTIMAL NUMERICAL METHODS, NUMERICAL STABILITY, AND NUMERICAL METHODS IN GENERAL

In 1964 and 1967, conferences devoted to numerical mathematics were organized. Emphasis was placed on the optimal selection of numerical methods and on numerical stability. These conferences, which took place in the castle Liblice, had a very informal working atmosphere. Leading numerical analysts and mathematicians from East and West participated, such as Bachvalov, Golub, Henrici, Marchuk,

Olver, Sobolev, and Tichonov. These conferences were, in my opinion, the very first meetings in the world concentrating specifically on the optimal selection of a numerical method. The various aspects of optimality—theoretical and computational—were discussed. Some ideas and results in this direction obtained in Czechoslovakia were presented in [13].

3. Computational Mathematics in the USSR

In this section I will make a few subjective comments about the development of computational mathematics in the USSR up to the mid-1950s.* For a systematic survey, see [18,19].

The theory of approximate methods has a long tradition. For example, the idea of the Galerkin method was introduced in 1915 in [20]. The Ritz method was investigated in a series of papers of Krylov and Bogoljubov [21–24]. The Galerkin method was investigated by various authors in the prewar period. The book of Kantorovich and Krylov [2] is likely the first comprehensive book about the numerical solution of partial differential equations. After the war this book was translated into many languages.

The Faddeeva monograph [25] may be the first comprehensive book about the methods of linear algebra. (It was later translated into English.) Michlin's work and books (e.g., [26,27]) on variational methods were important contributions to the theory of variational methods and computational approaches.

3.1. VARIATIONAL METHODS

As I have already mentioned, variational methods were investigated by many authors. The investigations addressed both the Ritz method based on minimization of a quadratic functional as well as the Galerkin method (sometimes called the methods of moments or weighted residuals) with the same or different trial and test spaces. The results based on minimization use the Friedrichs extension of the operator to a self-adjoint one. This approach was used by Michlin in many of his papers and books, and Michlin may have been the first to use the term "energy space." The analysis of the energy space played an important role, as well as the question (in today's terminology) of its equivalent Sobolev space. For example, in [27] this question was analyzed for basic problems in elasticity theory. For the mixed problem (e.g., a free-friction contact boundary condition), the equivalency was analyzed in [28]. The characterization of the energy space for the Poisson problem

---

* I give here the references to the originals in Russian. Translations of many of these papers and books are now available.

on an infinite domain was discussed in [29]. The convergence of the Ritz method in the energy space is then directly related to the best approximation. An effort was made to analyze the convergence in stronger norms $\| u \| = (Au, Au)^{\frac{1}{2}}$ [30] and weaker norms $\| \cdot \|_{L_x}$ [31]. The convergence of the Treftz method was analyzed in detail in [26].

The Galerkin method and general method of moments (also with different trial and test functions) for integral equations were studied in many papers by Krylov and his coworkers [23,32]. In applications to differential equations, Petrov [33] used different trial and test spaces, and the term "Galerkin-Petrov method" is used sometimes today. Keldyš [34] applied this method to a non–self-adjoint boundary-value problem for ordinary differential equations. This paper was very likely the first to establish the convergence of the method in a general setting when applied to a specific problem. The convergence of the Galerkin method was established by Michlin for operators of the form $A = A_0 + K$ where A_0 is a positive definite self-adjoint operator and $A_0^{-1}K$ is compact in the norm $(A_0x, x)^{1/2}$ [35–37]. In [38,39], Kantorovich discussed a general functional analytic scheme for a numerical method. The main idea is roughly the following. Consider $Kx = y$ with $x \in X$, $y \in Y$. The numerical method then solves essentially $K_h x_h = y_h$ where h is a parameter, $h \to 0$, and $x_h \in \tilde{X}$, $y_h \in \tilde{Y}$. There is a one-to-one mapping ϕ_h of $\tilde{X}$ onto $\overline{X} \subseteq X$ and ψ_h of $\tilde{Y}$ onto $\overline{Y} \subseteq Y$. One would like to show that $\phi^{-1}(x_h)$ is close to the solution of the original problem. For that, one essentially has to prove that $\phi_h K - K_h \phi_h$ is small. In [38] this approach was applied to a large class of illustrative problems.

The collocation method can also be understood as method of moments and has been treated [39] in the framework of the preceding approach. A method very close to collocation was applied in [40,41] by Vishik. In abstract form, the Galerkin method for nonlinear problems and a discussion of the approximate method are given by Krasnoselskij in [42] and in some of his other papers.

3.2. THE FINITE-DIFFERENCE METHOD

The basic theory of the finite-difference method, especially that related to stability, is in the book by Rjabenkij and Filippov [43]. A handbook of finite-difference schemes for partial differential equations was written by Panov [44]. For hyperbolic equations there is a series of results of Ladyženskaja and her coworkers [45–47].

In the case of elliptic equations, early work is found, for example, in [48,49]. For applications of the finite-difference method to parabolic equations, we refer, for example, to the work by Kamynin [50].

The general eigenvalue treatment by the finite-difference method is given, for example, in [51].

3.3. NUMERICAL TREATMENT OF DIFFERENTIAL EQUATIONS

In the previous sections some early works were presented. They played (in the author's subjective judgment) important roles in the development of the theory of numerical methods. It is interesting to mention that although the theory of variational methods was very advanced, the entire direction of the finite-element method was neglected for a long time, and the main emphasis was placed on finite-difference methods. Note that the finite-element method was until recently called the variational finite-difference method.

Finite-difference methods were later analyzed in the works of Samarskij, Godunov, and many others, and many monographs and text books are available today. In these works the emphasis is placed on the theory. The discussions of computational aspects, numerical experimentation, and analyses of the performance of the method on benchmark problems are rare. Very likely this situation is related to the state of computer technology in the USSR. Nevertheless, the computer situation stimulated various special methodologies such as splitting methods and various "tricky" iterative procedures that were used in scientific computations. In the area of mathematical modeling and scientific computations, important work has been done by Marchuk and his coworkers in many papers. The first of his books [52] addresses modeling and computational methods in reactor analysis. It is interesting to note that the idea of preconditioning—credited to Buljaev—is discussed there.

I have mentioned very few papers and results; nevertheless, I hope they give some illustrative picture of the character of research in the USSR in the early postwar period.

References

[1] V. Láska and V. Hruska, *Theory and Practice of Computations,* in Czech (Prague: JCMF, 1934).

[2] L. V. Kantorovich and V. I. Krylov, *Approximate Solutions of Partial Differential Equations,* in Russian (Moscow, Leningrad, 1936).

[3] J. von Neumann and H. Goldstine, "Numerical Inverting of Matrices of High Order," *Bull. Amer. Math. Soc.* 53 (1947): 1021–1099.

[4] R. Courant, K. O. Friedrichs, and H. Lewy, "Über die partiellen Differenzengleichungen der Physik," *Math. Ann.* 100 (1928–1929): 32–74.

[5] K. Rektorys, *Survey of Applicable Mathematics*, in Czech (Prague: SNTL, 1966). English edition (London: Iliffe Books, 1969).

[6] I. Babuška, K. Rektorys, and F. Vyčichlo, *Mathematische Elastizitatstheorie der ebenen Probleme* (Berlin: Academia-Verlag, 1960).

[7] K. Rektorys, *Variational Methods in Mathematics, Science and Engineering* (Boston: Dordricht D. Reidel, 1977).

[8] I. Netuka (ed.), *Development of the Mathematics in Czechoslovakia in the Period 1945–1985 and Further Perspectives,* in Czech (Prague: Charles University, 1986): 1–217.

[9] I. Marek, *Approximate and Numerical Methods*, in Czech, in *Mathematics in Czechoslovakia*, 127–43.

[10] I. Babuška and L. Mejzlík, "Calculation and Measurement of Thermal Stresses in Gravity Dams," VI Congress des Grandes Barrages, New York, Question 58 (1958): 1–38.

[11] I. Babuška, L. Mejzlík, and E. Vitásek, "Effects of Artificial Cooling of Concrete in a Dam during its Hardening," VII Congress des Grandes Barrages, Rome (1961): 1–13.

[12] E. Vitásek, "Über die quasistationäre Lösung der Warmeleitungs-gleichung," *Apl. Mat.* 5 (1960): 109–40.

[13] I. Babuška, M. Práger, and E. Vitásek, *Numerical Processes in Differential Equations* (New York: John Wiley, 1966).

[14] I. Babuška, "On Randomized Solution of Laplace's Equation," *Časopis Pěst. Mat.* 86 (1961): 269–76.

[15] J. Nečas, "Solution du probleme biharmonique pour le coen infini I, II," *Časopis Pěst. Mat.* 83 (1958): 257–86, 399–424.

[16] J. Nečas, "L'extension de l'espace des conditions aux limites du probleme biharmonique pour les domains a point angeloux," *Czechoslovak Math. J.* 9 (1959): 339–71.

[17] J. Nečas, *Les Méthodes Directes en Théorie des Équations Elliptiques* (Prague Academia, 1967).

[18] L. V. Kantorovich and V. I. Krylov, "Approximate Methods," in Russian, *Matematika v SSSR za 30 let* (Moscow, Leningrad, 1948): 759–801.

[19] M. K. Gavurin and L. V. Kantorovich, "Approximate and Numerical Methods," in Russian, *Matematika v SSSR za sorok let, 1917–1957* (Moscow, 1957): 809–55.

[20] B. G. Galerkin, "Rods and Plates," in Russian, *Vestnik inženěrov* 19 (1915).

[21] N. M. Krylov, "Sur les géneralisations de la méthode de Walter Ritz," *C. R. Acad. Sci. Paris Sér. I Math.* 164 (1917): 853–56.

[22] N. M. Krylov, "Application of the Method of W. Ritz to a System of Differential Equations," *Izv. Acad. Nauk* (6) 11 (1917): 521–34.

[23] N. M. Krylov, "Sur différents procédes d'intégration approchée en physique mathematique," *Toulouse* 19 (1927): 167–200.

[24] N. M. Krylov, *Approximate Solution of Basic Problems of Mathematical Physics*, in Russian (Kiev, 1931).

[25] V. N. Faddeeva, *Numerical Methods of Linear Algebra*, in Russian (Moscow, Leningrad, 1950).

[26] S. G. Michlin, "Variational Methods for Solving Problems of Mathematical Physics," in Russian, *Uspekhi Mat. Nauk* 40 (1950): 3–51.

[27] S. G. Michlin, *Problems of the Minimum of Quadratic Functional*, in Russian (Moscow, Leningrad, 1952).

[28] M. I. Edjus, "On the Mixed Problem of the Elasticity Theory," *Dokl. Akad. Nauk SSSR* 76 (1951): 181–84.

[29] S. G. Michlin, "Integration of Poisson Equation in an Infinite Domain," *Dokl. Akad. Nauk SSSR* 91 (1953): 1015–1017.

[30] S. G. Michlin, "On the Ritz Method," in Russian, *Dokl. Akad. Nauk SSSR* 106 (1956): 391–94.

[31] L. V. Kantorovich, "About Convergence of Variational Processes," in Russian, *Dokl. Akad. Nauk SSSR* 30 (1941): 107–11.

[32] N. M. Krylov, *Les méthodes de solution approchée des problémes de la physique mathematique* (Paris, 1931).

[33] G. I. Petrov, "Application of the Galerkin Method to the Problem of the Stability of Viscous Fluid Flow," *Prikl. Mat. Mekh* 4.3 (1940): 3–12.

[34] M. V. Keldyš, "Galerkin Method for the Boundary Value Problems," in Russian, *Izv. Akad. Nauk SSSR Ser. mat.* 6 (1942): 309–30.

[35] S. G. Michlin, "About the Convergence of the Galerkin Method," in Russian, *Dokl. Akad. Nauk SSSR* 611 (1948): 197–99.

[36] S. G. Michlin, "Direct Methods in Mathematical Physics," in Russian (Moscow, Leningrad, 1950).

[37] S. G. Michlin, *Variational Methods of Mathematical Physics*, in Russian (Moscow, Leningrad, 1957).

[38] L. V. Kantorovich, "Functional Analysis and Applied Mathematics," in Russian, *Uspekhi Mat. Nauk* 3:6 28 (1948): 89–185.

[39] L. V. Kantorovich and G. P. Akilov, *Functional Analysis in Normed Spaces*, in Russian (Moscow, 1960).

[40] M. I. Vishik, "Mixed Boundary Value Problems and their Approximate Solutions," in Russian, *Dokl. Akad. Nauk SSSR* 97 (1954): 193–96.

[41] M. I. Vishik, "Cauchy Problem for Equation with Operator Coefficients, Mixed Boundary Value Problem for System of Differential Equations and Approximate Solution," in Russian, *Matem. Sbornik* 39 81 (1956): 51–148.

[42] M. A. Krasnoselskij, "Some Problems of Non-Linear Analysis," in Russian, *Uspekhi Mat. Nauk* 9:3 61 (1954): 57–114.

[43] V. C. Rjabenkij and A. F. Filippov, *The Stability of Finite Differences*, in Russian (Moscow, 1956).

[44] D. Panov, *Handbook for Numerical Treatment of Partial Differential Equations*, fifth ed., in Russian (Moscow, 1951).

[45] O. A. Ladyženskaja, "Solution of the Cauchy Problem for Hyperbolic Equations by the Finite Difference Method," in Russian, *Leningrad, Uchen. Zap. Gosudarstvennovo Univ. 144, ser. mat.* 23 (1952): 192–246.

[46] O. A. Ladyženskaja, "Finite Difference Solution of the Mixed Problem," in Russian, *Dokl. Akad. Nauk SSSR* 85 (1952): 705–08.

[47] O. A. Ladyženskaja, *The Mixed Problem for the Hyperbolic Equation*, in Russian (Moscow, 1953).

[48] D. M. Ejdus, "Finite Difference Solution of Boundary Value Problems," in Russian, *Dokl. Akad. Nauk SSSR* 83 (1952): 191–94.

[49] L. A. Ljusternik, "Remarks to the Numerical Solution of Boundary Value Problem for Laplace Equation and Eigenvalue Computation by the Finite Difference Method," in Russian, *Proc. Stekl. Inst.* XX (1947): 49–64.

[50] L. I. Kamynin, "The Applicability of the Method of Finite Differences to the Heat Problem: I. Uniqueness of the Finite Difference Solution;

II. Convergence of the Finite Differences," in Russian, *Izv. Akad. Nauk SSSR* 17 (1953): 163–80, 249–68.

[51] L. A. Ljusternik, "Finite Difference Approximation of Laplace Operator," in Russian, *Uspekhi. Mat. Nauk* 9.2 (1954): 3–66.

[52] G. I. Marchuk, *Numerical Methods for Nuclear Reactor Computations*, in Russian (Atomizdat, Moscow, 1958).

The Contribution of Leningrad Mathematicians to the Development of Numerical Linear Algebra in the Period 1950–1986

V. N. Kublanovskaya

1. V. N. Faddeeva and D. K. Faddeev

The work of V. N. Faddeeva in 1950 marks the beginning of the investigation and development of computational linear algebra at the Leningrad Division of the V. A. Steklov Mathematical Institute (LDMI). This article contains a short review of the basic results in numerical linear algebra obtained by researchers at LDMI and their students.

First we discuss the work of Faddeeva and Faddeev, citing their inestimable contribution both in the development of numerical linear algebra and in the instruction of a generation of computational mathematicians.

They wrote the three monographs *Computational Methods of Linear Algebra* [1–3], which were translated into many languages and highly esteemed by mathematicians throughout the world. The first monograph (by Faddeeva), published in 1950, was acknowledged as one of the best books to have appeared in this field. It highlighted the concept of matrix and vector norms and also their application in the convergence theory of iterative processes. Without exaggeration it can be said that this monograph initiated the use of norms in studying the convergence of iterative processes.

The two other monographs, published in 1960 and 1963 and written by Faddeev and Faddeeva, present fundamental research on numerical methods in linear algebra. The books present a great many algorithms and methods, explain the basic principles of their construction, and classify them. Many of these methods were further generalized and improved. The survey articles [4–8] on computational linear algebra, and in particular on parallel computations, are excellent supplements to the monographs. The bibliographies [9,10], produced under the initiative and direction of Faddeeva, are also an inestimable service to specialists.

Primarily, the scientific investigations of Faddeev and Faddeeva are related to the solution of linear algebraic systems (chiefly ill-conditioned systems) and to tools for assessing computational results.

In [11,12] an ill-conditioned system is analyzed in terms of the singular-value decomposition of the matrix, permitting the extraction of the information that it contains. Various numerical measures of condition are considered—in particular, the H-condition-number is introduced: $H(A) = \mu_1/\mu_n$. Reference [13] considers an ill-conditioned system $Ax = f$ with a positive-definite symmetric matrix. The stable part of the solution is determined from the system $(A + \delta I)x_\delta = f$. An iterative method for solving it is presented.

Two articles are devoted to improving the condition of a matrix through scaling. Reference [14] poses and solves the problem of finding two diagonal matrices D_1 and D_2 that minimize the Turing condition number of $D_1 A D_2$. Reference [15] considers the problem of finding a diagonal matrix $D > 0$, solving $\min\| D^{-1}AD \|_2$.

The works [16–19] develop a new approach for estimating propagation errors in finite computational problems. The initial data and the result of a computation are considered as coordinates of vectors in appropriate vector spaces; the computational problem is interpreted as a mapping from the data space into the result space. The effect of propagation error on the result of the computation is investigated via the concept of natural domain as well as the related natural norm, allowing the most complete transfer of information from the data to the solution.

Since it is difficult to construct natural norms, elliptical norms are proposed as the closest to natural ones. The elliptical norms are constructed with the aid of accompanying matrices of ellipses. Using these matrices they consider the transfer from the norm in which the data are initially given to elliptic norms. They relate the accompanying and correlation matrices. It is shown that information (or estimates) about the natural domains can be used to analyze rounding errors.

Three articles, [20–22], are related to the solution of general systems. In [20,21], co-authored by V. N. Kublanovskaya, a geometric viewpoint is used to illuminate questions concerning the solution of rectangular systems. Independent of Golub's work, an algorithm is presented for factoring an arbitrary matrix into a left trapezoidal matrix (with a certain prescribed ordering of the elements) and a matrix of orthonormal columns (the normalized factorization). The singular values of the initial matrix are related to the diagonal elements of the left trapezoidal matrix. The normalized factorization is used to derive methods for solving rectangular systems and also to compute stable parts of the solution of ill-conditioned systems.

Reference [22] develops a new concept for estimating the quality of the numerical solution of $Ax = f$ based on the quality of the data. Three cases are considered: textbook (the initial data are exact), regular (the data are imprecise, but their perturbation is far from critical), and irregular (the variation of the data is critical or nearly so, leading to a qualitative change in the problem). In the textbook case, the character of the solution is determined by the correspondence between the rank and the dimensions of the matrix. The regular case requires the solution of a system with fixed data and the investigation of the influence of propagation errors on the result. In the irregular case, we seek an object close to the solution in some generalized sense and insensitive to small changes in the data. If the singular values of the matrix divide clearly into "large" and "small" groups, then the linear system should be considered as fully subdefinite and the solution as generalized-normal, and the singular-value or normalized decomposition of the matrix should be used to find it. The problem becomes improper if there is no sharp break in the singular values. In this case the authors resort to regularization. They present one of the regularization methods.

2. V. N. Kublanovskaya

The investigations of Kublanovskaya and her students went in the following directions:

- □ the solution of standard eigenvalue problems for matrices
- □ the solution of spectral problems for linear and polynomial matrix pencils of general form
- □ the solution of systems of linear and nonlinear algebraic equations
- □ the solution of inverse eigenvalue problems

These ideas are discussed in the subsections below.

2.1. EIGENVALUE PROBLEMS FOR MATRICES

In [23–25] Kublanovskaya proposed the following three algorithms, each of which finds, starting with the matrix $A_1 = A$, a sequence $\{\Lambda_k\}$ of left triangular matrices and a sequence $\{Q_k\}$ of orthogonal matrices according to the following formulas:

$$\Lambda_k = A_k Q_k \qquad A_{k+1} = \Lambda_k^T Q_k \qquad k = 1, 2, \ldots \tag{1}$$

$$A_1 = A \qquad \Lambda_1 = A_1 Q_1 \tag{2}$$
$$A_2 = \Lambda_1^T Q_1 \qquad \Lambda_2 = A_2 Q_2$$
$$A_k = \Lambda_{k-1}^T Q_{k-1} \qquad \Lambda_k = A_k Q_k \qquad k = 3, 4, \ldots$$

$$\Lambda_k = A_k Q_k \qquad A_{k+1} = Q_k^T \Lambda_k \qquad k = 1, 2, \ldots \tag{3}$$

$$\Lambda_k = A_k Q_k \qquad A_{k+1} = Q_k^T \Lambda_k - (t_{k+1} - t_k)I \qquad k = 1, 2, \ldots \tag{4}$$

Algorithm (1) solves the eigenvalue problem for matrices $A^T A$ and AA^T: The diagonal elements of Λ_k converge geometrically to the singular values of A; and the columns of the matrices $T_{2k-1} = Q_1 Q_2 \cdots Q_{2k-1}$ and $T_{2k} = Q_1 Q_2 \cdots Q_{2k}$ converge to the eigenvectors of the matrices $A^T A$ and $A A^T$ respectively. Algorithm (2) solves the eigenvalue problem for $A A^T$, but converges quadratically. Algorithm (3) and its shifted modification (4) solve the eigenvalue problem for an arbitrary square matrix A. For a long time, this algorithm was called the method of one-sided rotations in the Russian literature, and only after the work of Francis was it called by the generally accepted name of the QR algorithm. Version (3) was presented independently of the work of Francis and was first published in 1960. The authors of [2] kindly agreed to include it in a "Supplement" when the book was already in print.

In 1963 Kublanovskaya proved the convergence of the QR algorithm for an arbitrary matrix and also the quadratic convergence of the shifted modification for matrices of simple structure.

In [26] she presented an algorithm for constructing a canonical basis of a matrix, knowing its eigenvalues. Initially, an auxiliary orthonormal basis V is used to determine all the spectral indices (elementary divisors) for the eigenvalue $\lambda = 0$. Then the basis V is transformed to a canonical one. The study of the algorithm was continued in the works of A. Ruhe, Bo Kögsträm and P. Van Dooren. The latter used it for the analysis of the Kronecker canonical form of a linear pencil.

In [19,21] Kublanovskaya presented algorithms for refining isolated eigenvalues of a matrix (polynomial matrix) and computing their corresponding eigenspaces. The use of the normalized decomposition allowed us to move from solving the determinant equation to solving a scalar equation and applying Newton's method. An algorithm was considered for refining the real and imaginary parts of the eigenvalues of a real matrix while operating in real arithmetic.

In [30] Kublanovskaya and L. T. Savinova used the normalized decomposition to develop algorithms for solving partial eigenvalue problems: determining the eigenvalues in a given strip (half plane); finding groups of isolated eigenvalues, small (large) in modulus, of an arbitrary matrix; refining isolated eigenvalues; and finding their corresponding eigenvectors.

In [31,32] Kublanovskaya derived an estimate for the smallest eigenvalue of a positive definite matrix, and using this, with T. Ya. Kon'kova presented an algorithm to compute two-sided approximations of successive eigenvalues of a matrix (beginning with the smallest).

2.2. SPECTRAL PROBLEMS FOR PENCILS

To solve the full eigenvalue problem for a regular linear pencil, Kublanovskaya and T. V. Vashchenko presented algorithms AB and AB-1, allowing an arbitrary regular pencil to be reduced to an equivalent pencil of quasi-triangular (triangular) form [33,34]. Both algorithms preserve triangular Hessenberg form of the pencil: The first is based on planar rotations and is analogous to the QR algorithm for matrices; and the second is based on elementary nonorthogonal transformations and is analogous to the LR algorithm for matrices.

In [35,36] Kublanovskaya and V. N. Simonova considered modifications of the algorithms: a modification with shifts guaranteeing quadratic convergence; modified dimension-reduction for the pencils through separation of the null and infinite eigenvalues; and modifications exploiting a break between the groups of large and small eigenvalues of the pencil to approximate and refine the eigenvalues of these groups.

In [36,37] Kublanovskaya presented algorithms for the construction of Jordan chains corresponding to the computed eigenvalues of the pencil. For a singular linear pencil she presented algorithms [39,40] for computing scalar spectral characteristics (minimal and spectral indices), isolating a regular block, and constructing a basis from polynomial solutions. She also presented an algorithm for reducing the spectral problem for a polynomial pencil to the same problem for a linear pencil and algorithms that find vector spectral characteristics (polynomial solutions and Jordan chains) of a polynomial pencil without transforming it to a linear one [40–43]. Kublanovskaya and V. B. Khazanov developed algorithms that exhaust already-found spectral characteristics [43].

The works of Khazanov [44–46] are connected with spectral problems for polynomial pencils of general form: Spectral properties are investigated, and generalized methods of simultaneous iteration are presented for regular polynomial pencils.

2.3. SYSTEMS OF EQUATIONS

In [47] Kublanovskaya applies conformal mapping to accelerate the convergence of iterative methods for solving systems (preconditioning of systems). Let

$$X = \lambda A X + f$$

be a linear algebraic system, whose solution is sought for $\lambda = \lambda^{*}$ ($\lambda^{*} = 1$). If the topography of the eigenvalue distribution of A is known, so that a region D is known not to contain the poles of the Neumann series, then the convergence of the series

$$(I - \lambda A)^{-1} f = \sum_{k=0}^{\infty} \lambda^{k} A^{k} f$$

is accelerated using analytic continuation via the change of variables $\lambda = \phi(\eta)$. Where $\phi(\eta)$ conformally maps $|\eta| < 1$ onto the region D, and $\lambda = \lambda^*$ is transformed to the point $|\eta^*| < 1$. The new series

$$\sum_{k=0}^{\infty} [\phi(\eta)]^k A^k f = \sum_{k=0}^{\infty} \eta^k b_k(A) f$$

is guaranteed to converge more rapidly to the solution. A validation of the algorithm is given, and classes of matrices arising from physical problems are considered whose eigenvalue topographies are known.

Reference [48] classifies direct methods for the solution of linear algebraic systems with sparse matrices (having many zero elements) and presents factorization schemes for the inverse matrix and pivot rules that reduce the growth of nonzero elements during the solution of systems and inversion of matrices.

In [49,50], using the normalized decomposition, an algorithm is presented for solving linear systems that permits, under certain assumptions, the analysis of the condition of the system, the forward analysis of the rounding errors, and the refinement of the computed solution.

The application of orthogonal transformations to the solution of systems with rectangular, singular, and ill-conditioned matrices is outlined in [20,21,51].

In [52] Kublanovskaya presented the iterative process

$$x_{k+1} = x_k - \gamma_k \Delta_k$$

for minimizing a real functional $f(x) = \| P(x) \|_2$. $P(x)$ is a twice continuously differentiable transformation from Euclidean m-space into Euclidean n-space, and the Jacobian $J(x)$ for $P(x)$ is rectangular or singular in some neighborhood of the initial point. Here Δ_k is a generalized normal solution of the system $J(x_k)\Delta_k = P(x_k)$, and γ_k is an iterative parameter.

Under certain restrictions on the gradient of the functional and the initial approximation, it is shown how to choose the parameter γ_k to guarantee local convergence of the process. In particular, it is established that the gradient of the functional $f(x)$ decreases in the direction opposite to the generalized normal solution Δ_k. The iterative parameter γ_k and the generalized normal solution Δ_k are found using the normalized decomposition of the Jacobian matrix.

Kublanovskaya [53] presented an algorithm allowing the solution of nonlinear algebraic systems of equations to be reduced to the solution of a spectral problem for linear matrix pencils.

2.4. INVERSE EIGENVALUE PROBLEMS

The inverse eigenvalue problem arose during investigation of the stability of a system with a finite number of degrees of freedom. The inverse problem reduces to choosing parameters from their field of values, so the matrix has eigenvalues closest to the given numbers in the least-squares sense.

The inverse problem is reduced to a fixed-point problem for a real functional, together with an iterative process for solving it. Sufficient conditions for convergence are formulated in terms of the solved problem. An algorithm is presented for solving the additive problem. The results of these investigations were published in [54–57] by Kublanovskaya and Khazanov.

The works of L. Yu. Kolotilina [58–61] are related to the preconditioning of a system of linear equations. She presents a general procedure for constructing sparse approximations to matrices and their inverses, via the minimization of non-negative quadratic functionals. This procedure forms the basis for the construction of one-level explicit and implicit preconditioners. It permits the general treatment of a variety of known preconditioning methods and facilitates their comparison. Two incomplete block factorization schemes are presented for linear systems of block-banded structure.

Translated by Stephen G. Nash

References

The following abbreviations are used in the references:

- □ AS—Academy of Sciences of the USSR
- □ MIAS—Mathematical Institute of AS
- □ LDMI—Leningrad Division of the MIAS
- □ DCM—Division of Computational Mathematics
- □ JCMMP—Journal of Computational Mathematics and Mathematical Physics

[1] V. N. Faddeeva, *Computational Methods of Linear Algebra* (Moscow-Leningrad: State Technical Press, 1950), 240 pp.

[2] D. K. Faddeev and V. N. Faddeeva, *Computational Methods of Linear Algebra* (Moscow: Physmath State Press, 1960), 656 pp.

[3] D. K. Faddeev and V. N. Faddeeva, *Computational Methods of Linear Algebra* (Moscow: Physmath State Press, 1963), 734 pp.

[4] D. K. Faddeev and V. N. Faddeeva, "Computational Methods of Linear Algebra," in *Proc. 3rd All-Soviet Math. Congress* 3 (Moscow, 1958).

[5] D. K. Faddeev and V. N. Faddeeva, "Computational Methods of Linear Algebra," in *Proc. Sci. Seminar LDMI* 54 (1975): 3–222.

[6] D. K. Faddeev and V. N. Faddeeva, "A Look at the Development of Computational Methods in Linear Algebra," in *Computational Methods of Linear Algebra* (Moscow, 1977), 4–14.

[7] D. K. Faddeev and V. N. Faddeeva, "Parallel Computations in Linear Algebra," *Cybernetika* 6 (1977): 28–40.

[8] D. K. Faddeev and V. N. Faddeeva, "Parallel Computations in Linear Algebra," LDMI Preprint R–6–81 (Leningrad, 1981), 47 pp.

[9] V. N. Faddeeva, Yu. A. Kuznetsov, G. N. Grekova, and T. A. Dolzhenkova, *Computational Methods of Linear Algebra*, bibliographic index 1828–1974 (Novosibirsk, 1976), 418 pp.

[10] V. N. Faddeeva, H. D. Ikramov, E. A. Meinik, and G. G. Fursa, *Computational Methods of Linear Algebra*, bibliographic index 1975–1980 (Leningrad, 1982), 344 pp.

[11] D. K. Faddeev, "On the Condition of Matrices," *Proc. MIAS* 53 (1959): 387–91.

[12] D. K. Faddeev and V. N. Faddeeva, "On Ill-Conditioned Sytems of Linear Algebraic Equations," *JCMMP* (1) 3 (1961): 412–17.

[13] V. N. Faddeeva, "Shifting for Systems with Ill-Conditioned Matrices," *JCMMP* (5) 5 (1965): 907–11.

[14] D. K. Faddeev and V. N. Faddeeva, "Problems of Scaling for Linear Systems," in *Modern Computational Methods* (Materials of the international summer school, 1966) (Kiev, 1968), 76–84.

[15] V. N. Faddeeva, "Some Extremal Problems for Matrix Norms," *JCMMP* (7) 2 (1967): 401–04.

[16] V. N. Faddeeva, "Stability in Linear Algebra Problems," *Proc. IFIP Congress 68* (1969): 33–39.

[17] D. K. Faddeev and V. N. Faddeeva, "Natural Norms in Algebraic Processes," in *Questions of Precision and Effectiveness in Computational Algorithms*, Proc. of Symposium 1 (Kiev, 1969), 122–41.

[18] D. K. Faddeev and V. N. Faddeeva, "The Accompanying Matrix and Assessment of a Finite Computational Problem," in *Computational Methods of Linear Algebra* (Novosibirsk, 1973), 4–10.

[19] D. K. Faddeev, "On the Estimation of the Region Containing the Solution of a System of Linear Algebraic Equations," *Proc. Sci. Seminar LDMI* 90 (1979): 227–28.

[20] D. K. Faddeev, V. N. Kublanovskaya, and V. N. Faddeeva, "Linear Algebraic Systems with Rectangular Matrices," in *Modern Computational Methods* (Materials for the international summer school, 1966) (Kiev, 1968), 16–75.

[21] D. K. Faddeev, V. N. Kublanovskaya, and V. N. Faddeeva, "The Solution of Linear Algebraic Systems with Rectangular Matrices," *Proc. MIAS* 96 (1968): 76–92.

[22] D. K. Faddeev and V. N. Faddeeva, "On the Question of Solving Linear Algebraic Systems," *JCMMP* (14) 3 (1974): 539–58.

[23] V. N. Kublanovskaya, "On Some Algorithms for Solving the Complete Eigenvalue Problem," *Reports AS* (136) 1 (1961): 26–28.

[24] V. N. Kublanovskaya, "On Some Algorithms for Solving the Complete Eigenvalue Problem," *JCMMP* (1) 4 (1961): 555–70.

[25] V. N. Kublanovskaya, "Solution of the Eigenvalue Problem for Arbitrary Matrices," *Proc. MIAS* 66 (1962): 113–35.

[26] V. N. Kublanovskaya, "On One Method for Solving the the Complete Eigenvalue Problem for Singular Matrices," *JCMMP* (6) 4 (1966): 611–20.

[27] V. N. Kublanovskaya, "On the Application of Newton's Method to the Determination of Eigenvalues of λ-Matrices," *Reports AS* (188) 5 (1969): 1004–1005.

[28] V. N. Kublanovskaya, "Newton's Method for the Determination of Eigenvalues and Eigenvectors of Matrices," *JCMMP* (12) 6 (1972): 1371–1380.

[29] V. N. Kublanovskaya, "Toward the Solution of the Spectral Problem for Singular Matrix Pencils," *JCMMP* (18) 4 (1978): 1056–1060.

[30] V. N. Kublanovskaya, "Toward the Solution of Matrix Eigenvalue Problems," *Proc. Sci. Seminar LDMI* 70 (1977): 124–39.

[31] V. N. Kublanovskaya, "Some Bounds for the Eigenvalues of Positive Definite Matrices," *JCMMP* (5) 1 (1965): 107–11.

[32] T. Ya. Kon'kova and V. N. Kublanovskaya, "Two-sided Approximation in the LR-Algorithm," *Proc. Sci. Seminar LDMI* 58 (1976): 67–71.

[33] V. N. Kublanovskaya, "The AB Algorithm and its Properties," *Proc. Sci. Seminar LDMI* 102 (1980): 42–60.

[34] V. N. Kublanovskaya and T. V. Vashchenko, "On a Variant of the AB Algorithm for Solving the Eigenvalue Problem for a Regular Linear Matrix Pencil," *Proc. Leningrad. Korablstroitel Inst. Applied Math. and SAPR in Shipbuilding* (1982): 49–60.

[35] V. N. Kublanovskaya and V. N. Simonova, "Some Modifications of the AB Algorithm," *Proc. Sci. Seminar LDMI* 111 (1981): 117–36.

[36] V. N. Kublanovskaya, "The Eigenvalue Problem for Regular Pencils of Near-Singular Matrices," *Proc. Sci. Seminar LDMI* 90 (1979): 63–82.

[37] V. N. Kublanovskaya, "Construction of a Canonical Basis for Matrices and Matrix Pencils," *Proc. Sci. Seminar LDMI* 90 (1979): 46–62.

[38] V. N. Kublanovskaya, "Toward the Analysis of Singular Matrix Pencils," *Proc. Sci. Seminar LDMI* 70 (1977): 89–102.

[39] V. N. Kublanovskaya, "An Algorithm for Computing the Spectral Structure of a Singular Linear Matrix Pencil," *Proc. Sci. Seminar LDMI* 159 (1987): 23–32.

[40] V. N. Kublanovskaya, "The Spectral Problem for Polynomial Matrix Pencils," *Proc. Sci. Seminar LDMI* 80 (1978): 83–97; 111 (1981): 109–16.

[41] V. N. Kublanovskaya and T. V. Vashchenko, "Construction of a Fundamental Sequence of Solutions for a Matrix Pencil," *Proc. Sci. Seminar LDMI* 139 (1984): 74–93.

[42] V. N. Kublanovskaya, "Construction of Vector Spectral Characteristics of Polynomial Matrix Pencils," *LDMI Preprint* E–3–85 (1985).

[43] V. N. Kublanovskaya and V. B. Khazanov, "Exhaustion in Spectral Problems for Matrix Pencils," *DCM Preprint* 111 (Moscow, 1986), 33 pp.

[44] V. B. Khazanov, "Spectral Properties of λ-Matrices," *Proc. Sci. Seminar LDMI* 111 (1981): 180–94.

[45] V. B. Khazanov, "Some Spectral Characteristics of λ-Matrices," *Proc. Sci. Seminar LDMI* 139 (1984): 111–24.

[46] V. B. Khazanov, "Application of the Method of Simultaneous Iteration for λ-Matrices," in *Computational Methods of Linear Algebra* (Moscow, 1983), 219–32.

[47] V. N. Kublanovskaya, "Application of Analytic Continuation by Means of Change of Variables," *Proc. MIAS* 53 (1959): 145–85.

[48] V. N. Kublanovskaya, G. V. Savinov, and T. N. Smirnova, "Toward the Solution of Sparse Matrix Problems," *Proc. Sci. Seminar LDMI* 35 (1973): 57–94.

[49] V. N. Kublanovskaya, "Application of a Normalized Process to the Solution of Linear Algebraic Systems," *JCMMP* (12) 5 (1972): 1091–1098.

[50] V. N. Kublanovskaya, "A Normalized Square Root Method and its Application to the Solution of Certain Algebra Problems," *Proc. Sci. Seminar LDMI* 35 (1973): 56–66.

[51] V. N. Kublanovskaya, "Computation of a Generalized Inverse Matrix and Projector," *JCMMP* (6) 2 (1966): 326–32.

[52] V. N. Kublanovskaya, "Application of Orthogonal Preconditioning to the Solution of Nonlinear Systems," *Proc. Sci. Seminar LDMI* 23 (1971): 53–71.

[53] V. N. Kublanovskaya, "The Relation of Spectral Problems for Linear Matrix Pencils with Certain Algebra Problems," *Proc. Sci. Seminar LDMI* 80 (1978): 98–116.

[54] V. N. Kublanovskaya, "On One Approach to the Solution of the Inverse Eigenvalue Problem," *Proc. Sci. Seminar LDMI* 18 (1970): 138–49.

[55] V. N. Kublanovskaya, "Application of a Normalized Process to the Solution of the Matrix Inverse Eigenvalue Problem," *Proc. Sci. Seminar LDMI* 23 (1971): 72–83.

[56] V. N. Kublanovskaya and V. B. Khazanov, "On a Matrix Inverse Eigenvalue Problem," *Proc. Sci. Seminar LDMI* 23 (1971): 84–93.

[57] V. N. Kublanovskaya, "Toward the Solution of the Additive Problem for Eigenvalues of Matrices," *Proc. Sci. Seminar LDMI* 48 (1974): 12–17.

[58] L. Yu. Kolotilina, *On One Family of Explicit Preconditionings for Systems of Linear Algebraic Equations with Sparse Matrices* (Leningrad, 1986), 49 pp. (Preprint LDMI R–8–86).

[59] A. Yu. Yeremin and L. Yu. Kolotilina, "On Methods of Incomplete Block Factorization for Matrices of Complex Structure," *Proc. Sci. Seminar LDMI* 159 (1987): 5–22.

[60] A. Yu. Yeremin and L. Yu. Kolotilina, *On One Family of Two-Level Preconditionings Based on Incomplete Block Factorization* (Moscow, 1985), 43 pp. (Preprint DCM 103).

[61] A. Yu. Yeremin and L. Yu. Kolotilina, *On One Approach to the Construction of Incomplete Block Factorizations for Sparse Matrices of Complex Structure* (Moscow, 1986), 30 pp. (Preprint DCM 135).

References translated by a friend

List of Contributors

I. Babuška
Institute for Physical Science and Technology, University of Maryland, College Park, MD 20742.

Garrett Birkhoff
Department of Mathematics, Harvard University, Cambridge, MA 02138.

I. Edward Block
Society for Industrial and Applied Mathematics, 3600 University City Science Center, Philadelphia, PA 19104.

Oscar Buneman
Electrical Engineering Department, Stanford University, Stanford, CA 94305.

I. Bernard Cohen
Victor S. Thomas Professor (emeritus) of the History of Science, Harvard University, Cambridge, MA 02138.

James W. Cooley
IBM Watson Research Center, P.O. Box 218, Yorktown Heights, NY 10598.

George B. Dantzig
Operations Research Department, Stanford University, Stanford, CA 94305.

L. Fox
Emeritus Professor, Oxford University, Oxford, England.

Carl-Erik Fröberg
Department of Computer Science, Lund University, P.O. Box 118, S–221 00 Lund, Sweden.

C. W. Gear
Department of Computer Science, University of Illinois at Urbana–Champaign, Urbana, IL 61801.

Herman H. Goldstine
The American Philosophical Society, 104 South Fifth Street, Philadelphia, PA 19106.

Martin H. Gutknecht
Eidgenössische Technische Hochschule, CH–8092, Zürich, Switzerland.

Magnus R. Hestenes
Department of Mathematics, University of California at Los Angeles, Los Angeles, CA 90024.

Eugene Isaacson
Courant Institute of Mathematical Sciences, New York University, New York, NY 10012.

V. N. Kublanovskaya
Leningrad Division, V. A. Steklov Mathematical Institute, Soviet Academy of Sciences, Leningrad, USSR.

N. Metropolis
T–DO, B210, Los Alamos National Laboratory, Los Alamos, NM 87545.

J. Tinsley Oden
College of Engineering, The University of Texas at Austin, Austin, TX 78712.

B. N. Parlett
Mathematics Department and Computer Science Division of EECS Department, University of California, Berkeley, CA 94720.

Donald W. Peaceman
Annuitant, Exxon Production Research Company, Houston, TX.

John R. Rice
Department of Computer Sciences, Purdue University, West Lafayette, IN 47907.

R. D. Skeel
Department of Computer Science, University of Illinois at Urbana–Champaign, Urbana, IL 61801.

John Todd
Mathematics 253–37, California Institute of Technology, Pasadena, CA 91125.

James Varah
Computer Science Department, University of British Columbia, Vancouver, Canada.

Richard S. Varga
Institute for Computational Mathematics, Kent State University, Kent, OH 44242.

David J. Wheeler, FRS
    Computer Laboratory, Cambridge University, Cambridge,
    England.

David M. Young
    Center for Numerical Analysis, The University of Texas, Austin,
    TX 78712–1067.

Scenes from the Conference

John Rice

Oscar Buneman,
David Johnson,
Robert Vichnevetsky

Alston Householder,
Heidi Householder

Magnus Hestenes,
Gene Golub

James Varah

Beresford Parlett

Gene Golub

Garrett Birkhoff

Herbert Keller,
Edward Block

James Varah

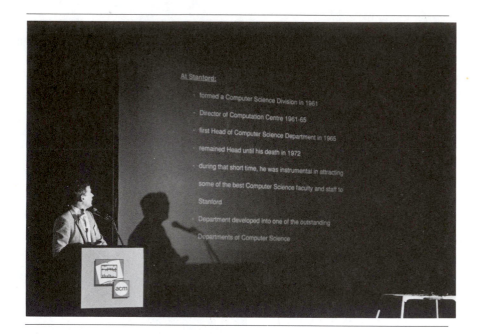

M. L. Juncosa,
David Young

Edward Block

Oscar Buneman

C. W. Gear

Index

Photo Credits